BUILDING BRIDGES

BUILDING BRIDGES
The Emerging Grassroots Coalition of Labor and Community

edited by
Jeremy Brecher and Tim Costello

Monthly Review Press
New York City

To the memory of
Ruth and Edward Brecher
and
Thomas F. Costello

The editors would like to thank the following, who have kindly given permission for the use of previously published material:

Labor Research Review, for "Noon at 9 to 5: Reflections on a Decade of Organizing," by Cindia Cameron, which appeared in #8 (Spring 1986), "Greenhouse: Why a Good Plan Failed," which appeared in #9 (Fall 1986), "'If All the People Banded Together': The Naugatuck Valley Project," by Jeremy Brecher, which appeared in #9 (Fall 1986), and "Asian Immigrant Women and HERE Local 2," which appeared in #11 (Spring 1988);

Zeta Magazine, for "Upstairs, Downstairs: Class Conflict in an Employee-Owned Factory," by Jeremy Brecher, which appeared in February 1988, "American Labor: The Promise of Decline," by Jeremy Brecher and Tim Costello, which appeared in May 1988, and "Labor and Community: Converging Programs," by Jeremy Brecher and Tim Costello, which appeared in July–August 1988.

"Camp Solidarity: The United Mine Workers and the 'People's Movement' Against Pittston Coal," by Jim Green, is a revised version of an article that originally appeared in *New England Labor News and Commentary*, November 1989.

Library of Congress Cataloging-in-Publication Data
Building bridges : the emerging grassroots coalition of labor and
  community / [edited by] Jeremy Brecher and Tim Costello.
    p.   cm.
  ISBN 0-85345-791-3 : $30.00—ISBN 0-85345-792-1 (pbk.) : $12.00
  1. Working class—United States—Political activity—Case studies.
  2. Trade-unions—United States—Political acitivity—Case studies.
  3. Social action—United States—Case studies. 4. Social movements—
United States—Case studies. I. Brecher, Jeremy. II. Costello, Tim.
HD8076.B85   1990
322'.2'0973—dc20   89-13808
                                                            CIP

Monthly Review Press
122 West 27th Street, New York, N.Y. 10001

Manufactured in the United States of America

10 9 8 7 6 5 4 3 2 1

Contents

Issue Campaigns

Part II

Perspectives

Programs

Contents

Preface

"Something is happening out there," wrote Studs Terkel at the close of the Reagan era. Grassroots movements "have never been more flourishing," he noted in *The Great Divide* in 1988, but they are "remarkably disparate in issue, ranging from local grievances—utility hikes, tax inequities, developers' transgressions—to matters more encompassing—Sanctuary, Pentagon spending, threats to Social Security." They are, he concluded prophetically, "a movement awaiting coalescence."

This book grows out of our recognition that such a "coalescence" is already under way. It presents the first fruits of a new social alliance which is unheralded at the national level—and virtually unreported in the national media—because it is being built at the grassroots.

Over the past few years, once-insular movements have been reaching out to cooperate at the local level. They have created literally hundreds of coalitions and alliances, large and small, formal and informal. This book presents a few dozen of them, "remarkably disparate in issue": coalitions to support strikes, run movement activists for public office, resist plant closings, secure working women's rights.

These coalitions have generally been created without the dominance of a single unifying organization, program, or leader. Rather, they have been constructed by active efforts of mutual outreach—by "bridge-building."

One of the most surprising, unanticipated, and significant aspects of these coalitions has been the frequent participation of unionists. The usual media images of workers for the past quarter century have featured "hard hats" beating up on peace demonstrators and "Reagan Democrats" abandoning traditional blue-collar loyalties in disgust at kooks and troublemakers from radical social movements. This book recounts a different reality: cooperation between grassroots union activists and activists from women's, African-American, Latino, Asian-American, gay, lesbian, environmental, farm, senior, student, handicapped, peace, human rights, anti-intervention, citizen action, consumer, and other movements.

This book focuses on labor's role in the emerging grassroots coali-

9

tions. Cooperation with other movements is proving to be an important means for renewing the labor movement and overcoming some of its widely recognized ills, such as isolation from the growing female and minority segments of the workforce, lack of rank-and-file participation, and public perception of organized labor as a special interest group rather than an advocate for the needs of all working people.

The separation of labor from other social movements has been a crucial barrier to social change in the United States, making it easy for those who benefit from the status quo to "divide and rule." An alliance of labor and community movements potentially represents the overwhelming majority of the population—a majority which is today largely excluded from political and economic decision-making, but which if mobilized would represent an enormous social force.

Compiling this book has in some ways itself been like organizing a coalition. We did not always know who to invite, and while we have corrected some glaring omissions along the way, we know that plenty of others remain. We apologize for them.

Most of the contributors to this book are themselves grassroots coalition activists; some are writers or scholars. Although they are generally sympathetic to the movements they write about, we have encouraged them to provide critical accounts. We have tried to select contributors who could strengthen the book as a whole; inclusion of an author does not imply our endorsement of one approach or political tendency over another in her or his movement or locality. The book aims not for a consistent "line" but rather for dialogue among different people rooted in different movements and experience.

Part I of the book presents case studies of four major kinds of labor-community coalitions: support for strikes and other labor struggles, efforts to preserve jobs and encourage democratically controlled economic development, strategies to run candidates for public office and hold them accountable, and campaigns addressing particular public issues. Part II presents reflections on the significance of labor-community coalitions and the putting forward of common goals, programs, and visions for their further development. Theory and practice are closely linked throughout: the case studies in Part I often include general reflections, while the thematic essays in Part II often discuss concrete examples in some detail.

The devastation of the human and natural worlds that marked the 1980s was only possible because the people hurt by it were divided from each other. Whether the 1990s will be a time of continued devastation or an era of creative renewal will depend largely on whether their divisions are overcome.

PART I

Labor Struggles

From its birth, the U. S. labor movement was rooted not only in workplaces but also in communities. During the past half century, however, U.S. unions have become increasingly isolated from potential allies and increasingly limited to representing the workplace interests of their own members. This tendency reached a symbolic peak when Ronald Reagan kicked off his presidency by firing 13,000 striking air traffic controllers—and few in the labor movement, let alone in the wider community, came to their aid.

Since that fiasco, labor activists have begun to reach out for allies. Virtually every major strike in the past few years has requested—and received—community support; day-to-day cooperation has expanded as well.

This section looks at forms of community-labor support for labor struggles. The accounts reflect some important developments:

1. The increasing proportion of women, people of color, and immigrants in the workforce has changed the composition of many unions. Unions are under increasing pressure to address the needs of these groups—and to seek cooperation with the community organizations in which they are represented.

2. The relation between various levels of union officials and the rank and file is complex and often ambiguous. Some of these campaigns, such as the Jobs With Justice, have had the blessing of top union officials. Others—like the strike of Hormel workers in Austin, Minnesota—have been conducted by rank-and-file groups over official opposition.

3. Widespread community support allows workers to use corporate campaigns and other tactics that confront employers far beyond the scope of a local production facility.

4. In many cases, what starts as community strike support leads to other forms of cooperation as well. The Community-Labor Alliance of New Haven, for example, which began with support for strikers at Yale University, became an ongoing institution mobilizing support for plant closing legislation, school lunch programs, and use of pension funds for local investment.

Camp Solidarity:
The United Mine Workers, the Pittston Strike, and the New "People's Movement"

Jim Green

When 1,700 members of the United Mine Workers of America (UMWA) struck the Pittston Coal Group on April 5, 1989, the miners had been working without a contract for months and the odds of winning a victory seemed long indeed. Faced with an intransigent employer dedicated to breaking a national agreement and to wringing deep concessions out of its union employees, the miners realized they were up against a corporation that would use every weapon available to break their union. Pittston's willingness to perpetrate economic violence became clear when it cut off health benefits to retired miners and widows.

Pittston attacked the union in a way that highlighted the main issues of labor struggles during the past decade by demanding cuts in health and welfare (also the main issue in the Communications Workers' strike of 1989) and by insisting on work rule changes and opening new nonunion mines, a practice known as double breasting. Furthermore, Pittston, like International Paper and U.S. Steel, justified its assault on the union by raising the specter of international competition. The leading U.S. producer of coal for export (mainly to the Japanese metal industry), Pittston made an issue out of the internationalization of the industrial economy.

In a bold decision to risk everything in order to win this strike, UMWA President Richard Trumka made it clear that the future of the union was at stake. Virtually everyone in the labor movement immediately realized that the Pittston struggle would be a decisive one. Another defeat, coming at the end of a series of discouraging losses, would be devastating, especially because the miners, long seen as the shock troops of American labor, had staked everything on the outcome. On the other hand, a victory could be the turning point for the labor movement, possibly a transformative event that would demonstrate paths to a union revival in the 1990s.

The outcome of the Pittston struggle was of special concern to union progressives, militants, and reformers of all kinds, who had been disappointed in the crucial strike campaigns of the 1980s for various reasons. Many criticized the unwillingness of leaders to mobilize and

15

empower striking members, or to encourage support from other unions and community groups, or to challenge unjust labor laws and
court injunctions by using civil disobedience. Indeed, throughout the
labor movement there was a general feeling of dismay that organized
labor had failed to effectively support the air traffic controllers' strike
in 1981 and had thus allowed the government to set a union-busting
precedent.

The UMWA leadership at the local, district, and international levels
indicated immediately that it would learn from the setbacks of the
1980s and do everything possible to maximize solidarity. So those
advocating change in the labor movement looked to the miners' fight
against Pittston with great expectations.

At this writing in early January of 1990 it looks as though the tentative agreement announced on New Year's Day will meet nearly
everyone's expectations. In the press conference announcing the settlement, held at the Department of Labor, President Trumka announced that the union miners had once again beaten the long odds.
"We've done something we didn't think was possible," he said of the
settlement.

In a phone conversation later that day, Trumka told me the union
had won the main things it was after in the area of health care and
job security. He also described the many concessions, including the
firing of hundreds of workers for illegal activity, which the union bargaining team, led by Vice President Cecil Roberts, had forced off
the table.

A *U.S. News & World Report* story on January 15 said Pittston's
union miners "appeared to score a major victory," especially in the
form of "new job security provisions" which limit the company's ability
to subcontract operations to nonunion firms. The study added that
"Pittston's attempts to shed some of the burden of financing health
care benefits . . . proved largely fruitless."

The details of the tentative agreement are being withheld pending
a ratification vote by the strikers, and though some of the legal charges
and some of millions of dollars in fines will be dropped, the union
still faces serious issues with the courts. Still, it seems clear that,
if the members ratify this agreement as expected, it will be the kind
of outcome labor needs to begin the 1990s. The nature of the settlement is crucial of course, but even if members are not happy with
all the details, it is clear that the way in which they waged their
fight will help show others the way forward.

When the strike began, Pittston's miners had been working without
a contract for fourteen months. Pittston withdrew from the industry
association, then stopped grievance arbitrations and dues check off.

In January of 1988 the company cut off health benefits to 1,500 retired and disabled miners and widows. The union filed numerous unfair labor practices charges with the National Labor Relations Board which later ruled in the UMW's favor. This meant at least that the company could not offer permanent jobs to the scabs they had imported and tried to protect with Vance Security guards.

No union members crossed the lines and the scabs found it tough going in Appalachia. During the spring the UMW mounted a massive civil disobedience campaign to impede roads and scab coal trucks. Thousands were arrested and the courts began to levy fines against the union for contempt and other charges that would add up to over $60 million. The union's defiance of the courts, part of its militant tradition, captured the hearts and minds of labor activists across the nation. The strikers, their families, and supporters dressed in camouflage to symbolize their involvement in a war of "civil resistance" against the authorities and the corporation. The uniforms also made it difficult for police to identify individuals accused of rock throwing or "jack-rocking" (hurling a wicked device of bent nails used to puncture scab truck tires). The women wore miniature jack-rock earrings as a kind of proletarian fashion.

The level of community support in the region was remarkable. It was estimated that 80 percent of the local merchants in the region supported the union. The UMW has drawn consciously on the tactics and principles of the civil rights movement and invited activists from the peace movement to help train miners in civil disobedience tactics. During the summer, even Lane Kirkland came to Virginia to be arrested with UMW President Richard Trumka, who was making a national issue out of the failure of labor law and the tyranny of the Virginia courts. Like John L. Lewis, Trumka decided to take on the government and to make the strike a political protest.

The strike leaders adopted a political tone from the start. On April 30, Trumka and Jesse Jackson spoke at the Wise County Fairgrounds to an enormous crowd. Although this is a rural area and although a driving rainstorm hit the area, 12,000 people came out to hear Jackson say the strike was not theirs alone: "This is the people's strike," he said. He referred explicitly to the influence of the civil rights movement, commenting that "the tradition of John L. Lewis and Martin Luther King, Jr. has come together."

To protest the unprecedented fines, restrictive injunctions, and what the union called "government union busting," thousands of West Virginia miners began a sympathetic strike in June which spread to ten other states and 46,000 workers. President Trumka sanctioned the walkouts on July 7 by calling for the miners to honor "memorial days" (which allow union miners to quit work without fear of penalty) in their contracts. Within a few days, however, the International asked the miners to return to work and they did. One of the lessons of the Pittston strike, as Staughton Lynd has argued, is that even with the enormous creativity and militancy employed, union contracts that bar sympathy strikes are a liability the labor movement can no longer live with.

Politicizing the Strike

The strike has been politicized by targeting labor law and judicial tyranny, but the core economic issues are also ones many unions are facing; they include Pittston's attempts to cut health care benefits and pensions in a time of rising costs and to shift work to nonunion subsidiaries. Like International Paper and other firms, Pittston played the foreign competition card, demanding flexibility of scheduling to meet the threat of competition. Like the Paperworkers, the UMW called this bluff and exposed the phony arguments about foreign competition; but they also fought a cultural battle which echoes through the social history of the American working class. One of Pittston's most onerous demands was to end the eight-hour day and to assign miners to Sunday work. "The world works seven days a week," declared Pittston Coal Group President Michael Odum, who enraged the miners by saying they were only "using church as an excuse" to avoid Sunday work.

In resisting Pittston's demands to schedule Sunday work and to scrap the eight-hour day, the miners defended community and union values against corporate imperatives. As the late Herbert Gutman wrote in "The Workers' Search for Power" and other essays, industrialization has involved a sharp conflict between capitalist "time is money" values and the traditions of rural working people with their habits of "passing" rather than "spending" time. To succeeding waves of industrial recruits to American factories and mines, the ten-hour day and the sixty-hour work week clashed with their own needs to celebrate holy days, wakes, and weddings. Pittston's demands showed contempt for regional culture, for Appalachians' deep-seated church-going traditions and for the miners' bloody struggle for the eight-hour day. The miners made their strike a "fight for community survival" and called up all the powerful values that contributed to labor-community solidarity in the past. The United Farm Workers' boycotts come to mind as another good example of the force moral and cultural arguments have in winning community support for unionized workers.

During the summer the strike continued as a stalemate, but the effectiveness of the resistance movement was hurt by the courts' restrictions on the mass pickets. The UMW also began to shift attention to other states, where Pittston was getting its orders filled by other coal producers. Still, the outpouring of solidarity was enormous, with hundreds of trade unionists caravanning from other states to the coal fields. A delegation of unionists from the International Confederation of Free Trade Unions (ICFTU) arrived in mid-October 1989 and may have had a catalytic effect. A representative of Solidarnosc, recently elected a senator in the Polish parliament, was especially outspoken— "shocked to see what is happening in the great democracy." The ICFTU group visited Pittston Chief executive officer Paul Douglas and helped persuade Labor Secretary Elizabeth Dole to visit the strike scene and talk to miners.

During a trip to the coal fields I talked to a retired miner, a fifty-year UMW member named Lloyd Davidson, camped out in front of Pittston offices in Lebanon, Virginia, "A lot of confusing things happen," Davidson mused. "Mr. Bush goes over to Poland, praises them guys over there for sticking up for Solidarity. Sends the U.S. marshalls down here on us. Does that makes sense to you? Somethin' wrong somewhere. Somethin' wrong with the system."

With the Poles in Virginia, Bush's hypocrisy became more embarrassing. With Solidarnosc in our coal fields, it was the labor movement's turn to play the "Polish Solidarity card." After the international delegation visit, Secretary Dole, perhaps anticipating Lech Walesa's visit to the United States in November, appointed a supermediator, William Usery, who pledged to finally bring Pittston CEO Paul Douglas face to face with UMW President Richard Trumka.

The strike has also involved a corporate campaign against Pittston, focusing on its stockholders and board members. The campaign has met with mixed results. In Connecticut, where Pittston headquarters are located, hundreds of clergy signed a petition of moral condemnation and pickets appeared regularly at the homes of the top executives. In Massachusetts a support committee based in Boston drew upon decades of strike support experience in targeting a Pittston board member, William Craig, a vice president of Slawmit Bank. Picketing of the bank began in the spring and then a family of miners arrived in early summer who met with many local union officials and members with good results. City Councillor David Scondras called for hearings on Boston's dealings with Shawmut Bank and President Trumka testified before the City Council, joined by fifty strikers based in Connecticut. Trumka also spoke to a militant rally of 300 workers in front of the Shawmut main branch, sponsored by the Boston building trades whose leaders promised to withdraw funds from the bank. Unlike earlier strike support activities in which left activists clashed with state and local labor officials, the UMW support work enjoyed a unified response.

Within a few weeks the Boston City Council voted unanimously to withdraw city funds from Shawmut Bank to protest Craig's involvement with Pittston. The cities of Cambridge and Somerville followed suit. The Painters Council withdrew $56 million and the Hotel Workers, Laundry Workers, and Boston Rainbow Coalition also made withdrawals. On October 19 William Craig was forced to resign as vice president of the Shawmut Bank, a major victory for the UMW's corporate campaign, which found the going tougher in other cities.

The key to success in Boston was a unified labor effort and the involvement of the City Council and of Mayor Ray Flynn. The union campaign against Craig was also assisted by the black community efforts to expose discriminatory lending practices by Boston banks and by the fact that the building trades resented the money the bank pumped into nonunion construction. Banks had been targets of corporate campaigns before, but this was the first time in Boston history that a big financial institution actually appeared vulnerable to labor–community and city government pressure. It set an important precedent. As Dominic Bozzotto of the Hotel Workers and I were lobbying before the City Council vote, one member told us, "If we pass this resolution, then people will keep asking the city to use its financial deposits to pressure banks when other social issues come up." Bozzotto, who conceived of the City Council action based on his own extensive experience in community-labor coalition building, just smiled and said, "Well, maybe so. We think these big banks need to be socially responsible."

The Occupation of Moss No. 3

In early October I spent several days in the Virginia coal fields. I traveled with a camera crew from a local television station, hoping to help somehow to shape their program on the strike. I stayed at Camp Solidarity and talked to miners, their families, and supporters from all over the country. I was deeply impressed with the strikers' determination. Mike Brickey, a picket captain, spoke of the rootedness of the miners and their families. "Since 1647 my family hasn't moved more than twelve miles," he told me after a scab coal truck rumbled by. "The coal's goin' to stay here. And the people aren't goin' to leave. This is their life."

I was eager to find out as much as I could about the daring occupation of the Pittston coal treatment plant (Moss No. 3) through which all Pittston's finished coal had to pass. As a labor historian, I thought this was highly significant in itself but historically the sit-down strike has had this curious tendency to spread. I had no idea how impressive the operation was until I heard about it from participants.

Led by Eddie Burke of West Virginia District 17, a dedicated student of labor history, ninety-eight miners and clergyman Jim Sessions appeared in orange hunting vests at the Clinch River treatment plant about 4:15 in the afternoon on September 17. Burke, who grew up in Cabin Creek, a storm center of labor struggle in West Virginia, called the plan "Operation Flintstone" after the 1937 Chevy strike. Like the Flint sitdown, the Moss 3 occupation depended on massive outside support, on getting enough people to literally surround the plant and protect the occupiers.

"When we got to the gate [of the Moss 3 plant]," Burke told reporter Paul Nyden, "there were two Vance Security guards there. I told them 'We are an unarmed, nonviolent inspection team of stockholders coming to inspect our investment. You will not be harmed.' The two Vance men left hurriedly. There were no weapons drawn."

The next day 2,000 miners and supporters lined the road in front of the plant protecting the workers inside, who refused to follow a court order to vacate. As the new deadline approached on Wednesday more than 5,000 workers surrounded the plant. The state police withdrew to a safe distance, as miners directed traffic. On September 20 at 9:20 P.M., hours after the court deadline passed, the occupiers marched out triumphantly out of Moss 3 having carried the UMW's campaign of civil resistance to a new level and demonstrating again the creativity and solidarity the miners have often shown.

Though miners in southwest Virginia are used to going it alone and relying on their own significant resources, they told me over and over again how important their supporters were.

One of the "camp czars," Fred Wallace, estimated that about 30,000 supporters stayed at the Clinch River Camp between June and September. Buzz Hicks, the co-director, declared: "Our people look at the solidarity we've got from people all across this country and the world. We look at the thousands of people who've come through the camp and we say 'With support like this, we can't lose.'" He assured me that Pittson is being hurt badly by the strike and only has "two ways to go, either sign a contract or go bankrupt."

At this point, he said, the struggle had clearly gone beyond the Pittston contract. "We've come to the point," Hicks told me over coffee in the commissary, "where we don't even call it a strike anymore. It's a people's movement."

"We're telling our people, 'Hey, if this things ends tomorrow, we've got people out there who need our help.'" What does the solidarity movement that has flowed through Camp Solidarity mean to Hicks?

"I don't think you'll ever see another situation arise in this country where one labor union will have to stand alone."

After talking to people in the Appalachian coal fields I quickly pick up an "us versus them" feeling. As UMW Vice President Cecil Roberts told thousands of supporters at an August rally: "This is class war. The working class versus the corporate rich and their allies in state and federal government." Roberts, still awaiting trial on criminal contempt charges, has become a cause célèbre. The court is clearly reluctant to try Roberts, let alone sentence him. "I'll tell you, it's old Cecil who's keeping the violence down in the country," said a picketer outside the Moss 3 treatment plant. "He's the one who's keeping it nonviolent. But if they put him in jail, there's going to be a war."

Camp Solidarity

There's another feeling running through Camp Solidarity. It's a "they're coming for us next" feeling. I camped out near Mike Dunbar, who had been a roof bolter in an Exxon mine in Southern Illinois for ten years. He told me how frustrated he was by the state police who ran him and his buddies off the picket line. The police were still "freaked out by Illinois license plates" from the summer, when hundreds of Midwestern miners traveled to Virginia to block roads. "I don't want this at home," he said. "We've got to stop it here."

Buzz Hicks, the president of the UMW local at Moss 3, put it this way. "We've got people suffering badly here. So let's go ahead and fight the fight here. There's no use in lettin' some other groups somewhere else suffer. Let's just have it all out right here while we're at it. Maybe this will show these large companies that we're going to stick together."

Camping in the Clinch River Valley, talking over a fire with miners from my home state of Illinois, made me think about how these kinds of encampments have marked out people's struggles in our history, like bonfires of solidarity in the national epic of dog-eat-dog "progress."

I thought of the patriots' camp fires circling Boston after the British redcoats closed the port and occupied the city in 1775 and the talk of revolution could be heard over the crackling wood. I thought of the many encampments of striking miners from Ludlow in 1914, where troops burned thirteen women and children to death, to Matewan in 1920 when Sid Hatfield stood up to the Baldwin Felts death squads after they fired on the strikers' tent colony. I thought of the Bonus March of vets on Washington in 1929 and the destruction of their encampment by the U.S. Army under Douglas McArthur's command.

And I thought of the other encampments for justice, pitched by

Americans on the move, kicked off their land, locked out of their jobs. The Okies and Arkies camped in California picking the "Grapes of Wrath" and looking out for the "Vigilante Man." The Poor People's March on Washington, after Dr. King was murdered, and the Resurrection City that grew up in that city to embody his dream. Camp Solidarity is part of this stream in our history, an encampment for social justice where people can talk and dream around the camp fires of resistance.

Two of the people I'll most remember from Camp Solidarity are Richard and Ruby Dishman. Richard grew up in Dante, Virginia, a town Pittston owned until the 1960s, and he put in thirty-two years in the company's mines. When the new management team took over a few years ago, they made things "mean" and shifted him, the second oldest worker in the mines, to a forty-two inch seam. As we drove through the hills in his truck, he said, "If you'd told me a year ago all this would happen, that I'd meet people from nearly every state in the union, from Denmark and Pakistan, from Italy and Germany, come here to help us, I'd have almost said you were a liar."

"When we first came out," said Ruby Dishman, "I never thought it would be like this. I never thought we would have all this support. That's really what has helped us. People should keep coming."

Of course, she also said, "God helps those who help themselves." Ruby Dishman is a Daughter of Mother Jones, arrested twice and almost a third time, when she eluded state police and motored up a back road to get "pop" to the strikers occupying Moss 3. Known as "Granny" in the camp, she really seemed like the kind of mother figure Mary Jones became to the miners a century ago. "The community is sticking together," Ruby told me at the camp lunch counter. "And we get stronger every day."

"We dearly appreciate the food and the money that is brought to the camp," Buzz Hicks concluded. "But the people who come in here mean more than anything. I don't believe there's ever been a strike won with money." Nor did he believe this strike would be lost because of money—"by the courts trying to break us financially." "They can take every dime," he said firmly. "But they can't take the union out of you."

Conclusion

In our New Year's Day conversation, Richard Trumka spoke about the many meaningful aspects of the Pittston struggle. He attributed the victory not only to his members' remarkable determination and fortitude and his leadership team's brilliance and creativity. He also credited the practical solidarity of miners, their families, and their neighbors in southern Virginia, Kentucky, and West Virginia. The stunning election of UMW strike leader Jackie Stump to the Virginia House of Delegates in an unprecedented write-in campaign highlights the political power mobilized by the solidarity campaign. Stump defeated the twenty-two-year incumbent Democrat whose son, Judge Don McGlothin, Jr., had fined the union more than $30 million for strike-related activities.

Stump's election not only suggests the return to an old UMW tradition of voting for actual miners to represent them; it also came as part of an overall effort to *politicize* the strike. The politiciation process began with the passionate hatred generated by the incumbent Democratic governor of Virginia, Gerald Balliles, who called out squadrons of state police to protect scabs and arrest strikers; it was sustained by Trumka and Roberts, who presented the strike as a political struggle against the courts and the federal labor laws.

Beyond this, Trumka emphasized the crucial role played by the thousands who expressed solidarity with these strikers who live and work in some of the remotest counties of Appalachia—support from church and peace groups as well as from union members and officials from all over the country and abroad. Even Lech Walesa played an important behind-the-scenes role when he visited the United States in November. In the reports about the settlement on public radio the local miners made a strong point of how much these demonstrations of solidarity meant.

The Pittston struggle does not suggest a single formula for the future but it does have many lessons. Trumka stressed the importance of unions being creative and relying on support from all friendly quarters, the kind of broad sympathy that helped rebuild the UMW and create the CIO in the 1930s. He hopes the miners' Pittston campaign will inspire a bolder, risk-taking approach to labor struggle for the 1990s—one that involves full mobilization of union members, their families, and neighbors, that opens the door to all of labor's supporters, and that directly challenges unjust labor laws, tryannical judges, and antiunion politicians.

Jobs With Justice:
Florida's Fight Against Worker Abuse

Andrew R. Banks

It was one of those rare moments I assume we all experience but a few times in our lives. It was one of those moments in which even the smallest of details are etched in your mind forever—the color of your shirt, the people you talked to and precisely what everyone said, and exactly what you were thinking about at every instant.

It was July 29, 1987, sometime between 7:30 and 8:00 in the evening. I was standing in the aisle, in the middle of a crowd of 12,000 union members, civil rights and women's rights activists, senior citizens and others. It was almost eerie because even with all these people the room was perfectly quiet. Everyone was intensely concentrating on the words of the woman at the podium, Dian Murphy, a black Eastern Airlines flight attendant from Atlanta. In the corner of my mouth I could taste that salty taste that tears leave. I looked around. The huge operating engineer sitting next to me was crying too, and so were his ten-year-old daughter and the three women wearing Communications Workers of America (CWA) T-shirts sitting next to them.

Murphy talked with a sharp and clear resonance which demanded attention from the crowd in the auditorium. She told her story. She had an outstanding record as a model employee for twelve and a half years at Eastern Airlines. She had made sacrifices along with Eastern's other workers to keep Eastern flying in the new deregulated environment. When Eastern chairman Frank Borman couldn't extract any more concessions from the unions he retaliated by selling the airline to Texas Air's Frank Lorenzo at a bargain basement price. Borman was later named as a director of Texas Air and paid $1 million. Murphy and the other Eastern workers knew it was only a matter of time before the notorious Lorenzo would try to crush the Eastern workforce. Already hundreds of flight attendants were being fired for minor incidents such as being $2.00 short on liquor money or being absent even on verified sick leave. On New Year's Day, 1987, these stories of worker abuse became very real to Dian Murphy.

In the presence of the 12,000 attendees of the nation's first Jobs With Justice rally Dian Murphy relived her nightmare. "On December 31, 1986, I came home from a four-day flight. It was approximately two o'clock in the afternoon. There was an intruder in my home who viciously attacked me. I was blindfolded, I was raped, I was terrorized for an indeterminate amount of time. My assailant threatened to kill me and my teenaged daughter if I called the police. I was so terrorized that he would return and hurt me that I left and called the police from a friend's house.

"I called Eastern Airlines the following day because obviously I couldn't take my four-day trip out that evening. Even though this was only my third absence in two years, I was so afraid that I would get in trouble for missing the trip I asked the police detective, Curtis Johnson, to call my employer and explain what had happened to me. The supervisor did not believe him so she called the Fulton County Police Department and asked to speak to, quote, a "white detective" to verify what Detective Johnson had told her. It seemed that the word of a black detective was not good enough for her.

"When I returned to work I brought medical documentation and a statement from the police department. Two weeks later I met with my supervisor and a manager and I was told that the incident would be counted as an absence under the company's new absence control program. I was told if I was absent again for any reason I would be taken off the payroll or terminated. There was no exception made for me.

"I could not believe that someone could sit across a desk and say the things to me that she said after all I had been through. It made no difference to them that I had been raped. They did not care. I am outraged by my employer's attitude and behavior. I feel hurt and I feel betrayed.

"I have given the best years of my adult working life to this company. I have given money and wage concessions along with all the other employees at Eastern because that's what the company said was needed to survive. Yet, when I needed compassion and understanding I was made to feel like I committed a crime.

"It's very difficult to stand here and talk to you about what's happened to me, but I feel it is important for people to realize how Eastern Airlines under Frank Lorenzo's Texas Air Corporation is treating its employees. I have lost so very much and to have Eastern Airlines further humiliate me and try to take away my dignity is appalling. I was victimized twice: once by a rapist and once by my employer, Eastern Airlines. And I *refuse* to continue to become a victim."

At this point, none of us could hold our emotions in check any longer. As those words—"I refuse to continue to become a victim"—reverberated from the huge sound system across the assemblage in the Miami Beach Convention Center the crowd jumped to its feet like the huge human waves football fans create at NFL games. In a spontaneous release of emotion the rally-goers cheered Dian Murphy for her determination to stand up and fight back. Now tears were streaming across her face too and her smile grew more confident, as if she was gaining strength from the thundering approval.

As the ovation carried on for at least another five minutes I looked around. I had never seen anything like this before. Blacks, Hispanics, whites, young and old, women and men. They were all shouting and all one. They held each other's hands and complete strangers from different walks of life cried and cheered together with their arms wrapped around one another's shoulders and waists. This was solidarity.

Jesse Jackson was there in the tenth row, flanked on the right by a cute freckle-faced five-year-old boy and on the left by Geneva and Irwin Miller, members of the Dade County Council of Senior Citizens. Jackson was the only presidential candidate to accept the local Jobs With Justice committee's invitation to sit with us and listen to what America's workers had to say.

Jackson and the others listened to workers who were victims of corporate greed. They listened to the victims of deregulation in telecommunications, to victims of privatization in mass transit, and, of course, to the victims of what Machinist president William Winpisinger termed "merger maniacs" in the airline industry.

It certainly was a different type of rally. Most of the speakers were rank-and-file workers like Dian Murphy. Other speakers included representatives of labor's allies: Molly Yard, president of the National Organization for Women, Reverend Joseph Lowery, president of the Southern Christian Leadership Conference, and the executive director of the Florida Consumers Federation, Karen Clarke. Their speeches all rang the same theme. Labor's issues have once again become civil rights issues, women's issues, and consumers' issues. They each welcomed the Jobs With Justice coalition declaration that rather than acting as a special interest, the labor movement was reclaiming its rightful role as leader in the fight for the public's interest.

As the cheering finally began to die down, I remember asking myself, "Is this it? A rally?" Or would this event kick off something even more special in Florida? Was Jobs With Justice merely another feel-good rally in which union members left the solidarity of that evening to return to the isolation of individual workplaces and separate unions? Or was Morty Bahr, president of CWA, correct when he opened the historic gathering with the prediction that "Jobs With Justice is the wake-up call for the American labor movement." As the coordinator for the rally and the Florida Jobs With Justice committee, I didn't want this magic to die. I also wanted to see the eighty local unions and twenty-four community groups who worked together in the two months of events preceding the rally continue their new-found solidarity and community-based unionism. As I looked around the seated crowd, I sensed that somehow this could be different. Jobs With Justice wasn't just another rally.

A Washington-Initiated Grassroots Movement

In December 1986, just weeks before Dian Murphy was to experience the dual assaults by a rapist and by her employer, workers in the Detroit area were experiencing attacks by their own employers. First, General Motors announced that it would be laying off 15,000 UAW workers and then open eleven new plants in Mexico. Later that week the wages of 3,000 downtown Detroit building janitors, all long-time members of the Service Employees International Union, were unilaterally slashed by 40 percent to $6.00 an hour. Third, just prior to Christmas, at the Detroit headquarters of the new telecommunications giant, MCI, 400 predominantly black college-educated women employees were told by management not to return to work the next day. Instead, they were to report the next day in groups of ten to area motels, from where they were individually escorted by security guards to get their personal belongings from their desks. At the motel they were notified that their jobs were being moved to Iowa. Months earlier a majority of these same employees had signed petitions for representation by the Communication Workers of America (CWA) and were waiting for the National Labor Relations Board to schedule a representation election.

The CWA organizing director, Larry Cohen, sat in his Detroit motel room stunned by the December massacres. He interpreted these events to mean that the problem in America wasn't a fight between two special interest groups, union leaders and corporate managers. The problem, to Cohen, was much more fundamental. Through such practices as mergers and acquisitions, deregulation, contracting-out, and the flagrant disregard for labor laws, as antiquated and watered-down as they were, corporate America was effectively depriving workers of job security, a decent standard of living, and a right to organize unions. As Cohen saw it, all of America, not just union members, needed decent jobs—jobs with justice. In a telephone conversation with CWA president Bahr, Cohen stated, "If they can do this to us in Detroit, a labor town, then I could be doing this job [organizing director] the rest of my life and not make a bit of difference."

Bahr agreed with Cohen and asked the Industrial Union Department (IUD) of the AFL-CIO to call a special meeting to discuss the issue. At this meeting ten international union presidents and their organizing directors agreed to form a Jobs With Justice Committee of the IUD. It was the strong belief of Bahr and the others that the committee would have no staff because Jobs With Justice had to be a locally controlled grassroots program which centered around community struggles emanating from the workplace. The national committee would assist in these efforts by providing printed materials, seed money, and technical assistance.

The backbone of the Jobs With Justice effort would be the "I'll Be There" pledge card. Individual workers and their supporters would be asked to sign a sacred pledge which stated in part, ". . . during the next year, I'LL BE THERE at least five times for someone else's fight as well as my own. If enough of us are there, we'll all start winning."

Detroit was targeted as the site of the first Jobs With Justice rally, with the United Auto Workers (UAW) taking the lead and the CWA and the Service Employees International Union (SEIU) playing strong secondary roles. However, some of the important union leadership groups in Detroit apparently felt threatened by an initiative which they did not start. So the Jobs With Justice Committee began to look for another city and the interest turned to Miami.

In April, Dan Miller, president of the Florida AFL-CIO, brought together various South Florida union activists and leaders. The purpose of the meeting was to discuss ways other unions could assist the Eastern Airlines Machinist and Flight Attendant unions in their fight against Frank Lorenzo. In conversation with IUD organizer Joe Uehlein, the leaders of the Flight Attendants (Transport Workers Union Local 553) learned of the newly formed Jobs With Justice Committee. Uehlein informed them that CWA was having its convention in Miami in July and would be willing to mobilize its 2,800 delegates for an airport picket line against Eastern. At the next national Jobs With Justice Committee meeting both situations were reported and later that month Dan Miller invited Jobs With Justice to assist unions and community groups in staging what would eventually become the largest labor rally in Florida history.

It is interesting to note that Detroit's failure to become the first Jobs With Justice site was in great part because of the top-down approach taken by the UAW. While many local Detroit labor and community activists were excited about Jobs With Justice, the top officials of the UAW (whose international headquarters is located in Detroit) were ambivalent about an approach which mobilized their members. Conversely, in Miami local labor was looking to Washington for assistance in mobilizing rank-and-file and community support for what they accurately believed was to become a major labor struggle—the fight against Frank Lorenzo.

Miami is perhaps the archetypal U.S. city of the late twentieth century. With a predominantly service economy and plenty of newly arrived immigrant workers, South Florida has been a tough place for unions to survive in. While unions from labor strongholds in the North function as players in the local political economy, South Florida labor is a numerically weak group and the few labor success stories from Miami have been tales of unions which tried new strategies and learned to fight from this position of weakness.

For instance, in Broward and Palm Beach counties building trades officials have created strong alliances with powerful senior citizen groups based in retirement condominiums. Many senior leaders are retired union organizers and officers and most of the condo dwellers held union cards when they worked in the Northeast. This labor-senior coalition has been successful in running slates for local elections and in passing a prevailing wage ordinance for construction workers in Broward County.

Likewise, the Eastern Airlines Machinist union, which is based in Miami, has received international labor acclaim for its innovative eight-year fight to extend real workplace democracy in the corporation and to fight management's demands for wage and work rule concessions.

In spite of these examples most of the unions in Miami were having a tough time just holding their own when the Jobs With Justice Committee first met with us in early May 1987. Most of the local unionists and community leaders welcomed their offer to help put on a rally in July, but expressed concern that a massive rally might drain energy which could be better spent on long-term efforts. We decided to make the July rally a kick-off of an ongoing Jobs With Justice effort rather than an end objective. We would build on the new relationships made between the various unions and between unions and important segments of the community. Moreover, we would develop new skills in mobilization and communications which could be adapted by local unions and community groups.

We also decided to use a media strategy which promoted the vision of unions as institutions which mobilized rank-and-file workers to fight what we termed "worker abuse" and which created alliances with other groups in the community that were also fighting "downtown" or the "establishment." Over eighty unions and twenty-four groups, such as the Florida Consumers Federation, Florida NOW, ACORN (Association of Community Organizations for Reform Now), and Florida State Council of Senior Citizens, signed our Florida Call for Jobs with Justice.

The Florida Jobs With Justice Committee implemented its media strategy by graphically demonstrating its rank-and-file and community-wide support at every opportunity. In early June, we held our first press conference to announce the formation of the Jobs With Justice movement and issued an invitation to the public to join us at the July rally. The press conference, held in front of Eastern Airlines headquarters, coincided with the moment when 3,000 Eastern mechanics walked off their jobs during their lunch break. They were joined by 500 officers and members of the Teamsters, Transport Workers, Plumbers, Carpenters, Teachers, and other unions, all carrying signs that demanded "jobs with justice."

Press conference speakers included victims of worker abuse from AT&T, Eastern Airlines, and the Dade County Transit Authority. Also speaking in support of Jobs With Justice were representatives from the clergy, NOW, the NAACP, and the Florida Consumers Federation. The Florida Consumers Federation produced over 2,000 signed postcards demanding that Congress hold hearings in Miami to investigate worker abuse.

Congress did hold the hearings, which were packed with an overflow crowd of rank and filers. This generated a lot of media discussion and anticipation for the upcoming rally, as did the 200-person Jobs With Justice picket line placed in front of the local offices of NBC, supporting the eight striking local members of the National Association of Broadcast Employees and Technicians (NABET).

The Jobs With Justice media approach reflects the movement's overall bottom-up philosophy of rank-and-file mobilization and community outreach. Unlike the top-down approach of the AFL-CIO's snappy $13 million Union Yes ad campaign, Jobs With Justice has spent almost nothing to get thousands of minutes of what most observers believe is the best media coverage unions have received in over thirty years.

More Than a Rally

For weeks after the rally my telephone rang constantly with energetic calls of local union people and community activists. They all had the same message—let's not let this die.

We decided to do two things. First, the Labor Studies Center at Florida International University agreed to sponsor a Breakfast Club once a month where interested labor leaders could pursue in-depth strategy discussion on issues such as white-collar organizing, privatization and contracting-out, and the threat of rising health-care costs for workers and their families. These meetings were very exciting and a lasting camaraderie was developed among these local leaders, who had barely known each other before. Based on this fellowship and the shared vision emanating from the Jobs With Justice activities, members of this group would eventually successfully elect one of their own, local Machinist president Marty Urra, to the presidency of the traditionally passive South Florida AFL-CIO.

Our second task after the rally was to computerize the thousands of pledge cards that we collected. This was done by senior citizen volunteers at the Florida Consumers Federation. This seemingly mundane task was to prove to be a crucial element in future labor-community struggles.

In October the local building trades council announced plans to picket the trade show of the notorious union-busting Associated Building Contractors (ABC) at the new Joe Robbie Stadium. After the construction unions requested Jobs With Justice support, we mailed postcards to all pledge-card signers, reminding them they had promised to "be there" five times in the next year. Over 3,000 picketers showed up, 1,000 of whom were not from the building trades. The trade show was effectively shut down, spelling major financial disaster for ABC.

The pledge cards were also used to mobilize 500 people for a labor-community rally on Martin Luther King, Jr.'s birthday, January 15, in support of unions in South Africa and the struggle of the predominantly black Dade County transit union, TWU Local 291.

Local 291 was in a fight for survival. Its leaders had publicly opposed the county commission's effort to expand the new rail system, which served primarily well-off suburban white professionals at the expense of the bus system, which serves the transit-dependent residents of black, Hispanic, and elderly neighborhoods. The downtown Miami business establishment and developers, who stood to rake in millions of dollars with the rail expansion, persuaded the County Commission's transportation chair, Commissioner Clara Oesterle, to try to bust the union by contracting out bus driver jobs and demanding $6,000 in concessions from individual transit workers.

After the successful labor-community rally and parade on King's birthday, TWU and Jobs With Justice announced a community-wide campaign to end what we termed "transit apartheid." The label was fitting for two reasons. First, the Dade County government was trying to export jobs and decrease wages of the mostly black transit workforce while increasing the wages of other county workers. At the same time the government and its Chamber of Commerce allies were promoting the building of a transit system for well-off whites at the expense of transit dependent minorities. The union demanded a halt to rail expansion until the bus fleet was increased from 400 to 1,000 buses.

In September 1988 the TWU leadership went to its labor and community Jobs With Justice allies for support in opposing the reelection bids of Clara Oesterle and two other incumbent county commission-ers. Jobs With Justice mailed get-out-the-vote letters to pledge card-signers, organized union retirees in the senior citizen condos, and worked on voter turnout with the major unions. Overnight, the bump-ers of county buses and thousands of union members' cars sported the orange and black (Oesterle's campaign colors) bumper stickers proclaiming "Throw Clara from the Train."

Although Oesterle out-spent the labor-endorsed candidate seven-to-one, and even though an incumbent had never been defeated in Dade County, all three were soundly defeated (Oesterle by over 20 percent). The media credited our success to the anger of union members and the public over the commission's transportation policy.

For the last three weeks of the 1988 Florida U.S. Senate campaign, Jobs With Justice troops picketed ultra right-wing candidate Congress-man Connie Mack in every one of his public appearances throughout Florida. Jobs With Justice picketers chanted loudly for an end to the "Big Mack Attacks" on working families, seniors, the environment, and education. Many attribute the thirteen-point drop in Mack's lead over Democrat Buddy McKay to the Jobs With Justice campaign. Un-fortunately, Mack won the race by less than one percent only after the absentee ballots were counted.

We have used the "I'll Be There" pledge cards to generate picket lines for striking Jai Alai players and for locked-out sign and display workers. Active Jobs With Justice committees have called for pickets and rallies in Jacksonville, Orlando, Tampa, Tallahassee, Boca Raton, and Fort Lauderdale.

A Nationwide Movement for Workers' Rights

In part because of the success of the Miami rally, Jobs With Justice actions have sprung up in over sixty locations throughout the country. Interestingly enough, the most successful of these efforts have been in locations where labor has not been traditionally strong, and has therefore been more willing to work with others and try new things.

Most unions in the stronger labor areas feel they can afford to con-duct their business by using strategies and tactics which are isolated from local labor and community concerns. To these unions, collective bargaining and even organizing is typically a private struggle kept from the public view.

From every corner of Texas over 2,000 unionists, civil rights leaders, and feminists paid $25 each to secure seats in chartered buses to tiny Nacogdoches in northeast Texas, where 3,000 people marched on Stephen Austin College in support of sixty black women cafeteria workers who had been struggling against employment discrimination and poverty level wages for fifteen years. After the Jobs With Justice march the cafeteria's management settled the contract and the Texas attorney general agreed to pay the workers back wages for past discrimination.

In Nashville 8,000 union members and progressive religious activists rallied to hear United Mine Workers President Rich Trumka and South Africa Mine Workers president, James Mlotsi, declare solidarity between the workers of both countries. A series of breakfasts between union and religious leaders which took place after the rally have evolved into a loose-knit coalition to deal with social problems. The new labor-religion coalition is credited with efforts to help house, feed, and employ Tennessee's growing homeless population. Likewise, this new alliance has played a key role in the IUD's successful organizing drives in eleven factories involving 6,000 workers in Tennessee.

On April 4, Jobs With Justice in Memphis initiated a month-long labor-civil rights pilgrimage through over forty cities in the South commemorating the twentieth anniversary of the assassination of Martin Luther King, Jr. The pilgrimage culminated in Atlanta where over 10,000 people marched arm-in-arm demanding justice for Atlanta's janitors who were seeking union representation by SEIU and justice for Eastern Airlines workers.

In Denver, the Jobs With Justice coalition has rallied massive support for janitors at the National Mint, musicians at the Philharmonic, and a boycott initiated by reporters and mailers at the *Denver Post*. The boycott was so successful that in the first three months over 20,000 subscriptions to the *Post* had been canceled.

The one traditional labor stronghold where Jobs With Justice pickets and rallies have been successfully implemented is Buffalo. Over 200 workers at Buffalo General Hospital had struck and been permanently replaced with no hope of regaining their jobs. Jesse Jackson led his supporters from the civil rights community and the Rainbow Coalition to picket the hospital with Buffalo area union members. Because of this public support generated by the Jobs With Justice activities all the strikers have been rehired and they once again enjoy the protection of a union contract. This stunning victory proved that a Jobs With Justice campaign can be effective wherever labor is willing to embrace a membership mobilization strategy which seeks the solidarity of other unions and the support of the wider community.

Both nationally and locally, Jobs With Justice committees are structurally loose and primarily play a coordination role. The structure of Jobs With Justice also reflects its emphasis on locally generated direct action. Nationally, representatives of the presidents of the twenty Jobs With Justice unions meet once a month to review requests for rallies or other actions around the country. It is almost automatic for the Jobs With Justice Committee to sponsor these actions by supplying organizing kits and materials such as pledge cards, posters, and banners. If at least two separate international unions want to sponsor a larger event, more resources are devoted to the local effort.

Almost always, local Jobs With Justice groups concentrate on multi-issue rallies or on organizing around a specific issue campaign. Local structures vary from place to place but most local committees emphasize "hands on" meetings where different unions and community groups take responsibility for one or more tasks in a Jobs With Justice project. Meetings tend to be very open and feuding unions are told to leave their past differences outside the room. In Florida we try to rule by consensus rather than by strict parliamentary majority rule.

The Labor Movement's Wake-Up Call

Now that I look back at that special moment in the July 1987 rally, when the throng cheered Dian Murphy for her courage and resolve to no longer be victimized, I realize that all the signs were right there that Jobs With Justice was going to be more than just a rally. In Florida and other places, Jobs With Justice has shown that grassroots efforts can be initiated and successfully supported by some of labor's Washington-based leadership. Without this support and encouragement Jobs With Justice would have been almost impossible. Their backing demonstrates that some of labor's top officials are willing to take chances and risk losing absolute control of an institution which is facing its greatest crisis of the century.

It is not easy for labor's top leadership to embrace a Jobs With Justice strategy because it demands such a different approach than that of service unionism which has evolved over the past few decades. Jobs With Justice means relying less on business agents solving problems *for* workers, and more on gaining public support for workplace issues through membership mobilization and local leadership development.

Many unions have spent years developing bargaining practices which only work when they are hidden from public view. A Jobs With Justice membership activation approach, with its involvement of seniors, environmentalists, feminists, the civil rights movement, and others, not only makes this method impossible, it complicates the bargaining process further by adding new players—the public and the rank and file. I can understand how frightening this could be to union leaders who already feel things are out of control with the labor movement's dramatic downward slide in the past decade.

While this hesitation by some is understandable, it should not be acceptable because labor's only hope for a comeback lies in its ability to articulate and *act* upon a vision of the world which can be widely embraced by workers and the community. Labor's foes in corporate America understand this and are effectively putting forth their alternative view of how society should look.

This is why the Jobs With Justice movement has ignited such enthusiasm in so many diverse places over such a short period of time. Jobs With Justice speaks about a future in which workplace issues such as job security, a decent living standard, and the right of workers to organize are embraced by the larger community rather than by one group of workers at one company. A core group of the AFL-CIO, twenty international presidents, have accepted this analysis and approach to one degree or another. Now is the time, they feel, to start working together on the arduous task of digging out of the deep pit of despair enveloping workers and their communities. Union leaders are turning to their members, the members of other unions, and the public for help—and they are receiving it.

Once every year, the AFL-CIO Industrial Union Department sponsors a national Jobs With Justice planning meeting where local activists and Washington labor leadership plan the next year's agenda and swap local war stories. The local folks are plugged into a growing national network of activists who are mobilizing within their communities around workplace issues. The national folks are getting out of the unreal world of D.C., back to the roots of the labor movement.

The 1989 meeting was convened in Memphis on the first day of the machinist, flight attendant, and pilot strike against Eastern Airlines. The symbol of the Eastern strike—the word "Lorenzo" in a red circle with a red slash—had been designed for the Miami Jobs With Justice rally. I remember, back at the rally, seeing a sea of these symbols on thousands of large placards, waving in unison with the cheers of approval for Dian Murphy's resolve. And I remember Murphy's final remarks.

"What has happened to me is just one of many incidents of worker abuse among my fellow flight attendants. I know of flight attendants driven to suicide and others who have attempted suicide because of the company's pressure to force them out of their jobs. We all know of countless other cases of suffering at the hands of corporate greed.

Its not just flight attendants who are suffering. We are all catching hell.

"I know it's not supposed to be this way. The history of the labor movement is filled with the accounts of brave men and women who've given their blood, their sweat, their tears, and their lives for jobs with justice. Let us all join together and say no to the Lorenzos, the Icahns, and the rest of the robber barons of corporate America—we demand jobs with justice."

Sisters at the Borders: Asian Immigrant Women and HERE Local 2

Patricia Lee

On one of my first days of work as a roomcleaner at a major downtown San Francisco hotel, I was stopped at the employee entrance by an immigration officer and asked to show my identification. Once inside the hotel, I saw many workers desperately phoning their relatives, others escaping through the back doors, and others using various delaying tactics in answering the officers' questions.

My first impression of this confused scene was that everyone understood what was happening that day—an immigration raid by "la Migra" (the U.S. Immigration and Naturalization Service). Despite the fact that most were either legal residents or naturalized citizens, all the workers felt threatened by the raid and understood their powerlessness in the face of such brute authority. But the guests, mostly businessmen and tourists from the Midwest, were completely unaware of the drama unfolding around them. They hardly noticed that the sheets were changed a little later than usual or that food service was slower.

Raids like the one I experienced that day have been repeated thousands of times in hundreds of workplaces, and have become a common feature in American life. With employer sanctions officially taking effect (under the Immigration Reform and Control Act of 1986), every place of employment became a target of this national witchhunt for undocumented workers. Each immigrant worker and naturalized citizen works under a cloud of suspicion as to the validity of their identity and documents. Nonimmigrants have been swept into the broad intimidation and repression that la Migra's raids encourage.

The main factor that prevents la Migra from making a clean sweep of the estimated 2 million undocumenteds who do not qualify for amnesty under the new law is that they are irreplaceable. Immigrant workers, both legal and undocumented, are part of the structure of this nation's economy. They perform the hard and dirty work the rest of us do not want to do—washing dishes, cleaning rooms, picking fruit, sewing garments, and assembling personal computers. Since they cannot be removed without damaging the entire economy, it is long overdue for institutions of this society to recognize their importance and extend to them the rights and benefits they deserve.

This article tells the story of a local union and a community group who, in pursuit of multinational and multiracial solidarity within their own organizations, have coalesced to help immigrants defend themselves against the exploitation they inevitably face in the workplace. In both cases, women provided the leadership that made these efforts possible, efforts that may harbinger a broader view of working-class solidarity in the American labor movement.

Immigrants and Unions

In a competitive society like the United States, there is no such thing as a free lunch—immigrants will not receive their due recognition until they get organized.

Traditionally, immigrants have gotten themselves together through two types of organization—labor unions and community agencies, including those operated by churches. Labor unions, the vehicles that worked so well for earlier Irish, Jewish, Italian, and Eastern European immigrants, have not been anywhere near as receptive to nonwhite immigrants. The fact of the matter is that labor unions in the past have too often been in the forefront of outright exclusion (as in their agitation for the Chinese Exclusion Act in 1882), against affirmative action for women and minorities, and have even been involved in union-busting of minority-led organizing drives (witness the United Farm Workers' problems with the Teamsters).

Today, however, unions are facing a generational crisis. While the leadership remains predominantly older white males, the membership is increasingly minority, immigrant, and female. The globalization of the economy has meant the loss of traditional blue-collar jobs to the third world and the decline of the once mighty industrial core of the AFL-CIO. In order to compensate for their reduced numbers, unions have turned increasingly to the workforce of unorganized service workers, mainly minorities, women, and immigrants.

Though unions are beginning to recognize that if they do not become more inclusive of immigrants organized labor will cease to be a force within American society, many union leaders cannot decide whether they should embrace or exclude immigrant workers. The AFL-CIO, for example, supported the Immigration Reform and Control Act, which is essentially a plan to force the firing of undocumented workers who cannot qualify for amnesty. One of the false assumptions of the union leaders is that "foreigners" are trying to take away jobs from Americans and are part of the cause of problems in the economy.

This naive point of view demonstrates that the union leadership does not fully understand the current transition in the U.S. economy.

The economic disruptions caused by employer sanctions and the increased interference by the INS into personnel offices will ultimately hurt all American workers. Solidarity with immigrants is the only way unions can protect their members.

Immigrant workers find the package offered by unions—higher wages, health insurance, pensions, and other benefits—to be attractive. But for many unions that package fails to include an aggressive fight against deportations and other problems immigrant workers face. A widespread perception among immigrant workers is that union leaders have maintained sweetheart contracts with employers and that while always ready to collect dues, many unions are less than eager to file grievances. Even when unions recognize immigrant needs, they have trouble getting their message to the unorganized because they are not equipped with enough bilingual staff and organizers drawn from the existing rank and file.

Thus unions have two major barriers to overcome in order to successfully organize and involve immigrant workers. The first is to promote immigrant leaders and develop programs that address immigrant needs. Second, unions must change their public image, which may sometimes require changes in their substance.

HERE Local 2

The Hotel and Restaurant Employees Union (HERE) Local 2, the union to which I belong, has developed a number of innovative programs aimed at greater immigrant participation.

HERE Local 2 represents 13,000 workers in the hotel and restaurant industries in the San Francisco area. More than half the members are women and about 70 percent are people of color, the majority of whom are third world immigrants from around the world. These are the roomcleaners, bellhops, dishwashers, cooks, waiters, waitresses, and bartenders who perform the job of making a pleasant stay for an ever-expanding tourist trade. A small percentage of the workers earn a good salary, but these are mainly white workers who are able to enter "the front of the house" jobs in the Class A restaurants. The majority of the workforce is locked into "the back of the house," unseen and unheard, performing menial labor. Despite these divisions, workers in San Francisco fare better than their counterparts in the rest of the country due to an aggressive rank and file and a leadership that has responded to the demands and issues of its members.

In the past seventeen years, Local 2's militant rank and file has reformed the union's organizational structure resulting in better representation and improved contract terms. These changes were due to a number of factors. One is that in the 1960s and 1970s the workforce dramatically changed from primarily European immigrants and black and white Americans to a rainbow of third world immigrants with a variety of languages and the cultural differences to match. As this group expanded, the union leadership of the time failed to represent them and their working conditions deteriorated. Following the transformation, a significant number of student radicals entered the industry, carrying with them all the militancy of the college campuses of the time. The meeting of the two provided an explosive combination that led to a tumultuous period of political strife within the local. As this dynamic duo set about organizing itself, women and immigrant workers filled the vacuum of leadership that eventually led to an overhaul of the union.

With many of the new members turning out to vote, union elections became a major forum for advocating demands and exposing atrocious working conditions. It became matter of fact that if you ran for union office, your slate had to represent the diverse ethnic make-up of the union, with women right in there.

In the 1985 elections, seven candidates vied to lead this greatly divergent and vibrant rank and file. The only two women running for the top office of president could not unify any of the slates around their candidacies. One of the factors was the belief that "our members will not elect a woman." But the two women, both in their early thirties, one of whom was Chinese, defied all prejudices and came in as the top votegetters, with the five men trailing far behind.

Today, with its first woman president, the local is in the process of a complete overhaul. A majority of the union staff is now women, with a large representation of minorities and many people who speak more than one language. A new committee structure has been developed to bring onto the committees members of every race, nationality, sex, age, and every department in each workplace to ensure full representation. The intent of the committees is to organize the workforce for contract fights, to win grievances, to organize nonunion establishments, and to take on such issues as the new Immigration Reform Law. While constituencies continue to organize along racial and gender lines, it has been mainly done by appealing to the support and unity of all members. Victories have come about when the committees have effectively organized around issues that cross racial and gender lines while addressing individual group needs.

Throughout Local 2's past seventeen-year evolution, women have been prominent leaders in the court of activity. Because of this, women's issues have often formed the rallying point for change.

The most dramatic mass movement in support of women occurred in the 1980 hotel strike, covering 6,500 workers, when there was overwhelming support for the demands of militant immigrant women roomcleaners who were protesting horrendous working conditions. In culmination of a five-year battle with hotel owners and a lot of anger directed at the union leadership, the whole union walked off the job in support of these women. The roomcleaners won all their major demands, which included a reduction in workload, participation of women in the grievance procedure, and a larger percentage increase in pay over the other crafts.

One of the programs the local has developed to serve our immigrant members is a legal counseling program, through which members get free legal advice on whether they qualify for amnesty or refugee status and legal assistance with other immigration problems. This is particularly important to immigrant workers because of the legal maze the INS has set up and the way employers exploit this maze to intimidate workers, but the counseling program is available to all the members.

The local has made an effort to develop a strong "core leadership" of shop stewards and house committee members who are bilingual in Spanish, Chinese, Korean, and other languages. As a result the local's field representatives can now conduct grievances and organize around numerous issues alongside bilingual rank-and-file leaders. The immigrant workers can fully express their testimony and opinions, and participate in the union structure and grievance process. Multilingual literature and translation at meetings has also proven effective, especially before and during contract negotiations. The local is able to survey the issues of concern to immigrants and get their input on all contractual terms before collective bargaining begins.

Through a developed committee structure of several layers, immigrant participation in the life of the union has been consistently high. Much of the committee work is aimed at "actions" during contract negotiations—actions like street rallies, demonstrations, nonviolent sit-ins, and "dinner-a-thons" where large groups of workers occupy a restaurant during peak periods eating soup, thereby filling seats that would ordinarily be taken by higher-paying customers.

While these programs have had a very positive response from both immigrants and the general membership, there is still far to go, especially in terms of developing immigrant leaders from the rank and file. Most of the immigrant workers have families, large rent payments, relatives in need back in their homelands, and many other pressures. Given their immediate situations, it has been very difficult for leaders to emerge and accept the added responsibilities of union leadership. The union will also soon face the difficult problem of sanctuary for undocumenteds and refugees who do not qualify for amnesty.

Asian Immigrant Women Advocates

As Local 2 developed these new programs, it often became necessary to seek help from organizations with roots in the various ethnic communities. We simply did not have the skills and elements to reach all the racial and national groups within Local 2's membership. One such group exists within the Asian community, the Asian Immigrant Women Advocates (AIWA).

The Asian immigrant population has expanded enormously because of Southeast Asians leaving the devastation of the Vietnam war, Filipinos and Koreans escaping political dictatorships and oppressive economic conditions, and Hong Kong residents migrating in anticipation of Hong Kong's incorporation into the People's Republic of China in 1992. Many of these immigrants begin their U.S. employment in the hotel and restaurant industries, most in nonunion jobs. For the most part, the Asian ethnic groups coexist harmoniously, with the main racial tensions occurring with whites who fear a "yellow peril" and non-Asian ethnic groups who are fighting to survive in already crowded communities with diminishing social services. There exists a dichotomy between recent immigrants and American-born Asians who feel the anti-Asian backlash of the overall population, but it is often the Asian-Americans who come together with their bilingual Asian counterparts to meet the challenges facing the Asian community. Such was the case with AIWA.

AIWA was the brainchild of Elaine Kim, a first-generation Korean-American who was then executive director of the Korean Community Center of the East Bay. Founded in 1982, AIWA was directed at women because of the pivotal role they play in the American economy by occupying many low-paying jobs such as maids, waitresses, and seamstresses. Exploited beyond imagination, the women are limited in their ability to contribute to the health of their communities. Ms. Kim and other Asian-American women saw the devastating impact on Asian communities of the poor working conditions the immigrant women suffer. In defiance of stereotypes and patriarchal cultural obstacles, AIWA went about the task of organizing these women to change the world in which they live.

Today, Yong Shin, Korean-American director of AIWA, and her multiethnic staff perform a crucial role in involving immigrant Asian women in the life of the union and within their workplaces. AIWA offers educational services to Korean, Chinese, Vietnamese, and Filipina working women. Instructors provide courses in English as a second language, structured to meet the needs of adult working women. AIWA also provides workshops on contract rights, federal and state labor regulations, health and safety rules, and hourly wage laws.

Most of Local 2's immigrant women members originate from countries where labor codes are weak and enforcement is practically nonexistent. In places such as Korea and Taiwan, for example, a complaint to the authorities will usually lead to harassment from employers or immediate firing. Since notices are not often posted in factories in such authoritarian societies, workers are not aware that they might have the right to complain. In contrast, the immigrant women now find themselves within a society which expects people to complain.

Managers often take advantage of the immigrants' ignorance of the contract and laws to illegally exploit them. Overtime without pay and denial of rest periods and lunch breaks are common abuses in the hotel trade. Blame for accidents is often put on immigrant room-cleaners and kitchen workers, instead of dangerous working conditions, such as slippery floors or exposure to dangerous chemicals. AIWA has informed the women about how to use the union grievance procedure and the laws to fight back.

While offering its services, AIWA has carefully maintained its non-partisan status in relation to the union and the employers. The role of AIWA has been to assist immigrant women in actively expressing their concerns to their employer, union, government, and the larger society. AIWA has independently helped immigrant women dialogue with their employers by offering translation services and organizational skills. The organization has also served as a bridge between the Asian community and Local 2.

In their job training programs, AIWA often encourages women to enter the unionized sector of the hotel industry, where many jobs require little English-language skill. A job in a San Francisco hotel is a major advantage over working in nonunion garment factories or restaurants, where wages fall below federal minimums and benefits are nonexistent. For the first time, these women will earn a decent wage and unheard-of benefits like medical, dental, and pension benefits, paid vacations, sick leave and holidays, a seniority system, and a grievance procedure. Although union contracts in the tourist trade often fall behind those of most industrial workers, a union hotel job remains a major improvement to these women's lives as they begin to make important economic contributions to their family units, which are the heart and soul of their communities.

AIWA has assisted the immigrant women in learning about unions, exercising their contractual rights, and increasing their participation in union affairs. In order to do so, however, the AIWA staff had to first "break the ice."

One of the large Nob Hill hotels employs Korean women as room-cleaners. Some of the women are wives of former U.S. military personnel, with little social contact with the larger society. Most are not very fluent in English and some belong to conservative churches. Because of the extreme anti-labor climate in South Korea, their attitude toward the union initially was one of fear and suspicion. AIWA organized Korean-style dinners for the women as an opportunity for social activity. The response from the women was overwhelmingly positive. The social meetings provided the women a chance to overcome their isolation and to reassert their cultural identity. These meetings also served to introduce the women to representatives from the local union in a manner less threatening than an invitation to a union meeting. Instead of the women coming to the union's "turf," the union was willing to meet them on their ground.

As a result of such activities immigrant women have become increasingly involved in union affairs, studying and enforcing the contract, walking picket lines, serving on committees, and taking their rightful place as union leaders.

Conclusion

AIWA stands as a multiethnic organization that breaks through the barriers between various Asian immigrant communities who can barely speak to one another, let alone work together. The difficulties in maintaining and expanding such an organization are substantial, but they are matched by the dedication and fervor of AIWA's leadership and by a group of Asian women who can see the value of crossing cultural and ethnic lines to pursue economic and political power.

The innovative work of Local 2 and AIWA is one of many examples throughout the country among hotel, restaurant, hospital, garment, and manufacturing unions and a diverse array of immigrant groups, including Central Americans, Mexicans, Haitians, and Asians. These programs are pushing unions and community organizations to reevaluate their traditional attitudes and policies in light of recent economic patterns. It is no accident that women, in the ranks and in leadership roles, are at the forefront of those doing the pushing.

There are very hopeful signs of change in the union leadership. At its last convention, for example, the HERE international voted to oppose the Simpson-Rodino immigration bill as racially discriminatory and anti-labor. The International Ladies Garment Workers Union (ILGWU) has taken strong measures, including class action court cases, against INS factory raids. Across the country many locals and local labor councils have become increasingly aware of the need to protect the civil and labor rights of immigrant workers.

Immigrant and minority communities also need to reexamine their traditional attitudes toward unions. The Asian-American community, especially, feels victimized and scapegoated by labor unions. Their experience with labor's past exclusionist agitation, advocacy of job discrimination, outright racist violence, and the recent wave of Asian-bashing has left a negative impression on Asians. Without overlooking these problems, however, community organizations need to recognize that unions have provided an important means for upward mobility for minorities and immigrants. Living conditions within the community are directly dependent on wage levels and employment benefits. Minority wage earners who are union members are able to provide for their families and the larger community far better than those locked into nonunion sweatshops.

Because of the internationalization of the world economy, local industries and communities have become very fragile. In this insecure environment, unions and community organizations are by necessity going to have to become far more interdependent. Both are going to have to learn to work better with people and institutions who are very different from themselves if multinational, multiracial worker solidarity is to be achieved. This process will redefine the social agenda as we have known it, and, if the experience of HERE Local 2 and AIWA is any guide, women will be initiators and leaders in this struggle.

Corporate Campaigns: Labor Enlists Community Support

Jane Slaughter

Most people would agree that the inventor of the corporate campaign is Ray Rogers, who runs the consulting firm of Corporate Campaign, Inc. out of New York City. Rogers masterminded the Amalgamated Clothing and Textile Workers' corporate campaign against the J.P. Stevens Co., which in 1980 finally forced the company to recognize the union.

Since that time other unions have run their own corporate campaigns, some with and some without Rogers' help. The Steelworkers targeted the copper baron Phelps Dodge Corporation. The Lumber, Production, and Industrial Workers battled Louisiana-Pacific because of L-P's demands for contract concessions. The Farm Labor Organizing Committee (FLOC) campaigned against Campbell, seeking union recognition for migrant farmworkers. United Food and Commercial Workers (UFCW) Local P-9 fought meatpacker Hormel and Company on concessions.

The record of corporate campaigns since that at J.P. Stevens is mixed at best. Many were clear failures, quietly fading away after initial flurries of publicity. In few cases—FLOC is one—have the union Davids succeeded in imposing their will on the corporate Goliaths. The question arises whether corporate campaigns, which would seem, on paper, to add a powerful weapon to labor's arsenal, are worth the time and money expended.

How It Works

The analysis behind a corporate campaign deals with rarefied levels of the business and financial communities which union members seldom encounter. The idea is to leverage different aspects of corporate power against each other, far from the daily grit and grind of the shop floor. In this way corporate campaigns are new and modern methods, appropriate to the age of information, the computer and the corporate raider. But the actual carrying out of a well-conceived campaign depends entirely on the hard work of the affected union members themselves and on the solidarity they are able to generate from other union members and from their communities. In this respect corporate campaigns rely on labor's very traditional weapons.

Rogers and others would argue that the corporate campaign has not been given a true test. In most cases campaigns have been started far too late. They have suffered from a lack of analysis, rank-and-file involvement, and commitment to follow through. In the case of Phelps Dodge, for example, the Steelworkers International did not begin the campaign until thirteen months after the copper miners' strike began; less than two months later scabs in the mines voted to decertify the union. At Louisiana-Pacific, the campaign began six months into the strike and consisted of a consumer boycott (of such products as fibreboard and particleboard) and an attempt to solicit proxies from L-P stockholders. The Lumber Workers' union was decertified after a year on strike.

In the best-known corporate campaign to date, there was a different obstacle to victory. The campaign of UFCW Local P-9 against Hormel in 1985–86, coordinated by Rogers, had an auspicious beginning. Launched well before the union's strike deadline, it generated more solidarity from the rest of the labor movement than has been seen in decades. Over 3,000 local unions contributed money to the Adopt a P-9 Family Fund. But Local P-9 lacked the support of its international union, which actively sabotaged both the corporate campaign and the local's strike against Hormel. The UFCW International refused to support P-9's efforts to extend its picket lines to other Hormel plants, and firmly discouraged locals of other unions from making donations. Eventually the international signed a sweetheart contract which left the strikers without jobs. P-9's failure to beat Hormel can be laid at the door of the union leadership rather than seen as an indictment of the corporate campaign strategy itself.

In January 1988 the United Paperworkers International Union (UPIU) began an ambitious campaign against International Paper Co. (IP), the largest paper company in the world. With the help of Corporate Campaign, Inc., it sought to beat back IP's demands for concessions. Although the campaign suffered the disadvantage of beginning very late—six months into a strike—it had the advantage of being backed by the top leaders of the UPIU, who hired Rogers despite the disapproval of their counterparts in other AFL-CIO unions. (As "dissidents" are often viewed with more alarm by top labor leaders than are the corporations themselves, Rogers has been persona non grata with many AFL-CIO union leaders since he backed Local P-9 in its conflict with the UFCW officialdom.)

Except for its late start, the corporate campaign against IP was in many ways a textbook case: backing of union leaders, enthusiasm in the ranks, Rogers' professionalism, a plethora of issues on which to attack the company. But by most measures it did not succeed. IP was not brought to its knees—it forced concessions on its local unions and replaced workers at three locations with scabs. The IP case illustrates both the strengths of corporate campaigns and why even the best ones need the (old-fashioned) ingredient of solidarity in order to win.

Starting a Corporate Campaign

The battle against IP began on March 20, 1987, when local unions at the company's Mobile, Alabama, paper mill said no to concessions. Several other IP mills, particularly in the South, had already accepted the company's demand that workers give up Christmas as a day off and premium pay for Sunday work, and had agreed to job cuts and subcontracting. When Mobile said no, armed Pinkertons escorted workers from the mill. In June three locals in Pennsylvania, Wisconsin, and Maine struck IP, refusing similar concessions demands. Nearly 3,500 of IP's 17,300 Paperworkers members were on the street.

The UPIU hired the Kamber Group, a Washington, D.C.-based consulting firm with close ties to the AFL-CIO hierarchy, to run a corporate campaign. Little was accomplished. Jewel Bragg, wife of a Mobile union leader, says, "The only thing the Kamber Group did was get a recommendation in some stock magazine [the *Wall Street Transcript*] not to buy IP stock. We weren't able to plug in. When Ray [Rogers] spoke to that meeting of 800 people in December [1987], that was the first time any of us really knew who owned IP." Kamber was let go and Rogers' outfit was hired, at the insistence of frustrated local union officials in Maine.

Corporate campaigns take advantage of the fact that no corporation stands alone but is, in Rogers' words, "a coalition of individual and institutional interests that can be challenged, attacked, divided, and conquered." Rogers' first step is to gather information on the company's big stockholders, its creditors, and the interlocks between its board of directors and other companies. The idea is to break the company's power down into manageable units. Rogers explains:

"International Paper is an $8 billion company. If I take International Paper head on, I'm dealing with $8 billion worth of power, and they'll use all that power to destroy me. As far as they're concerned, this is a life and death battle. When I go after Coca Cola, on the other hand, I'm not going after $8 billion worth of power, I'm only going after what the relationship *between* Coca Cola and International Paper is worth—maybe it's $25 million."

Coca Cola comes up because it shares a director, Donald Mc-Henry, with IP. Rogers looks for linked companies which are vulnerable to public pressure; besides Coke, IP also shares directors with Avon, Hershey, and Anheuser-Busch. It is easier to organize action against a company with a well-known consumer product such as Coke or Budweiser than against IP's many anonymous paper products.

The linked company is then subjected to a barrage of postcards urging it to kick the offending director off its board. All of the original company's sins are dredged up, and laid at the door of the linked company.

In IP's case, these sins include chairman John Georges' $1.1 million salary—87 percent higher than the average for the rest of the paper industry; getting caught dumping thousands of gallons of waste into a Maine river; being fined $242,000 for exposing workers to high levels of toxic chemicals; avoidance of taxes between 1982 and 1985, while raking in $667 million in pretax profits; hiring a notorious Alabama union-busting firm to provide strikebreakers; the erection of ten-foot barbed-wire fences around its mills; and the deaths of several scabs in mill accidents.

By sitting on the IP board, the outside director is tacitly or explicitly approving these actions—and so, by extension, is the linked company. "I am troubled about Avon's connection with a company that has shown contempt for thousands of its employees," said the campaign's pre-printed postcards.

Strikers and supporters attend stockholders meetings of the linked companies to attack the shared directors. They may picket sports events or other activities sponsored by the target. Since the Supreme Court's April 1988 ruling on secondary boycotts, unions may now go further, and ask consumers to boycott a linked company's products (as long as the unionists are not "coercive"). A boycott of Avon, with a mailing to 75,000 union leaders and activists, was part of the IP campaign.

Rogers also goes after the company's support system in the financial community. He found that one of IP's senior vice-presidents, W. Craig McClelland, was also on the board of PNC Financial Corp., the fifteenth largest bank holding company in the country. PNC has banks all over Pennsylvania, and one of the four embattled UPIU locals is in Lock Haven, Pennsylvania. The luckless Donald McHenry is also a director of the Bank of Boston, a major New England bank and thus easy for the Jay, Maine local to focus on. Both PNC and the Bank of Boston, which also own blocks of IP stock, became targets of boycotts, demonstrations, and actions at stockholders meetings. Central Labor Council presidents in Pittsburgh and Philadelphia and New England regional directors of several big unions sent strong letters to their affiliates urging them to boycott the banks, including withdrawal of funds. Corporate Campaign, Inc.'s own valuable mailing list was also used. Letters were sent to 14,000 union leaders and activists, with postcards enclosed to be forwarded to the banks.

A report was prepared recounting all the ways in which IP was not a good corporate citizen. Titled "A Clear and Present Danger," it was distributed in John Georges' toney hometown, New Canaan, Connecticut.

Rogers recounts his notion of what goes on after a corporate campaign begins to have an effect:

"All of a sudden within the IP board, instead of everybody sitting there with a rubber stamp saying, 'John Georges, you're right, you're going to kill that union'—it's 'Damn it, John, this is what's happening to me at Coke and this is what's happening to me at Bank of Boston. Me, Donald McHenry, former U.N. ambassador, and I am on the short list of six people who might become another ambassador or some big position if the Democrats win! I am Donald McHenry, former U.N. ambassador!'"

But Rogers insists that what makes such campaigns work is more than harassment: "You cannot embarrass or harass powerful corporate or financial power brokers into making decisions that are going to cost them millions of dollars. They only respond to really relentless, inescapable economic and political pressure.

"Coca Cola doesn't care what Donald McHenry does in his spare time—until it affects them. But they get letters from organizations saying, 'I was going to use Coke at my function, now I'm not.' They've got distributors calling them saying, 'I've got x number of unions, x number of wedding parties saying cut the Coke, take your damn machine out, we don't want any part of it.'

"So Coke goes to the guy on their board and says you either get this thing settled or you make a choice which board to get off of. What we're doing is dismantling the power structure."

The corporate campaign was eventually successful in severing ties between IP and three of its linked companies. Early on, the Jay mill's public relations chief resigned as director of the Livermore Falls (Maine) Trust Co. Richard Baker, a Hershey director who also sat on IP's board, retired from Hershey after strikers and supporters demonstrated at Hershey headquarters. And in February 1989 W. Craig McClelland resigned his IP vice-presidency, ending the boycott of PNC Financial. The Laborers union had withdrawn $200,000,000 from a PNC subsidiary. In no case, of course, did the directors say that their resignations had anything to do with the corporate campaign.

Mobilizing the Rank and File

Where do all the postcards and letters come from? This is where the campaign mobilizes the rank and file of the union. In the IP campaign, as at Hormel, union members organized themselves into "caravans" that traveled throughout their areas—in Mobile's case, all over the South—spreading the word to other unionists and to other communities. Overnight—usually spent sleeping on union hall floors—factory workers became public speakers, explaining why their fellow unionists should contribute financially to their cause and should get their friends and neighbors to write letters and boycott.

The caravaners found these experiences inspiring and eye-opening. Wayne Fisher, co-chair of the Mobile caravan effort, said, "We're treated as heroes. They think we have something they don't. We take pride that we were the first to tell IP no, and the other locals are saying thank goodness somebody did it. We find that people are the same everywhere, the people in other plants, the people who stay after the rallies to talk to us. Our people come back pumped up." Solidarity collections generated an average of $70 per member per week for the Mobile workers, in addition to their $100 per week strike benefits from the international union.

The campaign also included demonstrations that sought to mobilize support from throughout the labor movement. The largest were rallies of 8,000 in Boston and 6,000 in Jay.

The corporate campaign clearly had an effect on IP. In March 1988, nine months into the strike but only ten weeks after the revitalized campaign began, the company asked the UPIU for national-level negotiations. Until that time, IP had insisted that each strike or lock-out was a purely local affair. Its condition for coming to the bargaining table: cessation of the corporate campaign.

The UPIU complied, but the talks were brief and fruitless—IP insisted that all the strikebreakers be allowed to keep their jobs. The strikers voted overwhelmingly "no," and the corporate campaign resumed full force.

Internal Organizing

The strikers knew all along that it was not enough to target IP's financial connections. They believed that an equally if not more important tactic was to organize within the union so that they could, eventually, hurt production. The lack of previous communication among locals within the same company was startling. Each IP local had a different contract expiration date, and there were not even national meetings to coordinate bargaining strategy, although IP had been making concessions demands all over the country for several years. The Jay strikers, who played a leading role throughout, sought to remedy this lack from the bottom up, with a program they called Outreach '88. Outreach '88 involved caravans to other mill towns for face-to-face meetings to explain what the strike was about. The Jay people came up with a "25–1" program for internal education within the locals, in which one leader would be responsible for informing twenty-five fellow workers.

The aim was to convince other locals, as their contracts expired, to join the original four's coordinated bargaining "pool," in order to present IP with a united front. The results were impressive: in May 1988 leaders of over twenty IP locals met and resolved to "decline to participate in any company programs not legally or contractually required." They also decided on a "work safely" campaign, which if scrupulously carried out could cut IP's productivity measurably. By November 1988, twenty-three out of twenty-seven IP locations had rejected the company's concessions demands and were working without contracts.

But all the hard work and new-found solidarity came to nought. On October 8 representatives of the striking locals went to Nashville, UPIU headquarters, for a meeting of the union's IP Council. They expected to make further progress in the growing unity they had been building since the beginning of the year. They were unprepared to be sandbagged by officers of the International. President Wayne Glenn made it clear that he thought the strike a losing cause, emphasizing the depletion of the strike fund and the looming possibility of decertification votes. All the locals present were polled about going out on strike. As Ray Rogers tells it: "Every local was asked one by one if it could get its members to strike. Most of them said they couldn't guarantee it. The question should have been, 'Can you get a strike vote with the knowledge that there won't be a strike unless and until it's massive?' But that question wasn't asked." Morale hit zero.

The next day, after most local representatives had gone home, the International's attorney advised the three striking locals to call off their strike and make an unconditional offer to return to work. This would require the company, legally, to fill any jobs that opened up with former strikers. Feeling the rug pulled out from under them, the local leaders ended the strike. Less than three weeks later the locked-out Mobile workers accepted concessions and returned to work. Twenty-three hundred strikers in Jay, De Pere, and Lock Haven remained without jobs.

The International said that it would not abandon the former strikers. It would continue the corporate campaign, and would add another point—support for a bill introduced by a Maine congressman that would forbid companies to hire permanent replacements during the first ten weeks of a strike.

Corporate campaign activity continued apace. In December, UPIU members and supporters distributed leaflets about IP's unsafe policies at the New York headquarters of Avon and Pfizer, Inc. Ironworkers Local 7 in Boston announced in January that it had withdrawn $4 million from the Bank of Boston. A huge mailing was planned to state and local officials throughout the United Staes about the AFL-CIO's boycott of IP products, stressing IP's connections with South Africa. Solidarity rallies were held in five Massachusetts towns to raise money for the former strikers and to promote the boycott. Food banks continued to distribute aid.

But the hopes of building a united "pool" to take on IP all at once were dashed. Most of the IP locals which had rejected takeaways during the three locals' strike signed concessionary agreements soon after it was over. And other companies took IP's cue. In Rumford, Maine, not far from Jay, the UPIU local at Boise-Cascade signed a five-year agreement which contained the concessions that by now had become the industry "pattern."

The February meeting of the UPIU's executive board decided to end Corporate Campaign, Inc.'s contract. The corporate campaign would be conducted by headquarters staff, and three former strikers would be hired to continue the Outreach work.

How Well Does It Work?

The UPIU said all along that IP did not need concessions, and cited the company's profit figures as proof: $305 million in 1986, $407 million in 1987, the year the strike began. At the same time the union claimed that the strike was costing the company hundreds of millions of dollars. At its annual meeting in May 1988, Chairman Georges refused to answer strikers' questions about what 1987 profits would have been without the stoppage. However, figures for the first quarter of 1988 showed profits increasing at an annual rate of 77 percent, according to *Business Week*.

The truth is that IP's pocketbook was never badly hurt, partly because of a factor outside the strikers' control: the paper industry was booming, and IP could sell every pound of paper it made at an excellent price. Workers were out at only four of its 27 mills, and those four mills were all operated by strikebreakers—if not as efficiently as with experienced workers, at least well enough to get a product to customers.

Rogers pointed to McClelland's and Baker's resignations as signs that his strategy was having an effect. "But," he admitted, "we got one of their arms, but IP still has one arm and two legs and a head. When the company can sell everything it makes. . ."

The two most notable corporate campaign successes—at J. P. Stevens and at Campbell—both took years of patient organizing. Each succeeded in mobilizing tens of thousands of supporters inside and outside the labor movement, especially among church members. Workers were not on strike during these years; their goal was union recognition, rather than winning a fight against concessions.

Striking workers do not have years to organize. The law allows a vote on decertifying the union when a strike is a year old, with scabs voting and strikers excluded. Such elections are always lost by the union.

For IP workers, the hard fact was that unless they could hurt IP financially—the "economic pressure" Ray Rogers talks about—they could not win. The strikers' work in attacking IP's allies was enthusiastic, creative, and sophisticated. But it was not as effective as convincing their fellow workers at IP's other mills to walk out would have been. The strikers were working on that angle too—but their efforts came too late in the game and after too many years of disunity.

The strikers at Hormel faced a similar problem. They targeted First Bank Systems, Hormel's primary source of credit and a big stockholder. Millions of dollars were pulled out by P-9's supporters, according to Rogers, and the bank got an injunction forbidding the union to campaign against it. But the local's big problem was the failure to spread the strike to other Hormel plants. UFCW locals in Nebraska and Iowa were willing to respect roving picket lines, but the International would not permit them, and unilaterally ended the strike. "One of the biggest mistakes made," says Rogers, "was waiting for [UFCW President William] Wynn to act and not sending out the roving pickets a lot earlier."

Conclusion: Winning a Campaign

Four conclusions can be drawn from the UPIU/IP experience and from other corporate campaigns:

First, a well-run corporate campaign does an immense amount to educate and politicize the participants. It mobilizes members much more than the traditional staid, "picket the fence" strike. It can lay the basis for future solidarity and organizing. For this alone corporate campaigns are worth doing.

The outreach work that was part of the UPIU campaign was picked up and carried on by other IP locals. Five months after the strike ended the local at the Kaukauna, Wisconsin mill called a meeting of locals in its region to talk about "inside strategies" ("work to rule" and the like) and resisting concessions. Ray Rogers was there to advise on media strategies. "The locals in UPIU are closer now than they've ever been," said bargaining chairman Randy McSorley. "I know people in locals across the country, I know their problems. We're trying to teach ourselves that we're the bosses and our International officers are our employees."

Former Hormel meatpackers in Minnesota and IP paperworkers in Mobile alike say that they will never be the same again, that they will always see themselves as part of a larger community of the underdogs of the world. Candace Anderson, founder of the Mobile Ladies' Auxiliary, says, "Our original goal was to get the men back to work. But now that's not the end, it's the beginning. I will never close the door on the rest of the world again. I'll never stop."

Second, a corporate campaign à la Kamber, conducted purely at the level of Wall Street and which does not include mobilization of the rank and file, is worthless.

Third, a corporate campaign should be begun well *before* workers are forced out on strike.

Finally, a corporate campaign that targets power structures is a valuable tactic, but it must be combined with the ability to hurt the company's pocketbook directly. Usually this means withholding production, either through a strike or through a "working strike" or "work to rule" on the shop floor. It also means—easier said than done— finding a way to keep the company from continuing production with scab labor. This requires the willingness to face injunctions and arrests, and to ask allies to do the same.

A corporate campaign allows the union to garner large amounts of publicity and to be seen by the community as the side taking the moral high ground, two components of victory which are often lacking in traditional labor struggles. But the muscle of economic pressure—whether it comes from the company's erstwhile allies or from lost production—must come into play, and quickly enough to make a difference.

Supporting the Hormel Strikers

Peter Rachleff

No other labor conflict in the 1980s generated the sort of solidarity that was expressed with Local P-9 of Austin, Minnesota. More than 3,000 local unions sent material assistance, and 42 support groups were organized in 33 states. Some 600 workers at other Hormel plants were fired for honoring P-9's roving picket lines in 1986 or for promoting the boycott of Hormel products. Tens of thousands of rank-and-filers and local union officers visited Austin, from the fall of 1984 when the corporate campaign against Hormel and First Bank Systems was begun, until the summer of 1987 when local activists celebrated "Cram Your Spam" Days as a challenge to Hormel's effort to co-opt the 4th of July that year as the fiftieth anniversary of Spam. Rallies, parades, dances, picnics, food caravans, Christmas parties, and picketing and plant gate demonstrations over this period attracted the greatest outpouring of labor solidarity since the 1930s.

In the fall of 1984, based on an arbitrator's decision, Hormel unilaterally slashed wages at their flagship Austin plant by 23 percent. As the contract neared expiration in the summer of 1985, Hormel presented a complete rewrite of the labor agreement, gutting arbitration and grievance procedures, replacing plantwide with departmental seniority, ignoring safety problems, and continuing a pattern of wage and benefit givebacks. Local P-9 hired Ray Rogers and Corporate Campaign, Inc., to mount pressure on Hormel. A remarkable, participatory, energetic, creative battle was waged by the P-9ers. But they were not supported by their international union, the United Food and Commercial Workers (UFCW), and they were buffeted by a series of interventions by the National Labor Relations Board (NLRB) and the courts. The crowning blow came when Minnesota Governor Rudy Perpich sent in the National Guard in late January 1986 to bring scabs ("permanent replacements") through the picket lines. In the spring and summer of 1986, the UFCW placed P-9 in trusteeship, called off the strike, and negotiated a contract with Hormel that accepted virtually all of the concessions they had sought. The P-9ers were placed on a "preferential recall list"—but by the time of this writing (spring 1989), not one had been returned to work.

Although the Hormel conflict ended disastrously for the participants, it served as a powerful rallying point for the struggle against
concessions in the labor movement and the more general struggle
against the direction in which U.S. society was moving in the 1980s.
Support for P-9 reached well beyond the labor movement. Farmers,
peace and justice activists, poor people's organizations, even environmental groups, got involved. In part, this was because the leadership
of P-9 (and Corporate Campaign's Ray Rogers) actively pursued such
support. But it was also because so many people were able to see
themselves in this conflict: both their anger and frustration with the
"powers-that-be" and their hopes and aspirations that people like them
can indeed fight back and impose their sense of order, justice, and
fair play on the society around them. The following discussion thus
takes up not only the history of the strike but also the nature of
the broad mobilization that went on around P-9.

Support for P-9 carried a particular cutting edge to it, for both
those within and those outside the labor movement. As the United
Food and Commercial Workers (UFCW), P-9's international, disowned
the corporate campaign, limited the range of acceptable strike tactics,
undermined P-9's legitimacy in the labor movement, and finally im-
posed a trusteeship and accepted a settlement that left every P-9er
on the street and the jobs and union in the hands of the scabs, support
for P-9 became contentious, particularly within other unions. Conflict
between leaders and rank and file—sparked or exacerbated by support
for P-9—flared in union after union. No wonder the leaders of the
AFL-CIO closed ranks around the UFCW's $200,000-plus a year presi-
dent William Wynn. Interestingly, this sort of pressure increased P-9's
popularity among some union activists as well as outside the labor
movement altogether.

The support had a transformative impact on the P-9ers themselves.
Donations did not just materialize in the bank account. Massive food
caravans drove home a sense of solidarity. Checks were delivered
in person, often presented with a speech at a mass meeting. P-9ers
heard from farm, Native American, anti-apartheid, and peace and
justice activists, as well as from trade union militants from across
the country—or even the world. They came to see themselves in
global terms, as part of a world divided between rich and poor, powerful and powerless, justice and injustice. This development was particularly stunning—Austin is a small town (with a population of 23,000
and shrinking), virtually all white, located 100 miles south of the Twin
Cities (Minneapolis and St. Paul).

P-9 actively sought the support of local unions all over the country. At the beginning of the strike, P-9 artists painted a map of the United States for the purposes of noting the sources of solidarity—with a dot and a line to Austin. By the end of the strike, the map was so filled it was impossible to pick out lines or dots.

Ray Rogers and Corporate Campaign, Inc. urged P-9 to aggressively pursue solidarity well before the strike began, and they developed strategies and tactics to do so successfully. A communications committee organized speaking engagements and encouraged rank-and-filers to become public speakers. Their approach was rather simple: send hundreds of rank-and-filers on the road to speak to local unions, peace groups, church groups, civil rights organizations, and the like. Speakers were quite specific about their own experiences, but they also learned to draw parallels with the situations of their audience. P-9ers went in large group caravans—with motorcycles and school buses—to other Hormel plants. They leafleted at plant gates and invited other Hormel workers to their campsites for extended discussions. Small teams also went on tour, often away from home for weeks at a time.

Corporate Campaign, Inc. helped P-9 build structures to facilitate expressions of solidarity. Three months after the strike began, they launched an "Adopt-a-Family" program which had organizational as well as material goals. Local unions were matched with a specific P-9 family, and they would pledge a fixed amount of money per month for several months. The striker's family would send photographs and information to the local, personalizing the struggle, bonding them all together, and providing the sort of support that UFCW strike benefits of $45 a week just couldn't cover. Many were the homes and cars saved by this program. Many, too, were the long distance friendships that developed.

When a lively local union, characterized by rank-and-file participation, honest leadership, internal democracy, creativity, and resistance to concessions, reached out for solidarity, the floodgates opened. Many activists the country over had come to the conclusion that concessions could only be defeated through solidarity. Support came more often from plant gate and shopfloor collections than from formal union measures. Stewards at IUE 201 (General Electric, in Lynn, Massachusetts) explained in a leaflet they distributed on February 7, 1986, at their own plant gates:

> Working men and women in Minnesota have scratched a line in the cold hard ground and declared that they will give up no more of their pride, wages, or benefits. . . . Their victory will be hailed as the turning

point against concessions bargaining, or their loss will be another crushed union. What stands between their victory or loss is the resolve of all of us.

In addition to the traveling speakers and the "Adopt-a-Family" program, widely publicized rallies, both in Austin and elsewhere (the Twin Cities, Detroit, Boston, New York, Denver, San Francisco) contributed to the process of building solidarity. Union activists, frequently engaged in ongoing battles of their own, marched and expressed their solidarity with P-9, often drawing parallels between their own situation and the Hormel conflict. In this way, intense communication about—and among—a variety of struggles (shipbuilders in Pittsburgh, Maine, Los Angeles, and Alabama; steelworkers in Pittsburgh and Gary; autoworkers in St. Paul and Van Nuys; meat-packers in Chicago, Boston, Detroit, Nebraska, and Iowa) permeated Austin and the whole struggle involving P-9. "Solidarity" did not simply mean a one-way flow into Austin.

The P-9ers were as quick to extend their help to someone else as they were to ask for support. Family farming in southern Minnesota was in crisis for most of the 1980s, and P-9ers became visible participants in the round of "penny auctions" and foreclosure protests in 1985–86. Only weeks after their own strike had begun, a busload of P-9ers joined the IAM Local 459 picket line at the Union Brass Foundry in St. Paul. They joined in parades and demonstrations from the annual Minneapolis Mothers' Day March for Justice to the "Take Back the Night" march. After the Ottumwa workers were fired in early 1986, P-9ers shared their food shelf and other resources with them. They even pledged—through a democratic vote at a rank-and-file meeting—not to accept a return to work themselves until every worker fired for supporting them had been returned to work. P-9ers were also active in the campaign to free Amon Msane from South Africa's jails, when the union militant was detained without formal charges after a tour of the United States. Similarly, they made freedom for jailed Native American activist Leonard Peltier another of their concerns. Wherever there was a social struggle, P-9ers were present.

Solidarity and Internal Union Conflict

As the Hormel struggle wore on, conflict between P-9 and the UFCW leadership intensified. The national labor bureaucracy was kept well informed, and they flexed their muscles to block support for P-9. Just as often, however, their own members devised an end-run around their contrived obstacles or even launched a frontal assault on the citadels of power in their own organization. Thus, support for P-9 took on an oppositional character within the labor movement itself.

Let me give some examples.

In September 1985, the Minnesota State Federation of Labor, AFL-CIO, held its annual convention in St. Paul. Local P-9's strike against Hormel was about one month old and still enjoyed the official sanction of the UFCW (although everyone knew they were opposed to the strike). On the eve of the convention, the regional office of theNational Labor Relations Board (NLRB) had ruled the corporate campaign against First Bank to be a secondary boycott illegal under the Taft-Hartley Act. Local P-9ers and their supporters were eager to win the official blessings of the state labor federation, as that would facilitate the provision of material assistance, and it would give their morale a boost on the heels of the NLRB decision and the federal injunction that enforced it. But Minnesota state fed president Dan Gustafson seemed to dash those hopes when he ordered the shutdown of P-9's information table. While he offered the convention the excuse that P-9's literature included references to First Bank, he bluntly told the P-9ers at the literature table: "Your own international doesn't back you. We don't back you, and you're going to lose!"

The next day, hundreds of P-9ers formed a gauntlet outside the doors to the convention hotel. There, on the public sidewalk, they distributed their literature to the entering delegates. A core group of forty or so delegates, organized through the Twin Cities P-9 Support Committee, caucused, button-holed other delegates, and led the floor fight inside. When P-9 president Jim Guyette entered the convention, he was greeted with a standing ovation. The P-9ers got the official endorsement they were seeking.

The Machinists' Union (IAM) provides another instructive example. When UFCW international president Wynn condemned the "Adopt-a-Family" Program in a letter to AFL-CIO officers and affiliates just before Thanksgiving 1985 (he claimed the money would go to Rogers!), participation in this program took on an oppositional character. IAM president William Winpisinger (a supposed "progressive") was one of the first international officers to endorse Wynn's strictures and try to enforce them within his own organization. When the Minneapolis–St. Paul Northwest Airlines IAM lodge voted to send $10,000 to adopt several families, Winpisinger intervened. He claimed the authority to oversee any local expenditures greater than small change and refused to allow this gesture of solidarity. Under the prodding of an aggressive and imaginative shop steward, who was also a stalwart of the Twin Cities P-9 Support Committee, the local lodge convened an "emergency" meeting and paid out a constitutionally required $35

per diem to everyone in attendance. There was no other business
to conduct. As the meeting adjourned, rank-and-filers lined up to
sign over their individual checks to P-9. The total—slightly over
$10,000!

Structuring Solidarity

In some places, solidarity with P-9 spawned new organizations. Over
the course of the struggle, forty-two P-9 Support Committees were
organized around the country. They played an important role in raising
funds and in promoting the boycott. They also played an unintended
role in furthering cross-union communications at a local, rank-and-file
level. In some places, these committees went beyond their mandate
to support P-9 to organize support for a group of workers in their
own region who were engaged in a conflict. At times, these new
networks were extended beyond single regions or communities to
establish new levels of rank-and-file to rank-and-file communication.
In the spring of 1986, for example, the Twin Cities P-9 Support Committee organized a food caravan with the P-9 Support Committees
of Madison and Milwaukee, Wisconsin. Three separate caravans bearing more than 200 tons of food converged on Austin. A national organization (National Rank-and-File Against Concessions, or NRFAC) began
to take shape in December 1985, when 600 labor activists met in
Chicago. Over the next year it provided an important source of support
for P-9. Due to internal divisions, however, the NRFAC never developed beyond its initial stage.

The Austin United Support Group was the first and foremost of
all the support organizations. It was organized by several workers'
wives in the wake of Hormel's wage cuts and benefit take-backs. (It's
interesting that although there were hundreds of women who worked
in the plant, the United Support Group initially consisted of only
the wives of male workers.) They started well over a year before the
strike, first picketing the plant gates at shift changes, holding hand-
lettered signs reading "We support our husbands." They then began
holding outdoor meetings in a park and grew to some 400 members.
By the winter of 1984–85, they had moved into the Austin Labor
Center where there was heat and a sound system.

After the strike began, the United Support Group expanded its
membership and its activities. Though the leadership remained firmly
in women's hands, male retirees and husbands of women workers
joined in. An organization of high schoolers—"P-9: The Future Generation"—was launched, linked to the Support Group. In a variety
of critical activities—picketing, public speaking, peer counseling, the

soup kitchen, the clothing exchange, Santa's Workshop, answering mail, sending out flyers, t-shirts, buttons, hats, tapes, and so on—distinctions between P-9 members and Support Group activists faded. While there continued to be formal "rank-and-file" meetings at which only P-9 members could vote, nightly "mass meetings" (often for educational and inspirational purposes) grouped union members and supporters together. Weekly pot luck suppers ("The union that eats together, stays together") were another source of cohesion. The women in the Support Group were indeed, as one later emphasized to me, "beside" their husbands, not "behind" them.

In June 1986, the UFCW placed P-9 in trusteeship on the grounds that they had disobeyed an order to call off the strike. Armed with federal court orders, the UFCW took over the Austin Labor Center and began to expel the P-9ers and their supporters. From here on out, the United Support Group became the very center of the struggle. They rented a new office, maintained the food shelf, accepted contributions and donations that would have been derailed by the UFCW if sent directly to the union, promoted the Hormel boycott, and published the *Support Report* as the main vehicle of communications. Had it not been for them, the trusteeship would have ended the struggle altogether. Spouses, children, parents, neighbors, and friends joined union members at the very heart of the struggle. They, too, would be transformed by their experience.

The Twin Cities P-9 Support Group

In the Twin Cities, local union activists had come together to do sporadic strike support work in the early 1980s—a printers' strike at eight shops in the winter of 1982–83, the Greyhound strike, an eleven-month meatpackers' strike in South St. Paul in 1984. While a network had begun to take shape, there was little agreement about the proper structure or role for such support activity. We spent as much time in meetings disagreeing about the proper course of action as we did on the picket lines lending a hand. We were especially bedeviled as to our "legitimacy"—who gave us the authority to act in other people's struggles? As the Hormel conflict evolved, we were pushed in new directions, answering or transcending some of our old questions, but coming up against new, even more difficult ones.

In the fall of 1984, Twin Cities activists made several visits to Austin, for parades, rallies, and informal discussions. We were *very* impressed. On a Sunday afternoon in early March 1985, Rogers and Guyette spoke to fifty or so activists at the UAW Hall in St. Paul. They urged us to form a support committee. The idea was attractive and it made our legitimacy clear. We initially modeled ourselves after the "Committee of 100" which had played such a key role in the Minneapolis teamsters' strikes of 1934. Bud Schulte, a veteran kill-floor worker at Hormel and a picket captain in the recently concluded South St. Paul strike, was elected chairman. Our ranks already included autoworkers, steelworkers, rail workers from a variety of crafts, meatpackers, printers, hotel and restaurant workers, even a college professor. The Twin Cities group distributed a letter to other local unionists urging their support for P-9, and, over the next months, participated in demonstrations and leafleting at First Bank branches and the First Bank stockholders' annual meeting. It was becoming our struggle, too.

In the middle of the summer of 1985, as a strike looked more and more likely, we reorganized our committee. We began holding weekly meetings at the UAW Hall and staffing a regular office at the International Brotherhood of Electrical Workers (IBEW) 110's hall. I was elected chair and given the responsibility of holding together a rapidly expanding and increasingly diverse group. Other trade unionists began to attend our meetings, as did a variety of leftists, peace and justice activists, retired unionists, college students, feminists, and assorted sympathizers.

Active Solidarity

When the strike began in August 1985, we turned our attention to providing material assistance, particularly food. Our Support Committee was blessed with a priceless asset—Jake Cooper. A veteran of the 1934 teamsters' strikes and the 1948 packinghouse strike, Jake had long ago taken over a family grocery store after his blacklisting from the Minnesota industrial scene. His experience, his drive, his connections with suppliers, even his own beat-up tractor-trailer, made our food caravans huge successes. They were successes not only in terms of the amount of food delivered (which was in the hundreds of tons), but also in the publicity generated for P-9, the evidence of support we were bearing, and in the expanding network of people in the Twin Cities area who were getting involved in the strike. They also served as a model for other food caravans which would later be organized on an almost weekly basis. While the UFCW and the Minnesota AFL-CIO discouraged participation in our ventures, few unionists heeded their advice. These organizations even felt pressured enough to launch their own food caravans.

While we worked hard to expand our numbers, we were well aware that expressions of solidarity with P-9 had more to do with what was happening in Austin than with our own best laid plans. For instance, a Twin Cities rally we were organizing for mid-January 1986 took on new significance when the company announced its intent to reopen the plant and hire scabs.

On January 19, 1986, nearly 1,000 supporters from around Minnesota rallied at the UAW Hall in St. Paul, in response to a call signed by forty local union officers from the Twin Cities. (Conspicuous by their absence were the leaders of the state AFL-CIO, who had been invited to participate.) The dominant theme of the rally was the irony that production in the Hormel plant was scheduled to begin the following day—Martin Luther King Day. Some 450 rank-and-filers registered for a "Labor Solidarity Brigade," pledging picket line support to P-9. The breadth of support for P-9 is suggested by the list of unions and other organizations these rank-and-filers hailed from: aerospace machinists; sheet metal workers; letter carriers and postal workers; flight attendants; graphic communications; autoworkers; ladies' garment workers; hotel and restaurant workers; millwrights; office and professional employees; firefighters; federation of teachers and education association; communications workers; carpenters; teamsters; food and commercial workers (both meat-packers and clerks); public employees (AFSCME and Minnesota Assocation of Professional Employees); paperworkers; IWW; railway and airline clerks; Oil, Chemical and Atomic Workers; operating engineers; clothing and textile workers; steel workers; pipefitters; electricians; united electrical workers; plus, COACT (a low income neighborhood action group); Groundswell (statewide farmers' organization); Coalition of Labor Union Women; the Minnesota Public Interest Research Group; Women Against Military Madness; National Lawyers' Guild; the University of Minnesota Progressive Students Organization. The atmosphere at the rally was electric, from the greeting given Jim Guyette and such honored guests as Fred Dube, of the African National Congress, to the singing of "Solidarity Forever."

Early the following morning—Martin Luther King Day, January 20, 1986—hundreds of Twin Citians joined the P-9ers in a massive car blockade around the plant. A UAW activist stalled his car in front of the main gate. A gridlock resulted. By 9:00 A.M., the company announced it would not try to start production that day. Elated, some of the crowd went to the corporate offices, where a padlock provided by a rail unionist from Minneapolis was thrown on the gates of the company's expensive new fence. The padlock was not discovered until lunchtime, and the management and white collar employees were unable to get out of the facilities for lunch. The atmosphere got more festive. Folksinger Larry Long later commemorated these events in a verse lampooning the media: "They came looking for violence, but they got a song."

It was in response to this shift in *power* in Austin, a shift in which hundreds of Twin Cities supporters had participated, that Governor Rudy Perpich sent in the National Guard. This inspired even more impressive acts of solidarity. When Hormel reopened its Austin plant, P-9 sent roving pickets to the other Hormel plants where workers had been working overtime to make up for the loss of Austin's production. In Fremont, Nebraska, enough workers refused to cross the picket lines that production was disrupted for the day. Fift, were later fired. In Ottumwa, Iowa, 505 production and clerical workers respected the lines and shut down production altogether. Municipal workers refused to cross the lines to thaw out the plant's frozen sewer pipes. Hormel fired more than 500 of the Ottumwa workers—and UFCW President Wynn then announced that since the picket lines did not have his approval, the company was within its rights!

The firing of the Ottumwa workers and the imposition of martial law in Austin electrified activists the country over. In the Twin Cities, the Support Committee coordinated a noisy rally of more than 500 outside the governor's residence in $-20°$ weather and a sit-in at the governor's office at the state capital that lasted more than a week. College students, peace and justice activists, and P-9 retirees—folks who could afford to take a few days out of their lives—took the lead. Some seemed to have done this sort of thing before. During the day, the sit-inners lobbied state representatives and senators about withdrawing the National Guard and repealing the 1917 Criminal Syndicalism statute which had been used against Ray Rogers. Their presence set the tone at the capital. At night, they curled up in sleeping bags on the hard floor. Our weekly Support Committee meetings drew more than 100 participants for the next month.

Twin Cities activists brought special expertise to the escalating struggle. In February 1986, members of Women Against Military Madness (WAMM) came to Austin and conducted workshops in civil disobedience. When the governor pulled back the National Guard, P-9ers, the United Support Group, and WAMM members conducted a mass sit-in at the gates to the corporate headquarters. Women were in the lead all the way and retirees played a visible role, too.

The next month, Larry Long and a diverse group of Twin Cities musicians (a "New Song" duo; a feminist quartet; several folksingers; even a P-9er, Larry Schmidt, who had been arrested with the WAMM demonstration) organized a gala "Boycott Hormel" concert and released a locally produced cassette tape with the same message. Several of the songs had been written collectively with P-9ers on the picket line in Austin. The involvement of the musicians attracted the mass media and a lively audience. New "Boycott Hormel" t-shirts were sold by the Support Committee. Nearly 1,000 attended, enjoyed the great music, sang along, and expressed their support for P-9. Only two days earlier UFCW President Wynn had telegrammed P-9 to offer Hormel an "unconditional" return to work. But that very night 900 P-9ers met and voted overwhelmingly to continue their strike. The concert symbolically melded the P-9ers and their supporters.

It also marked a transition in the struggle and in the activities of P-9's supporters. Hormel announced that it had a full complement of workers, that the strikers had been—in the lingo of the new labor relations—"permanently replaced." In a punitive measure, Hormel also closed the Ottumwa plant. The company acquired FDL Foods, whose plants paid significantly lower wages than Austin Hormel, and expanded into new, high value-added, microwave-ready product lines, and into the poultry and catfish markets. Their profits looked good. Moreover, the international union was now on record as demanding the cessation of the strike—and had begun the process to place P-9 in trusteeship. Several efforts to block production via mass picketing were met with repression; not just Hormel's by the extensive private security force, or by the Austin police department (which accumulated more than 2,000 pages of "spy" reports and twenty-six hours of video-tape surveillance), or by the Mower county sheriff's department, but also by the State Highway Patrol (which closed a stretch of the inter-state to everyone but card-carrying scabs) and the National Guard. We later discovered that the FBI had had an informant in P-9's midst and that the U.S. marshals had a crack force of 150 standing by to enforce federal court orders in Austin. The company also employed the services of Gary Baker & Associates, a "dirty tricks" specialist with a track record of anti-union activities.

In early April, P-9ers and their supporters made their last attempt to shut the plant with mass pickets. Labor activists from all over the country flocked to Austin. A mass rally at the plant gates on April 11 was greeted with tear gas, police violence, and arrests with serious felony charges. Felony "inciting to riot" warrants were issued for Rogers and Guyette. The next day, thousands marched and rallied in protest. A day later, Jesse Jackson flew into Austin, prayed with the prisoners in jail, and proclaimed: "What Selma, Alabama, was to the struggle for civil rights in the 1960s, Austin, Minnesota, is to the struggle for economic rights in the 1980s."

But P-9 was now more than ever on the defensive. Supporters shifted their focus from picket line participation and material aid to defending the activists facing felony charges and promoting the boycott of Hormel products. Both projects were pursued in ways that continued to expand the network of people—inside and outside the labor movement—involved with P-9.

The Twin Cities Support Committee organized a legal defense committee, which secured experienced activist attorney Ken Tilsen (who had been a key defense lawyer in the Wounded Knee cases), and sent out a public appeal over the signatures of Meridel LeSueur, Tillie Olsen, Studs Terkel, and William Kunstler, among others. Thousands of people from all over the country responded with small donations and words of encouragement drawn from their experiences with their unions, their community groups, the Grey Panthers, Mothers Against Drunk Drivers, SANE, and others. Eventually, all the felony charges (there were eighteen defendants) were dropped.

Boycott Hormel

While the promotion of the boycott led to leafleting supermarkets as one might expect, there were also some creative strategies pursued. At this point of transition in the spring of 1986, for instance, the P-9ers called for a National Boycott Day. The day they picked, however, was fishing season opener. Our Support Committee was stymied. We felt a responsibility to set the pace for the rest of the country, but fishing season opener in Minnesota is a holiday equal to Christmas. We kicked around ideas and eventually settled on the following: we would station pickets (in "Boycott Hormel" and "Cram Your Spam" t-shirts) and leafletters at bottlenecks in the two highways leading to the "lake country," 100 or so miles north of the Twin Cities. Our leaflets proclaimed "Eat Fish and Boycott Hormel" and announced a raffle. To enter, one had to fill out a coupon and attach a non-Hormel union-made meat product. The prize: a boat motor. We reached thousands of people and got hundreds of entries. Expressions of support were numerous. All involved enjoyed themselves. Some of us distributed the same leaflets the next week at the Minnesota Twins' home ball games at the Metrodome.

Since then, P-9ers and their supporters have tried to keep pressure on the company via the boycott. Of course, the AFL-CIO and the UFCW have intervened to *promote* the sale of Hormel products ("union-made," they proclaim) and it has been difficult to get the boycott recognized as legitimate. But we've made a good try. Billboards urging "Boycott Hormel for Fairness and Justice" were leased by support committees in different cities. Here and there, there were benefit concerts and rallies. In November 1986, the Twin Cities Support Committee organized a major event—a concert featuring Holly Near, Arlo Guthrie, John McCutcheon, and Larry Long, which filled Minneapolis'

Orchestra Hall. In the lobby, a photo montage laid out the course of the conflict. I overheard someone say, "If the cops sealed the door, there'd be no demonstrations of any sort in the Twin Cities for years!"

P-9 had attracted this sort of support because they had stood their ground, had articulated their grievances in a language that made sense to lots of other people, and had actively reached out for support. By the mid-1980s, this approach proved successful (and would be used in the later 1980s by other unions). It was as if thousands upon thousands of people had been waiting for someone to take a stand like this. Their response made this a historic battle.

It was this committed participation by such a range of supporters that has allowed P-9 to continue its struggle even after being placed in trusteeship. It also broadened the network of people who were brought together by this struggle and transformed by their involvement in it. The entire Hormel struggle was a remarkable achievement for an incredibly diverse group of people. In the depths of Ronald Reagan's America, in the bowels of one of America's most bureaucratized unions, one local union was able to lead by inspiration, to pose as a rallying point for the many struggles and their supporters who slid ever backward over this entire decade.

The Community-Labor Alliance of New Haven

Barbara Richards

The Rally

In November of 1977, with the weather turning cold and Christmas approaching, the blue-collar workers of Local 35 of the Hotel and Restaurant Workers union had been locked in a bitter strike against Yale University for over two months. Vincent Sirabella and John Wilhelm of Local 35 asked the New Haven Labor Council to sponsor a community-labor rally in support of the strikers. Union leaders recruited a committee of community supporters to work together with them for three weeks to prepare for the rally.

As part of picket duty, striking workers blanketed the town with 50,000 flyers. The coordinating committee staged pre-rally events such as meetings between community leaders and politicians and the president of Yale. The local paper gave daily and prominent coverage to these events and to a barrage of press releases announcing endorsements by ministers, politicians, neighborhood leaders, women's organizations, minority groups, and others.

After some debate about the risk of a half-filled hall the committee reserved an enormous armory for the rally. The time was set for the end of the day shift at the local factories. The Rubber Workers at Armstrong, the Machinists at Pratt and Whitney and Olin-Winchester, the United Electrical Workers (UE) at Sargent, and the Amalgamated Clothing and Textile Workers Union (ACTWU) at Gant Shirt arranged busses directly from the workplace to the rally.

Fifty-five organizations signed a full-page newspaper ad just before the rally, and Yale took out an ad in response. Sentiment against Yale in the community was strong—not only due to the strike but because of the long history of arrogance and neglect by this wealthy institution occupying the center of the seventh poorest city in the nation.

In spite of Yale's influence among the local elite, the rally plans developed so much public momentum that virtually all local politicians of every faction not only endorsed the rally but also attended it. Over

4,000 people turned out for the rally. The diversity was astonishing—a fair representation of every age and ethnic group and neighborhood in the city. It was fun. People marched in the dark, accompanied by torches and a (Musician's Union) dixieland band, through the streets of the city to the posh residence of the president of Yale. The media covered the rally extensively—live on the largest local radio station, long stories on all local television stations, and banner headlines in the paper.

Yale and the union returned to the bargaining table within a week, and the strike was successfully settled within two weeks. Most people thought that the rally was a major factor in this victory.

Perhaps it would be well to interrupt this story now and at intervals throughout this article, to avoid presenting too sanguine a picture to anyone who might be inclined to try a similar venture. The narrative above is true enough, but there have been lessons learned in the work since that time which indicate that there is no simple recipe for this type of community–labor work.

Many good and imaginative tactics are less effective with each repetition. This lesson holds true to the extent that the tactics depend on the tolerance or lack of preparedness of the local media. Press releases on subsequent mass community–labor rallies in New Haven have been met with silence or one-time brief back-page announcements instead of daily front-page coverage. Local unions have had to escalate their tactics dramatically, culminating in massive civil disobedience, to force the press to cover the story.

As organizers, we rack our brains for tactics so novel that the press cannot resist covering them. This is something we need to do. But the problem of the press is symptomatic of an underlying weakness in our organizing efforts. If we depend on the press to provide communication with people on the streets, and as a vehicle for mobilization, we are subject to the whims of the owners and editors of that press. The only real solution is to develop a broad-based grassroots network, with its own means of communication, both in writing and by word of mouth.

There is a story about the North Dakota Non-Partisan League (NPL) that illustrates the depth-of-organization solution to the problem of press coverage. Robert Morlan, in his excellent book *Political Prairie Fire*, reports that the NPL organizers carried out an extensive door-to-door recruitment campaign before seeking any press coverage. After they had built a strong grassroots network, they began publishing a weekly newspaper. When the principal founder, J. C. Townley, went to the post office to apply for mailing privileges for the paper, the postmaster objected that the organization had to have a bona fide subscription list, paid up:

"'I have,' replied Townley. 'I have 18,000 paid subscribers scattered all over North Dakota.'

'What,' exclaimed the astonished postmaster. 'You say you have 18,000 subscribers, and I never heard of your paper or your organization?'

'You're right,' came back the wizard of farm organizers to the surprised postmaster. 'I have been organizing farmers, not postmasters.'"

When the NPL became public, it was attacked viciously in the regular press. Newspapers warned that "slick operators" were circulating, trying to bilk farmers out of dues money in the name of a fraudulent organization. The NPL was able to respond to these accusations and distribute accurate information to its members at meetings and through its newspaper.

In addition to the problem of press coverage, a sobering development shadowing the story of the New Haven rally is plant closings. In the years since the rally, the industrial unions which were the backbone of participation have been decimated. The large Rubber Workers and ACTWU locals are gone. The Machinists' membership has declined sharply at both shops. In Connecticut's increasingly service-oriented economy, the potential rally turnout at the plant gates has been drastically diminished.

If community–labor coalitions are to be strong, unions must be successful in organizing the service sector. New Haven has been lucky. The organizing drive among Yale's clerical workers by Local 34 of the Hotel and Restaurant Workers has revitalized the labor movement. But in New Haven and elsewhere there are far too many unorganized service workers. Community and labor activists need to lend support to union organizing drives and to efforts to pass legislation that would change the procedural stacked deck which makes organizing the unorganized so difficult at this time.

Formation of the Alliance

Before the rally, Local 35 organizers had expressed a desire to find a way for trade unions to work more closely with the community. They felt that from a union perspective such cooperation was complicated. The community was fragmented—represented by large numbers of organizations, many of them short-lived, linked by a complex web of mutual support, competition, or outright hostility. Union leaders are accustomed to more simplicity and stability. One workplace is represented by one union, and leadership turnover is slow.

The organizers of the rally saw it partly as a test of the potential of community–labor cooperation. If it went well, they hoped to develop an organization that would facilitate this kind of mutual support on an ongoing basis.

It was probably important that the initiative for the Community–Labor Alliance came from labor. Unions are often suspicious of community initiatives toward cooperation, partly because there is often a misunderstanding among community groups about the wealth of local unions, and many contacts from community groups to unions are in the form of asking for money. There is certainly suspicion on the community side as well, particularly among minority groups, but on the whole it seemed to work better for labor, with its strength and stability, to initiate the alliance.

The committee of volunteers which had coordinated the rally drew up by-laws for a proposed Community–Labor Alliance. One important feature of the by-laws was a requirement that organizations pay per capita dues. The monthly contribution meant that affiliation by an organization was taken seriously. And the per capita formula, with a small amount paid for each member, was familiar to the unions, as it was modeled after their payments to international unions and labor councils.

The alliance invited the ten largest local unions and eighteen important community organizations to be the first to affiliate. The use of invitations was another important step in building legitimacy for the alliance. Each invited organization had reason to expect that other groups representing significant constituencies would join. All twenty-eight agreed to affiliate, and the Community–Labor Alliance (CLA) was officially launched.

Invitations also provide an excellent way to guarantee that affirmative action is practiced from the beginning. The list of organizations can be drawn up carefully to reflect a broad spectrum of racial and ethnic groups, and to include organizations from all segments of the community.

There were some problems in the early days which might be instructive for others developing similar alliances. For example, although the CLA had been very thoughtful in preparing its initial list of organizations to invite, it gave much less consideration to the evolution of roles taken on by individuals.

The by-laws provided that organizations were entitled to send delegates to an Executive Board—the number of delegates to be based on the size of each organization's membership. Between meetings of the board, the work of the alliance was carried on by committees made up of people who volunteered at the board meetings.

This open volunteer method of forming working committees is common, but can create problems. For example, in the CLA, the first major task was recruitment of additional organizations as members.

The membership committee was made up of volunteers, who in turn volunteered to contact other organizations. One person went to ask a utility workers union to join and became embroiled in an argument about nuclear power—an issue on which the CLA had taken no position. That union henceforth refused to talk to anyone else from the alliance.

The volunteer committee system stemmed from a commitment to what was thought of as organizational openness or democracy. The day-to-day work of the CLA might have been improved had it been able to benefit from the later experience of Local 34, the clerical and technical workers union at Yale. Local 34 members have a well-developed analysis of the nature of individual leadership qualities. Committee assignments or responsible union posts are filled by either election or consensus, but only after extensive discussions among the membership about which people would best serve the organization. This process more closely approximates an ideal of participatory democracy. It involves more people in thinking seriously about the goals of the organization and the strengths and weaknesses of leaders. It also produces better leaders in important positions, and encourages those leaders to take their roles more seriously.

The CLA's problem with its membership committee touches on another basic issue which confronts any new community–labor organizing effort—that of the breadth of the coalition. Taking as a given that the coalition wants to recruit within the range of organizations which represent low and moderate income people, there is a choice to be made about how much of this range to bite off. A larger bite will offer representation of greater numbers of constituents with more diversity of viewpoints. A narrower one will limit size and diversity but allow for a higher percentage of agreement on issues.

It is probably helpful for new coalitions to discuss this continuum openly and make conscious choices about priorities. The discussion might help to avoid problems created by the illusion that one can simultaneously maximize breadth of membership and depth of consensus.

The CLA opted for a broad-based coalition. It made two early organizational decisions reflecting its desire for breadth. First, the invitations to labor unions and community groups were not limited to those which are sometimes referred to as "progressive." The list was based solely on the size of the unions' membership or the comparable base of the community organizations. The reason for this choice was a belief that most local union and community leaders are serious about serving their members. Since coalitions can be a useful tool in this service, there should be a common ground to work together. The alliance felt that the gradual development of relationships, common knowledge, and trust among people with divergent political viewpoints might be its most important accomplishment—more important than any victory on a specific issue. It never had reason to regret this decision.

The Issues

The CLA's second decision regarding breadth was the establishment of strict criteria for the adoption of issues. The group was aware of its diversity and wanted to avoid fights which would tear it apart. But it wanted to be able to do effective work on worthwhile issues which would serve to unite people.

Leaders expected that the alliance would receive requests for endorsement of hundreds of issues, and that many of those issues could involve the Executive Board in time-consuming and divisive internal debates. People discussed the fact that such votes of endorsement are virtually meaningless unless the organization dedicates time and resources to the issue in question. The CLA then established a policy of avoiding endorsement of any issue or event unless it was enough of a priority to warrant the establishment of a committee to work seriously on it.

This policy sometimes angered nonaffiliated groups which did not understand its origin and wanted endorsements, but it protected the alliance from endless wrangling on a broad range of issues. Because of this policy, the group held together and there was time at meetings to consider a smaller list of issues which might be pursued seriously. The criteria developed for the selection of issues were: (1) the issue should support the interests of low and moderate income people; (2) it should be of concern to both community and labor; (3) it should have broad support among the constuencies represented by the affiliated organizations (assured by a demanding procedure to approve a new issue—discussion at one meeting, written notice to affiliates that the issue had been raised, and a positive vote of three-quarters of the delegates at the next meeting); and (4) it should be one where the CLA could make a unique contribution by initiating and leading an issue campaign that would not duplicate the work of other groups. From its inception, the CLA raised enough funds to have at least one paid staff person. This gave the organization the capacity to lead effective issue campaigns. But since resources were limited, the fourth criterion necessitated a strict limit on the number of issues adopted.

Separate issue committees were established to coordinate the campaigns. The four major issues selected were:

1. School lunches—The goal was local preparation of the food in-

stead of importation of frozen lunches. This would result in more local union jobs, achievement of affirmative action goals in the school system, and better food for the children.

2. Yale—When the CLA asked community groups to support the original rally, it promised to do ongoing work to pressure Yale to contribute more to the New Haven community. An issue committee was established to develop a campaign to fulfill that promise.

3. Pension fund investment—The goal was divestment of city public pension funds from South Africa and reinvestment to benefit the local economy.

4. Plant closings—The object was the creation of a statewide coalition to press for a law requiring advance notice of plant closings, benefits for laid-off workers, financial aid to impacted communities, and technical assistance to save threatened companies.

CLA's initial discussions of possible issues did not adequately address the question of scale. The committees on plant closings and Yale tackled two of the most powerful institutions in Connecticut—the state's largest corporations and Yale University. Perhaps no one fully realized that, with the exception of the school lunch issue, the projects chosen would require years of sustained effort. The selection of issues that presented difficult challenges and required long-term multifaceted campaigns would have a profound impact on the organizational development of the CLA.

The members of the issue committees were recruited through the same open volunteerism which had caused problems in the membership committee. There was no mechanism to provide committees with a cross-section of views of the CLA as a whole. There was, however, some protection against maverick committees. The by-laws required that decisions of the committees be ratified by the Executive Board before actions were taken.

As time passed, the day-to-day work of the organization was increasingly concentrated in the issue committees. Single-issue campaigns of the magnitude taken on by the CLA are complex and difficult. As each issue committee learned to develop strategies to meet the unexpected twists and turns of the campaigns, the committees tended to take on an organizational life of their own.

There was no requirement that all delegates to the Executive Board participate in one of the committees. Once the board had finished its initial work of constituting the alliance and choosing the issues, board meetings tended to consist of reports from working committees and votes to ratify committee decisions. Frequent meetings for this purpose did not feel like an optimal use of the time of these dedicated and talented people.

The CLA model was designed to avoid some of the pitfalls of single-issue organizing by working under the umbrella of a broad alliance, and focusing on more than one issue. But because of the long-term nature of the issues selected, it sometimes seemed that the alliance was not much more than the sum of several separate single-issue organizations. The Executive Board provided only a weak link among them.

The problem of non-decision-making executive board meetings could have been addressed by holding the board meetings less frequently. This would have resulted in a further weakening of the bonds among the disparate elements of the alliance. An alternative which would have strengthened the integration of those elements would have been to require that all executive board members participate in at least one issue committee. This would have limited the pool of potential board members by requiring a higher level of commitment. It also would have failed to resolve the problems inherent in the model of single-issue organizing—problems which would still have been faced by each separate issue committee.

These problems will be taken up again in the concluding section of this article. For now it is important to note the strengths of the issue committee model. It did avoid splits in the organization, and in fact helped to cement ties among groups because the issues were carefully selected. And the work of the committees brought about major shifts in policy in areas which other organizations had not dealt with, and made the CLA a serious and legitimate force in the community.

The school lunch committee won a major victory when it united the PTA, the Hotel and Restaurant Employees (HERE), the American Federation of Teachers (AFT), and the School-Community Councils to force a reluctant Board of Education to build or reopen several kitchens, creating fifty-five new jobs and improving the quality of the lunches at many New Haven public schools.

The pension committee successfully pressured the city to divest part of its pension funds and use them for local housing. It also played some role in pushing the state to create a mortgage program with money taken out of investments in South Africa.

The Yale committee repeatedly and effectively raised the issue of Yale's contribution to the community. The long campaign culminated in the formation by the Board of Aldermen of a commission with seats designated for the CLA, the Central Labor Council, and two community groups as well as business representatives. The commission made a strong recommendation that the city negotiate with Yale for more direct payment in lieu of taxes. However, the city had no direct power to enforce this. Leaders who worked on the Yale issue learned that the state constitution in Connecticut, as in many other states, severely circumscribes the power of municipalities. This, when combined with the city's meager tax base, has led some of the CLA leaders to think about shifting to statewide work in the future.

The only statewide CLA issue committee dealt with plant closings. It started and staffed a loose statewide coalition with broad union participation and more limited community involvement. For several consecutive years, this Plant Closing Coalition introduced strong legislation, with advance notification and other provisions, in the state legislature. Each year the coalition brought hundreds of people to the capital for rallies, public hearings, and lobbying. The Connecticut Business and Industry Association spent tens of thousands of dollars on television and radio ads against the bill, which they called the "industrial hostage act" and a "foot in the door" for socialism. In spite of this, the bill came within two votes of passage in the House, and there was a good shot at an immediate revote. At that point the governor intervened and proposed his own, much weaker, bill, which passed. Its main provision was three months extended health coverage for workers affected by plant closings.

The committee that worked on plant closings was impressed by the extent to which a weak coalition could have a strong impact. The Plant Closing Coalition had no budget and was lucky if it could mobilize one phone call in some of the outlying legislative districts. Yet it almost succeeded in passing a bill which was one of the most controversial in the state for several consecutive years.

On the other hand, the committee learned that the legislative system was adept at avoiding major change. Legislators generally assumed that if they gave a bill to labor they had to balance it by giving a comparable one to business. Labor and progressive groups lobbying at the state capitol were unable to challenge this assumption without an extensive political machine to back them up. They were forced to think small—to make proposals for minor modifications of existing laws rather than sweeping changes. Even the moderate bills proposed in this context were then further "compromised" by the legislature.

In many countries, people with political views similar to those of labor and community activists in the United States belong to organizations with broad electoral bases. They seriously contend for power, and therefore frame their programs with the assumption that their proposals might be implemented. Consequently, their proposals for change are deeper, and contain more awareness of the linkage among diverse issues, the way changes must fit together into an integrated whole. In this country the vision of labor and community leaders is limited by our very limited political base, and vice versa. The Plant Closing Coalition experienced this dilemma.

The CLA issues committee on plant closings was unable to overcome this fundamental problem Without a broad grassroots base, its proposals for reform were initially circumscribed, and then further compromised.

Strike Support

The CLA continued to do support work during union contract struggles and strikes. There is little doubt that this is an important reason to have an ongoing community–labor coalition of some kind. It is difficult for a single union to effectively mobilize diverse community groups in a time of crisis. If a formal alliance of the CLA-type cannot be put together, a more informal network can be helpful. Hartford developed a community–labor alliance without by-laws or staff, where leaders of community and labor groups met periodically to offer mutual support at times of crisis. There was a tendency for it to drift apart as an entity by that name, but at least people came to know each other better, and could offer ongoing mutual support in other organizational contexts. Waterbury, Connecticut, and Providence, Rhode Island, both developed community–labor coalitions with levels of structure intermediate between the Hartford and New Haven models. For strike support, the exact structure of the coalition is less important than its existence.

The CLA organized mass rallies for the Newspaper Guild at the *New Haven Register,* the Machinists at Olin-Winchester, and Local 34 at Yale, and participated in other strike support actions organized by the Labor Council. The ongoing personal relationships among community and labor leaders in the alliance simplified the process of organizing such actions.

The strike by the Machinists at Olin-Winchester was particularly dramatic. During the strike, the company announced that it was going to import massive numbers of scabs for the 6 AM shift on a particular morning. The Machinists union, with the support of other unions and of the CLA, announced that there would be a mass picket that morning and that the scabs would not be allowed to pass. Everyone expected a dangerous confrontation at the gates. But the day before the deadline, the mayor was at a CLA fundraiser, where union and community people discussed the situation. The morning of the scheduled showdown, he ordered the plant closed to preserve public safety. Although his action was later overturned in court, it forestalled the confrontation, boosted the morale of the union, and de-railed the company's plans. The strike was settled without mass importation of scabs.

Strike support work by coalitions is important but it cannot be substituted for good union organizing, especially in tough battles. In Local

34, for example, there have been two major confrontations with Yale University. When the union was first organized, there was a long struggle culminating in an election, contract negotiations, and a strike. Throughout this process, there was significant community support. Hundreds of people were arrested, and thousands attended rallies, signed petitions, made public endorsements, or showed their support in other ways. But the success of the drive was unquestionably due to the skill and dedication of the people inside the union—staff and rank-and-file leaders. Years of tireless work, endless discussions of theories of organizing, struggle with uncommitted people, development of leadership structures with ever-increasing commitments by more union people, all paid off in the end. The community support was there, but only as background support for the union's effective organizing work.

When Local 34's contract was due to expire in January of 1988, the union again conducted a phenomenal internal campaign, with a comparable level of community involvement. In this case, the union began months before the contract deadline to build an atmosphere of crisis which would avert a strike by making everyone at Yale and in the community aware of the damage that would result from another strike. Some of the steps taken were:

—A committee of members visited bank presidents to secure commitments to postpone mortgage payments in case of a strike (one can assume that the bank presidents talked at cocktail parties to Yale officials about their desire to avoid this eventuality).

—Other members worked to enlist the support of community leaders, and succeeded in passing a resolution before the Board of Aldermen calling on Yale to negotiate seriously for the sake of the entire community.

—Another committee embarked on a voter registration drive among the membership, to put the local politicians on notice of the union's potential electoral power.

—Another did research on the members of the Yale Corporation (Yale's board of directors), and busloads of union members began visiting them at their homes and offices in cities across the country.

—Another worked on the details of the negotiations, which centered on problems of race and sex discrimination through job classification. The complex statistical and analytical work done by this group was a major reason for the union's victory.

—Another group worked on the media.

—Throughout the campaign, the union as a whole sponsored an escalating series of public events, involving more and more members and community supporters.

This ambitious program culminated in a total victory for the union without a strike. It is an example of what can be done with hard work and vision. Good work inside the union is a precondition for effective community mobilization, and for victory.

Local 34's ability to mobilize community support has also been enhanced by the nature of its struggles with Yale. It has consistently fought for contract provisions which address the needs of important sectors of the community. In a town whose population is close to 50 percent minority, the union's main focus in negotiations has been on wage discrimination and comparable worth—reclassifying jobs and upgrading salaries to redress longstanding inequities in the treatment of women and minorities. Local 34 has also addressed a widespread perception in the community that Yale discriminates against New Haven residents, and particularly minorities, in hiring. The union fought for and won the funding of a training program to prepare New Haven residents for entry-level jobs, and guarantee them jobs upon successful completion of the training. Local 34 has also joined in the campaign for divestment of Yale's endowment from South Africa. To the extent that unions in other communities uphold principles of fairness in their internal practices, suspicions about unions in minority communities will be allayed, and mobilization of community support in times of crisis will be easier.

Other CLA Activities

Sometimes having a community-labor alliance in place provides a vehicle for community response to an unanticipated crisis. At the same Olin–Winchester plant where the CLA had mobilized strike support, the owners announced several years later that they would sell or close the plant within a year. The CLA immediately began working with the Machinists Union and the Industrial Cooperative Association (ICA) to research the possibility of a worker buy-out. When ICA advised the union that such a buy-out was not financially feasible, the alliance successfully extracted from the company a promise to refuse to negotiate with any potential buyer who intended to move the shop out of town. The company kept its promise, and the CLA and the union worked closely with the city government to interview prospective buyers and arrange bank financing and city subsidies, which succeeded in keeping the plant open. It is still open, as U.S. Repeating Arms, and is still union. This was a case where the existence of an organization which encompassed both labor and community, which was acquainted with problems of plant closings, and whose previous work had already developed contacts and credibility within the city government made possible a quick and effective response to an unanticipated crisis.

The CLA also sponsored community cultural-educational events, some with thousands of people. And it organized a televised public forum where mayoral candidates were asked for yes or no answers on specific questions about CLA issues. Both candidates made commitments to support all the issues, and this was very useful in future work. For example, although the mayor of New Haven was not generally considered a liberal, he stuck by his commitment to help with plant closing legislation.

The CLA also played an inadvertent role in electing an excellent congressmen. He came to a CLA conference on plant closings when he was considered a hopeless long shot. The incumbent also spoke, and the difference between their attitudes toward labor was so striking that many of the labor leaders in attendance began discussions with the challenger. Those discussions led to a decision by the Labor Council to endorse a candidate in the primaries for the first time, and labor played a major role in his victory.

This kind of unintended consequence may be the most important reason to have a local community–labor umbrella organization. The act of bringing people together, whether for conferences, cultural events, meetings, or rallies, has an impact. They talk to each other, learn from each other, and make plans well beyond the formal agendas.

Another example of this process was the statewide plant closing group, whose meetings provided for many staff and rank-and-file leaders of different unions the only place they could regularly talk to each other. After each meeting, people were eager to talk about general developments in the state labor movement. These informal discussions led to interesting initiatives completely unrelated to plant closings.

Neighborhood Organizing

When the idea of a community–labor alliance was first discussed in New Haven, there were community organizers who pointed out that labor was clearly the more powerful of the two partners. Trade unions have large dues-paying memberships while many community groups consist of self-appointed boards with smaller staffs. The community organizations often service or indirectly represent large constituencies but lack the same type of broad organized membership base inherent in unions.

In order to partially redress the imbalance between community and labor, the CLA devoted a major portion of its resources to community organizing. It gradually organized a network of ninety block associations in two low-income neighborhoods. These associations functioned in part as crime-watch associations in cooperation with the Police Department. The crime watches provide a straightforward and broadly supported mechanism for organizing on the streets.

The CLA organizers utilized the crime watch framework to talk about a broader agenda. Meetings on each block developed campaigns to solve local problems such as a particular abandoned house or drug hang-out. Frequently an organized effort was able to quickly solve what had been long-standing irritations or menaces in people's daily lives.

In one case, neighbors were terribly afraid that a drug house on the corner would lead to involvement by their own children. The police were called repeatedly as drugs were sold openly on the street. But each time, the dealers would break up before the police arrived—there was some kind of sophisticated warning system in effect. Finally, the two affected block associations demanded that a police car be stationed at that corner twenty-four hours a day until the dealers moved elsewhere. This was done, and the dealers immediated moved elsewhere and stayed away.

In one of the neighborhoods, CLA organizers worked with small business owners to develop an association, which successfully pressured the city to inject major funding to revitalize the neighborhood commercial area.

Once the first few block associations had been established, CLA organizers invited block captains to come to a monthly meeting of all organized blocks in each neighborhood. These meetings developed issue campaigns based on broader neighborhood concerns, and became an effective vehicle for advocacy by the residents. They were able to improve city services such as street-cleaning and garbage collection, to stop undesirable developments and support or initiate constructive ones. Members who became involved tended to become more aware of neighborhood social service agencies, and to hold them accountable as well.

The city government was aware of the potential political importance of these groups. When the CLA block associations sponsored large neighborhood meetings to deal with questions regarding the city, the mayor brought all of his department heads with him and insisted that each meet the demands of the neighborhood immediately.

The neighborhood associations were entitled to representation on the CLA Executive Board, and a number of delegates did attend regularly. This was important for the people involved in gaining a broader perspective on the community as a whole, and on the labor movement in particular. It also helped the labor delegates to understand the low-income communities better. However, as was the case with the CLA issue committees, the link between the delegates involved primarily in the neighborhood work and those representing other organizations was weak. Neighborhood reports at Executive Board meetings were treated with respect, and block captains attended occasional large events sponsored by one of the issue committees or by the CLA as a whole. But the ongoing work in each neighborhood was carried on by the separate neighborhood groups.

The direct neighborhood organizing of the CLA did accomplish its major goal of balancing the participation of community and labor in the coalition. It also strengthened the voice of the people and improved life a bit in two neighborhoods which had serious problems. This kind of organizing requires a major commitment of resources, but in towns where there are not already effective grassroots community organizations, it is worthwhile.

The CLA block organizers learned that people in New Haven's poorest neighborhoods were quite sophisticated about the nature of power. For example, the low voter turnout was generally intentional. It stemmed from a distaste for the available candidates and a belief that none would cause great improvements in the lives of the people in the neighborhood.

At the same time, people in the block associations believed that political power was important. They were a little more skeptical of the community organizing. They participated in campaigns on neighborhood issues, but there was a sense that they did not see where the work was leading, or exactly why the CLA staff was spending time helping organize the blocks and develop the issues. Part of the problem was that the kinds of issues dealt with were of necessity peripheral—the main problem in the neighborhoods was lack of income, and the block associations were too limited in scope to do anything about that. If the CLA had offered a credible hope to win enough political power to affect the core issues of neighborhood life, people's commitment would have been deeper.

The block associations themselves are a vehicle which have the potential to exercise tremendous political power. When people on the street know and trust each other, they can choose collectively to support and work for a candidate. Some of the CLA blocks in some elections voted virtually unanimously for one candidate. But in general the political potential was untapped because of the limited goals of the CLA.

Funding Issues

The CLA was able to do the neighborhood organizing because of large grants from national churches and staff from the Federal CETA and VISTA programs. However, these funds were temporary, and the process of applying for the funding and reporting to the funding sources required massive and debilitating work. Grant-seeking created a weird sense of accountability in the wrong direction—grant reports got written and newsletters neglected. Many good organizers have gone on to other types of work because they had to spend as much time on fundraising as on organizing. Many good organizations have died because funding sources give seed money to innovative efforts and then abandon them even if they are successful, because they are no longer new.

To be fair, the funding sources are trapped in the reality that if a model organization works, others will want to try it and there just is not enough grant money to fund the breadth of organizations needed. It is important that community-labor alliances follow the example of unions and develop ways to raise money through their membership. This would help provide more organizational continuity, keep staff who really want to organize, and maintain accountability where it should be, to the members only.

Lessons for Community–Labor Coalitions

For those interested in forming a local coalition of community and labor organizations, the CLA experience provided some important lessons.

First, the development of personal relationships between leaders of the community and leaders of labor is more important than the specific organizational form. The relationships may outlast the coalition, and will certainly have unintended beneficial consequences for the organizations involved and for the community at large.

Second, per capita dues are a good idea. They augment the budget, make organizations take their commitment more seriously, and strengthen the credibility of the coalition in the broader community.

Third, strike support is one of the most important functions of a community-labor group, but it depends on strong unions, and will be more effective to the extent that the union involved is willing to take a stand against discrimination.

Fourth, it is probably better for the initiative for an alliance to come from labor, which is generally the stronger partner.

Fifth, a choice must be made between a broad-based organization and a narrower one with more internal consensus. Although the broader base limits the choice of issues and is trickier to hold together, it has major advantages. The involvement of large numbers of people gives the coalition strength and legitimacy, and allows the individuals involved to come to understand each other better.

Sixth, avoiding long debates on numerous endorsements of issues helps keep the group from splitting. Taking the lead on some carefully selected major issues is important.

Seventh, it would be good to take into account the power of the institutions being challenged, in terms of estimating the length and difficulty of the struggle. The CLA did not find that members needed immediate victories to sustain their commitment, as some organizing theories would suggest. But scale of issues is an important consideration.

Eighth, neighborhood organizing in low-income areas where no grassroots community organization exists is worthwhile if the resources needed to sustain it can be generated.

Ninth, the executive board of the coalition can function either primarily as an informal communication network in an organization without significant ongoing committees; or it can meet infrequently to approve committee decisions; or day-to-day work can be a requirement for board membership, in which case it would meet more often to make important decisions. It should not be asked to meet frequently without important work to do.

General Organizing Lessons

Some insights arising from the CLA experience apply to other organizing efforts as well. First, in founding an organization, carefully considered invitations to prospective members are useful to provide legitimacy and diversity.

Second, it is very important to find ways to generate the funding for the core budget from the membership.

Third, a model of internal participatory democracy which involves discussion of leadership qualities and leadership development, and careful thought about roles taken by individuals, will make an organization more effective and more open than the usual casual volunteerism. It will also help create an atmosphere where rank-and-file leaders take their roles seriously. This is necessary because we can never raise enough money for staff to do all the work that needs to be done.

Finally, both the issue of leadership development and the issue of the importance of relationships among leaders of diverse constituencies point to a deeper lesson. To the extent that an organization can generate awareness of the importance of both, it strengthens the process of what Paulo Freire and the liberation theology movement call *conscientizacion.* The organization consciously provides a place where people can grow—not only in specific knowledge and skills, but in empathy for the concerns and needs of other groups, and in sophistication about how particular small struggles fit into the broader system.

Lessons for the Future—Beyond the CLA

Persistent themes emerged in widely divergent experiences within the CLA. Throughout the work—in neighborhood organizing, in union support, in statewide lobbying—it became apparent that we need a vision and specific proposals which cover more territory and dig deeper than single-issue campaigns. People in neighborhoods want and need broad changes in the way government affects their lives. The labor movement is in decline, and needs systemic changes which would level the playing field in organizing drives and labor disputes. Single-issue campaigns in the legislature are unable to generate enough strength to produce such changes.

The single-issue work, whether it is about a plant closing bill or an abandoned house, takes a tiny piece which is intertwined with a broader problem, which is in turn related to many other problems, and tries to solve only the tiny piece. Even if there were hundreds of single-issues groups in the state, the gaps not covered would be much larger than the points which are. We need to find a way to develop and advocate broad, comprehensive, integrated policy proposals.

Because single-issue campaigns are often short-lived, a typical strategy of powerful institutions is to make partial concessions to a single-issue group, then wait until the group dies or goes on to a new issue. They are then free to reverse the advances made, or subvert the goals of the campaign through administrative means. We need organizations with continuity. They must include people who help develop ideas in each broad policy area, and have the expertise, motivation, and organization to hold both legislators and administrators accountable over the long term.

Single-issue groups also tend to have difficulty in reinforcing values of solidarity and empathy, or in developing relationships among divergent groups. Staff and leaders of single-issue groups are usually sympathetic to the concerns of other constituencies, but they are forced by the trade-offs of the lobbying process or the neighborhood advocacy fights to strategize in terms of narrow self-interest. Participating in a diverse organization and learning from the other groups encourages moral concern for the needs of others. It is also inspiring and fun, and we miss this when we work only in narrowly focused single-issue or single constituency organizations.

The CLA was fortunate in that it did bring together diverse groups. But it could not build a broad enough grassroots base because it was a coalition of organizations rather than individuals. One advantage of coalitions in comparison with direct membership organizations is that they build on the strengths of existing organizations, and provide a mechanism for the leaders of those organizations to communicate with each other. Any membership organization would need to be mindful of recruiting leaders of organizations for important positions, to try to maintain some of the strengths offered by coalitions. However, the experience of the CLA indicates that there are serious drawbacks to the coalition model, and that a membership organization offers greater potential for achieving the broad goals of community and labor groups.

Because the CLA was a coalition, the affiliated unions and community groups involved kept their own membership lists. They tend to do the same in similar efforts elsewhere, for understandable reasons. The lack of lists meant that if the CLA sponsored a rally, it had to ask the leaders of each organization to mobilize their members. The CLA could hope that the rally was a high priority for those busy leaders and that the leaders were skilled organizers. But it could not directly organize large turnouts, develop broad member education and leadership, or even send mailings to the memberships of the affiliated organizations. At one rally, a large union promised a busload of people and the bus arrived with six riders. A coalition is powerless in these circumstances.

This problem also minimizes the potential electoral threat of a coalition such as the CLA. Each affiliated organization, by itself, necessarily has a relatively weak network. A given street might have residents who are members of five different unions and four community groups, all affiliated with the coalition. But without access to membership lists of those organizations, a group of this type has no way to utilize this potential common ground on that street at election time.

The problem discussed earlier, of reliance on the media for effectiveness of tactics, is related to the coalitions' lack of effective organization of people at the base. A systematic block-by-block organization would provide an effective means of communication outside of the existing media.

For similar reasons, the CLA, as a coalition, could not have developed a comprehensive political program. Its work was limited to specific carefully selected issues which would be approved by virtually all member organizations. Some coalitions deal with this problem by compiling "laundry lists" of issue priorities of each separate organization. Since each has a limited membership base, none is in a position to demand sweeping changes, so the overall program is a list of moderate changes in existing law. And the program is not integrated—the gaps between the single issues are not filled, nor the connections between issues spelled out. A membership organization which develops its own district-by-district, street-by-street, block-by-block base is free to propose comprehensive policy changes without the least common denominator constraints of fitting into agendas of affiliated organizations.

Coalitions also have an inherent bent away from democracy. Leaders of organizations speak for their members, and there is no way to ascertain whether the positions taken by these leaders within the coalition are reached through a democratic process within their own organizations or are representative of the opinions of their members. Problems of internal democracy in affiliated organizations can lead to difficulties in mobilizing members to support coalition actions. Members who have no voice in an organizational decision are less likely to take action in support of that decision.

Local community–labor coalitions such as the CLA are important steps toward the work that needs to be done. They develop relationships, strengthen member organizations, and win victories on limited issues. They will not bring about a strong movement toward social justice. If we want to take another step toward this goal, we will need to develop organizations with two major components: a broad and practical integrated social policy program and a mass membership organization with a street-level political machine which supports that program.

Both components will require perseverance and cooperative efforts to improve our organizing skills. If we are to be democratic, the policy proposals must be developed through a broad-based process involving many people. And the grassroots political network can be created only through painstaking person-to-person organizing in neighborhoods and workplaces. To succeed we must somehow learn to concentrate a portion of our collective organizational and personal resources on the task of systematically building these two components together.

Jobs and Economic Development

As plant closings and unemployment swept U.S. industrial areas during the 1970s and 1980s, conventional trade union tactics were often ineffective in response. At the same time, communities as well as workplaces were deeply affected. This laid the basis for labor-community alliances designed to preserve and expand jobs.

Dozens of coalitions have been formed around new strategies for industrial retention and community economic development and empowerment. Our three case histories, from the East, Midwest, and West, show the complex ways such alliances must relate to various levels within the labor movement as well as between labor and community groups. These efforts also indicate how such alliances can help reshape community economic institutions in the future.

"If All the People Are Banded Together": The Naugatuck Valley Project

Jeremy Brecher

"All workers have to realize that we're responsible for our own condition. If we don't devote some time to our unions, our political party, our church organization, and the laws being enacted, we'll wake up and find ourselves with empty pension funds, bankrupt companies, disproportionate sacrifices and a run-down community.

"If all the people in the city are banded together to make it a better place to live, then it will be a better place to live. That's what Naugatuck Valley Project is all about."

Theresa Francis, chairperson,
UAW Local 1604's Century Brass Steering Committee

The Naugatuck Valley in western Connecticut was once the center of the American brass industry and one of the most intensely industrialized areas on earth. From its center in Waterbury, the region's major city, with a population of 100,000, the valley runs north through the towns of Thomaston and Torrington and south through Naugatuck, Seymour, Derby, and Ansonia. As in so many industrial areas of the U.S. Northeast and Midwest, its workers are primarily the descendants of immigrants from eastern and southern Europe, with more recent additions of blacks from the South and Puerto Ricans. During the 1960s and 1970s it could have been renamed "deindustrial valley," as dozens of plants were sold or closed.

Like those in similar areas elsewhere, the people of the Naugatuck Valley have found that their established approaches have given them little leverage over deindustrialization. Conventional union tactics have exerted little influence over companies prepared to close up or sell the shop. Legislation to affect plant closings has been difficult to pass, and when passed has had limited impact. Local communities have felt powerless in the face of decisions made in distant board rooms; until recently, few efforts have been made to affect those decisions, even when they have threatened the lifeblood of Naugatuck Valley communities.

Over the past three years, the valley has developed a regional organization of more than fifty religious, labor, community, and small business organizations. Called the Naugatuck Valley Project (NVP), its
purpose is to give workers and communities more influence over their
economic destiny.

The project's strategy grows out of its analysis of what has happened
to the valley's economy. While most valley companies were once locally owned, today they are mostly controlled by multinational conglomerates for whom local plants are mere specks on a balance sheet.
Project leaders trace much of the valley's economic distress to corporations which, instead of nurturing local companies, run them for a
quick profit and then "disinvest" by closing them, scaling them down,
or selling them off to owners who eliminate jobs.

Project leaders often characterize the NVP's preferred solution
to this problem as "broad-based local ownership." As NVP president Rev. Tim Benson put it, "When somebody in London or Los
Angeles owns a mill in the valley, you feel helpless and out of
control. When you are in charge of your life by being a member
of a democratically owned company, you're going to feel less anxiety than you would if somebody in Los Angeles is pulling the
strings."

The project draws on the experience and tactics of community organizing, but attempts to project those approaches into the economic sphere. It tries to mobilize concern about deindustrialization in
unions, churches, and other organizations that see the people of the
valley as their constituency. And it tries to serve as a vehicle through
which those groups can bargain with corporations, government, and
other powerful institutions over the economic fate of the valley. While
its strongest emphasis so far has been on employee buyouts, it has
also explored such other approaches as eminent domain, starting new
enterprises, and requiring that urban development be linked to job
preservation.

With chapters in six towns, hundreds of active supporters, and meetings almost daily in one or another part of the valley, the project
has become a vital force in the life of the region. This is a report
on its experience so far.

Origins of the Project

The Naugatuck Valley Project grew out of meetings of statewide
leaders of Catholic and Protestant denominations; the United Autoworkers, the Connecticut Citizens Action Group, and Ken Galdston,
an organizer experienced with similar coalition efforts in Chicago,

Buffalo, and elsewhere. Deeply concerned about the economic distress of their constituents in the valley, these groups decided to initiate an alliance that could assert worker and community interests in response to threats of plant closings.

With financial and in-kind support from these statewide institutions, Galdston began early in 1983 to call on community leaders in the Valley. He focused particularly on informing local trade unionists of the early warning signs of impending plant closings or sales. Almost immediately a local union leader identified such signs at General Time Controls (GTC), a 140-employee subsidiary of Talley Industries in Thomaston. The project alerted Thomaston union and church people, who met together and asked for a meeting with the president of GTC. After a story in the local paper and a call from a local minister, the GTC president agreed to meet with the NVP.

Having received this first degree of recognition in the form of the company's agreement to meet with them, the coalition had to decide what it wanted to negotiate for. Talley had announced that the plant was for sale. The workers at GTC, most of them over fifty years old, discussed, but did not support, a worker buyout. So the coalition decided to ask Talley to give preference to buyers who would keep the jobs in the Valley. Talley said yes, and in fact ended up selling two of its product lines to a company which moved the jobs to a nearby location.

Several lessons from this early experience have guided much of the subsequent work of the project. First, it established that a local coalition of diverse groups can be pulled together around the threat of a plant closing or sale if preliminary preparations have taken place and participants have some sense of what to do. Second, even a large absentee owner can be forced to recognize and bargain with a community coalition if enough pressure is brought to bear. Third, the union, as the representative of the majority of the employees, must be involved from the start. Finally, a certain degree of creativity is necessary to define a program which meets the needs of the community in a realistic way. All in all, the experience showed that the community and workers united were no longer powerless to influence corporate decisions.

A similar course was followed when a union leader at the Torin company, which had recently been bought by the conglomerate Clevepak, reported warning signs at the company plant in Torrington. Local management denied anything was in the wind; corporate management refused to meet with the union. The project thereupon went to the press with its analysis of the threat; Waterbury's auxiliary bishop Peter Rosazza called corporate headquarters to ask for a meeting. Workers in the plant, who were interested in exploring a buyout, did a home-made feasibility study. The mayor and the Torrington Chamber of Commerce joined the coalition.

Enough pressure having thus been generated, the president of Clevepak finally agreed to meet with the coalition. He conceded that Clevepak had been considering selling Torin, but said they had now decided not to sell it. And he agreed to come to the employees first if Torin was to be sold in the future.

Next, Emhart, another conglomerate, closed the casting shop at its subsidiary in Ansonia, apparently signaling the liquidation of the company. Emhart, too, refused to meet with the union to discuss the closing. A community meeting with union officials, clergy, the head of the Chamber of Commerce, and both candidates for mayor decided to ask for a meeting with Emhart. Over the weekend, the project gathered 1,500 signatures on a petition to Emhart, primarily through two local parishes and the Steelworkers local. Thereupon Emhart agreed to meet. It promised to give the project notice if it decided to sell any parts of the company. Whether or not in response to project pressure, the one building it has sold went to a company which has increased the jobs there.

Seymour Specialty Wire

Early in 1984, workers at the Bridgeport Brass wire mill in Seymour, a subsidiary of National Distillers, heard rumors that their plant might be sold. A UAW staff representative immediately steered the local leadership to the project and urged them to look into buying the plant. The project presented various options to the local, including employee ownership. Workers responded with a spirit of skepticism, but also with a sense that they wanted to pursue every angle that might help save the company's 250 jobs. The local voted to pursue the possibility of a buyout. To prepare a feasibility study, the project pulled together a team which included prestigious Connecticut law and accounting firms and the Industrial Cooperative Association (ICA), a consulting organization specializing in worker-owned companies. A Seymour chapter of the project was formed to support the workers' efforts; it persuaded the town and the state to kick in funds for the feasibility study. Personal contacts were made to win the cooperation of white-collar employees.

A steering committee of blue- and white-collar workers was elected. It hashed out by-laws, vesting procedures, and other plans for the proposed new employee-owned company. It proposed to limit owner-ship to those who actually worked in the company and to elect the board of directors on a one-person-one-vote basis—an approach that was confirmed after a subcommittee traveled to Hyatt-Clark Industries in New Jersey and Atlas Chain in eastern Pennsylvania, and learned about their difficulties with less democratic forms of employee ownership.

The feasibility study indicated the company had strong production capabilities and a desirable market niche. A market plan, drawn up with the cooperation of local managers, indicated the company could be quite viable.

Initially National Distillers declined to take the workers seriously as purchasers. The corporation later indicated that the community support effort, which included letters from two bishops and many political figures, gave the employee plan credibility. Eventually it donated $25,000 for the feasibility study and let its offices be used for its preparation.

The employees decided to make a bid for the company, based on an Employee Stock Ownership Plan (ESOP). After a last-minute bid was made and withdrawn by a competing company, National Distillers accepted the ESOP offer. A bank provided the financing. The union agreed to accept a 10 percent wage cut to ease servicing of the debt. In April 1985, Bridgeport Brass was reborn as "Seymour Specialty Wire: An Employee-Owned Company."

Seymore Specialty Wire is run by a board of directors of nine. There are two outside directors selected by the board, and the union and company presidents are automatically members. The other five are elected by all employees on a one-person-one-vote basis. Committees on personnel, operations, planning, education, and new business development assist the board's decisions. A management search committee, after reviewing 170 resumes, decided to hire the former manager of the local plant as president of the new company.

Economically, the first year of Seymour Specialty Wire has been a remarkable success. Sales have risen despite price increases. The handful of workers initially laid off have been rehired, and over a dozen new workers have been hired. A major new casting unit has been purchased to ensure the company an independent supply of brass. After six months workers received a bonus, and the 10 percent wage cut has been restored.

Seymour remains a UAW firm. Only minor changes have been made in the union contract, such as a streamlining of job bidding procedures. There has been little change in production quotas, though by all accounts peer pressure has led to tightening up of work practices. Some common work rules designed to protect bargaining unit jobs, such as prohibitions on foremen working or workers voluntarily helping others with their jobs, are left unenforced.

The transition to an employee-owned company has involved role changes which have been challenging for both workers and management. For the workers, employee ownership implied a much more active role not only in the production process but also in the governance of the company. An attitude of "I'll go in and do my job and let someone else worry about the company" became less appropriate, especially when the consequences were company policies that workers did not like.

For management, traditional managerial authority was suddenly transformed into something like democratic government. Management was initially concerned to protect its authority, but gradually came to believe that an employee-owned company must be run differently than a conventional company, with employees making decisions that management used to make.

While the union and the blue-collar workforce apparently accepted the necessity of managers making day-to-day decisions, they expected major decisions to be made by a process of discussion and consent. They wanted managers to be accountable for their actions. And they wanted personnel policies and procedures to be consistent for blue- and white-collar employees. Seymour's first year has been marked by a process of redefinition of roles that can be compared to that of a country which has suddenly been transformed from a monarchy to a constitutional republic, where rules and processes for decision-making must be reinvented almost from scratch.

Initially, day-to-day practices in the workplace changed little—leading to an accumulation of conflicts and divergent expectations. Near the end of the first year, as tensions mounted, this situation was addressed by a goal-setting process created with the help of ICA. Employees were divided at random into groups of fifteen to twenty, who met to express their concerns, identify goals for the company, and elect delegates to an ad hoc committee. This committee defined five goals for the company and developed a plan for meeting each of them.

The most crucial is a plan, dubbed "Workers Solving Problems," under which all the workers on each shift in each department will meet every two weeks to discuss all issues concerning the department and the company. An elected convener will chair; the foreman will take minutes, which will be posted in the shop. A company-wide council of shop representatives and foremen will pool reports from the departments and pass information back to the shop floor. Top management is responsible to the board for implementing the plan; ICA will provide training for participants.

The most obvious lesson of Seymour Specialty Wire is that, under favorable circumstances, employee buyouts can be an effective solution to the threat of a plant sale or closing. But a buyout is only the starting point for a process of transformation that cannot be expected to proceed without false starts and conflicts. The structures and practices of the workplace, evolved over generations, are not overcome simply by having workers elect the board of directors. Seymour's forthcoming attempt to develop new ways of running the company may be the most significant part of the entire effort.

Other Buyout Efforts

As the Seymour Specialty Wire buyout hit the headlines, workers at four other companies turned to the NVP for help.

Faced with threats of closing or sale, employees at the AMF Alcort sailboat company in Waterbury formed a steering commitee, conducted a feasibility study, and attempted to buy the company. After prolonged negotiations, the owners sold to another bidder, whose asserted intent to keep the company running locally has met with considerable skepticism. Workers at Judd Hardware Company, a plant outside the valley, also turned to the project to aid a buyout, only to find their plant sold to another buyer.

A few months after its meeting with the project, Clevepak decided to get rid of its Torin machinery division and, as it had previously promised, informed the workers of its intent. Workers in the machine division formed a steering committee, conducted a feasibility study, and made an offer for the plant. Clevepak agreed to sell but, despite the mobilization of U.S. senators and representatives, state and federal agencies, and many other supporters, repeated efforts to put together a financing package ended in failure. Torrington's mayor even raised the possibility of using eminent domain to prevent the shutdown of the plant, based in part on research and support provided by the project.

Clevepak eventually liquidated the company. The NVP has assisted a businessman who has purchased some of its equipment and has hired twenty-five former Torin workers. Although the new company will start nonunion, Torin union leaders who led the buyout effort are actively helping the new company in the hope of restoring jobs.

The Fight for Century Brass

The number of hourly employees at Century Brass, once Waterbury's largest industrial employer, has gone from 1,721 in 1976 to 438 in 1986. After a long series of union concessions and a classic milking of the company, Century filed for Chapter 11 bankruptcy. The bankruptcy court allowed the company to abrogate its union contract and renege on pension commitments.

Looking for a handle on the situation, the UAW local at Century asked the project to become involved, created a buyout committee, and sponsored a feasibility study. Century Brass refused even to discuss selling to the workers; white-collar employees, perhaps fearing company reprisals, did not join the buyout effort. While Century workers received a good deal of local sympathy, the kind of supportive mobilization that developed in the smaller towns did not materialize in the larger city of Waterbury.

In April 1986 the bankruptcy court allowed Century's hundreds of acres of valuable property running through the center of the city to be sold to the highest bidder, a real estate company from California. While the purchaser initially plans to lease the working plants back to Century, there is deep concern locally that this is only a step on the way to liquidation.

The state has allocated $250,000 to study the future use of Century properties. The UAW buyout committee and the NVP have responded by demanding that the mayor and other officials hold up the study until commitments are made to save the remaining jobs at Century. This required massive research and a series of community meetings to convey to the public that Century is not just another company but rather an unconscionable exploiter of the Waterbury community.

After a recent community meeting publicized Century's behavior, Century officials offered to talk with the minister who chaired the meeting and to other clergymen—but refused to talk with the NVP or the union. When the minister responded that the project, not the company, would decide who would represent it in any meetings, Century Brass changed course and has now held two meetings with project representatives and city officials.

Century Brass has raised a new series of questions for the project. It has demanded a search for alternatives where buyouts are not the answer. It has shown that the process of community mobilization in a city of 100,000 is considerably different from that in a city of 10,000 or 20,000. And it has posed the problem of how to proceed when a company initially refuses to make even a token response to community demands. But whatever else, it has meant that Century workers are no longer simply passive pawns but have become an extremely active and vocal force in trying to shape their own future.

Financing Buyouts

The Torin experience led the Naugatuck Valley Project to conclude that having sources of financing in place before buyouts begin can make a crucial difference in their success. Out of this awareness came the project's first major legislative effort.

In 1984, the Connecticut legislature had established a trust fund to subsidize interest on bank loans to employee stock ownership plans.

In 1985 the NVP drafted legislation to make money from the fund available for loans to employee groups seeking to buy their own companies. Several large community meetings were held; legislators from the valley and the state party leaderships were lobbied. The bill passed both houses unanimously.

The project is now exploring two additional possibilities for financing future buyouts. One is a revolving fund which would put money from credit unions, churches, unions, and other institutions into a mix of employee-owned companies and other socially useful local investments such as housing. The other possibility is establishment of a banking consortium to invest in employee buyouts. This should help spread the risk among different banks and at the same time alleviate banks' concern about the public relations effects of having to foreclose on an employee-owned company.

While the project's banking committee hopes that local banks will voluntarily support such an effort, they point out that most are not controlled in the Valley, and that at present most do limited commercial lending there. Muriel Moore, director of the Head Start program in Waterbury and head of the Naugatuck Valley Project's banking committee, stated, "The first task of the banking committee was to trace the amount of money banks had from depositors in the Valley. We found out that one of the banks reinvested less than 5 percent of its assets in the Valley. It awakened people's vision: What are the banks doing for us?" And at one project meeting a local pastor won loud applause for the proposal that "we say we are willing to deposit our money only in banks willing to help this valley."

The Organization

In each community where the NVP mounted a campaign, a local NVP coalition emerged, together with a growing core of people and groups committed to the project as a whole. The project as a whole was run by a steering committee which started with representatives of the initiating statewide organizations and gradually brought in more and more people from organizations in the valley itself. Staff worked hard to encourage a transfer of responsibility to participants from the valley. In October 1985, 250 delegates representing fifty churches, unions, community and business groups came to a convention in Waterbury to formalize the project as a permanent, self-governing organization with its own by-laws and elected officers.

The Naugatuck Valley Project is essentially a citizens' organization in the general tradition pioneered by Saul Alinsky's Industrial Areas Foundation. The mixed character of the participating institutions is particularly important. Catholic and Protestant denominations, the UAW, and the Connecticut Citizen's Action Group have remained its most important constituents; but Seymour Specialty Wire, the Chamber of Commerce of Northwestern Connecticut, and a variety of other organizations have also joined.

The broadest coalition was formed in the small factory town of Torrington. There, despite a long history of local industrial conflict, the project chapter includes the Chamber of Commerce as well as local union and religious leaders. The Chamber's small-business constituency is badly hurt by plant closings, and appears more than willing to accept employee buyouts if they preserve local jobs and payrolls. Local unions and the Chamber successfully lobbied together under project auspices for protection of the region's machine tool industry. Each welcomes this opportunity to combine forces where they share overriding local interests; neither expects the other to support it on issues, such as unemployment compensation reform, where they disagree. (Perhaps there is a parallel here to the many nineteenth- and early twentieth-century occasions in which local small businessmen supported local strikes against what were perceived as the encroachments of "outside" corporations. A strike in 1903 against a Waterbury trolley company that had been taken over by an out-of-town corporation, for example, won extensive sympathy from local businessmen.)

The only divided votes at the project's founding convention were on resolutions to support voter registration and to oppose utility rate increases. Both resolutions, presented by the Connecticut Citizen's Action Group, passed with slight rewording. What tensions would arise within the project coalition if it resorted to more militant tactics—for example, picketing unresponsive companies or their officers, boycotting banks, or attempting to buy companies through eminent domain—remain to be seen.

While its efforts at worker buyouts have received the most attention, the Naugatuck Valley Project is really focused more broadly on the issue of preserving and creating good jobs, especially industrial jobs. It is essentially a means by which workers and communities can influence economic decisions that affect the valley. Its focus on jobs makes its goals central to the lives of many people in the valley, and much of its energy has come from workers and communities directly threatened by plant closings. At the same time it has been able to show cumulative growth, perhaps because it is not limited to a single focus, such as saving one local plant. Those active in efforts around one plant often comment that they would remain active in the NVP even if their particular issue were resolved.

There appears to be a consensus among those active in the project that its central focus should continue to be jobs. How this should be interpreted, and what other issues should be dealt with as well, remains to be clarified. The project has already been involved in a successful effort to save a local branch of the state university; it is currently exploring the possibility of helping start a supermarket and organize a land trust. Visions of the future range from an organization focused on employee buyouts to one which will represent the full range of people's needs in the Naugatuck Valley. What seems to be agreed is that new spheres of action should emerge organically out of previous ones and out of needs perceived strongly by the project's constituency in the valley.

One future task that project staff identify as crucial is deepening the relationship between the project and its member groups. They have started providing leadership training programs to help member groups draw their own members more deeply into their own and project activities. They also see a need for the project to move toward financial independence, perhaps in part by providing services to member groups and employee-owned enterprises.

The project makes no effort to define itself in ideological terms. When pressed, some of its leaders portray worker buyouts as a form of capitalism; others see them as a democratization of the workplace. For most, they seem primarily a means for meeting the needs of local communities and workers, rather than an expression of a political or economic philosophy. If any single sentiment ties project activists together, it is a strong sense of community responsibility, coupled with a belief that Naugatuck Valley communities will be vulnerable to disruption as long as they do not in some way control their economic future.

While project leaders seem reluctant to state a vision beyond encouraging broad-based ownership of the valley's economy, Bishop Rosazza does say, "It would be great to make of the valley a little Mondragon." (Mondragon is a region in the Basque country of Spain with a series of worker-owned enterprises tied together with their own credit institutions, social security plans, and educational programs.)

In addition to its concrete successes, there can be little question that the Naugatuck Valley Project has transformed the issue of jobs and plant closings not only in the valley but throughout the state of Connecticut. Where two years ago closings were almost universally blamed on high wages and uncooperative unions, there is now a widespread awareness of the milking of the area's economy by outside corporations. Where corporate decisions were regarded as something the public simply had to accept, it is now acknowledged as legitimate for groups such as NVP to challenge business decisions and their human impact. And where the idea of workers buying and running their own companies was regarded as the height of absurdity, there is today a tremendous interest in the idea among politicians, community leaders, and especially among workers who feel threatened by plant closings.

Some Lessons

Project leaders and staff point out a number of lessons their experience might hold for those concerned with jobs and plant closings elsewhere. First, a project of this kind needs a clear focus, such as jobs and plant closings, but it also needs a multifocus framework that allows small victories and cumulative drawing in of additional people.

Second, much of the energy and legitimacy for the project comes from the involvement of those most directly affected. NVP efforts have almost always started with discussions with the leadership of the local union as the representatives of the largest group of employees, then gone directly to the membership of the local, and then reached out to white-collar workers and the wider community.

Third, it takes a certain creativity to bargain with companies over local jobs. Buyouts cannot always be the primary goal or focus because in most cases they are not feasible or appropriate and because defining a buyout as the only alternative puts all the bargaining chips in the hands of the company. It is crucial to develop bargaining goals that are appropriate to the situation and that allow partial victories: an agreement to give notice of any plans to sell, to give preference to a purchaser who will keep jobs in the community, to give workers the right of first refusal if a company is sold, and the like. A "carrot-and-stick" relationship is necessary toward the companies with which you are bargaining. It is often necessary to publicize a company's acts and even attempt to embarrass it.

Says Rev. Benson: "A lot of people like to keep everything quiet and peaceful, but my experience is that the quieter you keep it, the more likelihood there is of the whole deal being pulled out from under you. The more you're in the public eye, the more you're likely to get cooperation."

But a successful outcome may also require working with a company constructively and projecting an approach with which it can cooperate. At Seymour, for instance, the company at first had to be pressured into taking the employee buyout effort seriously; but thereafter it provided cooperation that was extremely helpful in making the buyout a success.

Fourth, much more sophistication about the business world than a community organization usually possesses is needed. This means a recognition of the need for the services of lawyers, accountants, and business consultants, and a search for ways that ordinary participants can learn to understand and research business issues.

Fifth, some of the project's strength has come from its independence. While many project leaders are active in politics, all seem agreed that the project itself should be independent of political parties—functioning in the political arena as a nonpartisan citizens' organization. In a recent contest for the Democratic nomination for governor, one project leader ran as a delegate on the slate of Governor William O'Neill while another apparently swung his town to O'Neill's opponent, Toby Moffett, with a charge that O'Neill had provided inadequate support for the Torin buyout effort. According to Rev. Benson: "In the by-laws, we tried to delineate that we need to keep a distance from the political process. We can't be in any political party's pocket, or any politician's pocket, because as soon as we are, we lose our effectiveness as an organization."

Conclusion

In many ways the Naugatuck Valley would seem an unpromising place for an effort of this kind. It is neither an unusually homogeneous area nor one with a strong progressive tradition. Before the project, there were hardly even modest responses to the threat of deindustrialization. While the region has some geographical unity and shared historical identity, there were few organizational or governmental structures tying together the valley as a whole. (In some ways this may have been an advantage, since before the project, the valley as a whole was not defined as anybody's "turf.")

Organizer Ken Galdston regards the existence of local and state organizations with a strong concern for the jobs issue and a prior history of cooperation as the biggest asset the region brought to the initiation of such an effort. And Rev. Benson points out that Naugatuck Valley towns are proud of their "milltown" identity and are therefore more willing than some communities to fight to keep their local factories.

Because the Naugatuck Valley is so typical of deindustrializing American communities, it is hard to see why efforts similar to the Naugatuck Valley Project might not be equally successful elsewhere. Of course, there are many aspects of the American and world economies that cannot be addressed from a purely local basis. But a proliferation of such experiments might not only help local communities solve immediate problems, but might also help transform the context in which national economic issues are debated.

Tri-State Conference on Steel: Ten Years of a Labor-Community Alliance

Charles McCollester and Mike Stout

On March 27, 1979, the Episcopal bishop of Pittsburgh convened the Tri-State Conference on the Impact of Steel. It drew delegates from western Pennsylvania, northern West Virginia, and eastern Ohio, all aging industrial areas, to discuss the potential economic impact of a proposed U.S. Steel "supermill" at Conneaut on Lake Erie. Impetus for the conference came from the activist Ecumenical Coalition of the Mahoning Valley which in response to a series of steel plant shutdowns had organized a potent community-labor alliance in Youngstown, Ohio.

For more than a year, the mounting plant closing struggle in Youngstown was to dominate the activities of the organization that grew out of the conference. Issues such as corporate disinvestment and the unaccountability of corporate decision-making were to remain central to Tri-State's concerns. Out of Youngstown the core idea of a community right over economic decision-making was born.

The early Tri-State effort had a strong ecology slant to it. Environmentalist allies were sought since it opposed the unspoiled, wooded "greenfield" proposed steel mill site at Conneaut, arguing that corporate reinvestment should be directed at existing industrial "brownfield" sites where workers lived and established communities existed. A regional approach was inscribed into Tri-State from inception, as was a commitment to conduct research so that collective action would be based on informed opinion and accurate analysis.

Youngstown also provided the Pittsburgh organizing efforts with a model in terms of style. Very consciously, both efforts attempted to link a radical and unconventional economic strategy with union activism and community organizing.

Tri-State's efforts in the early 1980s were directed toward sounding the alarm that Youngstown's demise was a foreshadowing of Pittsburgh's own fate. Unemployed organizing was an important activity but a clear delineation developed within the loose-knit organization from a group of unemployed committee activists who were to found the Mon Valley Unemployed Committee. While Tri-State remained involved in unemployed work through the efforts of several Tri-State board members who were officers in local unions and had helped form active unemployed committees in their locals, it saw as its primary task the development of an effective long-range plant closing strategy.

Early on, Tri-State also clearly distinguished itself from another activist group, the Denominational Mission Strategy (DMS, later DMX). This group of some dozen Protestant ministers were to unite with several militant union leaders to form a kamikaze outfit which harnessed much anti-corporate resentment, but provided no effective vision for change.

On the other hand, instead of loudly complaining to any available media people about the problem, Tri-State worked hard to develop a vision with a practical strategy for implementation. As its central organizing issue, it adopted the call for a public authority that could use eminent domain if necessary to stop plant closings as well as serve as a mechanism for community economic development. The authority proposal would provide a way for workers, community activists, and concerned citizens to be players in the economic decision game, not just its passive victims. It sought to structurally empower them to affect their own economic future.

Tri-State raised eminent domain as a battle cry in two plant closing fights in 1982, and came very close to successfully founding an authority in 1983 during the struggle to save the Mesta Machine Company.

Out of the Mesta struggle grew the attempt to found the Steel Valley Authority. In 1984, Tri-State's document calling for the establishment of the authority was released as plant closings became an almost weekly occurrence in western Pennsylvania. While public officials were skittish and red-baiting was common, several local unions and churches in the valley provided a firm base for Tri-State's organizing efforts.

What galvanized the organizing effort—and provided a powerful symbolic expression of the irrationality of the system—was U.S. Steel's closing of its Duquesne works, coupled with the announcement that Dorothy 6, the newest and most productive blast furnace in the valley, was to be dynamited and scrapped. The year-long effort to save Dorothy 6 saw the largest town meetings, demonstrations, and organizing efforts in the Mon Valley since the CIO organizing drives in the 1930s.

The Dorothy 6 effort, while failing to save the furnaces, had important consequences. Tri-State, which had been based on insurgent union forces, began to forge a working relationship with the United Steelworkers of America (USWA). More important, the Dorothy campaign provided the backdrop for an incredibly intense and complex organizing drive that eventually led two cities (Pittsburgh and McKeesport) and eight depressed mill towns to join together into the Steel Valley Authority (SVA). The Steel Valley Authority was formally chartered by the state and took up operation in February 1986.

The SVA was the institutional expression of the organizing effort born in Youngstown's Mahoning Valley. Unlike most authorities, top-heavy with corporate executives and/or government bureaucrats, the SVA was made up of dislocated workers, mill retirees, religious leaders, local businessmen, and elected politicians.

The SVA was born without funds into the height of a plant shutdown struggle involving the United Electrical Workers (UE) and American Standard, Inc. The authority immediately moved to get an injunction to stop the movement of equipment, which was blocked by the corporation's legal maneuvers. Entry to the plants by authority and borough officials for economic development purposes was legally enforced, but the plants were being dismantled too quickly to be saved. By the time the SVA won the right to have the merits of its case heard in court, critical machinery had been stripped from the plant.

Tri-State's goal of founding the SVA was achieved virtually at the end of the terrible wave of plant closings that eliminated more than 100,000 industrial jobs from Allegheny Co. Psychological and economic depression gripped the mill towns; young workers and their families fled in droves, while older workers were trapped in the ranks of the unemployed.

However, as the economy bottomed out in 1986, the bankruptcy of LTV Steel Corporation in the summer of that year posed both a threat and an opportunity. The immediate concern was the threat to retirees' pensions, which was the major remaining economic base for .many of the Mon Valley towns. The bankruptcy threatened to liquidate hard-won union gains, causing deep anxiety to workers who thought that their retirement was secured by a lifetime of labor. However, Tri-State also saw the crisis as a possibility.

For Tri-State the bankruptcy not only created the opportunity for a campaign to mobilize broad support for the retirees, it gave another opening to advance the possibility of reopening some facilities under a different form of ownership. From the very beginning, Tri-State linked the fight to save retirees' pensions and benefits to the effort to "recharge" the closed, LTV-owned electric furnaces in Pittsburgh's South Side. Retirees' benefits could be successfully protected and guaranteed only if younger workers were working, paying taxes to the government, and contributing to the pension plans.

During the summer of 1986, work had begun on a Metal's Retention Study, funded by the state of Pennsylvania. While the government people were envisioning a broad, general study recounting the ills of the steel industry, Tri-State fought for a study with an engineering emphasis focused on those elements of the local mills that had the best chance of reopening. In particular, it wanted special attention paid to the South Side electric furnaces.

Throughout the fall and into the spring of 1987, Tri-State activists held several large meetings of retirees in South Side and Hazelwood, helped organize busloads of retirees for rallies in Youngstown and Washington, D.C., and spoke to many community groups—always linking the struggle for benefits to the fight for economic rebirth.

In February of 1987, a breakfast in Homestead between Tri-State activists and four area state representatives on the ongoing Metals Retention Study produced the suggestion that an attempt be made to secure for the SVA a part of a large rebate that the Pennsylvania Public Utilities Commission had ordered Duquesne Light to pay to its customers. Of the $32 million earmarked for rebate only $28 million could be returned to those who had initially been overcharged. While some groups advocated turning the remaining money over to the same corporations that had shut down plants in the Pittsburgh area, the SVA proposed directing the funds toward restarting the South Side furnaces. Fittingly, the inability to return the money was directly related to the large numbers of dislocated workers leaving the area. Furthermore, the electric furnaces had once been Duquesne Light's single largest consumer of electric power.

On St. Patrick's Day 1987, Tri-State and SVA reported to a packed house at South Side's Brashear Community Center on a SVA-organized tour of the furnaces that included many local political leaders. Broad community support was garnered for two public hearings held in Pittsburgh by the Public Utilities Commission. At the hearings, an eloquent mix of former workers, retirees, and church and community leaders testified to the need for economic development money for the furnace project. Finally in August 1987, the PUC awarded the SVA $590,000 and for the first time the authority had solid financial resources to attempt something most people considered an impossible task.

In order to accomplish a worker-community-generated reopening of a steel mill, Tri-State began to work closely both with former workers and the community. In January of 1988, the Metal's Retention Study done by Arthur D. Little Consultants and Hatch Engineering was released. Front page banner newspaper headlines announced its conclusion that South Side's electric furnaces could survive as a semi-finished slab producer in a revived steel market with the installation of a continuous caster.

Having finally received "expert" sanction for its goal, Tri-State and the Steel Valley Authority moved to join the United Steelworkers of America in the formation of an electric furnace "Buyout Committee."

The committee's formation was announced to some 300 workers in a meeting at South High School in Pittsburgh. Joining Tri-State, the SVA and the USWA (local and international) on the Buyout Committee were former workers who wanted to return to work, retirees, state representatives, and South Side community leaders. Worker committees were established. The most active of these was a technical advisory committee, which did a detailed site evaluation concerning hazardous chemicals and provided advice and criticism to various hired consultants. More and more, longstanding Tri-State programmatic concerns like worker involvement began to require practical application.

Throughout 1988, the Buyout Committee launched a series of actions designed to move the project forward. Tri-State provided the organizing link to the community and retirees, while the SVA provided funding to supplement United Steelworker and local government support. Lazard-Freres, formerly involved in both Wierton and McLouth Steel employee stock option plans (ESOPs), was retained as financial consultant, with a local investment firm added later. Extensive engineering studies were undertaken for the needed continuous caster installation and the Allegheny county controller was retained as negotiator with LTV.

The SVA positioned itself to be the mill's landlord. As landlord, the SVA has proposed an innovative lease agreement with the mill's potential operators that ensures a clean environment, a fair tax rate beneficial to all, and a voice for the community in decisions that affect workers and community alike. A nonprofit Southbank Industry Association has been created to provide South Pittsburgh community organizations with an equity share and a direct voice in the project.

In early 1989 the SVA, on the advice of the USWA, hired a former Republic Steel plant manager, later industrial relations vice-president for LTV, and then consultant on the formation of the McLouth Steel ESOP, to produce a business plan. Much of his time has been directed toward securing critical customer commitments for the project. In February 1989, a decision was taken by the Buyout Committee to incorporate as South Side Steel of Pittsburgh.

Tri-State sees 1990 as the year of decision for the Electric Furnace project. LTV is dismantling many of the buildings around the furnaces because of the high price of scrap steel. They are pushing for a decision on the project so they can emerge from bankruptcy by mid-1990.

While both the SVA and Tri-State have a number of other projects underway, both organizations recognize the tremendous importance of the South Side steel project to the effort to empower community and labor in the process of job preservation and economic renewal. A restart in South Side could revive a plate mill at Homestead and generate other spin-off industrial projects. It would mark a major turning point in the steady erosion of the region's industrial, productive, manufacturing base as well as assist Tri-State's efforts to bring high speed, magnetic levitation (MAGLEV) rail production facilities to Pittsburgh.

For ten years the Tri-State Conference on Steel has stood firm against a hostile tide running full tilt against industrial communities and unionism. The organization brings together many different interests—unionists, many of whom were schooled in rank-and-file insurgencies; church-based social activists who were inspired by liberation theology, the Polish Solidarity union, and the hard times experienced by their congregations; veterans of the civil rights and anti-war movements who had gravitated toward the workplace as the battleground of the 1980s; community organizers who from their vantage point saw the intimate link between good jobs and neighborhood viability. This diverse group has sought to develop a strategy to counter the economic collapse happening around it; it has managed to link energetic newcomers to Pittsburgh with deeply rooted local people to create a sustained, consistent organizing effort over the past decade.

While local organizing remains fundamental, Tri-State recognizes the need to link up with other groups at the regional and national level. From a Regional Reindustrialization Conference in 1985 which spawned chapters in Cleveland, Ohio, and Wheeling, West Virginia, to assisting in the recent formation of the Federation for Industrial Retention and Renewal (FIRR) linking twenty local worker-community coalitions nationwide, Tri-State has seen the need for a broad political alliance to reinforce local struggles while working toward a national industrial policy.

Whatever the future brings, for even success brings its own baggage of difficulties and problems, Tri-State is proud of its defense of the industrial and union heritage of Pittsburgh, its hardworking towns and neighborhoods, and of its attempt to articulate for the country a vision of a more democratic economic order. There is a neanderthal capitalist viewpoint that thinks the way forward is to destroy unions, increase economic inequality, and heighten worker insecurity. Tri-State believes that a way exists to combine private investment and government support with community involvement and worker initiative to create a dynamic and equitable economic system. After ten years of wrestling with the problem, Tri-State believes that it is pointing the way to at least a part of the solution.

The Tri-State Conference on Steel is an example of democratic coalition building toward common long-range goals. The organization responded to a deep-felt community and worker need growing out of a severe economic crisis. It built gradually upon the most immediate level of community politics and has maintained a consistent focus on job retention and renewal. It has taken the route of building new, more democratic institutions as a way toward creating a more just society.

Labor-Community Coalitions as a Tactic for Labor Insurgency

Eric Mann

The Campaign to Keep GM Van Nuys Open has achieved one of the few victories that can be pointed to by the national movement against plant shutdowns that has emerged from unions and industrial communities in the past decade.

Jack Metzgar, *Labor Research Review*

The recent plant closing bill giving workers 90 days advance notice is certainly good, but it wouldn't have happened if it wasn't for farsighted movements like the one in Van Nuys, California that demanded a ten year commitment from General Motors.

Rev. Jesse Jackson (CNN interview)

The Campaign to Keep GM Van Nuys Open is almost as good as its press clippings. By organizing both workers at Van Nuys and the whole Los Angeles community since 1982—threatening GM with a boycott if it ever closed the Los Angeles area Van Nuys Assembly plant—it has thus far been able to keep the plant open. Hardly surprising that GM opposed the campaign; rather more surprising, however, the International leadership of the United Auto Workers (UAW) has targeted that campaign for severe repression, including colluding with GM management to allow the firing of the leader of that movement, former Local 645 president Pete Beltran. As a result of this repression, the campaign is seriously weakened but by no means defeated. In response, the Labor-Community coalition is organizing the campaign involving worker and community voices in the economy—such as an environmental campaign against corporate toxic air pollution—while also reorganizing the Van Nuys movement.

The battle at Van Nuys and within the UAW as a whole indicates that there is nothing magical or inherently progressive about labor-community coalitions. All coalition building must be evaluated—and in fact undertaken—as part of a clear political strategy. The Van Nuys Labor-Community coalition has won certain victories because its politics are adversarial, active, class conscious, rooted in a strategic alliance between the working class and communities of color, and in direct opposition to the disastrous policies of labor-management cooperation advocated by the present UAW International officers. Labor-community coalition building as a tactic within the strategic context of *labor insurgency* offers optimism about the long-term prospects for the UAW and the labor movement in general.

A Brief Outline of the Van Nuys Campaign

In the late 1970s, the California auto industry was booming; the main demand of most of its 25,000 workers in six plants throughout the state was, "Stop all this damn overtime." Within a few short years however, more than the overtime stopped. The Big Three automakers—General Motors, Ford, and Chrysler—facing greater international competition, adopted a two-pronged policy: (1) "reconcentration" of assembly in the Midwest in order to practice Japanese-style "just in time" inventory systems, in which parts manufacture and assembly are in close geographic proximity, and (2) cost reduction through speed-up, reduction in total workforce, and the closing of "surplus plant capacity." The implementation of both policies pushed the California auto industry (and autoworker) to the edge of extinction.

Between 1980 and 1982, the Ford plants in Pico Rivera and Milpitas, the GM plants in Fremont and Southgate, and the Mack Truck plant in Hayward, California, were all closed—permanently discharging 20,000 workers. By 1982, only the 5,000 workers at the GM Van Nuys plant in greater Los Angeles remained—and as the rumors of a Van Nuys closing began in earnest, union leaders at Local 645 decided that the last remaining U.S. auto plant west of Oklahoma would not be closed without an all-out confrontation with GM.

The Campaign to Keep GM Van Nuys Open was based on a strategy that was difficult to arrive at but simple to explain:

(1) The organizers saw that the GM Van Nuys plant was profitable, but not at profit levels high enough for GM. While GM did not want the labor of the workers at the Van Nuys plant, it did want the enormous Los Angeles new car market—the largest in the United States.

(2) Thus, they concluded the campaign could not be simply a "save our jobs" movement, based on, for example, withholding of labor through a strike, but had to be conceptualized as a broad community issue, in which the community's purchasing power could be used as a weapon against GM. In that the plant's workforce was 50 percent Latino and 15 percent black, the "community" in question centered on Los Angeles' large Chicano and black communities to combine issues of class exploitation with those of racial oppression.

(3) The main strategy was to build a broad united front, beginning with the GM workers, expanding to the Chicano and black communities, and then reaching out to students, professionals, white progressives, and directly impacted small businesses—to unite all who could be united against one common enemy: General Motors.

(4) The main tactic was to mount a public campaign of demonstrations, marches, rallies, press conferences, petitions, and letters, all directed toward GM management with the preemptive *threat* of a boycott. The coalition would not launch a boycott as long as the GM Van Nuys workers were still working but would demonstrate its capability for a successful boycott so that GM would keep the plant open rather than risk the loss of sales.

From 1982 to 1986 the Van Nuys Labor–Community Coalition in conjunction with the UAW local carried out a complex and multifaceted organizing campaign. I have discussed the details of that movement at length in my book *Taking on General Motors: A Case Study of the UAW Campaign to Keep GM Van Nuys Open*. But a few basic elements can be outlined here.

Over a period of four years, the campaign organized three rallies, each with 700 to 1,200 workers and community people; each generated substantial local and national press (the *Los Angeles Times*, the *Los Angeles Herald Examiner*, *Business Week*), and was covered by virtually every television and radio station in greater Los Angeles. The coverage was very positive—at a time of *uncontested* plant closings and the rise of probusiness, antiunion ideology, here was a local taking *preemptive* action and gaining broad community support. Throughout this period, the campaign flooded GM management with more than 2,000 individual letters pledging to boycott GM products if the plant ever closed down.

In January 1984, twenty-two leaders of the independent Labor-Community Coalition met with then GM President F. James McDonald at the Beverly Hilton Hotel and both sides threatened each other—McDonald with a plant closing if the workers did not become more "cooperative," the coalition with a boycott if McDonald ever closed the plant.

It was the view of all of us from the coalition who attended the meeting that McDonald was very impressed—in fact shocked!—by the strong representation from the clergy, elected officials, and Chicano and black communities, and the obvious willingness and capability of the coalition leaders to carry out their threat.

On November 6, 1986, GM announced the closing of eleven plants. GM Van Nuys, which had been predicted to be one of them by every business publication including the *Wall Street Journal*, was kept open.

The Evolution of the Van Nuys Movement

After the meeting with McDonald, both sides had lost the element of surprise and GM began to take the Van Nuys movement far more seriously. Over the next few years, GM's response evolved from disinterest to short-term retreat to cooptation to direct repression. But before going into the details of that repression, it is necessary to understand the conditions that allowed that movement to develop in the first place.

To begin with, the campaign evolved out of politically conscious activism. Mark Masaoka, Mike Gomez, myself, and several other workers at the plant had come out of the antiwar and civil rights movements of the 1960s and many had gone into the plants with the express goal of organizing a new union movement from the bottom up.

Second, the campaign was able to develop because of the involvement of a unique leader, local UAW union president Pete Beltran. Beltran was a Chicano whose family had come from Mexico. He had worked in the plant since 1958 when he was only eighteen years old. A self-taught scholar and political leader, a brilliant tactician capable of forging complex alliances in the local and a constant threat to the regional leadership, Beltran has always been both sympathetic to the left's general intentions and highly skeptical of its capabilities. Thus, when several activists from the local's Political Action Committee proposed the campaign to him in 1982, he agreed with it in theory, but gave it little chance to succeed. The obstacles to building a movement among the workers in 1982 were enormous. The problems of overcoming the workers' belief in management rights, ethnic tensions, anticommunism, fatalism, and a generalized inertia among the workers were formidable, but as those obstacles were overcome one by one, and as a growing core of twenty-five workers expanded to fifty, and as the second shift was laid off in 1982 pushing 2,500 workers into the street, the movement developed a mass character and Beltran came to take it far more seriously and put the full weight of his office behind it.

Beltran's successful leadership of the movement was multifaceted, and explains why his later firing by the company was such a blow. To begin with, Beltran was rare among today's labor leaders in that he was not in awe of top GM management. Rather, he had high self-esteem and an understanding that the interests of the autoworkers and the Chicano community were in direct contradiction to those of corporations such as GM.

Unlike the timidity too often shown by the local union official who is threatened by the development of new leadership, Beltran's confidence and his more strategic understanding that skilled organizers would both strengthen his administration and perhaps save the plant allowed him to put the full weight of his office behind the campaign and its organizers.

So, in fact, both the cadre of organizers and the progressive local president were essential for the campaign to develop. The organizers provided the strategy and the commitment to do the day-to-day shop floor organizing; Beltran provided enormous tactical understandings of the inner workings of union politics and the institutional legitimacy and resources of the local to give the workers at least some hope in the battle against the number one corporation in the Fortune 500.

Beltran also was a well-known and popular figure in the community, especially in the city's large Chicano community. The UAW local under his leadership was visited by virtually every progressive and community group in the city asking for contributions, endorsements, and worker involvement. Beltran was one of the few local presidents who were friendly to the peace movement, even becoming one of five citywide sponsors of a Jobs with Peace initiative.

Given the success of the campaign in not only winning the short-term goal but winning new interest in the labor movement, many union sympathizers, especially those with a well-deserved respect for the traditions of the United Auto Workers, cannot fully understand why the International union would attempt to suppress both this movement and such a progressive local union official as Beltran.

The Campaign and the UAW International

The campaign was initiated with the strategic understanding that the UAW international would be completely opposed to the long-term objectives of the movement, and when it was able to, would attempt to crush that movement up to and including a move to place our local in trusteeship. This assessment was helped by theory and reinforced by our direct experience in practice.

In 1980, for example, when the Pico Rivera plant was closed, another unusually gifted local president, Ron Delia, attempted to launch a movement to keep it open. Delia organized a caravan of buses to go to Sacramento, the California state capital, to ask for help from the legislature, but the UAW regional office opposed it on the grounds that it would embarass the Democratic Party. The UAW regional office canceled the bus contracts, froze the local's funds, and soon thereafter, Delia was brought up on completely false charges and removed from office so that there could be no organized opposition to the closing.

At virtually every rally called by locals to protest layoffs or plant closings, the international union spokespeople would argue that there was nothing that could be done except to (1) support import restrictions upon the Japanese and (2) get rid of President Reagan and elect more Democrats. By targeting foreign "enemies" and the Republican Party, the UAW worked to misguide the workers' anger away from the Big Three automakers themselves—and the Democratic Party's complicity in the rise of pro-corporate ideology.

In local after local, as plants closed, local officers who "cooperated" by not organizing any protests were given jobs in union-management "retraining" programs for permanently discharged workers, or given jobs with the international union. While the vast majority of workers received nothing but tragedy, for local leaders willing to sell out the members there were ample rewards.

The leaders of the Campaign to Keep GM Van Nuys Open, based on these experiences, pursued a strategy that anticipated an eventual direct confrontation with the international union but attempted a non-aggression policy as long as possible while the local carried out its campaign.

In the initial stages, the regional office of the UAW did not oppose the campaign, and in fact, members attended several of the rallies and pledged support. Their support was given for several reasons:

(1) to begin with, in the UAW regional directors are elected by delegates from their own region and in Region 6, the West Coast, Pete Beltran was a formidable, if long-shot, candidate for regional director. Too much antagonism to him might provoke a race against the incumbent;

(2) it was hard for the international to position itself against the campaign: with autoworkers and priests and Hollywood celebrities and other unionists all demanding that GM make a long-term commitment to the plant of at least ten years—it would have been politically suicidal for the international to openly oppose the campaign after it had done nothing to save the other five plants that had been closed; and

(3) few people took the campaign very seriously in its first two years; the rallies and marches were seen as "harmless." Almost before GM and the international understood the full scope of the campaign, the public support and visibility of the movement made it hard to suppress.

The international union's hostility toward the campaign was *strategic*, not personal. From the international's perspective, the U.S. auto industry is in grave danger due to foreign competition. As UAW Vice-President for GM Affairs Donald Ephlin expressed it, "The very existence of the auto industry is at stake." The key, from the point of view of the company (and not surprisingly the union officials) is to restore "competitiveness" and profitability—at which time the ample trickle-down benefits of the postwar period can be reestablished. Ephlin, to his credit, has been the most upfront about the argument. While certainly blaming management in words for much of the "culture of confrontation" on the shop floor, he expects the union leadership to stop it. UAW President Owen Bieber agrees: movements such as the one at Van Nuys, which directly challenged management's right to open and close plants as it saw fit, were not, according to Ephlin and Bieber, a progressive development, but rather a disaster for the industry and the union. For if communities were allowed to insist on the observance of workers' rights, and impose a sense of social responsibility and reduced profit margins on GM management, the whole damn industry might go down the tubes. (Based on this reasoning, in 1985, a feature length and laudatory article on the campaign, written by staffer Jeff Stansbury and already typeset for *Solidarity,* the UAW newspaper, was pulled at the last minute by Ephlin.)

So what was the alternate strategy to class confrontation at Van Nuys? Ephlin argued that in return for cooperation, the union would get a voice in the production process—bringing the long dreamed of "workers control" to the shop floor. So why was it not consistent with greater union influence to compel GM to keep one plant open in its largest market in the country? Ephlin argued that interference with such production decisions was not in the best long-term interest of the company and thus the union. (Ephlin's growing ability to talk interchangeably like a management executive led him to resign from the international in 1989 to take a position at the Sloan School of Management at MIT.)

Finally, this strategy of cooperation was extended only to management, for the full explanation of the international's strategy is *cooperation with management and suppression of union members who opposed cooperation.* The extent of this strategic vindictiveness is reflected in the international's response to the Canadian branch of the UAW, which had been increasingly opposed to both the strategy of jointness and the national chauvinism of the American leaders who offered the Canadians virtually no voice in the "international" union. When in 1984, the Canadians finally terminated what had been a fifty-year relationship with the UAW, and took 120,000 members to form their own Canadian Auto Workers (CAW), the response of the international union was "good riddance." Even though this weakened the union in its battle with capital it strengthened that faction that was proposing marriage with capital. And so the Bieber administration preferred to force out 120,000 Canadian brothers and sisters rather than tolerate a democratic debate on the union's future. (Able to run without the weighted shoes of the UAW "international leadership" the CAW has grown to 160,000 members.) In this international context, it is more understandable why the Van Nuys movement was seen as a threat to the policies and careers of the international union officials in Detroit.

Van Nuys and the "Team Concept" Model

In 1982, GM closed down its plant in Fremont, California—which had employed 6,000 workers when it was at peak production. In 1985 the plant reopened as New United Motors (NUMMI)—a joint venture of General Motors and Toyota Motor Company. While portrayed to the public as a bold new experiment in labor-management cooperation, the "experiment" began by giving former Fremont workers who had been scattered to other GM plants throughout the country the chance to apply for admission to NUMMI, providing they renounced their old "adversarial" ways. (Several new advocates of cooperation in the Fremont local begin speeches to university classes by saying, "While I used to be a militant, I now see the shortsightedness of confrontation and the value of cooperation." Some UAW observers call this recanting under duress "militants anonymous.")

Second, while the debate about the merits of tbe NUMMI system needs to be conducted elsewhere, workers on all sides of the debate admit that one key element of the system is a substantially speeded up assembly line and the goal of producing more cars with fewer people.

In terms of the Van Nuys story, however, the "team concept" at NUMMI then became the model for GM's and the international's counterattack on the campaign. While in the past the international union was vulnerable to charges that it had no strategy as to how to keep plants open, it could now claim to have "saved" or even "resurrected" the old Fremont plant.

Beginning in 1986, the GM Corporation, the regional UAW leadership, and significant numbers of Local 645 union officials began to advocate that the only way to keep the Van Nuys plant open was to tear up the existing local agreement and replace it with a "team concept" agreement à la NUMMI.

In the spring 1986 elections for delegates to the UAW convention, a well-organized slate calling themselves Responsible Representation, strong advocates of the team concept, swept the elections. The campaign organizers were temporarily disarmed: even many staunch supporters of the campaign advocated voting for the team concept since the company had made it clear that without a team concept agreement they would probably close the plant. In May 1986, after a long and bitter debate, the "team concept agreement" was passed by the narrow margin of 53 percent to 47 percent—and then only after GM promised to delay implementing the plan until they had delivered the commitment of a new car model that would keep the plant working into the mid 1990s.

But no sooner had the team concept been voted in than support for it began to unravel. The company took the vote as a mandate to abrogate the union contract, and the "living agreement" between local management and team concept union officials was used to virtually destroy the contractual protections of the workers on the shop floor. The new "team" players in the union turned the local into a patronage machine—as newly created "joint activities" personnel, appointed by union and management agreement, walked the floor with unspecified duties except to spy on union militants and to disappear from view for hours at a time. Finally, GM attempted to implement the new team system without keeping its promise of a new car model.

In reaction to these abuses, Pete Beltran decided to not run for re-election as president, in order to run for the position of shop chairman. The UAW operates with two strong centers of power at the local level—the president, who is the public spokesperson for the union, the leader of the executive board, and the primary controller of the union's finances; and the shop chairman, who is the highest contract enforcer and chief bargainer and controls the union activities on the shop floor. Thus, for example, while Beltran as president could authorize money for the campaign, hire shop floor workers as community organizers, and represent the union to the press, he had limited authority to deal directly with the team concept and a limited role in union negotiations.

Given this division of authority, Beltran argued, "What is the value of winning the demand 'Keep GM Van Nuys Open' if we just become another showcase for this company unionism they're calling the team concept? If I am elected shop chairman I can confront the team concept directly and help the workers on the floor who are crying out for protection." Others, such as Mark Masaoka and myself, argued that Beltran's control of the presidency was the plant's lifeline to the outside world, that the campaign provided the community support that would encourage the workers to fight against the team concept, that the temporary support for the team concept would make it hard to win election campaigning against it, and that it would make more sense to wait two more years until the workers had *direct* experience of working under the system—at which time rebellion would be more rooted in their own experience.

Critics of Beltran's decision worried that it was an all-or-nothing risk. Beltran's reelection for president was assured, while his candidacy for shop chairman on a platform of opposing the just-initiated team concept could threaten many frightened workers who were already being told that worker militancy was the main reason the plant was facing a closure.

Beltran, after listening to all the arguments, decided to run for the office of shop chairman. In April and May of 1986, more than 4,000 workers debated their options as dozens of leaflets were circulated—and read—arguing for and against the team concept. Finally, in June 1986, after overt company threats that a vote for Beltran would bring down the plant, Beltran was elected by a margin of 117 votes.

No sooner had Beltran won than the company began to move against him. First, when he began to protest the contractual violations of the team concept he was told by local management that they had no intention of dealing with him: they were told to bypass his authority and deal directly with the regional director, Bruce Lee. Then, when Beltran left the plant on union business, the company marked him absent and began to dock his pay. When Beltran asked the local president (his political opponent Jerry Shrieves) to provide a union excuse for those absences as was past practice, Shrieves refused. And finally, when local vice-president Mike Velasquez, functioning as acting president while Shrieves was out of town, *did* provide that union coverage specified in the contract, both Beltran and Velasquez were fired for "conspiring to defraud the company."

The willingness of the regional office and the local president to support the firing of their political opponents, even on grounds that were clearly in violation of Beltran's ability to carry out his duties, is consistent with the strategy of nonadversarial unionism in which colluding with the company to get rid of "militants" who will upset their arrangement is the highest priority—even if it means further weakening the *functioning of the union as an institution*. From this perspective, the union is no longer needed as a weapon to fight the company, since class conflict is replaced by the new class cooperation. Instead, the union becomes an instrument to crush grassroots opposition to the corporation.

The immediate response to the firing of Beltran and Velasquez was a marked reduction in rank-and-file activism. Many of the workers—at least temporarily—threw in the towel. The entire strategy of taking on both General Motors and the international union had seemed like a real long-shot, even among the most dedicated. Pete Beltran had been the main factor on which the organizing strategy rested. To the workers he was one of them, undoubtedly the highest reflection of what any of them had become, but still one of them.

With Beltran out of the picture the repression, at least temporarily, had accomplished its objectives. Many workers felt "If Pete and Mike with thirty years seniority can be fired, men who held union positions we felt were institutionally secure, then why bother fighting it. The company and union officials are in bed with each other and the hell with everything." It is a sad commentary on the behavior of the UAW's international officers that one of the key elements of their continued institutional power is an increasingly disillusioned and demoralized workforce—a product of their nonadversarial strategy. Of course, that is also reflected in growing anti-union sentiment and support of right-wing Republican candidates such as Ronald Reagan and George Bush by a large minority of autoworkers, but again, the international seems to feel that their continued rule is worth such costs.

Models of New Unionism and Labor-Community Coalitions

The UAW is undergoing a virtual Civil War, one that has direct analogies to the divisive issue of the American Civil War—slave or free labor. On the one side is UAW President Owen Bieber, most of the UAW bureaucracy, and of course the management of General Motors, Ford, and Chyrsler with their vision of a compliant, coopera-tive and "nonadversarial" workforce. On the other side is the growing New Directions movement, begun by the workers in Region 5 of the UAW and its present director Jerry Tucker, the 1989 candidacy of Don Douglas in the Detroit-Pontiac area, the outspoken and in-fluential criticisms of UAW pioneer Victor Reuther, and the encour-aging model of the Canadian Auto Workers. This battle exists within virtually every union local in the UAW and is generating a great de-bate among the 1 million members of the union. In this context the debate moves from the *tactic* of labor-community coalitions to the competing *strategies* of class-struggle unionism versus class-collabo-ration unionism.

The Campaign to Keep GM Van Nuys Open is part of a growing reform trend in the UAW that is in direct opposition to the policies of labor-management cooperation. The labor-community coalition in that campaign was based on the strategy of building a broad united front against capital in this society—only one of whose main elements was General Motors. The demand to *force* GM to keep open a profit-able plant at a lower rate of profit than management was seeking at least began to challenge certain basic management prerogatives and began to assert the rights of workers, their unions, and communi-ties of color. While not revolutionary, the demand that corporations should operate within strict guidelines set by a broader public, the idea that the interests of that broader public were in contradiction to those of corporate capital, and the idea that organizing, activism, and direct action were essential components of social change were a direct challenge to the right-wing ideology that was setting the terms of the debate in the 1980s—and that unfortunately had permeated the top levels of the UAW as well.

By contrast, the UAW international also attempts to organize labor-community coalitions. For example, at the UAW convention in 1986, Owen Bieber introduced Benjamin Hooks of the NAACP. Hooks said that the real heroes of the Chrysler turnaround were not the Lee Iacoccas, but the Chrysler workers who made all those concessions to save those jobs (not even mentioning that 57,000 jobs had been cut by Chrysler in the reorganization as part of the concessions). Bieber responded by telling the delegates to make checks payable to the NAACP. Then, Atlanta Mayor Andrew Young told of how he gave concessions to General Motors to keep open the Lakewood, Georgia, plant and how in today's competitive market urban centers should share with workers in giving concessions to big business. Again, Owen Bieber hugged Andy Young and many delegates cheered.

But while Bieber was hugging Hooks and Young, he was denying UAW founder Victor Reuther access to the microphone on the fiftieth anniversary of the Flint sit-downs that Reuther helped organize— because of Victor's opposition to the present direction of the union. And Bieber had just finished firing Jerry Tucker, a fourteen-year veteran of the UAW staff, for running for office in opposition to "the union's fall into management's embrace."

So, within the UAW there are actually two types of labor-community coalitions: labor-community coalitions to confront management and labor-community coalitions to cooperate with management and repress dissenters.

In that the Van Nuys campaign began with a clear understanding that the international would eventually move to crush it, the labor-community coalition was formed as a tactical way of putting independent pressure on the corporation to keep the plant open once the international moved against the local—as we knew they would.

As early as 1983, the campaign organizers began to anticipate the problems of carrying out the threatened boycott if GM actually closed the plant. To begin with, they anticipated GM telling the workers that while the plant would be "temporarily" closed, management was working on a possible "joint venture" with Toyota or Isuzu, and that workers should not do anything to jeopardize those negotiations. (For two years after it was closed, former Southgate workers continued to repeat "reliable sources" that it was going to reopen.)

Simultaneously, the UAW international would move in to freeze the funds of the local and place it in administrative trusteeship to prevent the boycott. They would argue that since our "brothers and sisters" in other GM plants were producing the cars we were proposing to boycott, it would violate "solidarity" to try to save our plant.

Then, they would offer the more pliable local officers jobs in retraining programs for the laid-off workers or jobs with the international on the provision they publicly condemn the boycott movement as "outside agitators" and "union malcontents" jeopardizing the workers' future. This company-international union system had developed the process of crushing popular movements into an art form, and the movement at Van Nuys *began* with the understanding of those obstacles.

In the Van Nuys model, therefore, the labor-community model went far beyond a simple "community support group" to become an *independent form of organization that could give both workers and community activists a vehicle with which to fight this new labor-management collusion*.

While the Van Nuys organizers had anticipated the company's strategy, they had not anticipated that they would fire the movement's leader—which is still another escalation of tactics in this war. Now, the labor-community coalition provides a base area for a counterattack, because the community has always been a strong supporter of the save the plant movement and has its own *independent interests* in taking on GM.

Rodolfo Acuna, a professor of Chicano studies, long-time movement activist, and co-chair of the Van Nuys coalition, expressed the new tactical initiative of the campaign, in a talk to a coalition meeting in August 1989: "The community and the Chicano community in particular is not a water faucet, to be turned on and off as the International Union wishes. Pete Beltran is a genuine community hero and the movement cannot be stopped by his firing. When Pete Beltran told us that the plant's future was critical to the future of LA's 3 million Latinos, we believed him. Owen Bieber and GM Chairman Roger Smith can't reverse that. For six years students from MECHA and faculty from the campus and priests from the churches have marched with the GM workers, but now some in the local union are telling us that our services are no longer needed. But we know that they were complicit in the firing of Beltran and we do not recognize their legitimacy. The community will serve notice on GM that if the plant is ever closed, many community leaders will carry out the boycott—and those GM workers with the courage of their convictions will march with us."

Regrouping and Reorganizing the Movement

Acuna's threat is real. The community, which originally came in as a "support" for the local, has now become an independent force in itself. Obviously, with the loss of the support of the local union leadership the campaign is severely weakened. Nonetheless, in the Van Nuys experience the labor-community coalition still gives that movement a fighting chance, by creating greater tactical flexibility—not just for the community but for many GM workers who still want to fight to save the plant. The campaign began within the local and then moved out to the community, but now its strongest support is in the Chicano and black communities (areas where GM and the UAW have limited influence) as it works to reorganize its base within the plant.

In April 1989, the labor-community coalition organized an exciting meeting with thirty GM workers and thirty community leaders to essentially re-initiate the campaign. The momentum for that reorganization was based on several key factors. First, after about a year of disorientation, many of the most active workers in the plant were ready to fight again, as the next wave of threats to close the plant in early 1991 became quite real. Pete Beltran agreed to run for delegate to the UAW convention, the Fighting Back caucus was reorganized, and in conjunction with the national New Directions movement there was a greater sense of hope.

Second, Mark Masaoka and Jake Flukers, long-time leaders of the campaign, had been elected to the executive board, there was growing dissatisfaction with the team concept among workers on the shop floor, and the continually divided local continued its complex oscillation between confrontation and cooperation—with the pendulum in spring of 1989 swinging back to the left.

Third, the opening up of the offices of the Labor-Community Strategy Center (described below) with its own independent budget and staff, and its commitment to keep the campaign going, moved the workers quite a lot. The "community" went from a somewhat abstract concept to a tangible institution only four blocks from the plant—with typewriters and meeting rooms and computers and staff and a community "board of organizers" and the involvement of GM workers in its leadership.

At the April 1989 meeting of the labor-community coalition, many GM workers told the community residents, "You have to understand that we have a divided local. We are afraid that if you call the president of our local, Jerry Shrieves (a supporter of the "team concept" and an opponent of the campaign) he will attack the campaign as contributing to closing the plant." The community leaders reassured the Van Nuys workers that the division of the local (and the division of the labor movement in general) was a matter of public record. That was not the problem. The problem was whether there was sufficient support within the plant so that when priests and ministers and other union leaders began to circulate letters pledging to boycott GM products if the plant was ever closed, there would be enough GM workers *active and visible* to demonstrate that there was *substantial* support for the campaign in the plant. The thirty GM workers in attendance, many of whom were officers of the local, agreed to expand their ranks in the plant for subsequent meetings. As this story is written the soap opera continues and the Van Nuys movement— after seven years—exhibits a power and resiliency and longevity under enormous duress that can offer some encouragement to other organizers.

The Creation of the Labor-Community Strategy Center

In January 1989 a new institution was begun in Los Angeles county, the Labor-Community Strategy Center, which emanated from the Van Nuys work but has expanded in conception and scope. The impetus for the strategy center came from many different historical forces: (1) the real possibility that the Van Nuys movement would eventually be defeated and the need to consolidate *organizational* victories from those years of organizing, both in terms of a *permanent citywide coalition* and a long-term future in the movement for the many GM and community activists who gave so many years to the struggle; (2) the rise of the *national* developments in the UAW focused on the New Directions movement, which placed greater national emphasis on our work; and (3) the pathetic campaign of Michael Dukakis and the election of George Bush, which indicated that the ideology of "business deregulation" would be continued—that is, complete carte blanche for the business elite at the expense of workers and communities.

Thus, the Labor-Community Coalition to Keep GM Van Nuys Open has been reorganized to become the Labor-Community Coalition—a citywide movement of labor and community activists of which the Van Nuys campaign continues to be a high priority, but just one of several organizing campaigns. As other work groups begin to plan campaigns in support of union efforts to organize immigrant workers, and community-based antitoxics struggles, the Labor-Community Coalition is using many elements of the Van Nuys model to apply to a broader agenda in a county of 8 million people.

This new coalition is now housed in the Labor-Community Strategy Center, a combination activist center and organizing think tank where union and community activists and scholars can get together to plan broader strategies for expanding an anticorporate politics in the county. The idea is to go beyond individual campaigns, or even a series of campaigns, to generate a *movement* that can reshape the debate not only about "corporate behavior" but about new concepts of democratic economic decision-making by alliances of workers and communities. We recognize the need for a politics that as in the 1930s and 1960s can once again more fundamentally confront corporate power and corporate capitalism itself.

As the Labor-Community Coalition is able to expand the scope of its work beyond the Van Nuys campaign, it gains a greater sense of maneuverability—not depending for its existence just on the uphill battle at Van Nuys. But as the coalition members make clear that they will not abandon the GM workers whose struggle launched the broader movement, they distinguish themselves from many established labor leaders who "cut and run" at the first signs of problems in an organizing drive. The long-term commitment is not just a question of loyalty. It helps to develop leadership that can fight through the inevitable downturns in the organizing work to make it clear to corporate management that the union is in the struggle for the long haul.

Finally, the strategy center allows organizers from various unions in the county to find a place where they can exchange ideas, meet with community activists, and get outside of the day-to-day intrigues and problems that all institutional work presents. There are many union officials in Los Angeles, most of whom are located in the unions' organizing departments, who reject AFL-CIO policy in Latin America (especially with so many of the city's workers being Mexican and Latin American immigrants), who do not accept the nostrums of labor-management cooperation, and who are looking for creative and bold ways of confronting corporate management. While this phenomenon should not be exaggerated, its existence in many Los Angeles unions allows the strategy center to generate radical ideas that are not always in direct conflict with every established labor official in the city and are frequently well received.

New Directions for the UAW

From its inception, the organizers of the Van Nuys campaign have understood that organizing breakthroughs at the local level had to be part of a national movement to bring progressive politics to the top levels of the UAW and to root out the "company boys" who are presently running it. But while for many years that vision had little

reflection in the reality of any significant, organized opposition, beginning in 1986, with the surfacing of the New Directions movement,
workers in every local in the country have felt a sense of hope for
the union's future.

In 1986, a group of local UAW leaders in Region 5 of the UAW
(an eight-state region including Missouri, Oklahoma, Texas, Louisiana,
and Kansas) who were fed up with the union's impotence in the face
of management's assaults implored the assistant regional director, Jerry
Tucker, to run on a reform platform against the incumbent director,
Ken Worley. Tucker had worked with many locals to rebuild the involvement of the members and to take on the company with diverse
tactics such as "running the plant backwards"—an "in-plant" movement to confront the company without going on strike. As in all coalitions, not all the New Directions supporters agreed chapter and verse,
but the most commonly expressed issues were: unifying white, black,
and Latino workers and women and men workers as opposed to the
"good old (white) boy" politics of Ken Worley—a New Directions sign
said, "List of all the women appointed to office by Ken Worley" on
top of a blank placard; re-establishing union democracy rather than
punishing local officers who did not support "labor-management cooperation"; paying attention to toxics as workers in a large pharmaceutical
firm complained of chemical spills and no union action; and an end
to the practice of "whipsawing" in which each local was told by the
company and international to "look out for number one" in the competition to keep their plant open (A New Directions sign said, "Justice,
not 'Just Us'"). Jerry Tucker, a fourteen-year veteran of the UAW staff,
approached president Owen Bieber to assure him that his candidacy
was not an attack on Bieber personally, simply a matter of disagreement about the future direction of the union. Bieber responded by
firing Tucker on the spot.

A few months later, at the June 1986 Constitutional Convention
in Anaheim, California, the New Directions movement took the union
by storm as delegates from every region in the country watched in
a large ballroom as the vote was totaled. The announced result, which
brought howls and charges of fraud from most delegates, was that
incumbent Ken Worley had defeated challenger Jerry Tucker by .2
of a vote—325 for Worley to 324.8 for Tucker.

More than a year later a Federal judge overturned the election.
He found that the UAW international had engaged in widespread fraud
and irregularity in its efforts to defeat Tucker. Finally, more than
two years after he was denied the office he had legally won, a new,
court-ordered election was held on September 2, 1988, in Tulsa, Oklahoma. Jerry Tucker was elected the new director of Region 5 by a
vote of 365 to 325. Owen Bieber administered the oath of office to

Tucker amid thunderous applause and many tears by more than 500 New Directions supporters. When Bieber finished, Tucker extended an outstretched hand but Bieber refused to shake it and walked away.

The election of Jerry Tucker is not an isolated incident, but the harbinger of long-term and structural change at the top levels of the UAW. For one thing, the far more assertive role of the Canadian Auto Workers, both on the shop floor and in the politics of their country, offers an alternative model for union organizing in the exact same industry with the exact same multinational Big Three. While the CAW is not a utopia and its officers are very careful not to interfere in the internal affairs of the UAW, the very existence of that union gives reformers and insurgents in the UAW a greater sense of confidence and orientation.

As this book goes to press, the New Directions movement has suffered some serious setbacks and simultaneously launched a major organizational initiative.

At the 1989 UAW Convention, New Directions supporters had hoped that Jerry Tucker would be reelected from St. Louis and that another reform candidate for regional director, Don Douglas, the president of a large GM Local in Pontiac, Michigan, would be elected in the heart of the auto industry. In Tucker's case, the enormous difficulty of taking over as regional director more than two years into his term, with less than six months before facing a reelection, denied institutional support from the UAW and sabotaged at every turn, created the worst of both worlds. Tucker was perceived by some as an "incumbent" regional director with all the expectations his victory created. And yet, denied the ability to function with the powers of elected office and attempting to serve the members in spite of that, he was unable to deliver either services or effective representation. On the other hand, his courageous efforts to function in that position also drained valuable energy from his uphill battle to win reelection, while the international union devoted their full resources to the candidacy of their new proxy, Roy Wyse.

Don Douglas, who ran an impressive campaign in Michigan and came out of the gate winning many upset victories, was finally defeated by the organizational muscle of the international, overt company-international interference in the election, and certain historical conflicts between GM and Chrysler workers in the region that were not successfully overcome. Similarly, Tucker could not recreate the power of his initial electoral coalition. Faced with the enormous resources of the international union—union staffers all over the country were assessed $500 each to develop a war chest of more than $100,000 to defeat New Directions—and again, direct interference in local plant elections by paid international union staff and corporate management in direction violation of federal election laws, Tucker was defeated for reelection.

At the UAW Convention in Anaheim in June 1989 the vision of two fighting regional directors on the International Executive Board was replaced with the sober reality of Tucker denied reelection, Douglas defeated, and the international officers proclaiming a mandate for the policies of cooperation. Despite brave words of continuing the fight, many New Directions delegates privately expressed a sense of despair and demoralization—as once again the power and dirty tricks of the corporate-international team had prevailed.

In November 1989 a founding convention of New Directions was called, and many founding organizers worried that they were throwing a party to which no one would come. But to the surprise of many, more than 500 auto, aerospace, and independent parts supplier workers came to St. Louis, Missouri, to listen to Victor Reuther, who gave historical context to their struggle; Ken Paff of the Teamsters for a Democratic Union, who offered encouragement after thirteen years of their own uphill organizing work; and mainly to listen to themselves reassert that the deteriorating conditions on the shop floor and within many union halls plagued by the virus of labor-management cooperation made New Directions a historical necessity. As the regional director of the United Mine Workers gave a rousing welcome, and the Canadian Auto Workers announced their newly written statement directly condemning the strategy of "jointness" with management, there was a sense that the New Directions project, with all its many obstacles, was rooted in the historical reality of an urgently needed labor revitalization. Jerry Tucker was unanimously elected organizing director and a twenty-person executive board was also elected.

The very existence of New Directions as a democratic, progressive alternative caucus to the previous one-caucus tyranny of the UAW international is a welcome historical development—but one that is faced with enormous institutional obstacles. Can New Directions develop a sufficient funding base to function effectively and can it survive several difficult early years to establish a firm organizational footing? Will the local leadership of New Directions be able to transcend the quagmire of day-to-day union politics at the local level to combine local campaigns for union democracy and shop floor battles with an organized national strategy? And will New Directions be able to go beyond a narrow shop floor focus to generate a broader social program for labor that will bring new community and political allies to the movement for labor reform?

In the short run, the organizational and political obstacles seem almost insurmountable. But the existence of an organized second caucus in a union of almost 1 million UAW members is an important development that contains the seeds of the early CIO—a movement that began as an insurgency against the existing AFL leadership and ended with an enormous expansion of union power as part of a broader progressive and left impact on American life. It is in this context that the tactic of labor-community coalitions can play a vital role—by serving as a model of a labor movement that can go beyond "complaining" or "criticizing" the "sell-outs" of the international union to develop a far broader political strategy for labor in a period of the enormous concentration of capital and the shrinking of workers' power. From that perspective, the efforts of Teamsters for a Democratic Union, New Directions, and other efforts to reform labor unions from within, combined with the creative ideas of progressive union officials such as Richard Trumka of the United Mine Workers and Tony Mazzochi of the Oil, Chemical, and Atomic Workers, offers that small ray of hope that working people can reclaim their unions from the control of management ideology and once again assert the role of the working class in American society.

Electoral Coalitions

The electoral arena has long been one in which social movements both amplified their power and risked seeing it dissipated or coopted. Labor-community coalitions have developed new ways of projecting power into the political process while retaining their autonomy.

The Legislative Electoral Action Project (LEAP) was the first of more than a dozen state-based organizations in which coalitions of social movements act together to develop and support candidates for state legislatures and other offices. At the same time, national and local Rainbow Coalitions have given social movements a new foothold in the Democratic Party and the electoral arena. Such groupings have elected hundreds of candidates at the state and local level and forced national attention on long-ignored issues and constuencies.

These achievements raise new issues of leadership, governance, and relations among different constituencies. This section examines the current state of coalition electoral efforts and asks how they can go beyond the election of representatives to the actual empowerment of ordinary people.

Connecticut LEAP:
A New Electoral Strategy

Bruce Shapiro

Ever since the end of the New Deal, progressives and activists interested in political change—whether organized into labor unions or as part of independent social movements—have sought a way to broaden their influence over the outcome of American elections. The collapse of the Roosevelt coalition in 1948 brought one answer: form a new political party and put someone charismatic or widely known at the top of its ticket. That was the strategy when Henry Wallace campaigned for president with the Progressive Party that year; it was the strategy again in 1980, with the Citizens' Party and Barry Commoner as an environmentally oriented alternative. A "third" party challenge is an exciting prospect, since candidates can articulate ideas unencumbered by the limitations of the two major parties, but it is not very effective. Since World War II, that strategy has never elected anyone to the presidency, Congress, or probably not even a state legislature; it has occasionally elected a mayor, such as the socialists Jasper McLevy of Bridgeport, Connecticut, in the 1940s or Bernie Sanders of Burlington, Vermont, in recent years.

Far more frequenetly, unions and activists have tried to use their influence—votes, campaign funds, organizational resources—to earn the loyalty of career electoral politicians already working within the Democratic Party. This has been the strategy followed nationally for the past forty years by the AFL-CIO, by the mainstream of the civil rights movement, by the National Organization for Women, and many other groups.

In 1980 in Connecticut, a coalition initiated by the regional office of the United Auto Workers (UAW), the grassroots Connecticut Citizen Action group (CCAG), and others undertook a new strategy: reach down into the ranks of activist groups themselves for new candidates for the state legislature. Train them, put resources behind them, manage their campaigns. And instead of expecting candidates to rise through the ranks of the existing Democratic political machine, challenge that machine in Democratic primaries. Build, in effect, a statewide progressive machine, from the ground up.

The coalition is the Legislative Electoral Action Program (LEAP).

That first year, it backed four candidates. By 1989, LEAP had achieved the most remarkable success record of any progressive electoral coalition in the nation. In the 1988 Connecticut General Assembly election, thirty-five of forty-two LEAP-endorsed candidates won state House and Senate seats, among them fourteen of fifteen "targeted" candidates who got LEAP technical help. The ranks of the legislature included former members and officers of the state nuclear freeze campaign, the Health and Hospitals Workers Union, CCAG, the Connecticut chapter of the National Organization for Women, and community organizations in two cities. Several LEAP legislators were set to chair influential committees. A third of all Democrats in the Democrat-controlled state House of Representatives belonged to the LEAP-organized Progressive Caucus. A LEAP-backed coalition had taken control of Hartford's Democratic Town Committee.

And LEAP's success convinced the UAW to hire the coalition's former director, Marc Caplan, to form similar coalitions throughout New England—coalitions which by 1988 were active in over thirty campaigns in every New England state. Thanks to these coalitions, at least ten activists from the ranks of progressive organizations were elected to New England legislative seats for the first time that year, including a labor leader and two environmentalists in Maine, two union leaders in New Hampshire, a peace activist in Providence, and the first Hispanic ever elected to state office in Massachusetts.

LEAP's notable success provides an important model—a new common strategy for unions and community activists around the country. The coalition's very success, though, raises important issues. Once progressives are elected to office, what agenda do they pursue and how far can their influence really spread? How can even an effective progressive coalition assert its power in more than a squeak against the overwhelming resources of the mainstream Democratic Party? How do "issues groups"—the diverse unions and community action groups in an electoral coalition—respond when for the sake of real-politik, officials they supported depart from their agenda? And can a strategy which has worked in Connecticut and elsewhere in New England—with small legislative districts and few large cities—be transferred to very different political environments?

The Elements of Style

For years prior to LEAP's founding, labor and grassroots groups were spending weeks at a time in Hartford trying to influence the outcome of legislation. "At some point we said, wouldn't it be nice to be in there ourselves, instead of just pounding on the doors," recalls one LEAP founder. In 1974, the youthful founder of the Connecticut Citizen Action Group, Toby Moffett, won a five-way Democratic primary and was elected to Congress from the state's mostly rural Fifth District. Though different in many respects from later grassroots campaigns, "we learned a few things from that campaign," says LEAP founder and former CCAG director Marc Caplan. "Among other things, how much easier it is to affect a primary than a general election."

LEAP's initial success in the early 1980s stemmed from the realization that Connecticut's assembly districts hold fewer than 20,000 people—and only a small percentage of those will vote in primaries. It is well within the power of volunteer-laden community-based organizations, LEAP strategists reasoned, to turn out a few thousand people. Thus within a few years, yet another former CCAG director, Miles Rapoport, was able to defeat an entrenched, incumbent conservative Democrat in a primary. A handful of initial successes culminated in 1984, when in the Reagan landslide the General Assembly became dominated by Republicans for the first time in fifteen years. In that generally devastating election, LEAP legislators managed to grow in ranks rather than be diminished like their more conservative Democratic colleagues. There were failures, too—most notably, a doomed LEAP-backed challenge by Toby Moffett to incumbent Gov. William O'Neill in 1986. But LEAP seemed to be riding high.

Among the key elements of LEAP's strategy from the beginning was a careful coalition decision-making process. LEAP's board of directors is composed of members of its constituent groups. Candidates seeking the coalition's support are interviewed both by the organization's staff and more formally by a coalition endorsement committee; candidates also fill out questionnaires about their stands on issues. LEAP actively encourages candidates and campaign managers to emerge from within its constitutent groups, offering numerous workshops, seminars, and other programs designed to pass on electoral skills.

Machine Backlash

By 1988, LEAP's performance had attracted national attention from the *New York Times,* electoral strategists, and prominent political figures like Texas Agriculture Commissioner Jim Hightower (whom Caplan refers to as "the Democratic candidate for president in the year 2002"). But it has also attracted attention of another sort: "regular" Democrats bent on quashing the upstart organization.

Although leaders of Connecticut's conservative Democratic establishment had been critical of LEAP, 1988 brought the first sustained backlash. Early in the year, AFL-CIO national president Lane Kirkland ordered the Greater New Haven Central Labor Council to cease supporting LEAP. After vociferous protest from Connecticut labor leaders, that demand was eventually dropped—indeed, Kirkland ended up, however grudgingly, endorsing LEAP's efforts. But later that year, party regulars mounted an aggressive and successful campaign to remove LEAP's president, New England UAW president John Flynn, from his seat as a member of the Democratic National Committee (DNC). So effective was the campaign that both Flynn and Mary Sullivan, another liberal and long-time LEAP supporter, were voted off the DNC and replaced by party regulars.

But the biggest challenge to LEAP's growing influence came after the 1988 elections, when the new General Assembly was sworn in in early 1989. Conservative Democrats and a handful of liberals in the state House broke party ranks and joined with Republicans to vote out two-term speaker Irving Stolberg of New Haven. Though not himself elected by LEAP, Stolberg was for years a liberal stalwart, a close LEAP ally who had appointed LEAP legislators to numerous influential committee chairs. Although the rejection of Stolberg in part reflected the internal and personal workings of the House, it was also a clear message: the days of unchecked growth of progressive influence in Hartford were over. Few LEAP legislators held onto their committee chairs following Stolberg's ouster; the Progressive Caucus, once seen as a rising political force, became just another bloc in a fragmented legislature.

Clearly, the coalition with Republicans showed just how threatening LEAP and the progressive legislative movement had become to the Democratic establishment. That, perhaps, could be seen as sign of success. But it also left LEAP legislators virtually without a way of exercising influence.

What About a Program?

The fallout from the loss of Stolberg and a state budget deficit in 1989 also underscored perhaps the largest gap in LEAP's strategy: lack of a coherent, ongoing legislative program. Since 1980, LEAP had concentrated on one thing: electing people to office. But while potential candidates were grilled on the issues prior to a LEAP endorsement, there was no attempt to forge a coherent legislative strategy. Rather, each of the "issues groups" in the LEAP coalition continued to function much as it always had—presenting its own bills, rounding up support from other groups and from LEAP itself. Thus in 1989, legislators would consider a gay and lesbian civil rights bill from a gay rights coalition, workplace safety legislation from unions, trash laws from CCAG. But those diverse goals were never woven into a comprehensive or long-term agenda. By 1988, LEAP and its legislative allies had organized a "Progressive Caucus" of legislators, but it seemed to function more as an organizational tool for individual bills than as a focus group for developing new approaches or a long-term plan.

"What we know how to do best is elect people. It is up to our constituent groups to develop a legislative agenda," says LEAP's current director, Nick Nyhart. Historically, there have been two weaknesses in that strategy—weaknesses exacerbated by the loss of committee influence. First, it has meant that despite the growing number of progressive—or to use LEAP's preferred word, "populist"—legislators, there has been no serious attempt to change many of the underlying injustices in Connecticut's political system and economy. Since 1980, a handful of clearly "progressive" environmental, health-related, and pay-equity laws have made it through the legislature. But the state—the wealthiest per capita in the country—has a regressive tax system that relies solely on sales taxes, some of the lowest per capital spending for key human services, and election laws that are more restrictive than those of any state but Utah. After eight years, LEAP legislators as a group were poorly prepared to consider "unrealistic" challenges to these gross inequities, instead concentrating on individual bills to serve consumers, workers, or other particular constituencies.

The problem is not lack of intent. Rather, it's that there is no long-term legislative strategy to parallel a carefully mapped electoral plan. This became devastatingly clear with the 1989 budget crisis. Throughout this crisis, LEAP legislators played an important role in fending off radical cuts to essential social programs. But they were unable to offer a serious progressive alternative to a series of regressive tax increases and spending cuts put forward by the governor and his allies. Stolberg and his allies continued to talk about an income tax, but their proposals scarcely made a dent in that year's budget debate.

LEAP founder Marc Caplan believes that such seeming limitations are a matter of evolution, that now that there is a progressive constituency in Hartford "to an extent impossible to imagine a decade ago," there is also a critical mass for more visionary politics. In the final weeks of the 1989 legislative session, progressive legislators had a series of meetings to map the beginnings of a long-term strategy. "I think there is a progressive response [to the budget crisis], but it has not been articulated well enough and coherently enough," Caplan says. He adds that the fall of Stolberg left a leadership vacuum that younger legislators weren't expecting. "I think there are people with ideas out there, but we've got to bring them forward. We never had to do that before."

The other problem to emerge—one that LEAP itself is perhaps in a better position to address—is difference of opinion among LEAP legislators and interest groups. One such gulf came in 1987, when a frequent LEAP ally endorsed by the coalition, state senator Joseph Harper of New Britain, proposed an amendment weakening a proposed gay civil rights bill by excluding religious institutions from antidiscrimination provisions. The amended bill was defeated anyway, and defeated once more—again with the Harper amendment—in 1989. "It really rankles," says one gay rights activist who asks not to be identified because of his continuing relationship with LEAP. "I got the feeling that this was a second-tier issue." This activist questions whether Harper should still get LEAP support. (The Connecticut Coalition for Lesbian and Gay Civil Rights remains a LEAP member, and in general LEAP legislators have remained among the unsuccessful bill's advocates.) The question raised involves the limits on a candidate's disagreement with an individual constituent group.

A problem with some different wrinkles emerged in 1989, when the Connecticut Citizen Action Group found itself working against one of its former leaders, state representative Mary Mushinsky, co-chair of the General Assembly's Environment Committee. As Connecticut began to consider solutions to its trash crisis, Mushinsky (the first candidate endorsed by LEAP) over the years became convinced that some incineration would be needed in addition to state-mandated recycling. CCAG opposes incineration; the group mounted a letter-writing and citizen-lobbying effort aimed at Mushinsky, eventually naming her to a "dirty dozen" list of incineration advocates. The case does not suggest, necessarily, the need for a "party line." But it and the Harper case go to the heart of what had traditionally kept Saul Alinsky-style community organizations out of electoral politics in the first place: accountability, the fact that even "friendly" legislators need to be constantly monitored and pushed by agressive constitutent groups. "We need both an 'inside' strategy and an 'outside' strategy," says Heather Booth, director of the Chicago-based Citizen Action. "What we've learned is that we need legislators, but that's useless if we don't continue agressive organizing outside the electoral arena."

Over time, LEAP's board and staff have made efforts to address constituencies uncertain of their role in the organization. LEAP has created political action committees aimed at promoting the civil rights of blacks, Puerto Ricans, and women; other "outside" constituencies, such as gay civil rights advocates, have also been invited in. These coalitions are under the leadership of independent activists; while generally not offering the grassroots membership of large citizen action groups and unions, they speak with a clear voice for their constituencies' interests.

Can You Fight City Hall?

One arena in which the LEAP strategy has brought little electoral success: big-city politics. Connecticut has three large cities with populations over 120,000: Hartford, New Haven, and Bridgeport. Each is a declining industrial center, and each is among the eleven poorest cities in the nation based on per capita income. Each has substantial black and Hispanic populations. In 1985 and 1987, LEAP committed serious financial and organizational resources to a mayoral primary in Bridgeport, backing a former Carter administration official, Charles Tisdale. Tisdale, who is black, was defeated both times, and eventually took a job in the administration of his victorious opponent. In 1985, LEAP organizations found themselves divided and therefore unable to make an endorsement in Hartford's city council race. "In general," says LEAP dierector Nyhart, "there are so many networks already at work in a city, so many different levels of debt and patronage, that it's hard for an outside organization to get a handle." It's worth noting that few minority communities in Connecticut are organized along community action lines.

In 1987, a group of Hartford community activists allied with LEAP came up with an alternative model, which won LEAP backing but followed a different strategy. People for a Change ran a slate of three candidates—community organizer Marie Birkley-Bey, former police officer and neighborhood activist Eugenio Caro, and teacher's union activist William Hagen—on its own line rather than as Democrats. The idea was to take advantage of the combination of Hartford's political structure—its powerful nine-member council is elected at-large, rather than by district—with a state law requiring minority party representation on such boards. Instead of running against incumbent Democrats. People for a Change ran for the Republican seats—and won two out of three of them.

At one stroke, that was a far more effective municipal campaign that LEAP's previous Democratic municipal primary efforts. It served as a reminder of an interesting historical fact of urban politics: while "third parties" have little impact on races for state or national office, purely local rivalries and the quirks of urban politics have often proved fertile ground for municipal challenges of that type. In Connecticut alone, besides People for a Change, two candidates cross-endorsed by a local Green Party as well as Democrats hold office in New Haven;

and the city of Norwalk, with population of about 77,000, boasts four active political parties. People for a Change was in some ways a special case, given Hartford's at-large council. But every municipality is, in its own way, a special case, and often such third-party challenges provide valuable alternatives. On the other hand, it is also clear that a successful third-party municipal campaign is unlikely to work as a strategy for higher level state or regional office, where citizens' voting patterns are far more rigid.

The most successful big-city campaign more or less following the LEAP strategy was not in Connecticut at all. In 1988, Nelson Merced, a Boston community activist, won a hotly contested campaign for state house from a newly created legislative district in Dorchester. He became the first Hispanic ever elected to state office in Massachusetts. Merced—a protégé of former mayoral candidate Mel King—won in an ethnically diverse district. His campaign was the first effort by the Commonwealth Coalition, a new LEAP-modeled effort. "The Merced campaign and the coalition worked in tandem," wrote LEAP's Caplan after the victory. "The campaign helped launch the coalition and the coalition helped ensure Nelson's victory. The Merced campaign built an impressive multiracial district organization, a model for future efforts."

Political Culture and Progressive Campaigns

In January of 1989, Merced talked about his campaign to a gathering of progressive electoral activists from throughout the Northeast about the special challenges of forming a coalition within ethnic urban communities. "Every community," he said, "has its own political culture, its own experience of politics—whether the black community, the Puerto Rican community, the gay community. As you forge an agenda, you must begin with the particular experiences of those communities—not expect them to come along with you."

Merced's comments suggest a vision of what it would be like to combine LEAP's brilliant strategizing with the cross-cultural, populist embrace of Jesse Jackson's Rainbow Coalition. As Merced makes clear, both the strengths and weaknesses of any coalition will lie in its underlying political culture. Thus LEAP, so influenced at the outset by activist unions, environmentalism, and largely suburban or small-town constituencies of CCAG, has had its greatest success with suburban, environmental, and consumer-oriented candidates emerging from those progressive unions; but like both the consumer movement and the contemporary labor movement, LEAP's legislators have rarely found a way to touch urban injustice in a systematic way.

Moving into the 1990s, it appears likely that many activists in many more states will emulate—with local adjustment—the LEAP strategy. In early 1989, for instance, Jim Hightower decided not to pursue his expected challenge to Democrat-turned-Republican Senator Phil Gramm, instead focusing on building a LEAP-style coalition within Texas. "My heart told me" to run, he wrote in the *Nation* (February 6, 1989), just a few weeks after he'd addressed the same LEAP-sponsored forum as Merced. But "campaigns are necessarily egocentric, leaving little behind in the way of a cohesive base. . . . Democrats generally and progressives specifically have spent far too much time waiting on the occasional 'good' candidate to ride in and save the day." He talked about Texas populists building their own "speakers' bureaus, small-donor solication programs, policy development centers. . . ."

There is both promise and peril in such coalitions. The promise is of electing a new generation of office-holders, trained not in the back room but in the union hall, in the waste-dump picket line, in the feminist movement. The peril is that in the rush to elect candidates, it could be easy to ignore true coalition building—coalitions that involve Nelson Merced's diverse communities in shaping their own agendas. Alone, neither the progressive interest groups that form LEAP's backbone nor the locked-out constituencies of the Rainbow Coalition can hope to form an effective bloc. Together, their strength is much greater. In fact, long-term political and social change will require not just legislators with a progressive agenda but coalitions behind them that in their very make-up suggest an altered political landscape. It may be that the key to genuine change through elective office lies in a coalition of these coalitions—a combination of innovative program, aggressive inclusion, and careful long-term strategy.

Rainbow Coalitions:
An Interview with Mel King

Janice Fine

Mel King is the founder of the Boston Rainbow Coalition, the model upon which the National Rainbow Coalition was founded. He has been a Democratic state legislator and a candidate for mayor of Boston and for the U.S. Congress. He has inspired countless successful community struggles in Boston and across the country. I was doing a lot of thinking about coalition work, and wanted to know what lessons Mel King had learned from his own experience in working in coalitions, particularly with labor: the circumstances in which they were most effective, their advantages and limitations. I was especially interested in how he viewed the Rainbow Coalition, which was then deciding how to continue in non-election years. I interviewed Mel King for this book at his office in Cambridge in June 1989.

Fine: How did you initially conceive of the Rainbow Coalition and why did you envision it as a coalition?

King: I thought about my involvement with a number of groups around their issues, groups I had met from working both in the Urban League and in the legislature. I had worked, for example, with the Latino community on issues of housing, community development, Cuba, independence of Puerto Rico, and Central America. I worked with gay and lesbian groups on equal rights legislation and on safety. I also worked with tenants' organizations, and numerous others.

I noticed that there was a kind of common issue, namely, how do you overcome the effects of a political process and its structures that deny access to these groups? And it was obvious that each group would gain some limited access, only on a one-by-one basis.

When I ran for mayor, I realized that there were two things that had to happen for my campaign to succeed. One is that I had to put together an organization which reflected the composition and concerns of the neighborhoods and the wards and precincts. Most of my work had been around issues, yet obviously the people with the issues lived in those neighborhoods. Therefore, the campaign needed to get those folks on the issues to see that one way in which those problems could be addressed could be by getting control of city government. In isolation they couldn't get control of city government, but collectively they could.

So I believed that if we could give the campaign a name and a concept we would have a chance. Then, as the campaign was moving and it was getting these groups together, we said, we've got a coalition and it's a rainbow coalition. Toward the end of the primary we started lifting that up and then I had a friend design buttons that reflected the rainbow.

We started with the statement that we may have come on different ships, but we're in the same boat now, which I used in my opening campaign speech. That was the beginning, because the natural folks who came to the campaign were the people from various oppressed or ignored or discriminated against groups.

From the outset we were direct about each group's own self-interest, saying that they had to lay out the issues that needed to be addressed. So they became the constitutent groups of the campaign. For example, the gay and lesbian constitutencies had to put together those issues for the campaign. The housing groups and health-care groups had to do the same for those issues. So I would work and meet with each of those groups.

Then they had to understand that they had to be willing to work together in order for the power to come into their hands, so that there could be some implementation of the programs.

Fine: My experience is that coalitions are tricky. Sometimes the strongest organizations don't want to come in because of questions of credit, or because coalition work will detract from their own agenda, or because of inequalities of power. It's one thing to say that oppression is something that groups have in common and another to overcome the reluctance of groups to join. How do you deal with that reluctance?

King: I went to a church in the black community and had this meeting in the basement with the preacher and his board of deacons. They said they had two problems with my campaign. One was my support for the pro-choice position on abortion and the second was my involvement with the gay and lesbian community. They said we can't support those positions. I went through the business of our common oppression and said, "I'm sorry, but I have to uphold the fact that you are making a mistake in not seeing the importance of overcoming all kinds of oppression that are in this society." It was tense. But they agreed that they wanted to support me, and they most certainly did.

Fine: Say there had not been a Mel King for mayor campaign, and you had had the same idea of putting together a rainbow coalition but not around a candidacy, how would you have fashioned a multi-issue coalition?

King: Well, where were the other places we tried to do this kind of thing? We tried to do it on district representation. And if you look at who's elected, it works. So it is around where power is that you obviously have to form your coalition. So with district representation, you could say to women's groups, lesbian groups, people of color, housing activists, whatever, "Here is where you can have an opportunity to have people run for office which reflect those issues." And since the campaign occurs in a much narrower area, you can have a greater impact on the way which people deal with those issues.

I think that the issues themselves do stand up. I don't think it's a question of personality. And I think local politics is the place in which there are people in those groups who say that this particular event and time represents an opportunity to get something that we need, if we can do it together. There's got to be some human link. More importantly, the issues must be compelling.

Fine: So you are saying the coalition should be more than the sum of its parts, each organization can multiply its power by recognizing a common oppression and deciding to come together. You are also saying that a successful coalition needs strong leadership, either from a candidate or from the constituent groups, as well as compelling issues.

King: And power, an understanding that if you capture power, you have an opportunity to get your issues addressed. This was true in the mayor's race. It was also true getting the district lines changed so that now Nelson Merced gets elected as the first Hispanic member of the state legislature. A wide coalition of groups came together to make that happen.

Fine: Organizations often initiate coalitions to share the burden of an issue that they cannot individually make a priority and none of them end up contributing enough resources or making a strong enough commitment to action. So the coalition ends up as meetings rather than as a dynamic organization. You seem to have been able to get people to take action.

King: One way you get people to move is generally around some crunch issue. If there isn't one that's defined by law periodically—the funding date, the election date—then it's when a government agency, such as Housing and Urban Development (HUD) says the time to save those units is going to be expiring. So there's always this crunch time that you get people to respond.

One thing about elections is that they are fixed, and so predictable. You begin a process and it reaches an end point, win or lose. And there's a defined piece of power involved. And so you can get the coalition coming together, again around the power. Everybody knows that between now and then certain things have to be done in order to be successful. So that makes it easier to get people out.

Also there has to be willingness on the part of the largest group to share power in their own interest.

Fine: How do you get people to understand that they aren't going to persuade people by the force of their arguments so that they have to use direct action, rather than just lobbying, having a meeting, seeking legislation, or whatever?

King: Sometimes you have to go through the first things and then you say to people, "Well these arguments didn't work. So you're still going to be left out in the cold." Sometimes you say, "The way you get that other thing to happen is you take direct action." So you strategize with folks about the appropriate action to take. Direct action never fails completely, because taking the action itself is, I think, a victory. One other thing is that you don't let anybody off the hook in the group because everybody can do something. "I won't go to jail," one person says. "Well, will you contribute 50 cents in case we need a bail fund?" "Oh, I can do that."

Or, we decide at our next meeting, we should have some food. A person says, "I don't have any money to contribute, but I can bake some bread." Or, "I'll come early and I'll set up the chairs. And I'll sweep up afterward." It's also important for people to have to come forth with what they can contribute and what they can't. And to have it on the table before a lot of action takes place.

Fine: In the early days of the Rainbow how formal was the structure of the organization? What was your structural vision and what was the relation between structure and accountability?

King: The Rainbow was built around an electoral campaign, and around trying to get power. The Rainbow was built because of an ideological, political difference between it and the other parties. What did I envision? I envisioned that we would have strength and power in our numbers. And that a simple structure would suffice.

What we were after is a way to relate to a particular problem with an all-of-us-or-none-of-us mentality that had people in the groups as representatives from their groups helping to shape the direction and activity. It was to be a structure that came out of the groups. And the groups were either issue-oriented or geographically based. There was to be a steering committee which was made up of all those folks in the meetings. I thought that this was a simple enough structure.

Why doesn't it work now? I believe because its initial focus has been electoral politics. A broad coalition represents a chance to get a big win, but if you don't (and I don't know what to say if you do) but if you don't, then people go back to their own struggles. Because if you're a tenants' group and you don't get your policies accepted, or people who will adopt them elected, you still have to go back and work on tenants' problems. And we must remember that the Rainbow Coalition can't be stronger than the individual groups that make it up. Each organization needs to have clear goals and a strategy. And member organizations in a coalition must agree on tactics and not be afraid of direct confrontations.

Fine: Over the years, what has been the relationship of the Rainbow with the labor movement?

King: The real labor movement or the corporate labor movement? The real labor movement has been pretty good. The irony of it is that you're talking about unions and not about a labor movement. There are unions that have been involved with the Rainbow locally because they have understood that what the Rainbow Coalition was about was in the interest of their membership and in support of the goals of the movement. And so you have the Rainbow working with the bus drivers, not necessarily the bus drivers union but people who are trying to exercise the same rights they would have if they had a union.

And then you have unions that have policies and approaches you have to organize people to challenge and confront—like in the building trades. The irony of it is that even with that, the Rainbow has been supportive on principle of the goals and objectives of the labor movement. At the same time knowing full well that some of those folks are standing in the way of other Rainbow members from getting access to a large number of jobs.

This discussion about the relationship between unions and the Rainbow is not very easy. Because the Rainbow frequently supports labor on principle, yet often does not get anything back from them.

Fine: How does the Rainbow address unions? Does it formally try to get those locals involved that share a vision? How does it hold labor accountable?

King: I don't know what the strategy is anymore. The accountability has to be a part of the relationship and the process. It has to be very, very clear. Part of the problem is that the Rainbow hasn't chosen to identify people from within the Rainbow to run for political office. To do so would be to be supporting candidates who advocate correct political positions, even when it means going against candidates that the union supports. I think we have to be clear about that and to say why the person the union is supporting is not worthy of being supported by the Rainbow.

We also have to raise questions at times other than elections about the policies of unions and to mobilize people to confront and challenge oppressive union policies. We haven't done that. What we have done is to support those unions that are trying to get a foothold: the laundry workers, for example. I think that's important. That's about where the activity is.

On the other hand, we have supported people who work at City Hospital, state employees, and a number of other unions. Overall, the affinity between the Rainbow and the unions is greatest where the unions are more democratic and participatory, or if not democratic, where they are more representative of people of color and women.

Fine: The backbone of the Rainbow has never been organized labor, but around the country there are coalitions forming that do have labor playing a major role. These coalitions are trying to form alliances among labor, women's groups, people of color, and other groups, yet it seems that often these coalitions are held hostage by labor in terms of the issues they can raise, the people they support, or the kinds of things they can do. How can you deal with this conflict?

King: I think that the broader group has to put out a vision and work to get people to join in the implementation of their vision. If the other group doesn't want to, then you just say, here's our vision. You just have to keep on moving. Because you have a broader vision and they're not correct.

What you have to do is get with the groups and build the movement on the basis of those who share the same broad vision. It's the same with the farmers and the paperworkers in Jay, Maine, and the Hormel meatpackers. The struggle takes its shape through the involvement and support of people who are oppressed. To the extent that there are parts of the labor movement who do not understand that it's in their interest to deal with oppression wherever it is, then they're part of the problem. And so you just have to keep moving and relate to people who understand what the correct politics and approach are.

Fine: Most unions currently seem unwilling to take that approach. On the other hand, the labor movement has very significant resources.

King: I don't agree with that. The evidence is quite the contrary. Whatever their resources, they haven't been able to hold their own membership when it comes to some of the national political stuff. You have the leadership saying one thing and then you have the membership obviously voting at another level. So I don't know what it means to say "their power and their resources." I'm not minimizing what they have, but there's something that has happened: members are dwindling, as is the percentage of people in the workforce who are in labor. What does that mean?

To the extent that this is the case, the potential for building the Rainbow does not lie with groups that support the oppressor or are losing their base of support. It doesn't seem to make any sense.

Fine: Labor participation in the Rainbow Coalition, the most prominent coalition in the country because of Jesse Jackson's work and your work, is spotty. In some places union participation has been major, especially unions that have a significant membership of people of color. . . .

King: And also those unions where they are strugglng against oppressive owners. That's why I talked abut the meatpackers, in Maine, for example; their support does not come from white elected officials. I may be wrong but it also seems that their support has not come from the major components of the labor movement. Their support has come from Jesse, from folk who relate on the principal issue of people being oppressed and exploited.

Fine: Labor needs to see why it needs coalitions. Often, unions only seem to see the need to build a coalition when they are backed against the wall and can plainly see that they need allies.

King: They have to see that they're in the boat; they don't. They have to ask themselves whether Jesse Jackson's vision is better for all people than Ronald Reagan's vision. And then if that is the case, let's move with Jesse. If they obviously think that Ronald Reagan's vision is better, that's where they're going to go.

The Rainbow is about people speaking for themselves. There are people at this stage that are not in the coalition. You go out and talk to them and invite them in. Or you can speak to their issues. Sometimes even when they're not speaking to them. Because you have some information. I'm saying we all have a responsibility to do that.

Mel King has been a tremendous force for progressive change in Boston and beyond. But no one can provide a hard-and-fast model for what the best coalition should look like. Coalition organizers need to continually ask themselves what are the best ways to organize in their own communities.

Constituency groups have a right to ask that the candidates they support and the coalitions they belong to put their concerns up front and not shrink from public association with them. But this has tended to intensify a basic problem of coalitions to date: presenting our program as a laundry list of unrelated issues promoted by diverse and apparently unconnected groups. It is clear that most voters do not see themselves primarily as members of specific constituency groups when they go into the voting booth. So we have to learn to represent a holistic vision that is more than the sum of its parts.

Probably the greatest heartbreak for labor progressives is the racist legacy and the racism that still exists in the labor movement. Labor is not going to recover its lost power and legitimacy till it hears, listens, and responds to Mel King's concerns and the concerns of working people of color. That's perhaps the greatest challenge to coalition organizers today.

The Story of New Mexico PRO-PAC: Community Empowerment Through Electoral Involvement

Max Bartlett

New Mexico conjures up easy visions of romance and enchantment, ranging from the historical to the fashionable: from the Sante Fe Trail to Sante Fe "style" and from ancient Indian pueblos to Georgia O'Keeffe.

The reality could hardly differ more: as former Governor Toney Anaya has observed, the system of power in the United States casts New Mexico as a "banana republic." The possibility of forming power structures accountable to its own people is weakened by a near total dependence on out-of-state corporations and the military-industrial complex.

New Mexico bears a striking resemblance to countries of the third world: local, sustainable cultures developed over centuries have been systematically undermined by the onslaught of market forces. For decades, railroads and extractive industries dominated the economy. Since the 1940s, as missile ranges and nuclear-weapons labs spread over the land, the Pentagon has become the dominant force: one out of every four working New Mexicans now holds a defense-related job.

This "colonial" system has led to a two-tiered structure of wages, with little or no benefit accruing to New Mexico's indigenous peoples. The unemployment rate in recent years has been among the highest in the country, reaching over 70 percent on some Indian reservations. New Mexico ranks forty-fourth among the states in per capita income and among the very worst in voter participation. Nearly one out of every five New Mexicans lives below the poverty level.

Yet, progressive activists in New Mexico have been building a political network that has already had a remarkable impact on the distribution of power. At the center of this story is PRO-PAC, New Mexico's Progressive Political Action Committee. Its five-year history can be seen as a concrete, practical attempt to resolve one question: How can people at the "grassroots" best empower themselves so as to be able to fulfill their real needs?

Shifting the Balance of Power

Before looking at the way PRO-PAC was actually created, it is important to understand both what is at stake in electoral politics at the grassroots level and exactly how powerful progressive activists can become by working together. An *astounding nineteen out of the twenty* legislative candidates endorsed by PRO-PAC *emerged victorious* from the 1986 general election. All were progressive Democrats. They won throughout the state, including districts that had been considered conservative strongholds. Given the political climate of the time, this grassroots success was extraordinary: in the very same election, the state's Democratic Party, led by a *centrist* candidate for governor, suffered its worst defeat in a generation in statewide races. What made this progressive victory possible?

PRO-PAC had foreseen and responded to a political crisis that threatened to unleash an unprecedented reign of Reaganesque terror on the people of New Mexico. After the 1984 elections, a caucus of Republican and conservative Democrats, generally known as the "Conservative Coalition," *formally organized* and took control of the state House of Representatives by a margin of thirty-six to thirty-four. The state Senate continued to be controlled, as it had been for years, by an old-boy network of political conservatives. The legislature proceeded to decimate the progressive legislative agenda of Governor Anaya. They also passed a state budget that grievously underfunded health care, education, child care, workers' safety, and other programs for New Mexicans of average and low income.

Since all state senators run for four-year terms in presidential elections years, no change could occur there in 1986. Moreover, PRO-PAC was convinced that a Republican was virtually destined to become governor in 1986 (no progressive candidate was even on the horizon). With ultraconservatives in control of *both* houses of the legislature and the governor's office, no obstacle would have remained to thwart their reactionary agenda. PRO-PAC saw one viable chance of countering this threat: the loyalist Democratic leadership in the House, if returned to power, would be the only force capable of blocking right-to-work legislation (a perennial issue in New Mexico), right-to-life proposals, and the host of other antiprogressive measures that would otherwise flood through the legislature to be signed into law by whichever Republican was elected governor.

Having grasped what was at stake, PRO-PAC set out in January of 1985 to "bust" the Conservative Coalition in the House. The plan had two phases: first to oust conservative Democrats in the primary election; second, to elect as many progressives as possible in the general election. Financial resources were concentrated in *marginal* districts, so limited funds would have the maximum effect.

"Marginal" districts are ones where the vote tends to split evenly between Democratic and Republic candidates. A district may be marginal, even where the Republican vote runs as high as 60 percent, if demographic data look promising (e.g., a high percentage of lower income residents). The opposite, where one party consistently wins, is a "safe" district. Safe Democratic districts are superb places to target during primary elections: very progressive victors can go on to easy wins in the general election.

In the June 1986 primary election, PRO-PAC supported candidates who were challenging incumbent conservative Democrats. They succeeded in four districts, including the top two priorities. The second phase required precise *targeting* to identify marginal districts, both (1) where incumbent Republicans could be defeated by progressive Democrats, and (2) where efforts would be required to protect incumbent progressives. The value of this targeting effort speaks for itself. Three targeted Republican incumbents went down to defeat, and *all* of the progressive Democrats were returned to office.

Besides targeting, other work led to the victory. First, PRO-PAC actively recruited progressive candidates and tried to ensure that only one entered each primary, so the progressive vote would not be split. Second, training programs for candidates and campaign workers were conducted, including a two-day Campaign Management School that offered progressives the latest campaign technology. Third, PRO-PAC worked within the Democratic Party to create a climate of opinion hostile to the Conservative Coalition: everything from resolutions of censure to "Coalition-Busters" buttons were used to isolate the Coalition Democrats from the "official" party. Fourth, funds were raised through direct-mail solicitation and other means in order to make monetary contributions to candidates endorsed by PRO-PAC.

Finally, PRO-PAC was not acting alone: other groups, notably the Trial Lawyers Association, the Plumbers and Pipefitters Union, the Southwest Voter Project, the Conservation Voters Alliance, and the Women's Political Caucus, engaged in parallel efforts. Neither PRO-PAC nor any other organization made any attempt to control this effort, dictate strategy, or even coordinate activities. PRO-PAC made its targeting information generally available, and other groups often shared information through informal contacts. One principle clearly emerged from this experience: progressive organizations can dramatically increase their power when they *work together* in an atmosphere marked by *openness* and *cooperation,* rather than by turf struggles and worries over who will "get the credit."

These victories did not come easy, nor did they occur in "safe"

Democratic districts. Most of the candidates endorsed by PRO-PAC had hard races in marginal districts. Yet, Democrats endorsed by PRO-PAC fared much better than Democrats who did not gain endorsement: while 95 percent of PRO-PAC Democrats won, only 70 percent of other Democrats did. The PRO-PAC candidates also had tougher contests: only two out of the twenty PRO-PAC candidates ran unopposed, while nearly half of the other Democrats (twenty out of forty-one) had no Republican opposition. Incidentally, nearly half of the Republicans who won had no Democratic opposition. Voters clearly favored the progressive Democrats who had strong beliefs and steadfastly championed them.

The state legislature has provided PRO-PAC with its best opportunity so far to impact on New Mexico's future. However, the decision to emphasize these races was made only after careful deliberation on practical, strategic grounds. Since these districts are small (the population averages 20,000 for the House), they are quite amenable to grassroots political action. The balance of power has also been very close statewide between progressive Democrats on one hand and conservative Democrats and Republicans on the other.

In different states or under different circumstances, the proper focus could well differ. Choosing the arena where grassroots progressives have the best chance of playing a *decisive* role is the crucial consideration. PRO-PAC avoids both "lost causes" and "sure things." Strategic goals are set on a two-year basis, tied to the election cycle, and the political context is reviewed at the start of each two-year plan. Since resources are very limited, PRO-PAC concentrates them where they will do the most good: to get, in other words, "the most bang for the buck."

Building the PRO-PAC Coalition

Creating PRO-PAC offered an opportunity for progressives in New Mexico to learn how to work together. PRO-PAC was founded in June of 1984, after eighteen months of informal "talks" and meetings. These preliminary discussions were vital for building trust and reaching a programmatic consensus among the forty activists who became the founding board of governors. The composition of this active core of the coalition was crucial: it required people who had established reputations for integrity and dedication within the progressive community.

Twelve people attended the first "organizational meeting" in January of 1984. It was held at the home of Rex Brasell, business manager of the local Plumbers and Pipefitters Union, and Diane Wood, a business agent for the United Food and Commercial Workers. A veritable network in themselves, they were active with a wide range of issues. Rex was indispensable to PRO-PAC's creation: his open style of leadership, in everything from conducting meetings to reaching out to a diversity of groups, helped inspire mutual trust and confidence.

Building a successful coalition also required a "founding core," drawn from a wide variety of progressive constituencies, including some people with experience in electoral politics. In the spring of 1983, Rex had run for Democratic Party chair in Bernalillo County (which includes 30 percent of the state's population). He came within two dozen votes (out of nearly 700) of defeating the incumbent. Perhaps one-third of PRO-PAC's founding members had gotten to know one another through this effort or earlier political campaigns. At least one-third had *no* prior electoral involvement, and most did not know each other. Of the twelve at the first meeting, few knew more than two or three other people (except perhaps by "reputation"). Almost all, however, were leaders (chairs, coordinators, past presidents, etc.) of progressive organizations: the New Mexico office of the National Women's Political Caucus, ACORN, New Mexico Conservation Voters Alliance, People United for Justice, the American Civil Liberties Union (ACLU), New Mexico Lesbian/Gay Political Alliance, Albuquerque Peace Center, New Mexico Democratic Council, and several labor unions.

The organizing process continued through three more exploratory meetings. Letters were mailed out each time, signed by those who had already attended, inviting additional participants to the next meeting. Each meeting included time for brainstorming to identify other activists who should be invited. *Inclusivity* was the byword: the founding board needed to match the cultural, organizational, and issue diversity of New Mexico's progressive communities. Given the cultural character of New Mexico, it was important for PRO-PAC to develop as an Hispano/Anglo partnership. This goal required sensitivity, openness, and the understanding that cultural, gender, class, and other distinctions may give rise to valid differences in styles of communicating, expectations, manners, and methods of decision-making.

Identifying the various activists in the state and providing a network within which they could get to know one another were seen as important by the emerging coalition. While seeking ways to move beyond single-issue concerns, the founders realized that other people from their own groups did not always share this goal. Much of PRO-PAC's work has therefore been devoted to uncovering the systemic character of society's ills and disseminating this understanding within the broader progressive community through publications and conferences. PRO-PAC has also backed other efforts to draw together diverse constituencies (such as the concern with toxic chemicals that linked environmentalists with labor union leaders on the New Mexico Right-to-Know Task Force). These steps, it was hoped, could lead toward a greater practical understanding of our *mutual interdependence*.

As PRO-PAC explains, "We are *working together* because we have come to understand that our concerns are themselves interrrelated: we see that the solution to any of the problems of alienation, violence, racism, sexism, and exploitation (of workers, the environment, or different cultures) is bound up with the solution to the others. To make lasting advances on any *one* requires us to make progress on *all* of them." PRO-PAC's appeal has prompted over 1,500 people to support its activities during the past five years.

All major decisions on policies and endorsements are made by a board of governors, now consisting of about 120 activists drawn from some sixty organizations that span the range of progressive interests. In order to maintain diversity and balance, newcomers join only with the approval of the executive committee. Decisions are made by mail ballot in order to facilitate participation from all areas of the state. Endorsements require 80 percent approval by those voting. Before candidates are considered for endorsement, they must respond to an exhaustive, four-page questionnaire on issues and budget priorities. Targeting data and other contextual information on the various races are also passed along to the governors.

PRO-PAC has structured its decision-making to facilitate acting together. A fundamental principle has been upheld from the beginning: *we agree to disagree*. It is acknowledged that not everyone will agree with every decision. Day-to-day affairs are conducted by a sixteen-member executive committee. At least eight members have always been women. The executive committee has evolved a consensus-building process for making decisions with general support (not necessarily unanimously), rather than by simple majority vote.

The founders decided to have leaders of other progressive groups join the board as *individuals,* rather than having organizations themselves join. PRO-PAC needed to be an independent legal entity with no formal ties to other organizations. The 501(c)3 tax status of many groups would have kept them from affiliating in any event. Also, a computerized program of direct-mail solicitation was envisaged that legally required PRO-PAC to organize as an "unconnected" political committee.

This structure has worked well because the board of governors is large and diverse. Formally, PRO-PAC is accountable only to its own board. Practically, its board members, who are themselves active within the interdependent context of New Mexico social-change movements, must "answer" to their constituencies for what PRO-PAC does. PRO-PAC is grounded within and accountable to the larger progressive community precisely because its board members have their "hearts in the movement" and are visible activists within it.

Beyond these basic considerations, there are both advantages and disadvantages to the organizational structure. On the positive side, PRO-PAC has the independence to make difficult strategic decisions and engage in its own long-range planning. Separating electoral activity from the lobbying activities of other progressive groups has also proven beneficial, since they occasionally need the support of legislators PRO-PAC has opposed. On the negative side, it is difficult to involve the membership of other organizations in PRO-PAC's electoral program. Communication problems and misunderstandings arise from time to time, especially since information about PRO-PAC's activities is passed along through purely informal links.

New Model for Electoral Politics

Through its work, PRO-PAC is developing a model for electoral politics that stresses self-empowerment, participation, and accountability. While the model itself needs time for refinement and its full implementation will require years of sustained effort, two central features have emerged: (1) recruiting candidates who have a proven record of commitment to progressive issues and (2) using the electoral process to develop grassroots, community-based organizations to which candidates must *remain accountable after they are elected*. Only a few of the candidates supported by PRO-PAC have been involved in campaigns that fully embrace this new model. While more have met the first criterion than the second, recruiting "movement" progressives to run for public office has become a top priority.

PRO-PAC's core principle has been its grassroots, decentralized emphasis. PRO-PAC does not embrace "trickle-down" theories of citizen empowerment and has therefore avoided presidential campaigns: the Rainbow Coalition, conversely, faces the dilemma of choosing whether it is a movement or a national campaign organization. Being a "campaign" entails the concentration of power in a hierarchic structure. Acting as a "movement" calls for the independent initiative of local groups, rather than centralized control from the top down.

If electoral politics is pursued as part of a coherent strategy of citizen self-empowerment, it offers a novel perspective on candidate accountability. Anyone experienced in community organizing knows that local politicians can be a serious problem. They are typically rooted to the status quo: expanding voter participation is seen as a threat to their own re-election; frequently, they are able to direct governmental resources away from community organizations that are committed to fundamental changes. Electing candidates who have been involved in progressive movements can increase their accountability to local communities; grassroots organizations can make an even greater difference, *if they are seriously committed to working in local elections.* Training programs to develop electoral skills are vital. Accountability follows readily where community groups are strong enough to make their central issues highly visible and to mobilize large numbers of volunteer campaign workers.

The voter registration and education programs of the Bernalillo County Voter Participation Coalition advanced the electoral model in 1988 by testing a number of techniques for voter empowerment. Velia Silva, a community activist who is currently president of PRO-PAC, served as director of the Voter Coalition. A door-to-door survey to determine the opinions of unregistered, potential voters in low-income, minority, and under-represented neighborhoods served as a vital component of the work. The act of surveying itself proved to be beneficial: people were intrigued that someone cared about their views. The survey also helped to establish a clear link in people's minds between the act of voting and their preferences on issues. Voting actually became more meaningful within the context of their daily lives.

One local community group, in particular, made extensive use of information garnered from the survey. With survey results as a guide, voter registrars were dispatched to register potential voters who shared the group's stands on the issues. They also developed a very sophisticated program to encourage first-time voters to vote by absentee ballot. The program produced a substantial increase, not only in the number of registered voters, but in actual voter turnout as well.

PRO-PAC's success has been achieved only because it was decided during the first meetings in 1984 that a grassroots fundraising base was mandatory. PRO-PAC has a computerized list of over 10,000 progressive New Mexicans and regularly conducts mailings to raise funds. Every two years a lengthy survey questionnaire is mailed to the list and the responses are used to help set priorities. PRO-PAC also raises money through house parties, phone banks, and direct personal solicitation. It has raised over $100,000 from in-state contributions, most of them in the range of $10 to $15.

Re-Visioning New Mexico

In addition to empowering people, the process of working both to elect candidates and to hold them accountable serves as a natural arena within which to link together single-issue groups. Since elected officials make decisions on a *wide range of issues*, electoral politics offers a concrete way to build progressive coalitions, without the need for choosing any one issue over another.

This advantage, however, gave rise to a problem. Initially, PRO-PAC's agenda looked like an endless laundry list: focusing on only the two or three top concerns of each of the various constituencies could produce twenty or more "key" issues. Developing a common theme or coherent program to unify all these issues in a positive fashion proved elusive. The only way to articulate a concise goal was by attacking or reacting negatively to the opposition: "Bust the (Conservative) Coalition," "Recall Reaganomics," and the like.

As the first step in formulating an agenda that could seize the attention of the media and return political debate to progressive terms, the board of governors of PRO-PAC convened a conference in 1985 called "Re-Visioning New Mexico." Co-sponsored by twenty-two organizations and attended by 250 grassroots activists from throughout the state, the conference initiated the work of "creating a *shared vision* of a progressive future for New Mexico and beyond." Three days of workshops, speakers, informal networking, and roundtable discussions produced a visionary look ahead to the year 2010.

The conference inaugurated a process of long-range planning within New Mexico's progressive communities. *Progressive economic development* has emerged as a unifying theme to provide focus to the entire range of progressive concerns. A consensus has formed around the idea that economic development is the core activity upon which the implementation of a broad-based progressive agenda must depend.

Re-Visioning New Mexico is now established as an independent, tax-exempt, educational organization. It forms the nucleus of a statewide, grassroots network that is being mobilized to develop and implement a strategic plan for bringing about a new economic agenda in New Mexico. The plan begins with an honest evaluation of the state's natural and human resources and then suggests patterns of development which would nurture these resources. Progressive economic development would enhance, rather than exploit or destroy, New Mexico's unique cultural and environmental life.

In addition to focusing the progressive agenda, Re-Visioning New Mexico enhances citizen self-empowerment and candidate accountability. Community power is created through the mutual interplay of three distinct activities. First, the program is developing economic policies and models that are responsive to people's real needs. Second, community-organizing efforts, including voter education and registration, are underway in strategically located communities throughout the state. Third, an ongoing program of leadership and skills training encourages independence and initiative on the part of all participants.

These activities interact synergistically. Policy development requires an avenue for broad, community-based input; implementing these policies brings about changes that have a real impact on people's lives; thus, effective community organizing both facilitates and is facilitated by this democratic interaction. Active participation in the formation of policy endows the community with an increased sense of power. The policies themselves provide a strict standard for candidate accountability, and the entire process creates local organizations with the collective power to enforce the standard.

PRO-PAC itself is keying into this process by recruiting and assisting candidates for public office who have strong grassroots support and a solid commitment to the progressive agenda. The long-term success of progressive economic development requires the creation of a permanent infrastructure that is capable of bringing about fundamental changes in the structure of power.

Power is the central issue. Existing economic, political, and psychological processes work relentlessly to bleed power from the majority and concentrate it in the hands of a few. If people are to empower themselves, they must interrupt this system of exploitation: it drains away the very power which they themselves create through their own work and activity. People need to institute processes that enable them to keep power in their own hands and in their own communities. As these novel institutions gain real purchase in their daily lives, they will be fashioning a world that is truly their own. In New Mexico. PRO-PAC is such an institution. Its story shows one way that grassroots activists can marshall their own political resources to start this process, even when the barriers to success might appear to be immense.

Issue Campaigns

Traditional "labor" issues have involved such matters as wages, hours, unemployment compensation, and the right to organize. But "bridge-building" has brought the labor movement into alliance with other groups around an enormous range of issues which go beyond such traditional labor concerns.

The examples in this section reveal some significant processes:

1. Sometimes campaigns around specific issues can help overcome long-standing antagonisms between different constituencies. In one locale, for example, a campaign to protect jobs by conversion to non-military production drew together hostile peace and labor groups and eventually led them to ally with many others in a broad electoral coalition.

2. Grassroots alliances can project their power into the national arena. This is demonstrated most vividly in the campaign against the nomination of Robert Bork to the U.S. Supreme Court, one of the largest and most diverse political mobilizations of modern American history. The interaction of local and national levels in such a struggle is tricky but potentially creative.

3. Coalitions often require cooperation among groups with enormous cultural differences and a history of interethnic conflict. But a positive response can be made to interethnic tensions by means of cultural activities that stress the positive value of varied ethnic traditions.

Making Minnesota Connections: From Economic Conversion to Progressive Coalition

Mel Duncan

"So this is the Karen Clark that wants to take my job away!" Thus began a 1984 meeting with a group of United Auto Workers (UAW), called by state representative Karen Clark and myself, as organizer for the newly formed Jobs with Peace campaign, to discuss a state economic conversion bill.

While one of the aims of the bill was to save jobs, union support was not automatic. Many union members viewed the peace movement with suspicion at best. Others perceived us to be an outright threat. This was the case of the UAW member quoted above who worked at a Food Machinery Corporation (FMC) ordinance plant in suburban Minneapolis. At that time FMC was Minnesota's second largest military contractor. The peace movement's reputation among union members was not totally undeserved. While some of the more forward-looking peace activists had always included a demand for no loss of jobs with any disarmament proposal, others were quick to condemn workers employed in military factories. All too often morally indignant demonstrators would pose the proposition: Which do you want, peace or your job?

Earlier in 1984 a small group had sat around Karen's kitchen table munching cookies and discussing strategies on how to localize the arms race. Karen had just returned from a conference sponsored by the Alternative State and Local Policies group to discuss, among other things, conversion, a planned transition from military to socially useful production. One of the others sitting around the table was a machinist laid off from a major military contractor. Another was a peace activist who had recently been arrested at a local weapons producer's headquarters. As they talked it became apparent that legislation creating a state economic conversion program would not only focus attention on the local impact of the arms race but would also provide a strategy to build a bridge between labor and the peace movement. Karen decided to author the bill in the state House of Representatives.

At that time I had just returned from picking cotton on the northern border of Nicaragua. I was deeply challenged by a need to find a way to integrate that experience into my life. When I heard that my friend Karen was introducing this bill, I volunteered to help lobby for its passage. I rationalized to my family that it was a short legislative session and that I would use the time networking to find a "real job."

An encounter at one of our first speaking engagements on conversion illustrated the painful choices many military workers confront. In the back of a church basement one evening I noticed a man scowling as we spoke. Near the end of the discussion period, he raised his hand. "I work at a factory where we produce parts for nuclear weapons," he began. "I have a wife and two daughters that I support. I carry their pictures in the top of my lunch box," he continued. "Every day I look at them at lunch. I know that I'm providing for their current needs while at the same time I'm helping to destroy their future. Thank God for what you're doing." Then he started to cry.

Quick reactions followed the bill's introduction in February 1984. Strong support from community, peace, and religious groups surfaced, as did stiff opposition from the weapons-making lobby, led by the Honeywell Corporation. Honeywell obtains 50 percent of military procurement contracts in Minnesota, producing a range of weapons including anti-personnel cluster bombs, nuclear missile guidance systems, torpedoes, and Star Wars technology. The corporation had been the target of numerous direct action protests. The previous October nearly 600 people had been arrested at the entrance to their international headquarters in Minneapolis.

We used the introduction of the bill as an opportunity to begin discussions with representatives of labor. Several unions, most notably the American Federation of State, County, and Municipal Employees (AFSCME), where the military budget is a bread-and-butter issue in terms of social service spending sacrificed to the military, endorsed the legislation. As the bill was worked through committee, it was expanded to provide conversion assistance not only to military-dependent industries but to other vulnerable and declining industries as well. Minnesota was experiencing a rash of plant closings. If conversion could be a tool to assist in transforming military-dependent industries to more stable forms of production, it should also be available to communities and workers facing other forms of economic dislocation. After vigorous lobbying, the bill was defeated on a tie vote before a major committee.

After that session we decided that enough support had been generated for this bill to build a campaign around it. Minnesota Jobs with Peace was formed. We spent the rest of the year speaking with groups and drawing the connections between increased military spending, decreased community services, and job loss. A committee was formed to redraft the legislation. Representatives from the AFL-CIO, AFSCME, the UAW, and the Amalgamated Clothing and Textile Workers (ACTWU) played an active role. The new bill embraced a broad approach to conversion for military as well as other vulnerable and declining industries and contained a provision for mandatory notification of plant closings. An impressive slate of supporters emerged including the Minnesota AFL-CIO, the Catholic Conference, the Urban Coalition, the Farmers Union, the state Council on Black Minnesotans, and the Nuclear Freeze Campaign.

In November 1984 something happened that we had not anticipated. The Republicans took control of the House, which had been controlled by the Democrats for most of the last decade. The new speaker of the House referred to the conversion bill as not the worst piece of legislation he had ever seen but certainly among the worst five. While we were flattered, our coalition of supporters had little influence with the new legislative leaders.

During the 1985 session we were able to append pieces of the bill onto another Senate bill. This resulted in an administrative agreement with the state commissioner of energy and economic development, Mark Dayton, to create a state Task Force on Economic Conversion with Representative Clark as chair and to focus existing economic development and training monies on the development of one or more model conversion projects.

The Task Force begin meeting in late 1985, and brought together an interesting mix of people: the worker at the FMC ordinance plant who had accused Karen of threatening his job twelve months earlier; the president of the Teamsters Union at Honeywell; reprentatives of the AFL-CIO, the United Elecrical Workers (UE), and AFSCME; the co-chair of the Freeze; the state economist appointed by the governor to advise the state on the economy; the assistant commissioner of agriculture; business development specialists; and job training people. Big business declined invitations to send representatives. Together, members of the Task Force struggled with understanding military spending not in isolation but in terms of how it impacted on the entire state's economy and related to other forms of economic dislocation and vulnerability. We crafted a conversion assistance program which would help eligible applicants obtain state economic development assistance, job training funds, and technical assistance. To be eligible a company, union, or community group would have to (1) present a plan to convert a vulnerable or declining business into one with growth potential; (2) demonstrate an effort to gain cooperation of management, employees, unions, and community groups; (3) preserve or create permanent jobs with liveable wages; and (4) not involve military contacts.

To no one's great surprise Honeywell did not apply. A few smaller businesses did show interest but the response was not overwhelming. A light manufacturing company producing land mine components as a subcontract for Honeywell submitted a plan to convert to making three-ring binders. The Task Force worked intensively with them constructing an attractive package for retooling and training. The day before the Task Force was to give final approval the company withdrew their application without explanation.

In 1986, taking advantage of Energy and Economic Development Commmissioner Dayton's departure from office for personal reasons, Honeywell moved to destroy the conversion program. Two days after taking office, the new commissioner notified us that the program was abolished and the Task Force disbanded. In a subsequent meeting the commissioner told us that economic conversion was "deeply offensive to Honeywell." While not successful in destroying the program, the action did result in shifting it to the state Department of Jobs and Training, where it remains today. The attack by Honeywell helped to solidify support among the task force for the program.

In addition to providing a forum to discuss the arms budget in the context of the state's overall economic health, the conversion effort created other connections, as we found out later.

The Democratic Farmer Labor Party (DFL) regained control of the state House in 1986. But the 1987 session proved disappointing for progressives. The legislature refused to pass plant closing legislation, did not approve a resolution opposing the deployment of Minnesota's National Guard in Honduras, and took away a tax credit for renters. Late in that session I sat in the gallery of the House numbly contemplating the significance of these failures. It was obvious that those of us working on issues of peace and justice were not being taken seriously by elected officials. As one rural legislator had told me when I lobbied him on the National Guard resolution, "Mel, I agree with you on this one, but you can't help me the way the American Legion can hurt me if I vote for this."

On the back of a House Journal I began jotting a memo to fellow progressives. Minnesota had a progressive political tradition. Many of us were doing impressive grassroots organizing around issues of peace and justice. Yet we were politically marginalized in the legislative and electoral arenas. I proposed that we needed to mount an effort that would directly link our grassroots activism (building a base) with electoral politics (contesting for power). All too often grassroots organizing shuns electoral and legislative politics and therefore does not contest for power. At the same time electoral politics ignores grassroots and thus becomes a politics without a base.

Labor, farm, civil rights, environmental, and peace activists agreed.

Through the fall of 1987 and early 1988 we struggled with the form that this effort would take. AFSCME, the Association of Community Organizations for Reform Now (ACORN), Citizens Organizations Acting Together (COACT), the Nuclear Freeze Campaign, the UAW, Clean Water Action, the League of Rural Voters, the Minnesota Education Association, the Gay/Lesbian Community Action Council, the Minnesota Peace and Justice Coalition, and Clergy and Laity Concerned all participated. By expanding the borders of New England, Marc Caplan of the Northeast Coalition Project was able to provide valuable consultation based upon the experience of LEAP in Connecticut and other New England coalitions. By April 1988 we had jointly developed a proposal to create a progressive coalition to express a clear progressive agenda that would both impact on the electoral process and create a system of accountability for elected officials. The proposal was circulated to activists throughout the state and informational meetings were held.

In June, the Minnesota Alliance for Progressive Action (MAPA) was formed. One representative from each of the member groups sits on the board. In addition to most of the groups who took part in the planning process, membership also includes twenty-one other organizations, such as the Coalition for the Homeless, the Working Group on Economic Dislocation, and the Philippine Study Group. At-large seats are available to constituencies not represented on the MAPA board but important to progressive politics. Major decisions have to be approved by an 80 percent vote and should reflect the support of each group's governing body. We started creating our common program, which included defining a progressive agenda, strengthening the coalition, and increasing voter participation in the 1988 elections. In the fall MAPA volunteers registered nearly 13,000 voters primarily in low income areas and the communities of color. We contacted over 14,000 voters with a voter education message in the two weeks prior to the elections. A universal voter registration day was established in St. Paul and Minnepolis. We sponsored training for human service agencies on implementation of a new law requiring them to register voters. We coordinated voter registration drives at the surplus food lines and homeless shelters.

Many of the same organizations are also involved in a state political committee, Minnesota PRO-Vote. PRO-Vote played a major role in the election of a progressive candidate from western Minnesota who defeated a reactionary former legislator who had tried to cut welfare benefits by 30 percent during the 1986 session.

During the fall, MAPA members also defined the common values that brought us together as progressives: justice, empowerment, community, self-determination, stewardship, and integrity. These principles helped inform us as we created our 1989 program at a December retreat.

A highlight of our 1989 program was successfully mobilizing joint resources for the passage of hate crimes legislation. The new law increases penalties for crimes motivated by race, religion, gender, national origin, sexual orientation, age, or disability. In addition, MAPA played a major role in the establishment of a progressive legislators group, assisted in bringing together an ad hoc coalition on race issues, provided voter registration and education in the St. Paul municipal elections, co-sponsored a conference with the progressive legislators group on building progressive power at the legislature, and continues to work with community groups for the passage of a police external review process.

In 1989 Minnesota PRO-Vote carried out a successful canvass and voter identification strategy in St. Paul to help elect Mayor Jim Scheibel, one of the most progressive elected officials in Minnesota since the 1930s. PRO-Vote also did a major voter identification and get-out-the-vote effort in a losing mayoral race in Bloomington, Minnesota's third largest city.

MAPA and PRO-Vote are still developing. Joint activities such as legislation or elections are significant themselves but also serve as methods for groups to build capacity and learn to effectively work together.

Meanwhile, the conversion Task Force is working directly with the International Brotherhood of Electrical workers (IBEW) local at Unisys in St. Paul developing and implementing an alternative use strategy. Workers on the shop floor have filled out surveys describing their skills and alternative civilian products that can be produced there. Both the state and the city of St. Paul have contributed funds to the alternative use process. On May 11, the union picketed the St. Paul Unisys site in support of alternative products. When the study is completed, the union will be presenting a list of feasible and marketable products to the company as an alternative to further lay-offs. Minnesota's governor as well as the area congressman are supporting the alternative use effort. In late October, the IBEW local, Jobs with Peace, and the Working Group on Economic Dislocation co-hosted a speech by Swedish Disarmament Ambassador Maj Britt Theorin, a world expert on economic conversion. She spoke to a union hall packed with trade unionists, peace activists, and other community supporters.

On May 9, the Task Force released a major study on the impact of military spending on Minnesota's economy. Especially significant was the finding that Minnesota's high-tech durable goods sector, the place where the economic development hopes of state political leaders rest, is heavily dependent on current levels of military spending. The study recommends ways that the state can help the transition to a peace-time economy.

Karen, now in her fifth term, chairs a newly created division of the House Economic Development Committee on Community Stabilization and Development. The division develops ways that the state can empower communities to create a stable economic base. They recently constructed the Community Stabilization Act that provides funding for pre-feasibility studies for communities threatened by plant closings, requires that communities be reimbursed for public funds invested in a facility prior to its acquisition, and mandates that a copororation closing a plant in the state pay into a community fund. The bill stands a good chance of passage in 1990.

We are still a long way from a progressive movement in Minnesota that effectively translates grassroots organizing into electoral and legislative power. The past years have impressed me with the patient, diligent work required to do that. Yet a solid base is being built. The early conversion work built relationships and broke down barriers among progressive groups especially between peace and labor organizations. Thus, as MAPA was being formed, trust and working relationships had already been established. Other collaborative efforts around farm issues and health care also laid groundwork for MAPA to develop.

MAPA and the conversion program both provide opportunities for various progressive constitutencies to actively engage each other in common struggles. We have not got it all figured out but we are learning how to combine our resources to increase our impact through common activities such as the hate crimes legislation and voter participation. Each activity gives us a chance to learn from each other, build trust, assess how we can be more effective, and define who we are as a progressive momvement. As the late Jim Dunn of the People's Institute for Survival and Beyond once reminded me, our values are always clarified by our actions.

Blocking Bork:
Grassroots Aspects of a National Coalition

Michael Pertschuk and Wendy Schaetzel

When in 1987 Ronald Reagan announced the nomination of Robert Bork to the Supreme Court, an astonishingly diverse coalition of national organizations came together in Washington to block it. Much of the credit or blame for Bork's historic defeat has been attributed to their brilliant or nefarious efforts.

But as the Washington-based coalition began to reach beyond the Washington beltway, it discovered that there was already another grassroots campaign beginning in dozens of states throughout the country. Ultimately the two forged a cooperative relationship that was crucial to their success—but not without some false starts along the way. What are the lessons for future campaigns which aim to project citizen power into the national arena?

Coalition stalwarts in Washington flinched when they heard that Maggie Kuhn, the mischievously resourceful founder of the Gray Panthers, proposed holding a mock funeral for the Constitution in Philadelphia one day before the Senate hearings began on Bork's nomination. At first, other leaders of the anti-Bork coalition in Philadelphia were doubtful, too, about the seemliness of such a spectacle, as they visualized scenes of exuberant mourning over the death of civil rights at the murderous hands of a Borkian Supreme Court. Let us stick to more sober, less aggressive activities, they argued.

But the concept took on life. This was, after all, Philadelphia, birthplace of the Constitution, in the very year of its bicentennial. And this was a coalition which had boldly called itself the "Philadelphia Ad Hoc Coalition to Save the Constitution."

The more the Pennsylvania coalition leaders talked, the more they liked the idea. The black churches and their ministers were at the heart of the Philadelphia coalition; their churches would be an apt setting for the "Funeral for Justice"—especially the Bright Hope Baptist Church of William Gray III, minister and respected black congressman, and chairman of the House Budget Committee. Why not lamentations over a casket symbolizing a post-Bork Constitution, bearing the ashes of civil rights, and borne by a rich diversity of pallbearers in a mass funeral procession through the streets of Philadelphia to Senator Specter's office?

And why limit participation to Philadelphia? Why not a "Train for Justice," originating in Pittsburgh, and stopping to take on mourners as it passed across the state to Philadelphia? So the plan grew. A special committee was established and assignments were made: organizing the program, the speakers, the props, the funeral and procession ceremonies. The "Train for Justice" required the joint planning of the two coalitions in Pittsburgh and Philadelphia, and all their constituent organizations. Energy poured forth.

Kate Michelman, co-chair of the Grassroots Task Force of the national coalition in Washington, was "absolutely panic stricken" about it, however. And their own affiliate in Philadelphia was working on the arrangements. "So I got on the phone with them," she explained, and said, 'What is this coffin garbage?!' I really felt that the coffin idea was just too hokey and I told her how worried I was about it because I had made a commitment to the national coalition to keep things on a dignified level."

By that time, all the national groups opposing the nomination had worked out a basic structure for a national coalition: four task forces were organized—Lobbying, Research/Drafting, Media, and Grassroots, each with four co-chairs. Frances Sheehan, executive director, of the National Abortion Rights Action League (NARAL) in Pennsylvania, tried to reassure Linda Schwartz, the organizer hired by the Leadership Conference on Civil Rights to work with several state coalitions including those in Pennsylvania. "I don't think this event *could* have boomeranged," says Sheehan. "It was a good even from the beginning of the concept, and they just didn't know the community well enough to know that. They didn't know the players; they didn't have the vision of the event that we did, and they didn't trust. I understand that. I think the thing about being in Washington is that you also hear all the nightmares."

The Washington worriers were not mollified. Nikki Heidepriem, who helped develop the campaign's themes for the national coalition, cringed at the concept: "Message has to do both with what you say, and how you say it. A 'Funeral for Justice'—now this was not consistent with our view of the line of the campaign; it was heart-stopping."

And all the "signals" from Specter's office were grim. The Senator would be offended; might be alienated; would be angered by intemperate attacks. The worst nightmare: Arlen Specter, one of four swing votes on the Senate Judiciary Committee, might even be goaded into voting for Bork to avoid any suggestion that he would succumb to intimidation! "We kept telling them it was stupid," says Jeff Robinson, Specter's subcommittee counsel. "You've gotta do what you've gotta do; but if what you're interested in doing is convincing him one way or another, that sort of thing has a zero impact, or a negative impact!"

In near desperation, key strategists of the national anti-Bork coalition pleaded with Senator Ted Kennedy's staff to get him to call the Pennsylvania organizers and urge them to call off the event.

He didn't—and their fears proved exaggerated. Some 1,200 people attended the funeral. It was a model of tact and decorum, and deeply moving in the depth of feeling conveyed by speaker after speaker and an overflow audience for the Constitution as a living shield against racism and injustice. Press coverage was excellent, and sympathetic, including national coverage by CBS, NBC, and ABC "Nightline."

In fairness to the worriers in Washington, the funeral did provide a chilling glimpse of just the kind of attacks the Washington insiders feared: one speaker departed from the prevailing respectful attitude toward Sensator Specter's careful deliberations, denouncing Specter and threatening to unseat Specter's wife from her long-held seat on the Philadelphia City Council. Such tirades, had they otherwise characterized the funeral, might well have infuriated Specter. And perhaps the alarms sent out from the Washington coalition at least reinforced the funeral organizers' insistence upon restraint, so that such bully rhetoric was confined to the one speaker.

But Mimi Mager, the national grassroots coordinator, cheerfully admits being flat wrong. "If there's one place where we should say a *mea culpa*," she told us, "it was that event. In fact, it was a terrific event. It got wonderful coverage and it was an example of where the event was done by the black community, primarily by the ministers. They knew what needed to be done, and they knew what was going to work. It really was the right event for that community and it did the job of energizing the people it was intended to."

Few events sponsored by state coalitions have provoked as much "creative tension" between "Washington" and the "the Field." Those shorthand labels themselves reveal the germ of the problem; they are "we-they" terms. The professional public interest lobbyists, media strategists, and organizers based in Washington tend to view their local members and activists in the field as a resource to be cultivated, then controlled. They are reluctant to leave any part of a national grassroots campaign untended; surely there must be a coordination process controlled by a central authority if there is to be unity of themes and strategies.

Grassroots activists, on the other hand, tend to view even their own colleagues and leaders in Washington as tainted by their surroundings, by the arrogance of the centrality of power. They feel they are closer to "the people," while Washington, and all who work within it, is isolated from the real country. They feel Washington appreciates neither their knowledge and learning, nor their strategic skills, nor their prudence and judgment.

There is some truth to both perceptions; but they can be exaggerated. And exaggeration leads to tension, both in strategy and in relationships. A campaign characterized by tempered decorum may suit senatorial notions of the judicial confirmation process, but activists, once alerted and engaged, may well have different notions of propriety. And all Americans, progressive political activists no less than libertarians, resent and resist dictation from Washington.

There was a consensus among most of the Washington-based strategists that the Bork campaign had to be far more decorous than a typical legislative campaign. Althea Simmons, veteran field general of the National Association for the Advancement of Colored People (NAACP), was clear as to the winning strategy: "A low profile. Don't tip your hand. No statements. No inkling of thrust." She recalled, "My gut feeling [was] that if we had the coffins, the caskets, and all that kind of crazy stuff we were going to turn off even our friends. The Supreme Court nomination has a status that is higher than other pieces of legislation. Those tactics would be perceived as a 'no, no.' In the NAACP literature I sent out, on page one of my cover letter, I said, 'Do not engage in demonstrations.'"

Kate Michelman agreed: "We had to be careful not to get lumped in with the crazies out there; we had to raise issues that had substantive research behind them, so our reason for not supporting massive rallies was that they can easily get out of control. We were worried that rallies would draw out the kooks, the anti-abortion groups."

Their convictions were widely shared among the members of the national coalition, but not unanimously. The National Organization for Women (NOW), in particular, demurred. Sheri O'Dell spelled out NOW's view plainly: "We looked at what role we could play here that was beyond just our members writing and calling and making constituent visits. We were well aware that some of the people working on the grassroots component didn't like the rally idea. They thought it was going to backfire. Our position was, "That's bunk." It's absolutely critical that there be constant awareness through the press and the public, getting people riled up sitting in their living rooms. By the time they got ready to take that vote, the public had spoken, and they said, 'You'd better not put this guy on the Court!' And I don't think that public opinion would have hardened against him without that level of activity, and without the very visible actions and the pickets and the rallies."

NOW and its members sought to draw media attention to the intensity of the opposition. Others, such as Simmons and Michelman, feared that the *medium* for gaining press coverage, boisterous rallies and events, would become the *message* that Bork's opposition was what President Reagan enjoyed labeling the "loonie left."

But, once roused, would grassroots activists be led? Would this widely diverse, activiated citizenry follow the carefully calibrated themes and campaign design emanating from Washington? And should they? The answer, as the "Funeral for Justice" illustrates, is: "Yes, and no!"

Washington could provide support, it could suggest, it could cajole, but it couldn't control. The field people believed they understood, better than distant Washington, the political culture of their own states, the salient issues, the local leadership structure, and the local media. Bill Robinson of the Lawyers' Committee on Civil Rights believes they were right: "Out in the country, this thing acquired a life of its own. You couldn't direct everything because there had been a snowball effect. Organizations in major centers had prepared information and gotten it out, but once it got out there, another level of leadership in the country took over and it assumed a life of its own."

While the national coalition, through its "desks," attempted to monitor the universe of grassroots activities, the coalition's Grassroots Task Force sometimes did not hear about planned events until after the fact. Unlike the "Funeral for Justice," there was a boisterous, unruly anti-Bork demonstration in Texas, which drew network coverage— conveying an image of unreasoning zeal, not reasoned opposition.

The Alabama coalition chose to appeal to churchgoers by making an issue of Bork's reputed religious agnosticism—an issue first raised by Senator Heflin. The raising of such an issue—personal and far afield from Bork's legal philosophy—was deeply troubling to coalition leaders in Washington. Such episodes led the coalition's national leaders, at times, to seek to discourage or restrain events enthusiastically planned by grassroots organizers.

Thus, the campaign faced a series of inherent conflicts: "inside" vs. "outside" politics (and Washington-based "insiders" vs. activist "outsiders"); central direction and control vs. the blooming of a thousand diverse expressions of opposition; decorum vs. intensity.

NOW President Molly Yard wears her Washington outsiders hat as a badge of honor. A great and courageous political organizer for unpopular causes or principle, she has as the *Washington Post's* Jacqueline Trescott put it, "nothing subtle about her, just an abiding attachment to unreconstructed liberalism." Yard expressed her concerns about the insider-outsider conflicts: "Our organization is on the cutting edge stating the problem. We recognize that other people are back here doing what is possible. They're doing what's possible because we're out there pushing, and both roles are perfectly legitimate. . . . My real distress is that I find a lot of our colleagues either not understanding how we operate or not willing to accept that it's a legitimate way of operating. I accept what they're doing as totally legitimate, and I think you have to have both. I don't think you get very far without both."

In retrospect a lot of learning took place, on both sides, during what was a relatively short campaign. And that was so largely because the principals, both in Washington and the field, were open to learning. The learning had to flow both ways. As Mager observes: "Many of the outsiders probably didn't know there were two games being played. Unless you were able to play in both of those fields, it never would have worked. A number of groups outside Washington didn't start off with a good taste for what Washington lobbyists do, and, equally, the people in Washington think, 'What could those people back home do that's going to make any real difference.' I think that all turned around."

While many issue campaigns of the 1970s and 1980s tended to be either Washington-centered and highly professionalized, or strong in grassroots energy but strategically weak, this Supreme Court fight succeeded in integrating both "inside" Washington-based leadership and "outside" networks and coalitions throughout the country.

The leaders of the anti-Bork effort in Washington knew that citizen action was essential to defeating Bork, and they invested resources, time, and respect in developing bridges to the field. And while the political force and much of the creativity of the campaign came from outside, the grassroots campaign was nourished by the intelligence, resources, and counseling of the Grassroots Task Force and the "desks" in Washington. Bork opponents learned that what was required to successfully challenge the White House with a just cause was not mysterious: the engagement of vast networks of activists on a national scale under the umbrella of a richly layered coalition of organizations.

The power of this grand alliance no longer seemed an illusion to many who participated in organizing the first grassroots campaign over a judicial nomination. Jewish attorneys and law teachers and NAACP community activists, white male labor leaders and feminists, libertarians and politically liberal baby boomers, consumer advocates, environmentalists, and small-business leaders—all came together in defense of their vision of the Constitution and the Court.

Civil rights attorney Bill Taylor observed, "No battle brought more diverse groups together. That's part of the legacy, because once people have worked together and found that they can work together, it provides a basis for doing so again." While the Reagan era had led many would-be activists to despair of progressive change, those who participated in the anti-Bork campaign experienced a renewed sense of civic empowerment and hope.

Noon at 9 to 5:
Reflections on a Decade of Organizing

Cindia Cameron

As manufacturing jobs have been automated, shipped abroad, and shut down for good, traditional sources of employment as well as of union members have dried up, with severe effects for the labor movement. For the past decade, job growth has been highest in the new "service economy," with office jobs becoming both the largest and fastest growing job category for the newest growth sector of the labor force—women. Fully one of every three employed women is an office worker. What effect has this shift had on organizing and on the union movement?

A new participant in labor issues in the past decade has been an organization known to many people because of a movie and hit song of the same name—9 to 5. As union organizers search for methods and strategies to tackle the new conditions, it is worth looking at this newcomer to see what contributions it can offer.

The purposes of this article are first, to look at the phenomenon of the 9 to 5 movement, the social forces that have encouraged its growth and have been its greatest obstacles; second, to describe its goals and methods, how they connect with or differ from those of traditional unions; and finally, to see what union organizers can draw from this experience that would be useful in attempts to build unions among this largest group of employed women.

The National Association of Working Women, 9 to 5, is a membership organization for women office workers. Since its founding in Boston in 1973, it has grown to 12,000 members in twenty-five citywide chapters, as well as at-large members located in all of the 50 states. Its purpose is to improve wages, rights, and respect for office workers through three methods: (1) individual job problem and legal rights counseling, (2) educational programs such as on VDT health hazards and job survival skills, and (3) public pressure campaigns which target corporate and public policies affecting office workers.

The organization combines women's issues (discrimination, pay equity, sexual harassment, respect) and union issues (higher pay, job posting, increased benefits) with a community organizing style (cor-

porate campaigns, locally elected boards of directors, personal empowerment).

Social Forces

What accounts for the emergence and endurance of this hybrid
women's workplace organization, and what have been the major obstacles it has faced?

By the early 1970s three social forces were building that resulted
in an immediate and widespread response to this new type of organization. First, there was a real change in the economic status of women.
More and more women had become wage earners out of necessity,
seeing themselves as permanent workers for the first time. Second,
the ideas of the women's movement had affected a majority of women.
Even the large numbers who described themselves as "not women's
libbers" had begun to accept the idea of equality for women, and
more importantly, were beginning to believe it was legitimate to
expect more. Finally, throughout the 1960s and 1970s, the nature
of office work itself was changing. The traditional private secretary
with a large amount of discretion and control over her office and
work was rapidly being replaced by data entry operators, word proc-
essors, and keypunch operators—all lower paid, more routine, and
monotonous jobs, with even fewer possibilities for promotion and
advancement.

As a result of these combined influences, working women's groups
with varying methods and agendas sprang up in several major cities
in the early 1970s. In 1977, five of these joined forces to found 9
to 5. The organization served as both a catalyst and lightening rod
for the concerns of this new breed of working woman. As an organizer
who worked for the Baltimore chapter in the late 1970s explained,
"I'd meet women for lunch to talk about 9 to 5 and would hear, over
and over, women expressing a sense of relief that finally there was a
group hearing and acting on their unspoken concerns and aspirations."

Even though these combined social forces have propelled organizing
efforts in cities across the country, 9 to 5 still has a relatively small
membership. What obstacles has it encountered in organizing among
women clericals?

The reasons traditionally cited by union leaders for not organizing
women office workers are all in some part true, but largely miss the
essential issues. For example, secretaries and other "elites" of clerical
work sometimes do identify with the power and prestige of their boss
or company, rather than with co-workers. But with more highly edu-
cated office workers and rising expectations, these women are often

precisely the ones with the self-confidence and skills to become the first leaders of a 9 to 5 chapter and to be the most convinced that they deserve more.

It is true that many office workers work in plush, clean, comfortable surroundings, and feel themselves to be somehow "above" blue-collar workers and their unions. There are, on the other hand, great numbers who work in large, poorly designed, stuffy, regimented worksites, with increasing numbers whose work is paced and monitored by computer and whose pay is based on production or piece-rate systems.

It is also true that many clerical women feel alienated from or hostile to unions. They have long been ignored by organized labor, and their special concerns—such as child care, discrimination, and lack of respect—have not, until recently, been addressed. Many unions do not have an organizing staff these workers can identify with, and they have few women and fewer with experience in issues of conditions of clerical work.

While all of these problems do exist, they do not add up to a useful explanation of why it may be difficult to make organizing inroads among women clericals. Within 9 to 5, there are three common observations about what the real obstacles are. First mentioned is fear. The real fear and hardship of unfair and discriminatory firings should not be underestimated, as women are increasingly the sole support of their families. But it is less likely that a woman will be fired for being open about 9 to 5 activity than it is that she will be harassed by management and isolated by co-workers. As one veteran staff members explains, "What many women really fear is stepping out of the mold—taking a stand for yourself first, before boss or company loyalty. Women are still brought up to put others before themselves. If they do change their behavior because of 9 to 5, it is often a threat to friends, family, co-workers, and their own self-images. This is the real fear."

A second obstacle is the tremendous job mobility of office workers in the 1980s. Younger workers especially are constantly leaving one job for another—motivated by boredom in a company with no challenge or advancement opportunity, by the prospect of better pay or conditions, or to escape a tyrannical boss or unfair conditions which they feel helpless to change. In cities, where clerical jobs are concentrated, there is always another office job. Maybe not a better one, but a different one, an escape. Because of this mobility, clericals do not have the incentive to stick it out, to stand up and join up to improve conditions.

The most significant obstacle, in my experience, was explained by an Atlanta member this way: "Why don't more women join 9 to 5? Because, in my seven years as a clerical, I can tell you, office workers

are never encouraged to join *anything*. To be a librarian or any professional, you *have* to join that association, but not clericals. It is actually
discouraged." Office workers do not have a history of political or civic
participation. Until very recently they have had no history of leadership or heroines, no social clubs or associations, no press or recorded
history, no experience of common struggle on their own behalf. As
an organizer for District 925 of the Sevice Employees International
Union (SEIU) observed on the founding of this first national union
for office workers, "A workforce cannot organize itself without organizational skills, leadership, a common identity and a collective sense
which gives it the *will* to organize."

Goals and Strategies

The central goal which has guided 9 to 5 over the past twelve
years is simply to introduce office workers to the idea, the experience,
and the value of organization. It has employed four basic strategies
to reach this goal. First is to raise the issues (pay, rights, and respect)
to the public in order to change the expectations of office workers.
Second is to create examples of change, to win concrete victories
which show that it is possible and worth the risk. Third is to educate
the constituency on issues and legal rights, in order to build a climate
of legitimacy for organizing and the knowledge of rights and how
to protect them. The final strategy is to develop leadership among
clericals, emphasizing both the empowerment of individuals and the
training of long-term activists within the constituency.

How have these strategies been put into action, and how effective
have they been?

The first steps in raising the particular issues of women office workers to the public were achieved by a combination of "street actions"
and the publishing of the Office Workers' Bill of Rights. The actions
took place in front of large companies, with colorful songs, speeches,
and visuals, such as the "Heartless Employer Award" on Valentine's
Day or "Scrooge of the Year" at Christmas. They resulted in consistent
press coverage of the issues—low pay, poor benefits, and discriminatory treatment—as well as in changes in some employer policies. Presenting what this new group was *for* as well as against necessitated
a rallying point. The slogan "Raises, Rights and Respect" and an
agenda, the Bill of Rights, were designed to raise the standards of
what was acceptable treatment for this largely underpaid and underval-
ued segment of the workforce.

To win concrete improvements, 9 to 5 had, in the early years, two
important weapons which are no longer viable: the element of surprise

and the threat of federal antidiscrimination agencies. Appearing on the doorstep of a company to dramatize conditions of unfair treatment was all it took to get some changes made. Companies were taken aback by this new phenomenon and were eager to get out of the press and public eye. But as word of 9 to 5 spread, the surprise element disappeared. Chambers of commerce and management consultants across the country now offer training sessions on how to control or "manage" white-collar workers and "militant feminists" like 9 to 5.

Early campaigns also relied on suing banks for noncompliance with affirmative action plans required of federal contractors. With the changes in funding, enforcement, and regulations since 1980, it is much more difficult to threaten companies or to win cases.

From 1974 till 1980, however, the combination of one-time actions on employers and year-long corporate campaigns and legal suits resulted in impressive victories—promotions and back-pay awards, job posting and grievance procedures, raises and child-care programs. Equally important, members changed their ideas about the possibility of change, their relationship to employers and government, and the value of organization.

The corporate campaigns had, in the eyes of some organizers, two weaknesses. First was that relying on the power and threat of government antidiscrimination agencies might encourage 9 to 5 members to see these agencies, rather than the power of their own organization, as the solution to their problems, Ironically, the changes in government enforcement under the Reagan administration have gone a long way toward curing members of this belief. Second, because of employer harassment and fear of being fired, women from the targeted company were sometimes not publicly involved in the leadership of corporate campaigns, thus presenting to some of the workers whose conditions were directly affected the lesson that "someone else will solve your problems for you"—a contradiction of the message 9 to 5 set out to convey.

Because of these changes, another approach to winning workplace victories has been developed. Using this model, job-problem calls are screened for individuals who can bring together a group of coworkers to meet with 9 to 5 to define their grievances, learn about legal rights, and develop a group strategy to pressure management for change. Similar to shop floor organizing, the goal is the solution to a specific problem: better lighting or equipment, a fair promotion or review process, or an end to mandatory overtime, not the recognition of their organization or union. With this model, change has been achieved and the message that there is power in organization has been learned and spread.

The third strategy is to provide a climate of legitimacy for organizing through educational programs on issues and legal rights. Workshops on sexual harassment, pay equity, or the health hazards of office automation are universally popular and well attended. It is through these outreach events that many women who go on to become chapter leaders have their first experience with 9 to 5. The programs are designed to give participants a chance to share common problems and solutions and to build a support network, as well as to teach skills.

The final strategy is that of developing leadership among women clericals. The trademarks of this style have been to develop those leaders who are most representative and can articulate the problems of this constituency: a single mother whose full-time pay still qualifies her for government assistance; an older women with years of training men to be her bosses; a keypunch operator who works rotating shifts and whose pay is based on production quotas. These are the people who speak to the press, to public officials, who address rallies and lead workshops. There is also a conscious effort to present a multiracial public image at all times. Leaders are often paired, black and white, for public or press appearances and even for leafletting. The aim of this style of leadership development is both to provide clerical women with the skills and experience to control their own organizations and also to use these leaders to convey to potential members that 9 to 5 is a group where people like themselves make decisions and make change.

Lessons for Unionists

Given that the goal of 9 to 5 is to build collective identity rather than collective bargaining units, what can unionists learn from the model and experience of this organization?

There are at least three areas in which 9 to 5 has broken new ground in reaching workers outside the traditional "house of labor." First, 9 to 5 has articulated the aspirations of the constituency and raised them to the level of public debate. Who should get the coffee in the office was not an issue in the minds of anyone but secretaries before the 1970s. Now in the most isolated and conservative town, bosses think twice before asking this service of their secretaries. Finding the gut issues and building a consensus on what workers should expect, then highlighting the gap between where they are and where they want to be, are the first steps in creating the *will* to organize.

Second, public outreach events such as educational workshops attract new potential members who then have an opportunity to become allied with the labor movement whether or not there is a union at their workplace.

Third, 9 to 5 has set a strong example in the area of public relations and media work, due in part to its emphasis on providing personal stories, well-researched issue papers, and a positive, aggressive approach to news stories. For the most part, 9 to 5 spokespeople are not paid professionals, but "real-life office workers" who can tell their own story in their own words—quite different from the popular stereotype of the union movement.

The major contribution of 9 to 5 for the union movement, out of which new methods and tactics can be developed, is in providing an example of a new phase in the process of organizing. This is a phase of building a collective identity and the will to organize which must precede the traditional union organizing methods, particularly among the new categories of workers in the service economy.

Update: 9 to 5 and the New Workforce

In 1985, when I began thinking about the implications of the 9 to 5 experience, the full impact of the shift from a manufacturing to a service-based economy was just beginning to be discussed within 9 to 5. The issues involved both worsening conditions for much of the workforce, and new opportunities and strategies for organizing.

Service industries now employ 75 percent of the U.S. workforce and account for nearly two-thirds of total Gross National Product (GNP). Recent studies show that these jobs are clustered at the lower end of the pay scale and account for the largest numbers of workers lacking health insurance and pensions. An estimated 44 percent of new jobs created from 1979 to 1985 yielded an annual income of $7,500 or less; almost one out of four workers in retail and business services has no health insurance and only 19 percent of retail trade workers (an industry which employs 17 percent of the total workforce) have pensions.

Working conditions which have prevailed for women office workers —low pay, few benefits, and no job security—are now becoming the norm for a wide sector of workers.

The "new workforce" is a term used by 9 to 5 to describe the result of two fundamental changes in our society: the shift to low-wage, less secure jobs, and the dramatic influx of women into the labor force, with consequent changes in family structure.

Thirty years ago, the typical U.S. worker was male, held a blue-collar job, worked in a large factory, and supported a family on a single wage. Unions, representing over a quarter of the workforce, provided a collective voice, and jobs provided the basic necessities of life for most ablebodied people.

Today there is almost a fifty-fifty chance that the typical worker is a woman and is part of a two-earner family, or a single head of household, juggling the dual demands of work and family. Her job is likely to be in an office or sales at a small worksite, while her employer is a multinational conglomerate. This typical worker is also far less likely to be a union member.

Organizers for 9 to 5 see, in the framework of issues described by the "new workforce," a potential new organizing strategy. For what truly distinguishes the new workforce from the old is not the difference between service and manufacturing sectors, but the terms and conditions of work—the social contract among workers, management, and government. The social contract of the 1980s changed dramatically; in fact, it lapsed.

Fifty years ago and more, the rise of the industrial age brought about similarly dramatic social and economic changes. Partly through the efforts of a massive labor movement, a new set of federally established minimum standards was legislated, including the minimum wage, social security, and the forty-hour week. Today we need a new set of standards to address the changed realities of jobs and families, including pay and benefits, work and family policies, jobs and training, and working conditions.

It is this need for new standards which could provide a new framework for organizing. Mobilizing for a new social contract would require cooperation among a broad range of community advocates and the participation of public officials. For those segments of the workforce and community with no tradition of self-organization, such a goal would provide a framework to express their needs and a vehicle to bring about solutions in new ways.

Chapters of 9 to 5 in several parts of the country have been experimenting with these opportunities. The Coalition to End the Abuse of Part-time and Temporary Workers in Milwaukee, Wisconsin, is one example. Formed in 1988 by 9 to 5 and several area unions, the group held a conference called "The Cheapening of the Workforce." The purpose of the event was to draw attention to the conditions of women and men in part-time and temporary jobs that these workers often had held for years, with no benefits or job security, earning less per hour than workers with the same duties who were classified as full time or permanent.

The coalition has met with city, county, and state elected officials and leveraged pay and benefit improvements for some classifications of public employees. They have also proposed several new policies, including a requirement that companies who apply for city development funds provide information on their use of temporary and part-time workers, and new ways of providing health insurance for uninsured workers.

In Georgia, the issue of family and medical leave sparked a new kind of local coalition. The need for basic job protection, for working families which no longer have unpaid caretakers because the wives and daughters are working full time, affects union and nonunion workers, retirees, and child welfare advocates. The coalition, founded in January 1989, includes 9 to 5, unions, women's groups, medical advocates, seniors, and other community organizations. In a state which ranks fiftieth in job security, and has no exceptions to the "employment at will" doctrine, the coalition faces serious opposition. However, it has already been successful in getting a study committee appointed by the legislature, in holding statewide hearings into the need for a law on family and medical leave, and in introducing a bill, modeled on the National Family and Medical Leave Act, in the Georgia General Assembly. This progress is a testament to the power of the issues and alliances born of the new workforce.

In Georgia as in Wisconsin, male, blue-collar workers from manufacturing industries, represented by powerful unions, will testify, rally, and lobby alongside black and Hispanic single mothers who support their children on a patchwork of part-time jobs with no health insurance. What these workers and a long list of community organizations face as common threats are the decline of the value of the minimum wage, the strain on social service budgets due to widespread lack of health insurance, and the crisis of families who have no one at home to care for infants, after-school children, and frail, elderly parents.

The lesson that 9 to 5, along with many allies, learned in the 1980s is that there is more than a single organizational step preceding unionization for women office workers. What we are seeing is that there is great potential for building a movement among whole new segments of low-income workers by forming alliances based on critical and widespread needs which are the result of a lapsed social contract. Using many of the same methods pioneered by 9 to 5 in the 1970s—surveys, hotlines, public hearings—issues as diverse as the minimum wage, access to health insurance, computer monitoring, and family leave can be addressed. Workers with no history of community or workplace organization can become involved, and be instrumental in building new coalitions and winning new policies. Such coalitions can have as a goal to develop a new social contract—in addition to or in the absence of the now endangered union contract.

The Chinatown-Harlem Initiative: Building Multicultural Understanding in New York City

John Kuo Wei Tchen

In mid-1989, the New York Chinatown History Project began an educational and cultural effort to improve relations concretely between the African-American and Asian communities of New York City. The Chinatown-Harlem Initiative (CHI) will facilitate the linking of *existing* human and organizational resources in a series of Afro-Asian dialogues and joint projects. The project represents an experimental attempt to improve cross-cultural understanding in New York City and facilitate the process of constructing a broader, more inclusive conception of what it means to be a multicultural citizen of New York City, New York state, and the nation. Much of what is proposed has never been tried between these two communities in New York City and I offer this early outline of our plan with the hopes that other coalitions across the country can share with us their experiences and also freely borrow from our ideas. First, let me offer some background about the History Project.

New York Chinatown History Project

The New York Chinatown History Project was founded in 1980 with the goal of developing a historical base of knowledge which could help empower residents to improve community life. The History Project staff have developed a variety of interpretive programs debunking persistent stereotypes about Asians and reclaiming the experience of what is now one of the largest Chinese communities in the Western hemisphere. These programs are presented in a variety of bilingual formats offering layers of public accessibility, including historical walking tours, changing exhibits, regular in-house media programs, a major library and archives, a small bookstore, traveling exhibitions and media programs, special events (such as issue-oriented conferences), and a triannual publication *Bu Gao Ban* (Community Bulletin Board).

The interpretation of the Chinese-American experience has been presented from a multicultural perspective. Whenever possible, emphasis has been given to the complex of shared experience in the

186

Lower East Side and New York City. For example, we have sponsored exhibits, programs, and conferences on: housing reform efforts during the Progressive Era; the comparable experiences of Puerto Rican women garment workers; Japanese-American family histories as a means to initiate a New York Japanese-American documentation project; and a multiracial roundtable bringing scholars and activists together in "'We the People' and Others: A Cross-Cultural Dialogue." The History Project serves several audiences: the burgeoning Chinese American community, the Asian New York community, and the general interested public.

Racism in the 1980s

While such tragedies as Howard Beach have captured national attention, ongoing ethnic and racial conflicts in New York City, often resulting in violence, continue, for the most part unnoticed. Ironically, while Asian-Americans have been heralded as the nation's "model minority," anti-Asian sentiments and violence have dramatically increased over the past few years. Korean and Chinese American businesses were recently boycotted in the largely Italian sections of Bensonhurst and Gravesend and in the black neighborhood of Bedford Stuyvesant. Asians have been accused of taking over local small businesses with "Moonie" money and drug profits, and of "sucking the blood" out of neighborhood economies like "vampires." Most alarming has been the rise of street violence selectively targeting Asians in the South Bronx, Flushing, sections of Staten Island, and elsewhere. One such incident resulted in the fatal beating in Hoboken, New Jersey, of Navroze Mody, a thirty-year-old Citicorp manager of East Indian descent, by a largely Hispanic youth gang known as the "Dotbusters."

Part of the context for this increasing anti-Asian hostility is the great increase in Asian immigration into New York City, which is a part of larger demographic shifts of race and nationality. The Asian-American Center at Queens College estimates that there are 310,000 Chinese and 600,000 Asians living in New York City today. As these immigrants enter the web of existing racial and ethnic relations, they have become entangled in a complex set of existing and newly developing frustrations and tensions. Not immune from ethnocentrism and racial stereotyping, many have accepted, at face value, previously existing racial attitudes and social inequities of the larger society. Many Chinese New Yorkers imagine all blacks to be muggers, lazy, and drug addicts. Chinese waiters often treat darker complected customers (including Asian Indians) badly. Few have any insights on the history of the African-American experience, nor do they have any understanding that the civil rights movement greatly improved the opportunities open to Asian-Americans, including the striking of racial quotas in the 1965–68 immigration reform legislation.

Outside of a bandaid crisis-management approach, New York City has not devised meaningful programs to deal with such racial tensions. Short-term attempts have been made to diffuse flare-ups, but long-term strategies have not been developed. This problem is a dual one of an insufficient effort to actually bridge communities and neighborhoods *and* of lacking a common conceptual language to articulate a revisioning of a shared public culture in New York City.

Multicultural Identity

Budget cuts, racial confrontations, and various other "emergency" issues often bring educators, human service workers, and cultural activists, among others, from these diverse communities together in temporary, short-term coalitions. Discussions inevitably lead us to note the paramount importance of building cross-community channels of communication. Yet when we return to our respective worlds to deal with everyday survival issues, we more often than not relegate these bridging efforts to the "to do" pile.

One of the most important components of any lasting strategy is the active promotion of mutual cross-cultural understanding between racially and ethnically defined communities. Great progress has been made in documenting the history and experience of many diverse peoples of New York City, but few of these educational and cultural fruits have been shared across what appear to be increasingly impermeable racial, class, and ethnic boundaries.

The "melting pot" notion of U.S. society, although still commonly referred to, has been effectively challenged in the arts, humanities, and human sciences with the general recognition of the right and importance of women and ethnicities to articulate their own experiences and interpretive theories. Originating from the progressive social movements of the mid-1950s through early 1970s, a spate of new scholarship has emerged. The terms "mixed salad" and "mosaic" are now often used to respond to a respect for and celebration of difference. Such terms are helpful, but little public discussion has been devoted to an alternative vision of what the unifying "bowl" or "board" might be. What does it mean to be an American? "Diversity" simply has not been a sufficient response. Such concepts also imply an equality and mutual respect within diversity, an implication of unfounded assumptions. Indeed, a pluralistic diversity is often accepted as already existing, while very tangible inequities of access to educational and

cultural resources continue and even grow. The simplistic neocon-
servative calls for a monocultural literacy and return to the "classic"
chestnuts (read: traditional white male texts) surely cannot do.

A unifying notion of *cultural citizenship* in a *multicultural democracy* begins to articulate what a New York City public culture might
look like.[1] "Cultural citizenship is an identity that is formed not out
of legal membership but out of a sense of cultural belonging, The
definition of 'cultural' is broad, and can include multiple and sometimes opposing determinations of nationality, ethnicity, gender, race,
and class memberships. It draws upon difference as well as commonality and helps us to understand the heterogeneity of constructed
identities."[2]

As each separate area of "minority" cultural expression and scholarship has developed, the experiences have proven to be highly complex
and resistant to generalizations. The Chinese laundry worker, for example, proves to have many layers of experience and many correspond-
ing memories and identities, often contradictory. He may have come
from a rural farming village, have been a merchant marine on a British
steamer, lived in Jamaica married to a creole woman, and then moved
with his family to the wealthy and largely white West Village, where
their child is perceived by Chinese New Yorkers as a *haak gwe*, a
"black devil."

Diversity, therefore, should not be understood simply among groups
and individuals, but also within individual and group experience. Once
this is recognized, deeper connective insights, such as the migration
experience, the breakdown and reformation of families, the subjuga-
tion of cultural "otherness," or the forging of new shared identities
in movements advocating greater social justice, can be understood
to undergird apparently "different" experiences.

The challenge is to understand these undergirding commonalities
while at the same time not diminishing the uniqueness of the diverse
experiences. Multilayered experiences and multicontextual identities
become a common ground for defining what it might mean to be
a fully participating cultural citizen. By helping the sharing process
of Chinese and black experiences across cultural boundaries via such
interpretive discussions, we can help locate and strengthen those
deeper experiential streams underneath.

Linking Existing Resources: The Year Ahead

The Chinatown-Harlem Initiative is primarily a process-oriented
approach that demands that the quality of interaction be as important
as, and intimately interlinked to, the concrete end products and pro-

grams of such interaction. Indeed, it is the dialogue process itself, targeting shared objectives, which will most concretely produce the insights and understanding needed to offer meaningful and engaging public programs between the Chinatown and Harlem communities, thereby greatly strengthening future work.

Year one of the Chinatown-Harlem Initiative will entail the following work process:

Forming an advisory board. It is our sense that the careful selection of the advisory board will be one of the keys to our success. If nothing else, the pulling together of people committed to multicultural work forms a basis for future cooperation. We have been in the process of identifying a mix of persons with track records in community work, the humanities, education, and arts who are all strongly committed to building multicultural New York communities. This combination of nontraditional scholars, activists, and creative artists will be the heart of the initiative.

Building a network. The CHI advisory board will have a roundtable discussion at the beginning of the project to strategize, further shape up to five pilot projects, and identify a network of people within both communities who should be involved in the specific pilot projects. The entire board will meet again during the fourth month to assess progress and provide further guidance.

Dialogues and planning. A series of small discussion groups will be organized to plan and articulate the content of pilot projects. These dialogues will explore the following cross-cultural issues, among others: (1) perceptions and attitudes of blacks and Chinese about each other in recent memory and how these representations contrast with self-images; (2) the values and struggles of everyday life in both communities, and how concepts of "self-determination" and "empowerment" are thought about and acted upon; (3) how boundaries between communities are established spatially, historically, and psychologically; (4) deeper unifying experiences between blacks and Chinese, including what a common New York public culture might be like; and (5) the social policy implications of a multicultural democracy. These discussions will be recorded and edited for the year-end report. Advisors, along with appropriate people who have been identified in the network, will lead these discussions.

Pilot projects. Five pilot projects, each to be refined by the advisory board and the dialogue process, are designed to leave long-term bridges between Chinatown and Harlem. Audience response and participation will be fundamental to the planning of each project.

1. Special Chinatown-Harlem issue of *New Youth Connections*. As part of a media/journalism strategy, a special issue of *New Youth Connections* will be produced. This magazine, published eight times a year,

reaches 80,000 high school students in New York City. The special issue will cover such topics as reports on the dialogues, how blacks and Chinese relate and do not relate to each other, the connections between racial stereotyping and scapegoating violence, and so on.

2. Walking tours of the original black community in Chinatown. William David Chin, community education director of the History Project, will research and conduct a series of walking tours of the Chinatown area with special emphasis on the area's original black community in Manhattan. Some twenty-five tours for groups of twenty from both the Chinese and black communities will be given this first year. The tour will then be integrated into ongoing tours offered by the History Project.

3. Chinatown-Harlem media exchange. Chinese-American scholars, activists, artists, and educators will be featured in theme-centered discussions in print and electronic journalism reaching the black community and vice versa. Given the great importance of community-based media for each community, we expect these contacts to be the foundation for long-term cross-cultural relations between the media establishment of both communities and to influence how the mainstream press represents ethnic and racial groups in New York City.

4. Black History Month and Asian-Pacific Heritage Week program exchange. A series of cultural and educational exchanges will be organized during the 1990 programming for both events. The interrelationships of both communities, such as the civil rights movement and the 1965 immigration reform laws or the comparability of Chinese laundry workers and black women washerwomen, will be explored.

5. Multicultural conference. A year-end conference will involve all pilot project participants and a broader multicultural network. Testimonies, reports, and exploratory sessions will be organized. The conference will reflect upon what was learned, help refine strategies, and recommend proposals for projects for year two (for example, bicommunity curriculum projects for the fifth grade, or translating "Eyes on the Prize" into Korean, Cantonese, Spanish, and Mandarin and then getting it aired on local Asian and Spanish-language television stations). Proceedings will be recorded, transcribed, and edited for a special publication for the end of the year.

Year-end report and recommendations. A year-end Chinatown-Harlem initiative publication will contain testimonies from advisory roundtables, dialogue sessions, pilot projects, and the conference proceedings. The pamphlet will be distributed free of charge, and a press conference will be held announcing its publication.

Given that we are just launching the project, we cannot offer reflections on what has worked and what has not. But it is clear that the basic concerns we are trying to address are not unique to Asian and African-American New Yorkers. Dramatically changing demographics, well-established pecking orders of ethnicity, race, and gender, and national insecurities about the continued preeminence of the U.S. way of life all conspire to create variations of conflicts and possibilities across the country. The challenge before us is one of long-term bridge-building. Can we forge strong multicultural linkages during the spaces in between the frequent crises which besiege us? Can we begin to change the terms of everyday "common sense" race relations attitudes embedded in the daily occurrence of racial conflict and violence? Clearly, our active efforts to form and support vibrant multicultural identities, without homogenizing real experiential differences, must be given priority in our everyday work. We must create tools and open free spaces for this process to flourish.

Postscript: Looking to the 1990s

Since this initial plan was written, a small advisory panel has convened and on their advice, the project has decided that we will expand the initiative to include Manhattan's largely Latino community in East Harlem. We believe that the initiative's intended multicultural emphasis will be further served by including a third racial-ethnic group. The project is now called the Chinatown-Harlem-East Harlem Initiative.

Notes

This essay is the result of many collective efforts by the New York Chinatown History Project staff, board of directors, and extended family of the History Project. Specifically, I'd like to thank Charles Lai, Fay Chew, Judy Susman, Howard Dodson, Marta Yega, Jualynne Dodson, Diane Morates, Keith Hefner, Joan Maynard, Leon Denmark, James Early, Henry Sapoznik, Rina Benmayer, William David Chin, John Gwaltney, and Ana Celia Zentella for helping to formulate ideas which have ultimately been expressed in this plan. The New York Chinatown History Project can be contacted at: 70 Mulberry Street, New York, NY 10013.

1. "Cultural citizenship" is a term being developed by the Inter-University Project for Latino Research (IUP) at Hunter College, City University of New York, of which Dr. Rina Benmayor, a CHI advisor, is an active member.
2. IUP Culture Studies Working Group, "Concept Paper," 1988.

PART II

Perspectives

The articles in this section address key questions raised by the emergence of labor-community coalitions:

- Why is a labor-community axis developing at this time?
- How can and should coalition efforts relate to struggles to reform or transform the labor movement itself?
- What are the implications for labor-community alliance of the drive for labor-management cooperation?
- How should such coalitions deal with the continuing problems of racism and sexism?
- How can trade unions and community organizations mesh their differing traditions of organization, leadership, and democracy?
- What strategic perspectives can help such efforts achieve their goals?
- Do new forms of horizontal linkage among movements open new possibilities for democratic social change?

The essays in this section provide a variety of approaches to these questions, focusing on the relations among different constituencies, the organizational problems of cooperation, and the external environment within which labor-community alliances must operate.

American Labor: The Promise of Decline

Jeremy Brecher and Tim Costello

First the bad news. The 1980s were the most disastrous decade for organized labor in America since the 1920s. Union membership has decreased by 20 percent since 1979. Today less than 18 percent of American workers are union members—a smaller percentage than half a century ago. Along with the decrease of membership has come a loss of labor rights in the workplace, a decline in bargaining power, a waning of political clout, and even, for many workers, a decline in real wages.

Worse still, the causes of this decline are deeply embedded in the structure and strategy of the labor movement. In a half-century that has seen American society and the world economy transformed, organized labor has changed less than any other major social institution. Without a profound restructuring, the movement is unlikely to revive even in a more favorable economic and political climate. As former *New York Times* labor reporter William Serrin summed up in a recent *Village Voice* article, labor is marked by "a helpless leadership, energyless unions, and a tamed rank and file. The movement cannot go on the offensive, cannot organize, cannot confront its enemies, cannot lead its members or join with others . . . in pushing the programs the labor people talk about. Labor is a toothless, ossified institution."

Now the good news. While conservative hierarchs continue to control organized labor at the top, their power to perpetuate the movement's petrified structure and strategy has sharply declined. In the space opened up by their declining power, grassroots activists are developing effective alternatives to longstanding labor practices.

The Labor-Community Axis

Changes in the structure of the labor movement have been envisioned in various forms: the capture of existing unions by reform movements and opposition caucuses; a split at the top of the kind that brought about the CIO; a spontaneous mass upheaval like that which created Solidarity in Poland; the creation of radical unions that, like the Industrial Workers of the World (IWW or Wobblies), would grow outside the official House of Labor.

What seems to be developing instead—with little fanfare but enormous significance—is different from any of these. The characteristic, almost ubiquitous strategy is for local unions and labor activists to join in alliances of unions and community organizations with goals that go beyond the traditional limits of collective bargaining. Such alliances are weaving a dense web of cooperation and enormously broadening labor perspectives. They promise to redefine the labor movement from its roots up and to create a new political force in America.

So far as we know, nobody has even attempted to count these local partnerships, but they must number in the thousands. Wherever there are unions, there is likely now to be some kind of labor-community alliance. This article is based mostly on examples from the New England region; many readers will know similar examples from their own localities.

So far, labor-community efforts seem to take four principal forms, not new in themselves, but far more widespread now than at any time in the past forty years. These are (1) strike support, (2) issue coalitions, (3) community economic self-help, and (4) political action.

Strike support. The transformations of the American economy have made the traditional economic strike an ever weaker weapon for the labor movement. Diversified multinational companies can shift production from one location to another; profits lost in any one division have little effect on their overall profitability. Public employees, who form a growing proportion of the unionized workforce, have no profit stream to cut off; they *must* base their strategy on influencing the public. So unions have been forced to look for allies. Community-labor support committees are now normal features of major strikes.

A dramatic example was the strike against the International Paper Company centered in Jay, Maine. A weekly union-community meeting regularly attracted over 1,000 people. Caravans of strikers fanned out across New England, building support for a "corporate campaign" against companies with ties to International Paper. In Boston, for instance, the caravaners created a network of support groups which included local progressive unions, church groups, university students and employees, and even Central American solidarity organizations.

In many cases, coalitions formed to support strikes have become institutions like the New Haven Community-Labor Alliance, which grew out of a strike at Yale, or the Waterbury Community-Labor Support Committee, formed to support striking nurses. Such groups have subsequently engaged both in strike support and in other joint activities.

Community economic self-help. Many labor-community groups are engaged in resisting plant closings and deindustrialization by developing worker buy-outs, local economic development authorities, and other means of saving and creating jobs. The Naugatuck Valley Project in western Connecticut, for example, is an organization composed of more than sixty local union, church, and community groups. It has helped workers buy a local plant, found alternatives to the closing of other local companies, and helped tenants fight condominiumization. The Tri-State Conference on Steel has developed plans for regional reindustrialization in the "rust belt" and has successfully promoted the Steel Valley Authority as an alternative to private development.

Political action. A strong trend at present is for these coalitions to project themselves into the political arena. In Pittsburgh last year, a thirty-member coalition won a referendum to eliminate an at-large city council system that virtually disenfranchised both Afro-Americans and much of the working-class white community. In Hartford, a coalition of Puerto Rican, black, liberal, and labor groups recently formed an independent ticket, People for Change, which defeated Republican candidates for the powerful City Council—thus becoming the city's recognized opposition party. Shortly after, activists with a similar base took over Hartford's Democratic Town Committee. Waterbury's Community-Labor Support Committee has recently given birth to the Waterbury Progressive Caucus, as a step to creating a political organization inside the city's influential Democratic Party. Some labor activists, particularly teachers, participate in New Haven's Green Party.

A pioneering effort to put such efforts on a permanent footing is Connecticut's Legislative Electoral Action Program (LEAP). LEAP is a coalition initiated by UAW Region 9A and the Connecticut Citizens Action Group, a statewide community organizing and lobbying organization representing the interests of low and moderate income people. LEAP now has twenty-three member organizations, including Machinists. Service Employees, District 1199 (Health Care Workers), the State Federation of Teachers, environmental, women's, gay and lesbian, Afro-American, Puerto Rican, and other organizations. LEAP has recruited activists to run for state legislature and provided them with training and volunteers. Those elected with its support recently formed the Progressive Caucus in the Connecticut legislature. Marc Caplan, LEAP's founding director, is now running the Northeast Coalition Project, which has helped set up similar coalitions in New Hampshire, Maine, Massachusetts, New York, and elsewhere in the Northeast.

Issue coalitions. Coalitions have used public education, lobbying, and direct action confrontations to push issues ranging from plant closing legislation to expanded medical programs, housing, voter registration, electoral reform, and many others. In New Haven, the Community-Labor Alliance pressed for increased contributions from Yale University to the city; use of city pension funds to finance housing; divestment from South Africa; and development of a local school lunch program to provide both nutrition and employment.

Labor Isolationism

The labor movement originally developed as part of the broad movement for social reform in nineteenth-century America. Local labor organizations entered the political arena with labor tickets and labor parties, usually in cooperation with farmers and middle-class social reformers. That tradition reached its acme in the Knights of Labor, which rejected the wage system and drew together all branches of organized labor under the slogan "An injury to one is the concern of all."

But the American Federation of Labor (AFL) abandoned this tradition and built instead craft-based unions with a policy of "pure and simple unionism." The AFL became the dominant organization in the American labor movement from the 1890s on, and its traditions continue to shape the labor movement today.

The Wobblies used to refer to the AFL as "the American Separation of labor," and with good reason. The AFL cut skilled craftsworkers off from the rest of the workforce and from potential community allies. Its doctrine of "craft autonomy"—the independent identity and organization of carpenters, bricklayers, garment cutters, and other skill groups—discouraged solidarity among unions in the same industry or even the same plant.

The AFL's contract-oriented unionism centralized control in national union bureaucracies which soon became self-perpetuating political machines. The combination of craft autonomy and bureaucratization made the AFL itself little more than a collection of jostling fiefdoms.

Samuel Gompers and the other hierarchs of the AFL actively opposed union participation in efforts at social reform and aid to less favored segments of the workforce. Under their guidance, unions participated in politics—but only to pursue their interests as bricklayers (for building codes) or as male tradesmen (for restrictions on the employment of women), not as workers or citizens. Gompers' "pure and simple unionism" advocated "rewarding friends and punishing enemies" but forbade involvement with political parties or social reform. In practice, the AFL formed local alliances with the Democratic Party in most cities. With the coming of World War I, Gompers abandoned the pretense of independence and the AFL became part of President Wilson's war government. Its reward was a government policy that protected the AFL and crushed the IWW and other militant unionism.

The AFL's alliance with President Wilson and the Democratic Party proved useless after the war when business counterattacked with an open-shop drive that virtually drove unionism out of American industry. By 1930, less than 12 percent of American workers were members of unions.

In the 1930s, the CIO split from the AFL and created new industrial unions designed to overcome the "separation of labor" by organizing all nonmanagerial workers in a workplace into a single unit and grouping those units into unions covering entire industries.

The survival of the new industrial unions depended in large part on government protection of the right to organize. They therefore formed an alliance with the Democratic Party and actively opposed efforts at independent political action within their own ranks. When CIO leaders in Connecticut threatened to start a Labor Party to protest their exclusion from the higher councils of the state's Democratic Party, national CIO leader Sidney Hillman simply ordered them to "cut out the socialist shenanigans."

After World War II, American business began a second counteroffensive against labor, signalled by passage of the Taft-Hartley Act. Recognizing that "what was won at the bargaining table could be lost in Congress or the legislature," unions greatly expanded their political efforts. After the merger of the AFL and CIO in 1955, these efforts were centralized in the Committee on Political Education (COPE), which was a major actor in American politics during the 1950s, 1960s, and 1970s.

The central goal of the AFL-CIO in politics was to protect the organizational rights won by unions and to encourage an economic expansion which would make possible continuing gains at the bargaining table. In pursuit of those goals, the AFL-CIO was willing to maintain paper coalitions with civil rights, environmental, and other groups—as long as it remained the dominant partner and could restrain these groups from militant direct action or efforts at major social change. The AFL-CIO enthusiastically supported and continues to support the expansion of America's worldwide economic, military, and political hegemony; in 1988, it budgeted ten times as much on foreign affairs as on civil rights and three times as much as on labor organizing in the United States.

Labor historian David Montgomery has compared the AFL-CIO in the Meany era to a great snapping turtle, "hiding within its shell to shield the working class from contamination" and "snapping out" at those outside forces who venture too close. In 1972, the turtle snapped hard at those who wanted to support George McGovern or other anti-Vietnam war candidates. In 1984, it snapped hard at those in the labor movement—primarily black trade unionists—who wanted to campaign for Jesse Jackson; most were coerced to support Mondale instead. In 1986, it snapped hard at those who supported the Hormel strikers in Austin, Minnesota.

If today's hierarchs of the trade union establishment had their way, labor would no doubt continue to define unionism as negotiating over wages and working conditions and would limit political action to supporting Walter Mondales. But they are unlikely to have their way.

How the Turtle Lost Its Snap

As in the 1920s, the hierarchs of today's tumbledown House of Labor seek to veto the very grassroots efforts that could rejuvenate the movement. But the good news is, their veto power has declined along with their positive power. Few labor activists are intimidated any more when the turtle's jaws snap.

In 1987, for instance, AFL-CIO head Lane Kirkland campaigned against labor participation in the April 25 anti-apartheid, anti-contra aid demonstrations. A decade earlier, the veto would have prevailed. This time, dozens of unions, hundreds of locals, and tens of thousands of union members joined the marches.

Another indication is the inability of the AFL-CIO officialdom to control the movement's political course. Large numbers of both black and white trade unionists support Jesse Jackson, who represents everything the AFL-CIO has opposed within the Democratic Party. The AFL-CIO does not even try to repeat the anathema it leveled at Jackson in 1984.

Another litmus test is the AFL-CIO's acceptance of Ray Rogers, head of Corporate Campaigns, Inc., in the International Paper strike. This represents a quick switch from their open opposition to Rogers' role in the Hormel strike in 1986, when Lane Kirkland instructed local unions not to support the strikers.

A particularly dramatic and previously unreported example of lost veto power took place in Connecticut in 1987. Soon after the Northeast Coalition Project began to spread the LEAP model to other states, national COPE Director John Perkins sent a chilling letter to the AFL-CIO affiliates attacking "attempts—sometimes successful—by some community action groups not merely to work with labor in behalf of issues or candidates but to inject themselves into our endorsement and decision-making process. In one state, the community action group calls itself LEAP—Legislative Electoral Action Program. In other states they have other names."

Perkins also held meetings with Connecticut labor leaders at which he demanded that Central Labor Councils and all of their principal officers withdraw from LEAP. Many of those present expressed unexpectedly strong support for LEAP and outrage that national COPE was trying to tell them what organizations they could join. As one union leader put it, "Their goal was to shut down LEAP. Perkins' script was hard line. A lot of people took him on in the meeting. He was very surprised. The AFL-CIO then decided to rethink the issue: to their credit, they knew how to count."

LEAP-affiliated unions got national officials like William Winpisinger of the Machinists, Owen Bieber of the United Auto Workers (UAW), and John Sweeney of the Service Employees International Union (SEIU) to put pressure directly on Kirkland to back off from the Perkins demand. At a follow-up meeting, much to the surprise of the LEAP leadership, Perkins and AFL-CIO secretary-treasurer Thomas Donahue backed down completely, and Lane Kirkland subsequently decreed that participation in LEAP "would not be contrary to the AFL-CIO's rules or policies."

Significance of the Community-Labor Axis

The impulse toward labor-community alliances transcends "separation of labor" unionism based on craft or industrial sectors. It moves from a concept of "labor" as an exclusive group toward one which includes all working people, unionized or not, at work and in the rest of their lives. It moves toward decentralization of the labor movement and away from its control by a national bureaucracy.

The labor-community axis promises to be more than a coalition-of-convenience. It begins to redefine union locals not simply as units of a national union, but equally as expressions within the workplace of goals shared by the entire community of working people, locally, regionally, nationally, and internationally. What it means to be a good union member is beginning to include a responsibility to that wider community—to people who live across the street from the plant and people who live in South Africa, Poland, and Central America.

All forms of community-labor action seem to share this broadening effect. For example, a thirty-year old striker from Jay, Maine, when asked how the strike there had changed him and other strikers, answered, "It's made us very much more politically aware. There are now 1,200 people who are more involved in community affairs, state affairs, and ultimately world affairs." Says New Haven organizer Barbara Richards, "Our plant-closing campaign got union people together with people from other groups and unions. It built networks and trust rapidly."

UAW international representative Hank Murray adds, "Ten years ago, the UAW CAP had a defensive legislative agenda, featuring issues like protecting unemployment compensation regulations. Today LEAP represents their agenda—and LEAP's agenda is very broad, including even such issues as gay rights. It's impressive to see local leaders enthusiastically embrace such a program as their own."

According to Marc Caplan, this broadening of perspective outlasts particular efforts. "LEAP has created a climate supportive to collective action on many issues. Building trust through working together is part of the effort. LEAP by example encourages people to think in terms of coalitions and allies. The key is that movements more and more make these initiatives collectively." This, he adds, requires unions that are willing to work as equal, not dominant, partners.

One of the vicious effects of the "separation of labor" has been its separation of worker-as-worker from worker-as-citizen, as human being, as member of the human family and resident of the global ecosphere. Allegedly in the interest of jobs for workers, unions have lobbied for weapons systems that make war more likely and for nuclear reactors that threaten to make workers glow. Labor-community alliances are beginning to reunify workers-as-workers with their other roles in life. Only a labor movement that allows for the full humanity of working people will be able—or deserve—to grow.

Organization

Some labor-community alliances function purely as networks which create ad hoc organizations to campaign around particular issues. Some have a formal organization with officials, delegates from organizations, and regular meetings; some even have their own offices and staff. So far, no one form has established itself as ideal. Form needs to follow function, and labor-community organizations tend to evolve in response to changing needs and conditions.

Drawing together disparate groups requires an active willingness to cooperate combined with a sensitivity to the need of each group to retain its independence. Much of LEAP's success, for example, resulted from its identification of a political strategy on which many movements could agree: the backing of a select group of political candidates with strong activist credentials. At the same time, each LEAP-affiliated organization retained its own autonomy, including its own independent endorsement policies. An attempt to merge the twenty-three constituent groups, or even their political action efforts, would have been doomed to failure.

Some, such as Barbara Richards of the New Haven Community-Labor Alliance, point out advantages of organizations based on individual membership. "They're more democratic because individuals can participate directly, not just through leaders of the member organizations. And you aren't bound by the official policies of dozens of other groups."

Yet many of the most successful alliances so far have organizations as members. Groups such as the Naugatuck Valley Project (NVP) and LEAP characteristically are run by boards made up of officers of constituent organizations. Supporters of this approach point out the relative ease of building on existing organizations, the importance of drawing on their clout, and the value of drawing existing groups into a dialogue around common interests.

Many community-labor partnerships are hybrids. Much of the money and clout even for the membership groups actually comes from unions and other established institutions. Conversely, such groups as NVP and LEAP often develop a cadre of activists who identify directly with the organization and participate in its work as well as remaining active in constituent groups.

Perhaps the goal needs to be stated not as movement toward a single conglomerate organization that subsumes all distinct groups—the role aspired to, for example, by most European mass parties—but rather as an ever-extending *process* of cooperation. What we need may look like a single organization for purposes of the issues shared in common, but like a coalition of distinct groups with respect to other issues.

The Political Arena

Community-labor alliances are increasingly entering the electoral arena, becoming a new political force in many communities and providing much of the local muscle for the impressive victories of Jesse Jackson's presidential campaigns. This poses many questions, not just questions of tactics and strategy, but more fundamental questions about the relation of electoral and nonelectoral activity, how to keep elected officials accountable, and how to retain the movement's independence.

Labor-community alliances have taken very different approaches to electoral politics. Groups such as the Naugatuck Valley Project may propose legislation and lobby for it, but remain strictly nonpartisan in elections; this allows opponents in the political arena to cooperate within the organization. Such an alliance may win support from politicians of both parties on locally important issues. Says NVP leader Rev. Tim Benson, "In our by-laws, we tried to delineate that we need to keep a distance from the political process. We can't be in any political party's pocket, or any politician's pocket, because as soon as we are, we lose our effectiveness as an organization." Groups such as LEAP, by contrast, actively recruit and campaign for political candidates.

Because resources are so often in short supply, there may be direct competition between electoral and nonelectoral organizing. In many communities the decline in resources available for door-to-door community organizing has been aggravated by the shift of organizations such as the Connecticut Citizens Action Group (CCAG) to an electoral focus. Steve Schrag, a former community organizer and now an SEIU health and safety staffer, is active in electoral campaigns but suspects that "if we put as much energy into direct action as we're putting into elections, it would tear the power structure apart." Conversely, electoral activists complain about those who remain aloof from crucial electoral efforts.

Electing responsive officials is necessary but not sufficient for social change. As Jerry Brown, Secretary-Treasurer of Local 1199 (health and hospital workers), put it, "There are a lot of levers of power in this society. Economic power is the most direct. But now economic power requires political power."

Perhaps electoral action can best be seen as part of a "constellational" strategy in which the electoral arena is recognized as one, but only one, battlefield—along with workplaces, communities, media, education, and others. While electoral and nonelectoral forms of action may contrast in theory, in practice they are often synergistic. Political action won extended unemployment benefits for the International Paper strikers in Jay, Maine; conversely, the strike experience and Jesse Jackson's widely publicized support for it is credited with Jackson's unanticipated success in the Maine primaries. The Naugatuck Valley Project's first step in a recent housing campaign was a voter registration drive for tenants. Hartford's People for Change city council ticket grew out of support efforts for strikers at Colt and a three-year struggle for a program of "linkage" which would force downtown developers to contribute to urban needs.

Such synergism can itself be a goal. Doreen Del Bianco, long a CCAG activist and one of LEAP's first legislative candidates, says, "During my campaigns I focus on the same issues I worked on as an activist—environment, plant closings, and health care—and I stage events with local groups around these issues."

Worldwide, social movements have been developing many new

models for coordinating efforts to change society. The German Green Party, for example, has simultaneously run candidates for parliament, organized mass direct-action confrontations with the government, and fostered independent countercultural institutions. Adam Michnik, a leader of the Polish independent opposition, asks, "Should people act by creating independent institutions unrecognized by the authorities or by struggling inside official institutions with the aim of winning them over? This question resembles the classic problem, 'Should I wash my hands or my feet?' Both!"

The LEAP model is one possible form for such a policy of "walking on two legs." Like the German Greens, it involves running a ticket of movement activists; but because LEAP remains a coalition, not a party, it may be less likely to exacerbate tensions between militant direct action and electoral efforts.

Labor-community coalitions are encouraging and training activists to run for public office. They are creating political organizations, such as Hartford People for Change, the Waterbury Progressive Caucus, and the New Haven Green Party. They are also running for Democratic Party positions; a group backed by labor, Hispanic, and various other organizations, for example, recently won party delegate elections and took over the Democratic Town Committee in Hartford, Connecticut. Similarly varied strategies can no doubt be found in other parts of the country.

How such efforts should relate to the Democratic Party seems to be largely a tactical question. LEAP became a significant power in Connecticut politics when it successfully ran candidates in primaries against conservative incumbent Democrats. In Connecticut, election laws still give party committees most of the power to select candidates, yet the Democratic Party organization itself is fairly weak in terms of its ability to deliver votes. This has led to a strategy of trying to expand representation on Democratic committees in major cities. LEAP co-director Nick Nyhart points out that in states where candidates raise their own funds and recruit their own volunteers, capturing party organizations may be less important.

These varied efforts and others like them in other parts of the country have demonstrated that alliances of labor and community can elect candidates who call themselves progressives. But, as historical experience has repeatedly shown, it is easier to elect candidates to office than to hold them accountable. Says Jerry Brown of District 1199, "Many politicians have used the labor movement to rise to power and then have ended up as part of the problem." Many a political boss was a reformer once. Two techniques are being used to encourage accountability. One is described by Marc Caplan: "In today's political environment, progressive organizations too often talk in terms of an 'us-them' relationship in which candidates and elected officials are 'them.' The LEAP approach is to make it 'they are us' by running a candidate who is 'one of us.' We are building a movement. Politicians remain part of it. All this helps keep them accountable." Leap co-director Rebecca Doty adds, "The Progressive Caucus in the legislature helps keep our legislators accountable to each other and to their progressive constituency."

The other technique is the ability of organizations to withdraw support. Says Nick Nyhart, "Accountability comes down to a power relationship. Even those legislators who don't have a movement background want to stay on the good side of LEAP so they can get support to move up. LEAP is either an asset or a problem for people who want to run, say, for governor."

Organizations sometimes attempt to enforce accountability by announcing clearly defined programs which a candidate must support as the price of endorsement. But such clear definitions are hard to reach in a coalition; LEAP, for example, has been built on the assumption that it is easier to get different groups to agree about candidates than about program details. Says Nyhart, "LEAP doesn't hold people to a 100 percent standard for endorsement, but it will fight them when they go too far astray." What that means in practice has yet to be fully tested.

Underlying the problem of accountability is a reality that no electoral strategy can overcome. As long as society contains undemocratic power centers such as corporations and entrenched bureaucracies that can influence politicians through financial contributions, patronage, media access, inside information, and flattery, political representatives will never be fully accountable to their constituents. Capitalist democracy can therefore never be truly democratic. Representatives can be truly accountable only when the power of corporations and government bureaucracies is devolved to socially responsible institutions.

Throughout history, social movements that enter the electoral arena have been changed by the processes at work there. The search for votes leads to a reduction in the movement's demands. More insidiously, success itself can present real dangers. Unionists or reformers can become part of the inner councils of the power structure, for example in the Democratic Party. After a while the boundary between their base and the Democratic Party becomes vaguer, their loyalty more doubtful. Party candidates and officials are expected to support the entire party ticket, no matter how offensive some candidates may be. A union official who recently contemplated running for office was told that he could not run as a Democrat unless not only he but also his union supported the head of the Democratic ticket.

Because representative institutions cannot be made fully accountable within the present structure of society, social movements must retain independence from the electoral arena. Jerry Brown of 1199 warns: "There is a danger of the push into politics. The more you sit down with politicians, the harder it is to get up from the table and call them SOBs. The only reason they sit down with us is because if they don't, we can call them SOBs. But it gets harder each time you sit down with them.

"There are real dangers in success. It would be wonderful if the governor, legislators, and mayors looked to LEAP as their mentor. But a union has to jealously guard its ability to fight with them. If we elected someone governor, the first thing we would have to do is pick a fight with him. It's important to fight for those who will advance your cause, but then you must maintain a reasonable pissing distance from them.

"Labor must be in opposition until workers run the society. Even if coalition gets our people elected, we're still going to be fighting Colt.

"In the labor movement, you always make compromises; just signing a contract is in a sense a sell-out of permanent struggle. The purpose of power is to get a seat at the table, but once you get there, it is harder to get up and and get away. It's a delicate thing to balance the importance of being insiders to help our members with an ability to attack from outside."

Social progress in the United States has often come from a dialectic of insurgency and reform—interactions between anti-slavery abolitionism and the Republican Party, industrial radicalism and the New Deal, the civil rights movement and the Great Society. It is often politicians' fear of social disruption and of losing their mass base that leads them to institute reforms.

Despite inevitable tension between working inside the system, confronting power holders, and building independent institutions, all three can potentially work together as elements of a common strategy. Part of the key to such synergism lies in developing a set of goals that can unite disparate elements of a labor-community bloc. The need to formulate such goals has become a common concern of activists of many stripes.

Impediments to the New Communalism

Temma Kaplan

There is cause for optimism in the United States right now. Although old, blue-collar unions are declining, new unions of clerical and health workers are blooming. Non-Traditional Employment for Women (NEW) is setting up apprenticeship programs to train poor women for the lucrative jobs in construction work from which they have been excluded. Polluters are meeting their match in broad-based community groups, many of them led by women fighting for their families' survival. Peace movements, dominated by women, have made an impact on the superpowers and have compelled arms reductions. Groups such as the Sisterhood of Black Single Mothers take on the welfare system and generate ideas about new kinds of family-support systems. Jesse Jackson's presidential campaigns and the organization he has built based on local movements all over the country has set the stage for a confederation that could unite the energy of local, sometimes single-issue campaigns with the power to seize the initiative and vie for office at the state and national levels. A new kind of communalism has emerged.

By "new communalism," I mean political associations of people organized around concrete issues affecting everyday life. Such movements are generally dedicated to social justice, to righting wrongs, to reshaping political and social life for all people. They try to unite life and work and they realize that human dignity—an essential part of human life—entails providing the entire community with all the goods and benefits it needs. Instead of endorsing abstract doctrines, they promote a more democratic version of what they already know, what they have already experienced that they want to enhance in the future.

Communalist movements go beyond traditional hierarchical organizations in trade unions, political parties, and church groups to create new kinds of associations or transform the old ones. Cooperation, often through committees devoted to specific tasks, undergirds most of these organizations, which generally eschew traditional systems of authority. They use informal neighborhood and friendship networks to create strong bonds among people. Since people in the United States are generally grouped by friendship and housing according to race and class, this lends homogeneity to many communalist movements. The new communalists view themselves as capable of shaping their own lives if only they remove the collective forces grouped against them: with government or corporate interests gone, the group could function more effectively.

In their democratic goals and their attacks on hierarchical relationships the new communalist movements, no matter what their percentage of women, echo practices that have characterized grassroots organizations of women. Many social movements of women are unconsciously organized according to "female consciousness," a term I coined to explain what drives so many social movements in which women have engaged.

By "female consciousness," I mean what most women are taught to think are the proper rights and obligations of women. The content varies by class, culture, and historical period. What does not vary is that all children are taught what their society thinks is appropriate gender behavior. From childhood, most girls learn that they are the people responsible for feeding, clothing, housing, and preserving their family and community. But if they learn these obligations, they also learn that they have the right to do what is necessary to fulfill them. This has brought women into conflict with governments and other authorities around food, housing, sanitation, schools, and efforts to win peace. Unions and political groups have often put women and children up front when confronting repressive forces because the men, as well as soldiers and police, often recognize these special rights of women acting in the interests of their communities. Governments' and organizations' reluctance to attack women and children pursuing traditional survival interests sometimes gives women the leverage men of their class and race lack.

Some examples of what I call "female consciousness movements" come to mind. In February 1917, Russian women protested against the cabbage and bread shortages of World War I and ignited the first in a series of revolutions that destroyed tsarism. In South Africa today, refugee women whose homes were bulldozed in areas now reserved for whites created a community capable of providing sanitation, health care, and education for their children. In today's Chile, Mujeres por la Vida, Women for Life, mobilizes women of all classes, organizing spectacles that amount to guerrilla theater to protest against the deteriorating conditions of life in Pinochet's Chile. They mobilized the "No" campaign that forced Pinochet to consider stepping down in 1989.

The new communalist movements often resemble female consciousness movements in that communalists place human survival and improving the quality of life rather than ideological struggles at the forefront of politics. They assume that politics is a means to an end, and that end is preserving and enhancing life.

The new communalism suffers from some of the same structural problems that have historically beset grassroots movements in which women predominate. The committee form of organization, though highly democratic, means that there is very little division of labor and very little time off. The rate of burn-out of activists is extremely high. Because direct rather than representative democracy is the prevailing ethos, people who cannot spend a lot of time in committee meetings can seldom get their views across. As Oscar Wilde foresaw about socialism, communalism requries too many evenings at meetings. This practice erodes the possibilities that women with families can participate to the same degree as men, who bear less responsibility for child care.

Both communalist and consciousness movements are subject to charges of racism and sexism if they do not directly confront both of these issues along with any others they pursue. Women's movements at least incorporate the interests of some women, although they are sometimes wildly insensitive to racial differences. Communalist movements—no matter how many women or people of color they have in them—often presume that sex and race make no difference. They frequently hold their own trickle-down theories, according to which improvement in the condition of nonelite people will necessarily help all women and people of color. When white men do not stipulate race or gender, they get sucked into the undertow of the prevailing cultural beliefs. Unfortunately, in the United States, these cultural beliefs are both sexist and racist. Without special efforts to overcome the cultural drag, the communalist movements are doomed to incorporate the worst traits of American society.

The movements based on female consciousness have flaws of their own. Unlike feminists, who attack the division of labor by sex and challenge attributes and roles assigned according to gender, grassroots women's movements operating according to female consciousness do not confront stereotypes about women; they use them to proclaim a higher law, a more important community than the municipality or the state. Women enter resistance movements when housing and food shortages, unpopular wars and violence, pollution, or lack of health care, housing, educational facilities, or child care inhibit poor women's ability to care for their communities in a way they think is not only their obligation but their birthright. Traditionally and cross-culturally, these are the "women's issues."

Although movements around survival issues are highly political, even when they begin around economic issues, and although such movements have been the primary organizational form among poor women of all races here and abroad, they skirt important power relations. Squeamish about confronting men of their class and race, the members of these movements seldom raise questions about marital rape, battering, or other forms of private violence against women; hence they preserve gender relations. On the other hand, female consciousness, insofar as it is synonymous with social consciousness, has shaped American feminism. In electoral politics this has sometimes appeared as the gender gap, according to which women are on the whole more sensitive than men to such issues as health care, housing, aid to the disadvantaged, and educational reform.

The most far-reaching impact feminism and female consciousness have made has been on unions of clerical and hospital workers. New unions, made up of previously unorganized—and seemingly unorganizable—women and people of color, incorporate the social concerns, especially of the civil rights movement, of the past twenty years. The local of the American Federation of State, County and Municipal Employees (AFSCME) at the University of California Los Angeles (UCLA) Medical Center is an example. This group began life as a committee of African-American workers. When they decided to carry out a unionization drive, they made child care for the entire university population one of their main demands. The fact that the staff was overwhelmingly women who bore primary responsibility for children made the need for child care obvious. The UCLA local, with its feminist concern to win equal wages for women and its female consciousness, attuned to the importance of social issues such as health care and child care, would not choose between the needs of families and improved working conditions; they fought for both simultaneously. Increasingly, demands for child support from employers have become a regular part of union struggles, as they are consistently with District 65 of the United Auto Workers (UAW) in its negotiations with Columbia University.

Questions about parental leave, flex time, and child care would not have been raised in unions without the extraordinary increase in labor-force participation of women with young children. Half of all women with children under one year are now working for wages. And the rise in the number of single mothers who head households has led women to organize their own groups; Sisterhood of Black Single Mothers, a multipurpose grassroots organization, is an example. Parent-teacher associations and organizations dedicated to improving education, moreover, have always been the special concern of women. Women overwhelmingly make up coalitions to house the homeless and countless other efforts to improve life for themselves and the broader community. Now that so many grassroots organizations exist,

the next step seems to be in confederating single-issue groups throughout the country. And that step is slippery with moss.

Most communalist movements in which women do not predominate
try to win women and people of color to struggles in which the main
outlines have already been set by white men. Men concerned with
workplace reform or improvement in medical care seldom recognize
protection of women's fertility or federally financed abortions or support for the anti-battering movement as primary goals. These generally
remain subordinate issues delegated either to women members or
to women's organizations. The issue of comparable worth never arises
unless people of color or women raise it themselves, increasingly
through new unions. On the other hand, movements which choose
a racist or sexist course, even as a short-run strategy, risk becoming
part of the order they claim to oppose.

One particularly egregious example of making concessions to racism
in the name of other goals—in this case feminist goals—came during
the 1988 electoral campaign. The National Abortion Rights Action
League (NARAL) participated on behalf of a mild supporter of abortion
rights in the electoral campaign in Queens, a white, lower-middle-class
borough of New York City. A leading student activist who happened
to be black was asked not to campaign in Queens because she would
promote a racist backlash. No movement can agree for expediency's
sake to accommodate racism unless it is willing to incorporate racism
into its movement, as so many grassroots movements have. It is especially important in fact to build an anti-racist commitment into every
social movement in America, no matter what its primary goal. In
a racist country, not to oppose racism as a fundamental principle dooms
the entire movement.

The same is true of sexism. In the communalist movements, as
in the traditional hierarchical parties and trade unions, it is common
for leaders to embrace issues affecting women and children and then
delegate women to articulate and pursue the associated political tasks.
Peggy McIntosh, writing about the development of women's studies,
has spoken about the "add-women-and-mix" syndrome. By extension
to communalist movements, this means anything having to do with
women is included as an appendix to the organization's main issues.
Most grassroots movements that are not specifically organized around
so-called women's issues, including child care and reproductive rights,
have never incorporated these demands as part of their primary goals.
To do so would entail the reorientation of priorities and procedures.
Unions, for example, would have to prioritize paid maternity leave,
subsidies for child care and care for aged relatives, medical plans
to pay for abortions, and demands for comparable worth. Only by

stressing issues that pertain to all women can a movement overcome the always-present menace of racism and sexism.

It is not racists and sexists who are the greatest threat to the new social movements; it is, unfortunately, the people of good will who have not yet recognized how deeply embedded racism and sexism are in the new movements. Here in this book as elsewhere, the words "community" and "labor movement" are even today used without specifying whether women and people of color are differentially affected. This blind spot occurs despite women's predominance in some segments of the labor, peace, and ecology movements and the struggles to win rights for the homeless.

Some of these problems, which afflict even the community-based unions, are carry-overs from traditional labor culture, which is saturated with sexism in its language, jokes, and lifestyles. The male bonding that typifies these organizations—drinking together, telling dirty jokes, fistfights on picket lines—has traditionally been part of what has given them their strength. Quoting Jerry Brown of District 1199 (health and hospital workers) about the dangers of labor's incorporation in representative institutions, the editors of this volume echo the message that "It's important to fight for those who will advance your cause, but then you must maintain a reasonable pissing distance from them" (see "American Labor: The Promise of Decline").

Cheap jibes aside, the problem remains. Despite Jeremy Brecher and Tim Costello's optimistic view that "What it means to be a good union member is beginning to include a responsibility to that wider community—to people who live across the street from the plant and people who live in South Africa, Poland, and Central America" the reality is that it is just as hard in those countries to raise issues about women as it is in the United States. In Nicaragua, only the women's solidarity groups were willing to discuss the fact that the greatest cause of death of women in their childbearing years is related to childbirth and septic abortions. Since the Sandinistas' governing junta has two Jesuits and no women, it is perhaps not surprising that it was considered uncomradely in Nicaragua—as well as in U.S. support groups—to raise questions about providing abortions for the women who need them in Nicaragua.

Except in communalist movements particularly devoted to women and people of color, commitment to so-called women's issues or matters of special concern to people of color has seldom been a priority. Groups such as the now-defunct Massachusetts Fair Share—while dedicating themselves to reducing the cost of utilities and defeating a right-wing judge—refused to address issues about neighborhood segregation among its white ethnic constituency.

The successes of the Rainbow Coalition and Jesse Jackson's personal commitments to scores of strikes and multiracial community action projects show that anti-racist coalitions are possible. A man who originally opposed abortions, Jackson came to recognize the importance of free choice for all women. He also consistently brought up the issue of gay and lesbian rights, even when there was no political gain to be made. By not underestimating ordinary people, the Jackson campaigns have done a great deal to knit together groups that have often been antagonistic.

This leads to a consideration of whether people are limited by their own sexual and racial histories or whether they can go beyond their own experiences to comprehend the meaning of what other people have undergone. If white men take their own experiences as emblematic of the experiences of all people, the tilt is always going to be toward racism and sexism. White men have an obligation to comprehend what people of color and women have suffered, not the reverse. The same goes for white women in relation to men and women of color. This seems obvious, but it is one of the principal stumbling blocks in most communalist and consciousness movements.

Problems aside, it is possible to incorporate the specific needs of different groups into a common program. An early reproductive rights organization called CARASA has continued in its pursuit of free choice for women. African-American and white women originally had bitter disputes about where to place the emphasis in struggles over reproduction. While white women thought they were struggling for all women by demanding "Free Abortion on Demand," women of color were distraught about sterilization abuses that occurred in all major metropolitan hospitals. The acronymn CARASA stands for the Committee on Abortion Rights and Against Sterilization Abuse, which links the demand of all women for free, safe abortions with the demands of women of color who still suffer forced sterilizations in many regions of this country.

There are other examples of mixed groups who work together. The Center for Constitutional Rights is a civil liberties group with a broad range of concerns. But its women and men have chosen to concentrate not only on "generic" civil liberties issues, but on issues such as abortion—regarded by many as a "women's issue." And it has done so in a way which focuses on how limitations on abortion affect poor women and women of color.

There do not seem to be many alternatives to integrating the main concerns of women and people of color into the communalist movements if we hope these movements will provide models for future democracy in the United States. It is not up to women and people of color to overcome the gravitational pull of racism and sexism; it is up to the people who have never viewed themselves as subject to its vagaries to overcome these particular inequities daily, in everything they do. Women and people of color can help white men and women gain new perspectives, but only if white people and all men recognize that there is something important at stake.

There is great cause for hope. The emergence of the new communalism and its increasing consciousness about race and gender promises new possibilities for this country. The strengths of consciousness movements, which are also their weaknesses, provide new models for political practice if they can be modified. The same women who often form committees, work on projects, go home, and then reactivate their telephone trees when the next crisis comes along need more consistent organizational forms.

But the sense of solidarity built up over many struggles can go a long way toward correcting the hierarchical character of traditional male organizations. The crystallization common to the communalist movements, which often are coalitions, can help overcome the fluidity of the movements governed by female consciousness. A lot has happened to everyone in grassroots movements over the past few years, and it would be an all-too-American tragedy to let these organizations drown in racism and sexism.

Building a Labor Movement for the 1990s: Cooperation and Concessions or Confrontation and Coalition

Kim Moody

The decline of American trade unions is by now recognized by all and the genuflection to the need for new strategies as firmly entrenched in the ritual of the labor hierarchy as in the demands of union dissidents. Yet, there are two very different responses to the crisis of unionism taking shape in the United States: labor-management cooperation versus labor's traditional adversarial role in determining workers' standard of living and shaping the workplace. Among the latter, those who see the conflict between labor and capital as unavoidable, the apparent weakness of U.S. labor's major defensive institutions and tactics has produced an increasing willingness to experiment with broader social alliances as a means of strengthening and supplementing traditional labor solidarity.

Organized labor's decline as a numerical proportion of the U.S. workforce has been long and fairly gradual. Union membership as a proportion of nonfarm employment fell from 32.5 percent in 1953 to 16.8 percent in 1988. This decline was very gradual in the 1950s and 1960s, but accelerated in the 1970s and 1980s, losing about six percentage points in each decade. The collapse of U.S. labor's major institutional lines of defense, on the other hand, was rapid and spectacular. In only a few years, by the second half of the 1980s, the national multi-employer, industry-wide contracts established in most basic industries during the 1940s was almost completely dismantled. Known as pattern bargaining, this system that had advanced wages and benefits for millions of workers for nearly forty years was rapidly replaced with a decade of wage deceleration. Long-term contracts, once sanctified as immutable, were routinely opened and reopened at the whim of management to yield contractual concessions of all kinds. Business norms of competition replaced labor's historic fight to "take labor out of competition" by standardizing wages and benefits.

The official explanation for the virtual collapse of the major pillars of postwar business unionism focuses on foreign competition and imports. As with labor's organizational decline, the roots of concessionary and competitive bargaining are presumed to be external. Yet, as real as the forces of global economic integration are, this economic reductionism is more self-serving than illuminating.

The integrity of the union contract and wage and benefits pattern ultimately rests either on employer tolerance, which ran short during the 1970s and 1980s, or on the union's own ability to enforce the integrity of these protective institutions. The bureaucratization of union structure, the near monopolization of the bargaining process by the national headquarters, the suppression of political pluralism, and the virtual gutting of shop-floor organization accomplished by the CIO leadership in the 1940s effectively demobilized the rank and file of the new industrial unions. The removal of grievance determination from the shop floor and the shop steward to the union's regional or central office dampened the energy and incentive in workplace contract enforcement. Contract enforcement, like negotiations, became the monopoly of the central bureaucracy in almost all of the industrial unions. Even unions with decentralized bargaining structures typically adopted the practice of making the international union a signatory to the contract in order to place final legal authority in the hands of the top leaders. In effect, the bureaucracy itself became the contract enforcer. The membership, on the other hand, became the demobilized recipients of contract benefits and other union services.

So long as the economy allowed management to leave contractual integrity in order, this system appeared to work well enough. This set-up, it was thought, was backed by the law of the land. Contract enforcement became a fairly routine matter of administration by the early 1950s and remained so for over two decades. The occasional withdrawal of labor was sufficient to produce progress when employers occasionally showed resistance. When the effects of global integration pushed management toward a more hostile and aggressive posture in bargaining, including the use of scabs in more and more cases, the U.S. labor bureaucracy was unprepared for this attack and unable to draw the line. The generation of top union leaders that commanded the unions by the end of the 1970s had never experienced "class warfare," as former UAW president Doug Fraser put it in horror in 1978. They were administrators of demobilized organizations who believed the law and the Democratic Party would save the day. When neither the law nor the party proved reliable, the labor leadership reeled from one retreat to the next.

The hope that union concessions were a temporary phenomenon of the 1980–82 recession or limited to "troubled" firms and industries collapsed by the mid-1980s, as givebacks swept from auto and steel into every unionized sector of the economy, including services and public employment. Average private sector wage increases shrank from

9.8 percent in 1981 to 1.2 percent in 1986. In manufacturing, 1986 saw a decline of -1.2 percent, the first such recorded average decline since the early 1930s. By the late 1980s the real wages of manufacturing workers were below the 1973 level.

Resistance, however, was not an easy choice for most workers. The employers clearly meant business and most union leaders sent the unambiguous message that resistance was futile. First, they joined the corporate chorus by teling their members that they would lose their jobs if they did not submit. Second, when workers did not simply surrender, the leaders allowed passively waged strikes to drag on until the workers accepted some level of concessions or, worse, until scabs had replaced the strikers and decertification lay just around the corner. Strikes such as those at Phelps Dodge (1983–84), Greyhound (1983), and Wheeling Pittsburgh (1985) seemed to prove that the strike was no longer effective and militancy would be self-defeating. Not everyone, however, drew the intended lesson.

Resistance and New Tactics

Almost from the start, many local unions and a handful of smaller international unions began to experiment with new and old tactics. Some of these involved simply breaking the business unionist notion of solidarity as something limited to those workers immediately affected and began reaching out to others. An example that surprised almost everyone involved was the 1984 strike at A. P. Parts, a small auto parts producer in Toledo, Ohio. By the standards of the 1980s, this strike of about 300 members of Local 14 of the United Auto Workers (UAW) should have been a loser. But on May 21 this conventional strike took Toledo's business community by storm when some 3,000 workers showed up for a plant-gate rally on two hours' notice. For most of the day, the demonstrators fought scabs and police in what seemed to many a reenactment of the 1934 Toledo Auto-Lite strike. The UAW international stepped in to prevent any more mass actions, but the A. P. Parts strike became a cause célèbre with many UAW locals in Ohio and Michigan. With financial and material support from many locals the strikers held out for nine months, beat most of the concessions, and got the scabs removed from the plant. If spectacular events like the May 21 demonstration remained rare, material and financial solidarity became an increasingly common feature of strikes in the 1980s.

Increasingly, a broader range of innovative tactics were employed where strikes seemed inappropriate or inadequate. In Region 5 of the UAW, running from Missouri down to Texas, Jerry Tucker, then assistant to the regional director, experimented with an in-plant strategy he called "running the plant backward." Instead of walking out in a conventional strike and allowing the company to bring in scabs, the workers took action in the plant itself. This was guerrilla warfare on the shopfloor: employing old tactics such as the slowdown, a bit of workplace street theatre, outside demonstrations by spouses and other supporters, and occasional "quickie strikes" where workers remained at their jobs but performed no work. What was most unconventional, from the vantage point of classic business unionist practice, was that the union allowed the contract to expire. This freed the workers from the contract's no-strike clause and, in theory, granted them the protection of the Wagner Act's "concerted action" provision. This inside strategy worked well at Moog Electronics in 1983 and later at an LTV Steel plant in Texas. This innovation received a measure of official endorsement when the Industrial Union Department of the AFL-CIO published a how-to manual entitled "The Inside Game."

One of the most innovative struggles of the 1980s was the fight against concessions at the Morse Cutting Tool plant in New Bedford, Massachusetts. Gulf & Western bought Morse in 1968. Rather than investing in the plant, however, G&W milked it for profits. Looking at Morse from a global perspective, G&W decided it was no longer competitive and began pushing for concessions in 1981. In spite of the threat to move the work elsewhere, the union, United Electrical Workers Local 277, resisted. The UE international union, one of the few with a no concessions policy, stood behind Local 277. A campaign was waged in New Bedford to convince the community that either concessions or a closing at Morse would hurt the town's economy. A Citizens Committee to Support the Morse Workers was formed, including thirty-five other unions and various community groups. A strike by Local 277 in 1982, backed by much of the town, forced G&W to back off for the moment. When G&W renewed its demands and threats, the mayor of New Bedford was persuaded to threaten the use of eminent domain if G&W tried to move any of the equipment out of the plant. G&W sold the plant in 1985. Local 277 eventually made some concessions in 1986 to keep the plant open, but the labor-community coalition organized by the UE remains a model of creative resistance.

Reaching Out

One of the major lessons learned by those who chose to resist management aggression, whether it was fighting for union recognition or resisting concessions and plant closings, was to reach beyond the union or even beyond organized labor to other constituencies. In one sense, this was really the relearning of an older practice. Typically, the early strikes that led to the formation of the CIO involved massive community mobilizations as well as coalitions with other social groups, such as farmers in the 1934 Minneapolis Teamster strike, unemployed workers in the Toledo Auto-Lite strike of the same year, or Detroit's black community in the organization of Ford at the end of the 1930s. The dramatic General Motors (GM) sit-down strike in Flint, Michigan, in 1936–37 not only mobilized the entire working-class community of that city, but brought in thousands of workers from around the Midwest to support those in the plants.

The idea of community outreach and broad social coalitions, how-ever, also springs from the dramatic changes in the relationship of working-class communities to the workplace. The global integration of the U.S. economy, the migration of industrial plants from the central cities to suburbs and exurbs, and the fragmentation of working-class communities that accompanied their suburbanization in many cases all contributed to a growing physical separation of residence and work in the decades following World War II. Thus, even the mobilization of working-class community groups came to require a special effort and a sense of strategy to accomplish what came more naturally to earlier generations of workers. When the CIO was built, the only major coalition that required a special approach was that between a largely white labor movement and the black community, a result of America's historic separation of white and black workers and the bitter oppression of the latter. Thus, with this significant exception, the very idea of a labor-community coalition is neccessarily a new one.

Nevertheless, the growing history of lost strikes led many of those who dared to resist to adopt some form of community outreach as a part of strike strategy by the mid-1980s. The Hormel workers from United Food and Commercial Workers (UFW) Local P-9, the Watson-ville cannery workers of Teamster Local 912, the United Mine Workers at A.T. Massey mines, and the United Paperworkers (UPIU) locals at International Paper all employed aggressive community outreach as part of their strike tactics.

The mass media hardly ever discuss the real issues in a labor strug-gle, let alone try to provide a national audience with a forum on strategic subtleties. At the same time, there are few communications links between members of different unions or even among members of the same union. Thus, drawing lessons from previous strikes or campaigns, like the building of coalitions, requires a special effort. Yet it seems clear that by the late 1980s more and more labor activists were attempting to synthesize the experience of that decade. A few small-circulation journals such as *Labor Notes*, the *Labor Research Review*, and *American Labor* attempted to draw out strategic ideas and spread the news, but most labor activists had to glean their tactical arsenal from fragments of information. For this reason, no clear pattern of "improved" coalition efforts is clear as yet. What is clear, however, is the generalization of such efforts to most corners of organized labor and a broadening of the scope of outreach.

Often these outreach efforts consisted of new tactics such as the corporate campaign, old ones such as the boycott, and other tactics designed to create a coalition of forces capable of pressuring the employers. These coalitions, whether ad hoc or more long-term, increasingly included not only church and community organizations, but civil rights and peace organizations. Corporate connections to South Africa were emphasized in the Massey, Hormel, and International Paper strikes to make links with black community organizations. The appearance of Jesse Jackson at numerous strike rallies from 1984 on became symbolic of this quest for coalition. In the Watsonville strike the Mexican national identity of the strikers was key in building community support that ran from California to Mexico. Reflecting a stronger orientation toward mobilization than the conventional strike, a growing number of strikes also included spouse-based support groups and innovative self-help and fundraising programs.

Similar tactics have been used in the service sector. At Yale, Harvard, and other universities, extensive community outreach and coalitions with women's organizations played a key role in successful clerical organizing drives. Hotel workers in Boston combined multilingual organizing and the threat of lobby sit-ins with a community-based campaign against the insurance companies who were the financial backers of many of the hotels. Possibly one of the most interesting labor-community coalitions occurred in Philadelphia in 1988 when sanitation workers belonging to the American Federation of State, County, and Municipal Employees (AFSCME) joined with black community organizers to stop Mayor Wilson Goode's attempt to privatize the city's sanitation services. What was for the sanitation workers a fight for jobs was for the community a struggle against the further deterioration of a vital service. The coalition caught Mayor Goode off balance when they turned out some 3,000 demonstrators at City Hall. The privatization effort was abandoned.

Though the greater emphasis on mobilization and community outreach enabled these and many other struggles to sustain themselves, the tactics were not always a guarantee of victory. Particularly in the private sector, where plant closings or the use of scabs proved more than a threat, even a broad coalition or deep community support was not enough to tip the balance of forces in favor of labor. While the success or failure of this or that campaign is always a complex and unique question, there are some inherent problems in the notion of labor-community coalitions that need to be addressed if this approach is to become a central part of labor (or community) strategy in the 1990s.

Community and Labor: Working Together

"Community" is a vague concept. Since the working class tends to be less organized or politically articulated than the middle classes at the community level, partly because of the separation of residence and work mentioned earlier, the "community" in labor-community coalitions tends to refer to organized constituencies that are multiclass in nature and frequently middle class or professional in leadership. The limited commitment of middle-class coalition partners in a potentially nasty fight can undermine a coalition effort or cause the union to pull its punches in order to preserve the coalition. This means that, in practice, coalitions with community-based groups tend to be limited to oppressed racial or national groups, liberal churches, social movement organizations, or liberal political office-holders. In today's America most "liberal constituency" groups are weak or unpracticed at real mobilization, while most politicians, liberal as well as conservative, are notoriously indebted to corporate interests. Thus, in practice, it is often the union, as the one organization with a clear set of limited goals and a unitary class base, that both creates and sustains the labor-community alliance.

But organized labor also contains internal contradictions that inhibit resistance to corporate aggression and thus undermine the effectiveness of labor-community coalitions. These include, of course, a legacy of racial and gender discrimination that weakens class solidarity. For the purposes of this discussion, however, the most basic and universal problem is bureaucracy.

Labor-Management Cooperation as Bureaucratic Strategy

In the absence of official resistance, capital went beyond demands for ad hoc concessions and sought the means to institutionalize the union's participation in cost-cutting and profit maximization. Corporate America presented labor with a choice: "If you can't beat us, join us." In the imagination of the business unionist leader there was no question about which way to go. Faced with a choice between a level of confrontation with corporate America that they could not imagine, let alone lead, the majority of the top labor leadership took the path of least resistance. During the postwar years of a strong U.S. economy this generation of leaders practiced a form of bargaining based on national productivity pacts between capital and labor. As long as productivity increased, which often meant the adoption of job-cutting technology, capital allowed wages to increase. When industry began to severely contract however, and union membership declined sharply, these leaders moved to a more intimate level of cooperation in hopes of making "their" employers more competitive and, thus, salvaging as many dues-paying members as possible. So entered the new era of nonadversarial labor relations.

In the 1980s, large corporations began to aggressively push programs such as Quality of Work Life (QWL), Employee Involvement, and Team Concept. Some of these existed on paper in auto, steel, and telecommunications in the late 1970s, but it was in the 1980s that management got serious about these programs. The 1985 Saturn agreement between the UAW and GM was the archetypal plan for eliminating "restrictive" rules and job descriptions on the shop floor and blurring the union's role by substituting "problem solving" and consensus techniques for grievances and conflict.

Whether sold by the carrot of "having a say" or by the stick of unemployment, this turn to cooperation has been costly to both unionism and community solidarity. On the shop floor it has meant self-designed speed-up enforced through peer-group pressure, with management prerogatives thoroughly intact. Job rotation is among deskilled, motion-timed, Taylor-made assembly-line jobs. Since problems are "solved" within the team or circle, grievances are discouraged by union leaders and management alike. The consensus and competitive norms of these programs obscure the "we" versus "they" social dichotomy which leads workers to form unions in the first place and undermines the economic solidarity that allows them to maintain unions over time. For some labor leaders, what began as a pragmatic adjustment to hard times has become a full-fledged ideology. Cooperation is seen as a bold new social experiment. In one of the more extravagant claims for the new labor relations, UAW West Coast director Bruce Lee announced in the *New York Times,* on Christmas Day 1988: "The workers' revolution has finally come to the shop floor."

Obviously, a revolution that abolishes conflict between labor and management has little use for anti-corporate coalitions. Indeed, the coalition partner of choice for labor leadership has become the corporation. Insofar as any sort of broader coalitions might be envisioned within this new framework they would probably reflect the sort of government-business-labor partnership embodied in the corporatist approach to international competition favored by neoliberals. Conventional legislative coalitions around moderate labor goals will certainly continue, but confrontational anti-corporate labor-community coalitions are unlikely to originate within the labor hierarchy.

Equally problematic is the fact that labor leadership has tended to regard such confrontational coalitions as a threat to its own vision of the role of U.S. labor today. Thus most international unions deliberately put a brake on most attempts to move beyond the conventional strikes. The most extreme case of this was the strike by UFCW Local P-9 against Hormel's Austin, Minnesota, plant, where the UFCW's top leadership publicly and actively opposed the strike. In that event, not even the broadest national solidarity campaign since the United Farm Workers (UFW) grape-boycott of the 1960s, a corporate campaign, and a unique infrastructure of support organizations in Austin could defeat the Hormel/UFCW axis.

Less visible were the steps taken by the UAW to stop mass picketing in the A.P. Parts strike and those of the United Steelworkers in the case of Phelps Dodge. Other cases of the bureaucratic undermining of coalition-based campaigns include UPIU President Wayne Glenn pulling the rug on the IP strikers and their corporate campaign, the Carpenters ditching its corporate campaign against Louisiana-Pacific, the Machinists' termination of the corporate campaign against Brown & Sharpe, and the UFCW's decade-long opposition to including the Farm Labor Organizing Committee (FLOC) boycott of Campbell Foods on the official AFL-CIO boycott list. In all of these cases, a fledgling or existing effort at coalition was undermined or deserted by the union hierarchy, sometimes resulting in a defeat. Almost as debilitating is the common practice of endorsing a project or campaign on paper, but withholding any real resources or efforts at mobilization.

An important and perhaps hopeful exception to the fear of mobilization that characterizes most of the labor leadership has been the conduct of the United Mine Workers strike against Pittston Coal that began in April 1989. Although only 1,900 miners are directly involved in the strike, the struggle to force Pittston to sign the UMWA's national contract has mobilized virtually the entire community of Southeastern Virginia, where Pittston's mines are located. High school students staged strikes. Women, organized as the Daughters of Mother Jones, seized buildings. Forty thousand coal miners throughout the eastern coal fields struck illegally for over two weeks. Thousands of miners, members of other unions, and community supporters have been arrested in the union's campaign of mass nonviolent civil disobedience. And, for a few days, ninety-eight miners and one minister occupied Pittston's major coal cleaning and sorting plant, Moss 3 in Carbon, Virginia, while thousands of supporters outside blocked attempts by the police to remove the occupiers.

UMWA President Trumka has supported the campaign of nonviolent civil disobedience, even though it has endangered the treasury of the union. Vice-President Cecil Roberts has participated in civil disobedience and been arrested. Trumka did eventually call the 40,000 wildcat strikers back to work, but in general the leadership of the UMWA has approved or even helped plan this unique effort in labor-community mobilization. But, then, the UMWA never adopted any of the labor-management cooperation schemes so many other unions have. So far, the positive role of the UMWA leadership in the Pittston strike remains an unusual example of bold leadership.

The Dissident Response

Ironically, the sharp turn toward union-management cooperation may be an inadvertent source of rank-and-file mobilization, independent activity, and outreach. The complicity of the union leadership in concessions is itself a reason that many local unions turn to various forms of outreach. The top leadership retreat has also brought forth movements within labor to change the unions. This is clearest in the UAW, where the New Directions movement swept throughout the union after the election of Jerry Tucker as director of Region 5, in the election of long-time tactical innovator and health and safety activist Tony Mazzocchi as secretary-treasurer of the Oil, Chemical, and Atomic Workers (OCAW), and in the new growth of the Teamsters for a Democratic Union. But it is also apparent in local struggles in many other unions. The leaders and activists in these new movements along with those of such struggles as P-9 or the International Paper (IP) strike are among the most aggressive advocates of labor-community coalitions. Often they see the need for new methods of struggle as an integral part of building a new, more responsive, and democratic kind of unionism. It is here in the grassroots of labor that the hope for new forms of struggle appropriate to the era of global economic integration lies.

Since labor's hierarchy is by no means monolithic even in its most bureaucratic manifestations, one might expect a growing tension between rebellious elements of the rank and file or local level officialdom and the top bureaucracy, combined with employer intransigence, to create political fisures or changes at various levels of the hierarchy. In the relatively democratic OCAW for example, Tony Mazzocchi's decade-old efforts to move that union toward more creative strategic thinking, along with the aggression of the powerful multinational oil and chemical firms OCAW deals with, led the leadership to abandon labor-management cooperation efforts and to turn to Mazzocchi for a leadership alliance.

This sort of response at the top, however, is relatively rare and generally confined to smaller unions with a politically progressive or militant heritage, such as the UE or the United Mine Workers. The response of the UAW leadership to the New Directions phenomon, like that of the Steel Workers' officialdom to the earlier rebellion led by Ed Sadlowski, has been to adopt increasingly undemocratic methods in defense of their positions and cooperative approach to management. One reason for the relative rigidity of the national or international bureaucracy is that most U.S. unions are really two-level structures. International executive board members are usually regional directors and virtually all regional staff are appointed by the international executive board. Thus, in reality there is no intermediate structure in most industrial unions within which the expected splits might occur.

At the same time, outside the structures of the international unions, informal coalitions of local union leaders at the local level or occasionally official local or state labor bodies that are composed mostly of local leaders have experimented with new alliances. In the Boston area, for example, the Massachusetts Labor Support Project has helped mobilize both labor and community support for many strikes and organizing drives in that area. In some parts of the country, notably Colorado and Florida, the semi-official Jobs With Justice committees have done similar work. Obviously, coalitions of this sort which are supported by more farseeing officials offer an opening to rank-and-file activists. Indeed, their viability depends on attracting activists beyond the limited number of office-holders who often initiate them. The fact that these labor based coalitions carry out functions that are supposed to be the jurisdiction of central labor councils (but which they seldom perform) has brought down considerable heat from the AFL-CIO headquarters in Washington. An encouraging sign is that this pressure from above does not always have the desired chilling effect.

No Tactical Panaceas

The building of a vital labor movement in the United States involves more than saving today's shrinking unions or winning tomorrow's strikes. It will take a reshaping of unionism from the bureaucratic norms of today into democratic expressions of the broadest interest of working-class people. It will certainly require organizing the millions of low-paid workers in both the service and goods producing sectors. It will take a new, active internationalism and a politics that transcends the exhausted liberalism of the Democratic Party. There are no tactical shortcuts or panaceas to accomplish such goals. We will need every tactic and combination of tactics within the reach of our imagination and resources.

In this regard, it is a mistake to dismiss the strike as an economic and political weapon. Geographically dispersed but highly integrated systems of production are often vulnerable at certain key points. Just-in-time inventory set-ups magnify this vulnerability. The German metal workers strike of 1986, the British Ford workers strike of 1988, and the threat to cripple Chrysler production by closing a few key parts plants in 1988 are clear examples of this. Furthermore, intensified competition among employers is a source of potential power for labor as market loss becomes a central obsession of capital.

Nevertheless, the list of problems plaguing the strike is impressive. New technology, dual-sourcing, off-shore production, and the sheer size and financial resources of many corporations allow them to take a strike at one or more operations almost indefinitely. The introduction of scabs can spell victory for any firm willing to wait long enough. Thus, creative tactics involving the broadest social mobilization possible have become an essential aspect of contemporary labor struggle.

Such mobilizations can be as simple as the outpouring of support for striking mechanics, flight attendants, and pilots at Eastern Airlines. Here, the support, almost unsolicited by the Machininists' leadership, came from other unionists and social movement activists who saw this strike as a pivotal confrontation with one of capital's more vicious representatives, Frank Lorenzo. Or it can involve the complex of roving organizers, spouse-based support organizations, and corporate campaigning employed by the IP strikers. Almost always they must include national fundraising throughout labor and among sympathetic constituencies. But it is the activation of people that is ultimately the key. For a demobilized labor movement, this is the hardest lesson to implement.

It is instructive that labor's rebels and new thinkers must often turn to the language of another era or to that of other social movements (above all the civil rights movement) to find the first clues to the unleashing of labor's greatest potential source of power—mass action and collective decision-making. Some mistake the evocations of past struggles as mere nostalgia. In fact, because there is so little in labor's recent official practice or thought from which to draw, today's innovators have no choice but to search history, look to other social movements, or draw on the experience of unions abroad for new strategies and tactics.

Ultimately, the barriers to mobilization and confrontation presented by the bureaucracy within organized labor point toward the need for new leadership and a democratic reorganization of the unions. This reorganization must include the rebuilding of workplace unionism as well as the abolition of top-heavy bureaucracy. Change from within the unions, however, is not, by itself, a strategy for the revitalization of labor any more than coalitions or innovative tactics are a guarantee of victory in any particular struggle. Rather, these are all part of a bigger task in which the broadening of labor's social objectives and a willingness to confront capital in the workplace, in the streets, and in the political arena combine to awaken the unorganized and the demobilized of America.

Organizational and Leadership Models in Labor-Community Coalitions

Louise Simmons

Organizations generally enter coalitions to achieve goals beyond their individual reach. In the contemporary era of economic restructuring with important consequences for both labor and community forces, it seems quite logical for these forces to forge coalitions to confront such issues as plant closings, strikes, neighborhood matters, housing needs, and even electoral possibilities. Yet good intentions and the sincere desire for labor-community solidarity do not automatically translate into successful coalitions. Different styles, different organizational structures, practices, and traditions, unless carefully attended to and respected, can produce formidible obstacles to coalition building.

Community and labor struggles in Hartford, Connecticut, in recent years produced interesting coalitions in which these different styles and practices confront each other. While a number of coalitions have emerged over a variety of issues, two are particularly instructive in demonstrating several problems which can surface when labor and community forces coalesce. One coalition, the Community-Labor Alliance (CLA), formed in 1986 around the four-year strike at Colt Firearms by members of United Auto Workers (UAW) Local 376. The other coalition, People for Change (PFC), emerged in 1987 as an electoral coalition of community, labor, and civil rights forces, running candidates for the City Council, and capturing two of the three seats it sought. Both efforts attempted and in varying degrees succeeded in bringing labor and community forces into functioning coalitions.

Each of these coalitions grew out of the concrete social problems and social movements in Hartford. The city has the unfortunate distinction of being the fourth poorest city in the country: over a quarter of its population lived below the poverty line as of 1980. Hartford also has massive wealth within its 17.2 square miles: corporate headquarters of several major insurance companies and the defense giant, United Technologies. Its downtown has exploded with development in the 1980s, while its neighborhoods, largely African-American and Puerto Rican, remain severely impoverished. Three active neighborhood organizations who employ the neighborhood organizing methodologies developed by Saul Alinsky operate in several sections of the city. Other activist concerns contribute to many other social movements. Despite a decline of manufacturing in the area and a substantial growth in service-sector employment, dozens of unions remain active in the greater Hartford region.

Within the context briefly outlined above, the Community-Labor Alliance (CLA) and People for Change emerged. The remaining comments highlight some of the lessons from these efforts, specifically the problems of unions and Alinsky-style organizations attempting to define and achieve common goals. It must be noted that as organizations, the neighborhood groups did not formally participate in PFC, although many individual neighborhood activists played key roles and one was a successful candidate. These comments are informed by Ira Katznelson's illuminating work on the dichotomy of work and community in American social consciousness, *City Trenches* (1981), and by the wealth of literature on economic restructuring, as well as extensive personal observation.

To begin with, one should recognize the different rationales for entering a coalition on the part of a particular union or neighborhood group. Specifically in the Colt strike, the UAW approached building the CLA as a necessity in potentially winning the strike. Locally and nationally their experience with plant closings, strikes, and union-busting has led them to elevate coalition work to a central strategy for survival. Other area union activists likewise felt the need to build bridges and were impressed with the organizing capabilities of the neighborhood groups—groups who could potentially be helpful not only in strike support and discouraging their constituents from becoming replacement workers, but also in future organizing drives. The local Alinsky organizations were some of the first groups approached by labor to build the CLA.

Even though Saul Alinsky fashioned his neighborhood organizing methods after labor organizing techniques he learned through his association with the CIO, contemporary Alinsky organizers generally do not share a prior association with labor and have developed their own unique methodologies. In terms of coalitions, many of the neighborhood groups approach them somewhat differently than do unions. Being newer types of organizations, not feeling the same types of assaults in recent years as unions have, and having different conditions of membership may cause these organizations to approach coalitions more as a specific tactic in relation to a specific issue rather than as an overall strategy for survival. They have no equivalent of a "union shop" so they must devote a major amount of resources to ongoing organizing activities and developing loyalty among their members. Coalition work may drain organizational resources.

When the CLA began to function, the neighborhood groups did formally participate for some months, but this gradually dwindled and eventually ceased, although they remain available for specific support activities. After discussions with neighborhood organizers as to why this transpired, several issues were identified, some of which later resurfaced in the PFC effort. These issues have to do with the differences in agenda formation, styles of decision-making, and the definition and role of leadership within the two respective types of organizations.

First, with respect to agenda formation, when neighborhood organizations have formed coalitions in the past among themselves, generally a set of steps is followed in which the first actual meeting is preceded by careful negotiations to ensure the equal participation of all organizations. Process issues are as important as substantive issues. No single organization can dominate: meeting sites and chairpersons are rotated. Agendas involve concrete planning items and task assignments. "Citizen leaders"—individuals who live in the respective neighborhoods and who are elected by annual community congresses—generally speak for the organizations and the open role of paid staff is secondary. This method of work is oriented toward building consensus and is extremely task-oriented. It is all very different than the way in which the CLA operates.

Within the CLA there is a tacit understanding that the UAW has the ultimate authority in decision-making on Colt strike issues (as is the case with other unions bringing their issues to the group for support). Even though the UAW leadership is extremely open to suggestions from non-UAW members, if the UAW feels a particular suggestion conflicts with its overall approach, that plan will not be adopted. Moreover, since the CLA has met continually during the four years of the strike, the sense of urgency to accomplish tasks within a short time frame has diminished and some plans are never thoroughly followed through to conclusion. These practices are not what neighborhood group members are used to and probably contributed to their dwindling participation.

In the PFC experience, the issues were almost reversed and some labor leaders experienced frustration with the more process-oriented meetings in the early stages of the coalition. In that situation, a small number of neighborhood activists and union leaders convened the effort and new participants were continually brought into the process. Since the formation of a third party was uncharted territory for the organizations and individuals involved, nobody wanted to move too quickly and risk alienating a segment of the evolving coalition. Rather than putting many matters to a vote early on and solidifying "factional" blocs, the process dragged on. Union leaders were used to being able to come to a decision, vote, and move forward with a plan of action. PFC now has a greater sense of permanency and has adopted procedures and policies which alleviate these problems to some degree, although meetings are still quite process-oriented.

Another major difference between the two types of organization which surfaced in the CLA and elsewhere is in the definition and use of leadership by each type of organization. Elected union officers generally are the full-time functionaries of the union and are constitutionally vested with the authority to make and execute many types of decisions. Even active rank-and-file groups who might be opposed to an existing leadership work within this framework. However, the full-time staff members of neighborhood organizations are not the elected leaders: they are usually hired by the organization's board of directors, which consists of volunteer citizen leaders. When neighborhood organization staff are contacted about particular plans, they generally check with the elected citizen leaders and work through planning committees to make decisions. This creates a situation where leadership of these organizations is shared between the staff and citizen leaders.

Now there is some commonly held criticism of this arrangement charging that although Alinsky organizations claim to be based on participatory democracy, they in fact are often manipulated by their staff. This argument is countered by the assertion that neighborhood organizations attempt to meet their constituents "where they are at," not where others might wish them to be. Staff must develop members and organizational loyalty carefully since there is nothing mandating membership other than a belief in the goals of the organization—hence, the careful consultations. Union leadership, particularly in a strike situation, does not always have the latitude for such processes, even when their locals have active rank-and-file groupings.

One rather critical difference between the two types of organizations that impacts on coalitions is their respective relationships to legal processes and attorneys. Much of modern labor relations is bound by laws, precedents, and legal interpretation. Even the right to represent workers at a particular worksite requires certification by the National Labor Relations Board. In certain strike situations, when other alternatives are precluded, many unions can come to rely heavily on lawyers and legal strategies. Neighborhood groups are much more able to create their own rules and have a real aversion to relying on attorneys and relinquishing a large measure of control of an issue to a court. Their relative freedom from the types of laws and regulations which circumscribe many union activities makes for frustrations on their part with what they consider tedious and cautious processes employed by unions in various situations.

Perhaps because unions are so affected by laws, regulations, and political processes, many unions are actively involved in electoral politics. Participation in PFC became a quite logical extension of the UAW's experience in the Colt strike in which many elected officials were called upon for specific types of support, with varying responses. The UAW, the New England Health Care Employees-District 1199, the teachers federations, and other unions were substantially involved in the PFC effort. However, the neighborhood organizations could not become formally involved. Their funding depends upon their tax-exempt, nonprofit, nonpartisan status, and entering electoral politics would preclude such funding. Moreover, many of the neighborhood organizers are philosophically opposed to their organizations entering electoral politics even if funding were not an issue. They believe that the neighborhood organizations are more effective if they hold office-holders accountable from an independent, nonpartisan base rather than allowing themselves to be viewed as either partisan or a political stepping stone. Despite the fact that many of the individual convenors of PFC were involved in these neighborhood organizations and they viewed electoral politics as the logical response to the City Council voting down a "linkage" ordinance which all of the neighborhood groups supported, many of these staff people remain quite firm in their convictions. Union leaders have some difficulty with this stance.

Finally, there is the important element of "ownership" of issues. In order for coalitions to attract and retain both kinds of organization, there must be a sense that the goals or issues of the coalition are directly relevant to each organization, or at least the belief that the coalition effort in and of itself is directly relevant to each organization. This can be difficult to achieve. In the Colt strike, union leaders—within the UAW and other unions—feel that the strike is relevant to the entire labor movement and, moreover, to the standard of living enjoyed by the larger community. Neighborhood organizations do not see this issue as directly relevant to their members and constituents in the sense that they are willing to be involved on a weekly basis in strike support activities. They may be extremely sympathetic, but it is not *their* issue—it is the UAW's or labor's. Developing a sense of shared agendas and shared importance of issues is critical to retention of both labor and community organizations in a coalition effort.

The problems and issues raised here *are* surmountable. They need not become barriers to developing alliances. But they have to be acknowledged, expected, and addressed to develop successful coalitions.

Coalitions and the Spirit of Mutuality

John Brown Childs

In a world that tends toward monolithic centralized control by power-ful governments and multinational business, the recognition and cele-bration of grassroots local diversity is an important positive step in beginning to combat such power. But we are often overwhelmed by what seems like an avalanche of different ethnic, cultural, gender, labor, and political groups, so diverse that they seem to have nothing in common. Dispirited by apparent barriers between and among such distinct groups, put off by the apparent differences that separate peo-ples, we often feel that we have little to do with others. Sometimes, our sense of isolation and difference from others results in our thinking negatively about each other, as competitors rather than allies, even though underneath it all we often share some fundamental concerns.

I believe that diversity is not the problem. There is nothing wrong with farmworkers emphasizing the dangers of pesticides in the fields, while a tenants' group focuses on poor housing and high rents, as clerical workers at a university battle for a union that will be speak for them. Not surprisingly, these are different agendas, with different concerns and contexts. The problem, however, is more the absence of meaningful efforts to communicate among ourselves about such differences so that we can understand what others are doing, and why their priorities are different, and what we can do together. Often, instead of going through the difficult process of understanding other approaches, some people want to simply put their one agenda into control over others. The danger with this one-agenda method is that it ignores and usually antagonizes those for whom other issues are more crucial. What we need, then, is an ever-widening opening for a wide range of many groups and many agendas. Within this opening, people can engage in actions that are meaningful to them while also working on ways to constructively link those actions with different groups with different agendas.

How can such interaction take place, given the differences among various agendas? There is no doubt that working with other different groups is difficult: it requires a willingness to listen to other groups' concerns, to not put them down for being interested in areas not of ones' own immediate interest. Listening to other voices can help to clarify both the gaps and the common ground between groups. But such actual commonality is not enough by itself. Mutual interaction among groups also requires a willingness to look for ways in which we can learn from and support one another without giving up the essence of our own distinctive approaches. In short, there has to be genuine communication—a sharing of voices—for the interaction of diverse groups to work. And, there has to be toleration for differences combined with an active search for linkages among those differences.

The search for, and the creation of, linkages among different groups cannot take place in a hierarchical structure of organization and decision-making. There can be no orders "from the top" for a group to give up a key issue in order to sacrifice all for another group. Such central direction is too rigid and too heavy-handed to be able to deal with the shifting subtleties and complexities of highly diverse groups and needs. Rather, this linkage can only work horizontally through expanding the correspondence—the awareness of, and communication among—different groups.

For example, imagine one group that has toxic waste dumping at the top of its agenda as an issue to work on. Another group has made the creation of more day-care centers its top agenda item. At first glance these groups would seem to have nothing in common. There would seem to be no ground for interaction. But, both of these groups' agenda items are based on the shared desire for a better society in which people can lead meaningful lives without being poisoned by industrial wastes and in which working women can gain meaningful employment without sacrificing their families. The anti-toxic waste group could issue a statement supporting the day-care group, and vice versa. Members of one group could attend some of the others' meetings on occasion. They could send representatives to march in each others demonstrations, sign petitions, send letters, distribute fliers. All this could be done without giving up the priorities of either group. Simultaneously, misconceptions and ignorance or just simple unawareness of each group about the other would be overcome. The possibility for more effective interaction would be increased. In times of crisis for one group, such a knowledgeable ally might be crucial to survival. Such mutualistic interaction among diverse groups, as I have argued at length in *Leadership, Conflict, and Cooperation in Afro-American Social Thought*, is antiparochial, yet pro-local. "Each separate group constantly reaches out to the wider world of other groups, and it welcomes the particular contribution that each group can make from its own vantage point. In becoming aware of and acting with others, each group enhances itself by ending its isolation and embedding itself in a larger, more powerful process."[1]

Is this a pipe dream, or can mutualistic interaction that reaffirms group differences while contributing to greater cooperation among groups actually take place? Yes it can, and it is. Today we can see powerful global evidence of the sharing of voices among highly diverse groups. For example, the battle over the fate of the Amazon rain forest is only partly an environmental struggle involving ecologists and developers. Indigenous Brazilian Indian peoples, whose ancient communities are in that rain forest, and the Brazilian rubber tappers union, whose members extract latex from the trees without harming them, are also deeply concerned about destruction in that region. The rubber tappers union, whose leader, Francisco Mendes, was assassinated in 1989, employs nonviolent tactics such as sit-ins that mirror earlier U.S. civil rights and Gandhian approaches. Native American groups elsewhere have supported Amazonian Indian efforts as part of a large-scale struggle to protect what some call the "Fourth World" of indigenous peoples. An Italian environmentalist organization has proposed Mendes for the Nobel Prize. In short, this is not just an ecologist "pet project": it involves complex links between those concerned about global environment, Indian communities, unionists, Brazilian environmental groups, and sympathetic organizations in other parts of the world. The situation in the Amazon admits no easy solutions given that there is great concern in South America about U.S. interference, in all its forms. But it is also clear that this is an issue that cuts across national lines and organizational differences in a variety of ways.

Current grassroots, women-based movements in India are another important example of mutualistic intertwinings among distinctive groups and agendas. There, diverse concerns including environmental and women's issues are being woven together by people who want to improve conditions, but without the ecological degradation and social distress that multinational "development" often brings. As Kamla Chowdhry of the Vikram Sarabhai Foundation in New Delhi points out, poverty in India is closely connected with land degradation. "If poverty in the country is to be tackled, then environmental issues such as deforestation, soil erosion, pollution, use of common lands, and fuel and fodder development need to receive the highest political attention."[2]

Chowdhry and others point to important grassroots movements, often spearheaded by women, that are taking on these problems. Amrita Basu notes the intertwining of issues in India that connect democratization, ecology, women's liberation, and the protection of ethnic minority group rights."[3] Chowdhry agrees. Writing of the Chipko movement, spearheaded by women in Uttarkhand in the Himalayas to protest government contracts on cutting forest trees for industry, she notes that the movement was supported by voluntary agencies as well as students, teachers, scientists, and other local groups. "In general, the various environmental groups have adopted Gandhian tactics to protest and change existing laws in favor of conservation, sustainable growth, and protection of the rights of the poor on common property resources."[4] Such grassroots activity, she concludes, requires decentralization of power to local agencies.

For Chowdhry there is often a mutualistic cooperation of women's groups, environmentalists, teachers, students, and scientists. In turn, gender, class, and environmental issues are interactive. As Basu points out, the environmental impact of commercialization in many cases has been especially significant for women. The cultural shaping of women's work brings them into direct contact with environmental problems. The result is an especially active effort by women to organize around environmental-gender-cultural domains. Thus to consider those problems adequately requires addressing gender inequality as well. Consequently, issues of gender, ethnicity, class, caste, tribe, ecology, and capitalist impact on India, interlock and collide. The complexities of this situation are a clear indication of why Western-focused environmentalists, feminists, and others interested in connections across national lines must tread with alertness, care, and respect for cultural, political, and economic differences. But the fact that issues of gender, class, and environment are being struggled over in India indicates that there is the potential for some cross-communication with women's groups, environmentalists, and other analogous grassroots efforts in "Western" countries in ways that might allow for the sharing of information and resources. Such sharing would have to be mutualistic—people would have to be alert to, tolerant of, and willing to learn from the complex social, cultural, economic, and political circumstances of India while looking for parallels and analogies that allow for communication. Chowdhry, arguing that "only voluntary agencies can act as counterplayers in the fight for change," suggests an analogy exists between grassroots movements in India and the African-American civil rights struggle in the United States.

Meanwhile, in the United States the Rainbow Coalition made the environmental crisis part of its agenda, which linked it to environmentalists in Brazil and elsewhere. Other parts of the Rainbow agenda included the fight against racism, economic justice for all working women and men, support for the African National Congress (ANC) and the Congress of South African Trade Unions (COSATU) in that country. In the 1986 organizing convention of the Rainbow Coalition, Free South Africa activists, members of the predominately white North American Farmers Alliance, inner-city organizers, Latinos, Asian-Americans, trade unionists, and others gathered together. Many who had not previously been in touch with each other, such as white farmers and African-American unionists, worked together in that convention.

Significantly, white people working with the Rainbow Coalition were not doing so to "help" people of color. They were doing so because the Coalition addressed issues that were of importance to them. The Texas Department of Agriculture's populist Jim Hightower's involvement in the Rainbow's activities was a particular example of these overlaps between diverse groups. Whatever its limitations, the Rainbow was itself a living example of diverse groups with different agendas interacting across ethnic, political, and national boundaries. In its environmental and South African objectives, the Rainbow linked itself to mine and factory workers in South Africa, and to environmentalists and Green movements in Europe and other parts of the world. Meanwhile, in South Africa, COSATU sent a message of support to the Solidarity movement in Poland which was also supported by various environmental and anti-authoritarian Green organizations in Europe.

Notice the way in which different groups with distinctive objectives and methods become intertwined in this setting. Amazonian Indian peoples, the Brazilian rubber tappers union, environmentalists, women's grassroots organizations in India, Gandhian voluntary organizations, the Congress of South African Trade Unions, European Greens, Polish Solidarity, a variety of Latino, African-American, Asian-American, and Anglo-American groups intersect at certain moments in an ongoing global action. They do so differently, from many different vantage points. But they share a general direction toward a more egalitarian and just world.

Within this general direction actual interconnections among widely separated and different groups can and do arise. For example, the destruction of the rain forest would affect large numbers of people, both there and around the world. Consequently, it is an issue that has brought together people who previously had no contact. Similarly, the success of the Free South Africa movement is directly linked to the strengths and weaknesses of sanctions against trade in weapons, coal, and other materials with that country. The success of these sanctions in turn depends partly on efforts by unions and anti-apartheid organizations in Europe and the United States. For example, the United Mine Workers (UMW) union in the United States has joined in demonstrations against apartheid and in support of sanctions. So interconnectedness among locally grounded organizations is not just a hope. It is real, although not nearly as fully developed as it could be. Such mutualistic connections between groups are often fluid and complex. The participants shift in the degree and the direction of their involvement depending on victories and defeats in their own areas. Networks are constantly developing, being reshaped and broadened through an increased sharing of information which in turn increases awareness about commonality and shared concerns, problems, and solutions among different groups around the world.

This fluidity and openness is a source of strength. There is no one world leader or leading group that must be depended on and whose failure or assassination could disrupt hierarchical organizations. Moreover, there is no one set of experts to issue directives to others. California farmworkers, welfare rights groups, organizations of the homeless, Brazilian rubber tappers, and Indian peoples have a knowledge about their concerns that no outside expert can duplicate. The result is a vast and intertwining array of knowledge that consists of many different perspectives, grounded in particular circumstances, battles, and strategies.

But a major weakness of this vast fluid bubbling mix of groups is the more common thinness of actual communication among them. If we do not attempt to correspond with other groups, and do not recognize what other people are doing, we lose the opportunity to make actual shared and overlapping concerns more direct and overt. If we fail to recognize commonalities running through diversity, we fool ourselves into thinking that we are isolated (while governments and multinational corporations look very well tied together and, as such, overwhelming). Conversely, if we overlook diversity and imagine unitary homogenous commonality, as the term "global" is sometimes used, for example, we ignore the highly varied, intricate, and contradictory complexities of the different cultures in this world.

For example, in some cases, Western white environmentalists, women's groups, and leftists, while proclaiming the universality of ecological, feminist, and socialist issues, have sometimes failed to understand the way in which those issues are being addressed by people in other cultural contexts. Often those of us who live within more privileged powerful places in the world—no matter how much we criticize those settings—assume that our particular cultural knowledge is universal. In fact it is one form of knowledge among many. Willingness to learn from those who are more knowledgeable about their own areas is therefore vital. Failure to do so erodes the possibility of cross-cultural communication and interaction.

Sometimes the opposite happens, and people assume that their concerns are only of relevance to them, and that only they have something to say about them. For example, occasionally some environmentalists have assumed, quite wrongly, that ecological issues are only of concern to white middle-class North Americans and Europeans. Such assumptions ignore deep African, Asian, South American, and Central American concerns about land degradation related to lumbering and mining; toxic waste dumping in the third world by industrialized nations; and the impact of dams, along with other ecological/economic issues. By assuming lack of common themes, activists cut themselves off from potential connections with others. Mutualistic communication is crucial to our understanding simultaneously complex similarity and difference among diverse groups. If we do communicate—if we share voices—about these similarities/differences then, to varying degrees, real interactions can be shaped *around and within* those complexities. For example, Chowdrhy's description of Martin Luther King's "inspirational and challenging" relevance to movements in India in no way suggests that India is simply the same as the United States. At the same time it recognizes a common theme cutting across racial and national barriers. Such commonalities are not exceptions. They are persistent possibilities that await being brought to fruition through mutualistic thinking and action.

To accomplish this sharing of voices and resources is not easy. It requires toleration for difference, and the willingness to communicate, while simultaneously being alert to other agendas among quite distinctive groups. It can also require transformation of some aspects of some agendas, such as the necessity that men recognize the importance of gender, and of transforming male-dominated organization into more egalitarian forms. When to accept, when to transform, and where to do it are obviously difficult and contentious questions. There will be inevitable arguments and disagreements. There is no blueprint or formula to answer such questions; they must be worked out by the people involved. But to even recognize the difficulty is a step forward insofar as it removes us from the arrogant assumption that our particular group's way is the best and the most important. As difficult as it is to attempt linkages among diverse groups, the benefits of such interaction are huge. People around the world, who lack the power of the centralized monolithic institutions, have the possibility of creating a globally expanding complex fluid networking of groups who work separately, while also working together; who are local and global at the same time; and who have different priorities but who understand the threads that tie them into a commonly held communication. Such groups potentially come to know that, in the midst of their own distinctive struggle, they are not alone in the world, and this is a mighty understanding.

Martin Luther King, who devoted his life to civil rights for African-American peoples, also spoke about the importance of world peace and economic justice. For King, civil rights was a key domain of profound importance. But he did not stop with that. Rather he saw that struggle as tied to other important questions of economic fairness and peace. He did not ask people to subordinate or abandon their concerns for civil rights. But he did ask them to look for the ways in which linkages with other peoples in other places could be understood and developed. I believe it is King's flexible mutualistic ability to focus both on the struggle of African-Americans and on the larger world, that helps Chowdhry, an Indian writer, to cite this African-American activist as an inspiration for what is going on in India. In this vein of thought King wrote:

> We have inherited a large house, a great "world house" in which we have to live together. . . . However deeply American Negroes are caught in the struggle to be at last at home in our homeland of the United States, we cannot ignore the larger world house in which we are also dwellers. Equality with whites will not solve the problem of either whites or Negroes if it means equality in a world society stricken with poverty and in a universe doomed to extinction by war.[5]

King advised us all to be both particular and general, local and global, aware of others, yet rooted in our own concerns. Today King's "world house" is growing. The doors between rooms are opening. There is conversation and movement in the corridors. Simultaneously there is the increasing recognition that the people in each room have their own distinctive views out on the world. Some rooms face the heat of the south wind. Others are chilled by northern gusts. Some have too little light. Others are in need of shade. For the world house to be a place of benefit to all requires recognition of, and communication about, such different problems and solutions while we also recognize the way in which all are living together in a common structure. Such mutualistic understanding accepts differences while seeking paths toward communication and shared action.

The real interconnections among everyday people today are global, but they are also grounded in complex cultural and local realities. They reach round the world, but they are rooted in township and factory, rain forest and orange grove, sweatshop and ghetto, shipyard and village. There are many different people in these rooms of the world house. Working together they can make this house a home for all.

Notes

1. John Brown Childs, *Leadership, Conflict, and Cooperation in Afro-American Social Thought* (Philadelphia: Temple University Press, 1989), p. 8.
2. Kamla Chowdhry, "Poverty, Environment, Development," *Daedalus* 118 (1989): 141–42.

3. Amrita Basu, "Grass Roots Movements and the State: Reflections on Radical Change in India," *Theory and Society* 5 (1987). See also Brinda Rao, "Gender and Ecology in Contemporary India" (Ph.D. diss. University of California at Santa Cruz, forthcoming).

4. Chowdhry, "Poverty, Environment, Development," pp. 150–51.

5. Martin Luther King, Jr., *Where Do We Go from Here: Chaos or Community?* (New York: Bantam, 1968), pp. 195–96.

Programs

Developing common objectives is one of the most important but also one of the most difficult problems facing labor-community alliances. The pieces in this section aim not so much to present a fully developed program as to show a process by which concrete cooperation around common problems and issues is creating elements of a program which links the objectives of many potential partners. Those elements range from alternatives to unchecked corporate economic power to the conversion of military spending to meeting human needs.

Labor and Community: Converging Programs

Jeremy Brecher and Tim Costello

The search is on for a program that can draw together a wide range of labor and community movements. The results of that search may reshape American politics in the post-Reagan era.

As we argued in "American Labor: The Promise of Decline," the American labor movement is being transformed at its roots by the development of local and statewide labor-community coalitions. These alliances are rapidly becoming a new force in American politics.

These coalitions have usually started in response to specific issues or limited political objectives, rather than around broad philosophies, ideologies, or programs. Many of them are now trying to define goals that can transform these temporary alliances of disparate elements into a labor-community bloc.

Neither Laundry List nor Transmission Belt

A coalition must formulate its program differently from an organization with its own unified decision-making processes; three of the most common approaches are likely to lead to unfortunate results. First, there is the "laundry list" approach, in which the various proposals of the different coalition partners are just strung together and called a program. Second, there is the model, exemplified by the many AFL-CIO initiated coalitions, in which one dominant partner defines the common program, with at most a pro forma consultation with the others. Third, there is the "transmission belt" model, in which one political group formulates a position it believes will represent the interests of the movement as a whole and then demands that the other coalition partners accept it; this is the traditional model of Communist and other Leninist parties in relation to their front organizations.

A more constructive model comes from the Montana Alliance for Progressive Policy (MAPP), a coalition of citizen groups representing conservationists, low income people, senior citizens, women, workers, and teachers. To develop an economic program for the state, MAPP

245

first prepared information packets on the Montana economy, then brought members of their constituencies together for workshops to consider the data. According to MAPP director Don Reed, "Participants sit in small groups and discuss the information and draw their own conclusions." More than forty such workshops around the state have focussed on the Montana economy in general and on such specific topics as agriculture, taxation, toxics, and women in the economy. One product of this process has been a Montana Bill of Economic Rights.

Another good model comes from U.S. farmers. During 1983–84, Jim Hightower, the populist Texas commissioner of agriculture, and Jim Nichols, his Minnesota equivalent, held hearings around the agricultural regions of the country to get the ideas of farmers and other rural residents on alternatives to agribusiness-dominated farm policies. The goal was to unite small farmers who belonged to different organizations, grew different products, and farmed in different parts of the country.

The result was the Save the Family Farm Act, designed to provide (in Jesse Jackson's memorable paraphrase) "parity not charity." The program, supported by all general farm organizations except the American Farm Bureau, was narrowly defeated in Congress in 1985; it became a focal point in the 1988 presidential primaries. Of course, such an approach can be used by others besides public officials and made highly participatory. A group of activists from different movements, for example, could hold hearings and function somewhat like a jury— hearing from all kinds of witnesses, but drawing conclusions based on their own role as citizens.

What's a Program Good For?

The initial objectives of many struggles tend to be formulated in negative terms: stop a highway, stop aid to the Nicaraguan Contras, or stop nuclear testing. A program reformulates such objectives into positive goals and expresses them in a form that applies to situations beyond the immediate one.

A program needs to perform four basic functions, in relation to diverse elements respectively within the movement, the wider public, the opposition, and the world to be changed. While there is bound to be tension among these functions, an effective program must integrate them fairly well.

First, a program must unify the concerns and approaches of the different parts of a coalition. At the most obvious, this involves addressing the needs of racial, ethnic, gender, occupational, geographic, and other constituencies. At a deeper level there are different political philosophies, such as liberalism, libertarianism, Marxism, the Green orientation, and tactical orientations toward working inside and outside the system which an appropriate program may draw on to create a stronger whole.

Second, a program addresses the uncommitted. It appeals for support for particular projects and can be used to recruit movement participants.

Third, and less often noted, an effective program can fragment, neutralize, delegitimate, or even win over parts of the opposition. The initial Reagan program, for example, effectively divided working people by racial and gender appeals and by cutting public programs for middle-income people far less than programs for the poor.

Fourth, a good program proposes solutions appropriate to the problems of coalition members and of society as a whole. These must not only be solutions that would work if tried, but also ones that can in fact be implemented. A good program, that is, must take into account the realities of power. Its elements must be compatible with each other. And the changes advocated must be deep enough not simply to catch transitory political winds but to provide a viable alternative to the status quo.

Basic Values

While program formation requires many pragmatic considerations, it must take place within a framework of basic values. Values do not provide concrete answers to questions of policy: they develop over time, they are subject to different interpretations, and there is bound to be conflict among them. But they do provide a framework for dialogue, a touchstone or set of criteria in light of which concrete policy questions can be evaluated. A valuing of human life does not solve the population problem, but it rules out eating babies for breakfast as a policy option.

Values are inevitably expressed in different rhetorics, symbols, and traditions, religious and secular. Our social movements have articulated values in a way that forms a rich heritage. Part of Jesse Jackson's importance has been his ability to articulate those values in a way that has resonated among a wide range of individuals and movements.

Whatever the rhetoric, at the core of both the labor movement and its community partners has lain the positive value of human solidarity, a sense of common humanity. Conversely, there has been a refusal to reduce the goal of human life to dominating others or chasing a buck. These movements have asserted the importance of other values: of human individuality, of interpersonal relationships, of family, community, and nature.

The Established Labor Program

In some ways the labor-community program can resemble, or at least draw on, the established program of the labor movement and its liberal allies. The labor movement, after all, grows out of some of the same core values of solidarity, democracy, and equality.

But there are important ways in which today's community-labor axis implies a reconstruction of basic labor movement policies. First, it needs a program for a coalition in which labor is an equal, not a dominant partner; hence, the concerns of the other partners must be integral, not additions to a laundry list. Second, the existing labor program represents not only the democratic impulses of the labor movement but also the tendency of labor organizations toward bureaucratization and the representation of narrow, separate, at times even antisocial interests. And third, any program must recognize that the world has changed radically since the established labor program was developed.

The unique and unsustainable dominance of the United States, with its 6 percent of the world's people, over the rest of the world has inevitably begun to fade. Internationalization of the economy has made traditional national economic policies self-defeating. The potential destruction of the ecosphere has impugned the goal of unlimited industrial growth. The impossibility of defending against modern weaponry has made established national security policies counterproductive. And new values have come to the fore, including feminism, environmentalism, and cultural pluralism. Unless a program deals realistically with these changes, it may be able to appeal to the American electorate, but it will be unable to address the problems that really need solving.

The modern American labor movement developed in a period of intense nationalism and expansion of the importance of nation-states; its program has focused on the national level. A program today must differ in two respects: our basic problems—economy, environment, security—cannot be solved at a purely national level; all require a global response. Yet our institutions for addressing them are at present primarily national. We must create transnational solutions for problems that transcend national borders.

At the same time, the national institutions, government and private, have come to be, and to be perceived by a large proportion of the public as being, remote and out of control. Decentralization of power and the empowerment of local institutions directly controlled by their participants must be an aspect of any labor-community program; otherwise it will be rightly regarded as simply a renewed attempt to expand unresponsive national bureaucracies.

This does not mean that the national level has become unimportant. Rather, it means that a labor-community program should aim to devolve powers now held at the national level upward to global institutions and downward to regions and communities. Our vision should be of a series of levels of social regulation, no one of which is dominant.

The traditional labor program looked positively on both capitalism and the state. It aimed for a strong private economy combined with a strong national government to take care of social needs unmet by the private sector. Today, both corporations and government are widely perceived as out-of-control power centers which threaten and exploit people as much as serve them. A labor-community program needs to address the desire for community-based forms of enterprise through which people can earn their livings and meet their needs.

All these differences imply a fresh approach to power. The traditional labor program generally sought to achieve its aims and to limit the power of private business by increasing the power of the national government. A new labor-community program must aim to transfer power from corporations, national government, and other existing powers centers to independent institutions directly controlled by their participants. The arenas of struggle will include not only government but workplaces, neighborhoods, schools, and many other institutions. An effective program will help make synergistic the construction of independent institutions, resistance to corporate and governmental policies, and efforts to transform the political structure from within.

The Workplace

At the core of conventional unionism lies the workplace and the relationship between the union, as bargaining agent for the workforce, and the employer. The basic program consists in the right of workers to choose a union to bargain on their behalf; a contract with a grievance procedures; seniority and other protections against discrimination; protection of established work processes; protection against unhealthy conditions; and a share for workers of increases in productivity. Beyond these spheres, unions have generally accepted "management's right to manage."

Labor-community alliances have pushed far beyond this framework.

Many of their actions directly challenge "management's right to manage." Opposition to plant closings, attempts to pressure managements to preserve local jobs and act in other socially responsible ways, and pressure for plant-closing legislation have been a major focus of labor-community programs. So have challenges to corporate rights to pollute the environment inside and outside workplaces.

At the core of a labor-community program should lie an expanding right of workers, communities, and others affected by corporate decisions to participate in making those decisions. Initially this is taking the form of demands that corporations bargain with labor-community coalitions over such crucial issues as plant closings and environmental pollution.

This practice can be expanded and eventually established as a "right to bargain" for labor and community groups. The specific forms in which such a right can be institutionalized will of course have to be developed through time and experience. Several existing models can indicate possible directions. Collective bargaining by unions can include an expanding set of issues and can include community as well as labor representatives. Labor-community coalitions such as the Naugatuck Valley Project and the Tri-State Conference on Steel are already pressuring corporations to meet and bargain with them.

Environmental legislation, with its requirements for impact statements, public hearings, and a right to public input on decisions, can be used as a model for "job impact," "social impact," and similar evaluation procedures. Unions and individuals supposed to represent "the public" are increasingly represented on corporate boards of directors; while such token representation often means little, especially in the absence of mechanisms to hold such representatives accountable, they could play a significant role in connection with these other forms. Finally, direct ownership of companies by worker and community groups is becoming increasingly widespread; where this occurs it gives another avenue of labor-community power over corporate decisions.

The traditional structure of work in America, based on a concentration of authority in management and a sharp division between workers and management, is being eroded—not by labor intransigence but by low productivity and new technologies. Managers are attempting to use this situation to increase their dominance still further—often under the guise of "quality circles" and other schemes that purport to improve the quality of work life. A genuine democratization of the workplace implies, by contrast, high levels of autonomy, skill, education, cooperation, and self-direction throughout the workplace. Such democratization provides a way to increase productiveness without resort to speed-up and union busting.

The Domestic Economy

Labor's economic policy has centered around Keynesian techniques of economic expansion and public works designed to maintain high employment and thereby maintain labor's bargaining power. Unions have often been happy to see the development of strong national corporations able to pay high wages and compete effectively in world markets. They have also supported minimum-wage and prevailing-wage laws designed to protect unionized jobs from nonunion competition. Unions have often given indiscriminate support to economic development projects, even those that destroy communities (highways and urban renewal) or threaten the environment (nuclear power plants).

The new labor-community alliances have pioneered alternative approaches to ecnomic problems based largely on local initiatives to strengthen community economies. These grow in large part from a sense that where government and business have abandoned an industrial community, that community must take economic initiatives itself.

The Naugatuck Valley Project, for example, besides bargaining with corporations on behalf of workers and the community, has helped employees buy one company and has explored other buyout possibilities elsewhere; it has created a revolving loan fund for future worker buyouts, has stimulated the creation of a state investment program for buyouts, and has launched a land trust for cooperative housing efforts. It sees these as creating a network of worker and community controlled enterprises, somewhat like the famous Mondragon Valley in Spain.

The Tri-State Conference on Steel, a similar coalition in the core of the rust belt, has stimulated the creation of the Steel Valley Authority, a public agency which can buy, sell, and run companies, float bonds, and use the power of eminent domain where company property is needed for a public purpose. Its immediate goal is to prevent plant closings by threatening companies with taking ownership by eminent domain unless they allow workers and the community an opportunity to try to keep them going. Its long-range goal is a program of "regional reindustrialization": rebuild rustbelt industry via public investment and a market based on rebuilding the country's transportation and other infrastructure systems.

Another approach, pursued by coalitions in Boston, Hartford, and other cities, is "linkage," a requirement that those seeking development rights and other benefits of building in a city be required to contribute to such urban needs as housing, job training, and employment of city residents. Linkage is both a means to shape urban development to community need and to extract resources from corporations for social needs.

These initiatives point to a strategy of economic development that is neither private nor government sponsored but based on a "community sector" of worker and community controlled enterprises producing goods and services for public need.

American cities and states are now involved in a growing range of entrepreneurial activities, most of them guided by a conventional business philosophy. A more progressive model might resemble the various economic development programs run by Labour governments in British industrial cities, such as the Greater London Enterprise Board of the Greater London Council (abolished by Mrs. Thatcher). These utilized community development funds for a carefully targeted set of social and economic objectives, including the preservation of local employment, affirmative action for minorities and women, expansion of high-quality, skilled jobs, encouragement of cooperatives and worker-community-run enterprises, unionization, and expansion of workers' rights and powers within privately owned firms. Where necessary they also aided the restructuring of key local industries and helped companies develop plans in accord with the future of local development.

Such economic strategies can be initiated at the local or state level. They can be even more effective if supported by proper national policies, such as Staughton Lynd's program for "reindustrialization from below." Lynd points out that funding public works is an established and universally accepted function of the federal government, even in the Reagan era. This has at times been extended to production for public needs: the Tennessee Valley Authority (TVA) expressed the principle that, where private enterprise fails to produce socially needed goods or services, the public sector must step in to provide them. Lynd proposes a reindustrialization program based on large-scale investment of public funds in needed productive enterprises as well as traditional public works.

Lynd points out, however, that TVA is completely undemocratic, and that people rightly fear a centralized national bureaucracy with powers to shape the entire economy. He proposes instead decentralized, community-based democratic planning boards to administer public investment funds. Such institutions could function along the lines envisioned by the Greater London Enterprise Board, encouraging the development of a local "community sector" of worker and community controlled enterprises oriented toward local and regional needs.

The Federation for Industrial Retention and Renewal, a new national organization of local movements that have been fighting plant closings, is currently developing a set of policy initiatives which embody much of this approach. They recommend a plant closing law which would require companies closing workplaces not only to give notice but to consult with labor and community groups and to provide them all the information needed to develop an alternative. They propose the creation of a National Industrial Development Fund to help fund local and regional development. The fund would channel resources to regional jobs authorities modeled on the Steel Valley Authority.

Such an approach could be used to encourage local and regional production for local use, rather than export—putting local communities more in control of their economic destinies and minimizing disruption by uncnrolled forces of the world market. It would increase control by those who have a local stake, not irresponsible multinationals. It would move toward smaller scale, more environmentally sound economic development. The "community ecnmic sector" would inevitably be interstitial at first, utilizing both market and state. Combined with democratization in the workplace, it might ultimately lead to a recognition that ownership is a "bundle of rights," each of which can be assigned as appropriate to workers, communities, and wider regulatory bodies, local, regional, national, and global.

International Relations

Traditionally, the American labor movement has welcomed the expansion of American world power. It supported expanding military spending and U.S. intervention in Korea, Vietnam, Central America, and elsewhere. It directly encouraged foreign labor movements that were tools of repressive governments—as long as they were anticommunist.

Until the 1970s, the labor movement supported the lowering of tariffs and other barriers to international trade. Now it has shifted to a protectionist policy that is no solution to the problems of the U.S. economy.

Labor-community coalitions have embraced very different foreign policy goals. Divestment from companies with investments in South Africa and an end to U.S. military intervention in Central America have been their most common foreign policy issues. "Jobs with Peace" campaigns in many localities have attempted to reduce local dependence on military production and win support for a shift in national priorities from military spending to human needs.

One of the most important contributions of Jesse Jackson has been to articulate a framework for restructuring international relationships that has found wide acceptance among the kinds of groups which participate in labor-community coalitions. This framework emphasizes a respect for world law, support for the labor and political rights of all peoples, and a world economy managed to meet the development needs of poor countries. It provides an alternative to policies which use U.S. economic and military power to support regimes which suppress the rights of their workers, thus buttressing the "foreign competition" that drives down wages and closes companies in the United States.

Even at a local and regional level, economic development policies can support conversion from military to useful production, encourge production needed for third world development, and create markets for third world exports produced under nonexploitative conditions. "Sister cities" and other forms of person-to-person international outreach can start "peacemaking from below." Nuclear-free zones can begin to disengage comunities from the arms race. Central to economic and foreign policy must be an alternative to both protectionism and export expansion. Protectionism hurts many domestic constituencies who produce exports or use imports and encourages cartelization and economic stagnation; export expansion requires workers to accept Korea- or Brazil-style labor conditions, and puts community economies at the mercy of uncontrolled global economic forces.

The "Save the Family Farm" bill promoted by progressive farm organizations suggests an alternative. It starts by recognizing the right of all countries to relative self-sufficiency in basic resources such as agriculture, and therefore rejects the agricultural trade offensive promoted by the Reagan and Bush administrations. It calls for multilateral trade negotiations "to ensure stable and equitable prices for producers in all countries" rather than the current drive to open all markets to U.S. products. Within such an international framework, domestic supply and demand can be managed to provide a stable basis for family farms.

This approach fits the broader model developed by third world countries for a New International Economic Order. These countries point out that the chaotic world economy hurts the industrialized nations as well as the developing ones—an argument borne out by a decade of global stagnation and the inability to collect third world debt. They proposed a "North-South dialogue" which would restructure the world economy to regulate global market forces in the interest of the development process. The core concept was price and production policies and long-term sales agreements designed to allow orderly development of production and trade. The goal would be global management of world resources and relative self-reliance for countries and regions.

The Environment

The labor movement has in general supported environmental legislation; but where major employers have claimed that environmental regulations would cost jobs, unions have often asked for their modification. Labor has frequently supported environmentally threatening development projects, notably nuclear energy plants. In general it has supported the development of large-scale, centralized production systems oriented toward production for the national or world economy, without regard to the environmental implications.

Many local coalitions, with and without labor support, have fought against chemical dumps, polluting industries, and other degradations of the environment. Many have fought to save open spaces from destructive development.

Such efforts reflect the threat posed to the entire biosphere by an industrial economy guided only by the drive to maximize profit. Acid rain, the destruction of the ozone layer, Three Mile Island, and Chernobyl—all indicate the necessity for production systems to respect the natural ecology of the earth and its regions. Stopping the most blatant polluters is of course an immediate minimum goal. But beyond that, an ecologically sound society requires that each locality and region live in harmony with the potentials and limits of its environment.

A growing community sector should serve as a model for such environmentally sound development. National, regional, and local planning should orient development toward smaller scale production units and mixed, low-impact utilization of local environments. Public policy aimed at providing jobs and rebuilding economic infrastructure should insist that publicly supported development evolve toward such ecological balance.

Equality

The labor movement has supported civil rights legislation and affirmative action to end racial, gender, and other forms of discrimination, although it is only now beginning to oppose discrimination based on sexual preference. It has opposed overt discrimination in the workplace, although it has often defended seniority systems that covertly perpetuate such discrimination.

Labor has generally supported policies, such as progressive income taxes, that redistribute income from wealthy to other groups. It has supported full employment and welfare policies that tend to favor lower income groups. It has generally acquiesced, however, in a system of "dual labor markets," through which unionized workers in major industries, predominantly white and male, receive far higher incomes and better conditions than workers in the more casualized labor markets in which women and minorities are concentrated.

Labor-community coalitions have mobilized initially to protect existing social programs from conservative assault. These efforts reached their peak in the campaign against the appointment of Robert Bork to the Supreme Court.

Our society remains marked by racial, ethnic, gender, age, and other forms of discrimination. These can only be corrected by a continuing expansion of the principle of affirmative action, ultimately including a right to equal access to socially produced wealth.

Our society has also been marked by the cultural domination of male over female, white over black, and established ethnic groups over newer arrivals. It has also often attempted to impose social codes regarding sexual preference and other forms of individual behavior. Equality means valuing a diverse, multicultural society and recognizing the human right of all individuals and groups to pursue lifestyles that are not harmful to others.

Social Policy

Unions traditionally have supported unemployment compensation, social security, and other programs providing support for those who cannot or should not work. They have also supported free public education, a national health care system, public housing, and similar services.

Many labor-community coalitions have focused on such matters of social policy. Welfare, housing, and similar coalitions have been common. Defense of federal programs was the origin of many coalitions, expansion of state programs has been a goal of many others.

There is growing public support for major new programs for day care, health care, jobs, housing, and education. These can be made part of a growing community economic sector. Day-care programs, for example, can be treated as a means of community-building, of providing training and employment, of creating feminist, multicultural, antiracist education and of ensuring social responsibility for children, not just a subsidy for Yuppies and employers. Health care programs can include neighborhood clinics, expanded opportunities for paraprofessionals, and preventive health and safety programs, not just high tech hospitals and specialists.

The Political System

The American labor movement has been a strong supporter of the expansion of government power at the national level. The social reforms it has championed have occurred largely through national legislation and the creation of specialized federal agencies. Labor has accepted large-scale public bureaucracies as a necessary social form, even when they have proved largely unresponsive to democratic control. Labor has largely accepted the rules of the game of interest-group politics, with all their favoring of corporate interests, as long as the narrowly defined interests of organized labor were protected.

Labor-community alliances have focused largely on local and state levels of government. This results in part from the weakness of progressive forces at the national level during the Reagan era, but also because the goal of increasing the opportunities for direct participation and control is far more achievable at the local level. Coalitions have lobbied, demonstrated, run candidates, and otherwise attempted to make political institutions responsive to their needs. They have tried to make the political process more accessible by such means as reform of voter registration and reapportionment. They have used the planning powers of city governments to increase democratic control over urban development. And they have experimented with new forms of government institutions, such as the Steel Valley Authority, which let local communities be players in the industrial economy.

This approach implies a democratization of the entire political system. It erodes the "iron triangles" of private interests, government bureaucracies, and politicians in which undemocratic power is entrenched. It challenges the power of money over politics and media. It proposes a new openness in government and economy supported by new media in which knowledge of and debate about public policy can be equal rights of all.

Democratization also requires the expansion of vehicles for direct participation at the local level and an increasing power to control the forces which shape community life. Forms of town-meeting democracy can be revived at the neighborhood level. Environmental legislation provides a possible model that can be expanded to other forms of social impact of government decisions.

A Summary

Such a program can be summarized as a move away from pursuing worldwide military, political, and economic domination and toward building communities that encourage people to live in solidarity with each other and in harmony with their environment. At its core lies the expansion of a "community sector" of worker and community controlled enterprises using available resources to meet community needs. These will be supported by public institutions which channel resources to "third sector" enterprises in ways which meet defined needs for education, skill development, affirmative action, environmental improvement, third-world development, and other social needs.

Such a development will need other changes to support it. Workers and communities will need expanded power over private corporations. New forms of planning will be needed to encourage balanced, ecologically sound local and regional development that can lead toward relative local and regional self-sufficiency.

A reduction to a defensive military, an end to military interventionism, and the liquidation of capabilities designed for interventionism can allow the transfer of resources from the military to the community sector. A New International Economic Order designed to stabilize the world economy through long-term trade agreements and support for human rights, especially labor rights, worldwide, with encouragement of a worldwide "level playing field" for labor conditions, can replace international competition with cooperation.

Equality can be approached by expanding the "affirmative action" principle, eventually to include equal right of access to productive property. Government can be democratized via decentralization and opening institutions to public participation.

From Protest to Economic Democracy: Labor-Community Ownership and Management of the Economy

Staughton Lynd

We hear about the disappearance of the industrial working class; about how workers, even when they do traditional blue-collar jobs, think of themselves as members of the middle class; about the way the car and the suburban shopping center destroyed the ethnic neighborhood close to the mill in which a sense of class community flourished; about "hard hats" and "middle Americans," and working-class racism, nativism, and overall obscurantism. If all this were so, it would hardly be significant to speak of labor-community coalitions. Labor, having absorbed the reactionary values of the larger community, would have no independent contribution to make. "Labor" and "community" would be but two words for the same unpleasant reactionary reality.

But it is not so. Twenty years ago, as the son of two upper-middle-class professors for whom the Depression was something that happened to other people, as a Harvard graduate and a Columbia Ph.D. who later added a J.D. from the University of Chicago, as one who (so friends told me) even if he became a steelworker would always be known as "the professor," I set out to strike up a conversation with American workers. I did so because the new left movement of the 1960s seemed to me to have painted itself into a corner. Its members were students. When they protested at universities, working-class parents across the country wondered how kids could fecklessly throw away the opportunity to go to college. The kids, sensing this disapproval, escalated their tactics to make up for the absence of off-campus support. The new tactics (burning things down, calling policemen "pigs," etc.) further alienated blue-collar America. I wanted somehow to interrupt this downward spiral. I wanted to find out if American workers would relate to the language of the Port Huron Statement, the 1962 founding document of Students for a Democratic Society (SDS) that talked about the right to participate in decisions that affect our lives, or if some new, Marxist language was needed to be able to communicate.

My wife and I have conducted this experiment, first as historians and then as legal services attorneys, in Chicago and Youngstown, Ohio. We are ready to report some results. We do this not in a belief that the most important things happen in northeast Ohio, but in the spirit of Thoreau's comment that all any of us have to say to each other is what we have personally experienced.

We Still Don't Know What We Mean by "Economic Democracy"

A generation after SDS promulgated the Port Huron Statement in 1962, those who seek to create a more democratic society have given very little content to the vision of "economic democracy."

The Port Huron Statement called the United States a "Remote Control Economy." The mass of people are excluded "from basic decisions affecting the nature and organization of work, rewards, and opportunities." Economic minorities "not responsible to a public in any democratic fashion make decisions of a more profound importance than even those made by Congress." Government influence is marginal: "the basic production decisions, the basic decision-making environment of society, the basic structure of distribution and allocation . . . is . . . determined by major corporations with power and wealth concentrated among the few."

All this was true when it was written, and remains at least as true today. Concentrated wealth administered from the top down still stands opposed to the common wealth, the common thing *(res publica)*. Economic democracy should still be at the top of the agenda for any movement of social change.

But when it came to outlining the forms of an economic democracy, the Port Huron Statement stuttered. A "way must be found to direct our economic resources to genuine human needs," the statement declared; "the anarchic actions of industrial leaders should become structurally responsible to the people"; there should be "increased worker participation in management decision-making."

A few nuts and bolts were suggested. Public ownership is appropriate (1) when a resource has been discovered or developed with public revenue, (2) when monopolization seems inevitable, and (3) when national and business objectives conflict. Local, regional, and national economic planning is needed, as well as "experiments in decentralization." Specifically, there should be a "proliferation" of public authorities such as the Tennessee Valley Authority (TVA), and a breaking up of cities into smaller communities "powered by nuclear energy."

All this is—or seems to me—pretty thin soup. But the soup is not much more substantial today. Fashionable remedies such as employee stock ownership plans or quality circles on the shop floor catch on partly because the Left has had so little that is specific to suggest. Do we or do we not favor public ownership? If so, under what circumstances? And how do we plan to forestall top-down management by a *state* bureaucracy? What do we have to say about the role of unions in publicly owned enterprises? Should workers manage, or does the wider community also have a legitimate voice? To whatever extent community input is appropriate, how should it be expressed? And what are the mechanisms—eminent domain, for example—by which a change in ownership arrangements can be brought about?

A long list of such questions requires detailed response. Of course, specific suggestions are hard to make when it is so difficult to make specific experiments. The rising bourgeoisie within feudal society appears in retrospect to have had ample social space in which to create new institutions, such as free cities, Protestant congregations, corporations, guilds, and finally, nation-states. Within the belly of the capitalist whale, new institutions—particularly new *economic* institutions, permitting persons to make their livelihoods in a new way—seem far harder to bring into being.

This essay will explore the question of how labor-community coalitions can move toward the creation of economic democracy. First, I will argue that labor-community coalitions such as Polish Solidarity and the solidarity movements in Youngstown, Ohio, prefigure the sort of democratic, decentralized, participatory economic institutions that we might wish to see in a more democratic society. Second, I will suggest that when such movements address the problem of social ownership of enterprises, they tend to become more pragmatic and conservative, and more likely to sacrifice the values of solidarity and community to the goal of survival in the marketplace. Third, I will conclude by contending that we must seek to imagine, to project for acceptance, and to construct, kinds of ownership and management that are consistent with the values of solidarity and community, and I will suggest what seem to me some relevant first approximations, using as examples the Legal Services Corporation and the "land trust" model in an industrial setting.

Some "Labor-Community Coalitions" Are a Lot More Democratic Than Others

The term "labor-community coalition" is quite abstract. It can be applied to movements that differ greatly with respect to how much they express the values of solidarity and community, and how much they practice the participatory democracy sought to be created in the 1960s.

"Labor," to begin with, is an ambiguous word. There is a tendency to use the word as if it meant national trade unions and their leaders.

But if this is what "labor" means, then one has to question to what extent "labor" as it presently exists in the United States is part of the solution to the problem of undemocratic institutions, or part of the problem.

Top-down, bureaucratic unions mimic the top-down, bureaucratic corporations with which they purportedly do combat. The government of even so seemingly liberal a union as the United Automobile Workers resembles a one-party state in the Soviet bloc (in fairness to the Soviet bloc, perhaps one should say a one-party state before *perestroika* and *glasnost*). There is no concept of a loyal opposition. Opposition tends to be viewed as betrayal, deserving of repression by means fair or foul. Moreover, these unions believe in control of the world of work by means of legally enforcible contracts negotiated far from the shop floor. Contracts routinely give away by means of no-strike clauses the worker's most necessary tool, the right to strike. Efforts to improvise participatory democracy on the shop floor are routinely stamped out by union leaders, acting as policemen for the boss.

Such unions are institutional dinosaurs, which caricature rather than express a vision of the labor movement based on solidarity, militancy, innovative strategies, and most important, rank-and-file democracy. They are not models for a democratic future. They are cautionary horror stories that tell us what to avoid.

Local unions are often more democratic, and are the natural starting point for labor-community coalitions. But local unions that belong to "international" unions are severely circumscribed in what they can do. From their beginnings in the 1930s, international industrial unions have discouraged contact between different locals (for example, General Motors locals in the Detroit area), insisting that locals communicate with each other through national headquarters. At least in the Steelworkers Union, the national union signs every contract, and insists that each local clear with it the possibility of action that might expose the international to liability for contract violation. The local union that insists on hiring its own lawyers and pursuing its own strategy in a local crisis such as a plant shutdown risks being put in trusteeship in any union in the United States, including those with the most liberal reputations.

Finally, the community organizations with which labor cooperates in labor-community coalitions are often undemocratic, too. Many such groups are organized by organizers trained by Saul Alinsky and his followers. Alinsky (whom I knew personally, and in whose Industrial Areas Foundation Training Institute I was a teacher) was a brilliant organizer and a great admirer of John L. Lewis. Like Lewis in the 1930s, Alinsky organizers typically create top-down structures held together by hatred for a personalized enemy. Particularly offensive is the common assumption among organizers trained in this tradition that ordinary human beings are motivated by money, sex, power, and not much else, and are incapable of complex political decisions. Just as in the organizing of unions, Alinskyan organizers do battle until they are recognized, at which point, having been given a piece of the action, they put their feet up on the table and break out the cigars with their erstwhile enemies.

Accordingly, I believe that any discussion of labor-community coalitions as harbingers of a more democratic future must carefully define at the outset what *kind* of labor-community coalition we are talking about. In what follows I shall be speaking about a kind of labor-community coalition for which there are many models, but which may be atypical in the United States: class-conscious, raucously democratic, militant mass movements based (for the most part) not on existing labor organizations, but directly in the rank and file.

The Workers' Solidarity Club of Youngstown*

We wanted a place where rank-and-file workers could go to get strike support without a lot of hassle and delay.

We were disillusioned with big national unions that encourage their members to "pay your dues and leave the rest to us."

We were called "rebels" and "dissidents" but we believed in solidarity, and we wanted a way to see each other regularly, share experiences, laugh at each other's jokes, and dream up plans to change the world.

The Workers' Solidarity Club grew out of classes at the hall of Utility Workers Local 118, where the club still meets. Local 118 had been through a long strike a couple of years earlier. There was a core of members who were eager to give tangible strike support to other workers on strike. In the fall of 1981, we held a series of discussions at the hall on the topic, What has gone wrong with the labor movement? We talked about all kinds of things, for instance the new encyclical by the Pope called "On Human Labor." As the discussions drew to a close, we realized we did not want to disband. We gave ourselves a name and started to meet monthly.

From the beginning, the club has been extremely informal. There are no officers except a treasurer. Two members get out a monthly notice describing what is expected to happen at the next meeting. Individuals volunteer (or are volunteered at the last moment) to chair

---

*This description of the Workers' Solidarity Club of Youngstown appeared in a slightly different form in *Labor Notes*, April 1989.

particular meetings. If there is a speaker at a particular meeting, the person who invited the speaker is likely to become chairperson. There are no dues, but by passing the hat we have raised hundreds of dollars for legal defense, publications, and travel expenses. We also raise money by selling bright red suspenders with the words "Workers' Solidarity" silk-screened in black. Beer at the end of every meeting, and annual picnics and Christmas parties, keep us cheerful.

The Workers' Solidarity Club is like a Wobbly "mixed local," or a local branch of Polish Solidarity, in that its members come from many different trades and unions. A recent leaflet was signed by twenty-five people. Of these, seventeen are current employees; they work for Ohio Edison, Schwebel Baking Company, LTV Steel, and other enterprises. Six of the seventeen are stewards or local union officers. The remaining signers are retired or unemployed. The signers include present or former members of the Utility Workers, the Laborers, United Steelworkers (USWA), the Bakery Workers, the Teamsters, United Mine Workers (UMW), the Ohio Education Association, and the Amalgamated Clothing Workers.

Our first big action came in the summer of 1982. Service and maintenance workers at Trumbull Memorial Hospital in Warren, Ohio, organized in an Association of Federal, State, County, and Municipal Employees (AFSCME) local, went on strike. Two members of the club visited the picket line. The club put out a series of leaflets that appealed to strikebreakers not to cross the picket line. The first leaflet began: *"THINK* before you cross a picket line. Think before you take your neighbor's job."

The leaflets also invited members of other unions to rally every Wednesday afternoon in front of the hospital. The rallies grew larger and larger. People brought homemade banners and signs, and chanted such slogans as: "Warren is a union town, we won't let you tear it down."

On October 13, 1982, there was a confrontation with the Warren police. Thirteen demonstrators were arrested, including three members of the club: Ed Mann, retired president of a steelworkers' local; Greg Yarwick, a member of Local 118; and Ken Porter, laid off from a local cement company. The other arrestees entered agreed-on pleas for lesser offenses, and paid a fine. Ed, Greg, and Ken pleaded not guilty, and were convicted of conspiracy to riot and resisting arrest. With the help of the American Civil Liberties Union (ACLU) they appealed to the Court of Appeals and the Supreme Court of Ohio. In the end, not only were they acquitted, but the club recovered $1,000 in court costs from the City of Warren.

As a result of all this mass activity the AFSCME local survived the strike. After the strike, the club conducted classes for sixty to eighty members of the AFSCME local at the hall of Local 1375, USWA.

Other club activities have included weekly picketing at the Bessemer Cement Company, which closed and cut off benefits (only to reopen as a nonunion ship under a different owner), and strike support for the Food and Commercial Workers. Although there are three lawyers in the club, we all agree that legal activity should reinforce mass activity, not the other way around. A local bakery became notorious for its many discharges. Club members were involved in picketing, bringing National Labor Relations Board (NLRB) charges, and a lawsuit, and the number of discharges has decreased dramatically. Executives of one of the very few businesses to move to Youngstown since the steel mills closed, Avanti Motors, told the local media that if a union were organized they might leave town. The Workers' Solidarity Club filed a charge with the NLRB, and Avanti Motors was obliged to post a notice promising not to threaten a shutdown. The United Automobile Workers is now organizing the plant.

In evaluating the Trumbull Memorial Hospital strike, many club members felt that our role had been essentially reactive. Union leaders made decisions about strategy. Rank-and-file union members and strike supporters had to live with these decisions whether or not they agreed with them. The sentiment was expresed that the club should seek ways to do its own organizing.

This has been a long process, and of course we are still learning. Club members have been involved in three attempts to organize unions. One was successful. A small group of visiting nurses and home health aides formed an independent union for which they (not we!) chose the name Visiting Nurses Solidarity. Two other organizing drives, at medium-size metal fabricators, have failed.

The most dramatically successful organizing in which Club members have taken part involves retirees from LTV Steel and other steel companies, and workers disabled by exposure to toxic chemicals at the Lordstown General Motors (GM) plant. These people are not union members but they are affected by union decisions. In the case of LTV Steel, for example, contracts are ratified by 20–25,000 active workers that affect the pensions and medical benefits of over 40,000 hourly retirees. By organizing independently retirees have been able to bring some pressure to bear on union decisionmakers, although retirees still have no formal voice. At GM, chemically disabled former workers and the relatives of deceased workers have joined forces with curent rank-and-file employees to try to do something about occupational hazards.

In all this activity, a solidarity-building process is at work. Youngstown-area LTV retirees, organized as Solidarity USA (again a name chosen wholly by those involved), have reached out to other LTV retirees in Canton, Ohio, and Aliquippa, Pennsylvania, and to retirees from other, smaller steel companies. The GM group, known as Workers Against Toxic Chemical Hazards or WATCH, has been sought out by the employees of other companies who are exposed to similar hazards. And some of the leaders of both Solidarity USA and WATCH have become new and valued participants in the Workers' Solidarity Club.

What is the purpose of the Workers' Solidarity Club? What is its long-range contribution to rebuilding the labor movement?

There may be as many answers to these questions as there are members of the club. At a recent meeting, one member characterized the club as the local labor movement's SWAT team. One of the founders of the club remarked: "We don't fit in. We shouldn't. We're free-flowing." Another longtime participant commented on the hundreds of persons who have passed through meetings of the club during its eight-year history. What we've shown, he added, is that you have to get people involved; you can't just throw money at problems, but must be able to build a mass movement in your own back yard.

Recently, it has begun to seem that the club is on its way to building that mass movement. The first 1989 meeting of Solidarity USA attracted an estimated 400 persons. The Mahoning County AFL-CIO Council has invited Solidarity USA to send a delegate to its meetings on behalf of retirees, and Ed Mann attends.

There are a couple of things we would like to share with others who might want to try something similar.

First, from the very first meeting a majority of those present have been rank-and-file workers, or retirees. Rather than fast-speaking professionals or academics setting the tone, it has been the other way around. While lawyers and academics (including the director of labor studies at the local university) take part, they are minority voices.

Second, we have discouraged lecturing, and rarely make long presentations. We think that a broader consciousness has grown naturally from the experience of talking and acting together. Having lived through the way big corporations trampled on people's lives in Youngstown, we find it easy to relate to corporations doing the same thing to Indians in the Southwest, or to workers and peasants in Latin America. In April 1988 four members of the club went to Nicaragua along with steelworkers from Aliquippa and Pittsburgh, for two weeks. Most of the group worked at the Metasa steel mill near Managua. In February 1989 one of the group, an electric lineman, returned with a fellow worker and helped to string electric lines to bring electric power to a hospital in northern Nicaragua.

Third, we do not feel the need to come to a group decision about the correctness of a proposed action before a member does something. Instead, the member will say: "I'm planning to do so-and-so. I need help. Any one who wants to give me a hand, meet me" at such-and-such a time and place. Acting in this way gives us a chance to try things out in practice. It's like the experimental method in science. We're able to draw conclusions from what works and what doesn't.

Personally, I think that the Workers' Solidarity Club of Youngstown is doing what the line in "Solidarity Forever" talks about: in its small way, it is bringing to birth a new world from the ashes of the old. All around us is a capitalist society that believes in dog eat dog. We in the labor movement know that at its best our movement practices a higher ethic, the ethic that an injury to one is an injury to all. The thing is, though, we have to *live* that ethic, not just talk about it. The basic idea is, simply, that if we believe in solidarity, we should start living that way here and now.

Polish Solidarity

And then, of course, there is the inspiration of so much that all of us have done since 1980, the Mother Church of labor-community coalition: Polish Solidarity.

Like the movement in Youngstown, Polish Solidarity grew out of strike support work. This activity was conducted by the Committee for the Defense of Workers' Rights, or KOR. They raised money for people who had been fired and their families. They got lawyers for people who had been jailed. They started committees, without tight membership requirements, that came to include thousands of people. They decided to continue on as a movement for workers' rights and to democratize society, with the key strategic idea that the way to democratize Poland was to create a new, independent trade union movement. They developed a program called "Charter of Workers' Rights" and began running it in every issue of their underground newspaper *Robotnik* (The Worker).

During the years when Solidarity's leaders were in and out of jail, and Solidarity functioned underground, the time was hardly conducive to detailed blueprints of economic reform. But if we go back to the 16 glorious months in which Solidarity was able to function freely (August 1980–December 1981) we can identify a number of specifics, which, while far from containing the full vision of the future needed in Poland as well as everywhere else, go considerably beyond the Port Huron Statement.

The following are programmatic elements Solidarity has expressly endorsed:

(1) "Union pluralism," that is, the right of more than one union to exist and to represent workers in a particular workplace. This idea is nearly as revolutionary in the United States as in Poland. As of January 1989, it had been accepted in principle by the Communist Party of Poland but not by labor unions or by labor law in the United States.

(2) A workers' council in each enterprise. Consistent with union pluralism, "several unions could co-exist in a plant, but would send representatives proportionally to a workers' council that would bear full responsibility for negotiations with management" (*New York Times,* January 20, 1989). Workers' councils have been championed by Polish Solidarity since 1980, when Point 6 of the Gdansk Agreement declared that economic reform "must be based on the strengthening, autonomous operation and participation of the workers' council in management."

(3) Authority of the workers' council to take part in investment decisions and in the hiring and firing of management. The draft program of Polish Solidarity, developed in 1980–81, said that workers' self-management bodies should exercise authority, not just on the shop floor, but "should have the right to exercise control over the assets of the concern, to decide on the aims of production and sales, the choice of production methods, and investment goals. They should also decide on the distribution of the profits of the enterprise." One thing is especially necessary, the Solidarity draft program continued: "involvement of workers self-management bodies in the recruitment and dismissal of directors."

(4) A "clear separation" between the workers' council that participates in the management of the enterprise, and the union that defends workers' immediate interests. We in the United States have reason to appreciate the importance of this element of the Solidarity draft program. At Rath Packing, Seymour Specialty Wire, and Weirton Steel, local union presidents sat on the enterprise board of directors and have experienced an inevitable conflict of interest.

When solidarity movements address the problem of social ownership of enterprises, they tend to become more pragmatic and conservative, and more likely to sacrifice the values of solidarity and community to the goal of survival in the marketplace

It might seem at first glance that when "mere" strike support movements turn their attention to worker-community ownership and management of enterprises, it would indicate a growing radicalism, or produce a radicalization of those involved.

The evidence is that the reverse is the case. Alternative ownership of enterprises typically presents itself in the aftermath of an announcement that a particular workplace will be closed. This generates conservatism in two different ways.

First, because the focus of attention in a plant closing context is on a single endangered enterprise, the struggle to save that particular plant typically gives rise to a collective egoism, an attitude that this particular enterprise must be made to succeed at whatever cost to workers elsewhere. Thus when Weirton Steel was struggling to survive, officers of the local union told David Moberg of *In These Times* (December 15–21, 1982), "If there is going to be one steel company alive in this country, we intend it to be Weirton," and "I don't feel bad about undercutting them [Weirton's competitors], if that's what we're doing. We're stockholders. That's the way big business is. I'll be an equal owner of a big business." And at Seymour Specialty Wire, where worker-owners belong to the UAW, they compete for survival with members of their own union in other plants.

Second, the effort to save a particular enterprise requires those responsible for the effort to garner support from *existing* institutions, not from institutions as we might wish them to be in some future society. This is above all the case with respect to obtaining capital. Where the plant sought to be saved has closed because of the failure of conglomerate owners to invest in up-to-date equipment, one must seek capital not only to buy, but, far more expensively, to modernize the facility. Thus, in Youngstown, we could have purchased any one of the mills we sought to save for $15–20 million, but in each the existing open-hearth technology had to be replaced by steelmaking devices (basic oxygen furnaces or electric furnaces, plus a continous caster) that cost roughly ten times as much. At U.S. Steel's Duquesne Works, where in 1984–85 a mighty battle sought to reopen the "Dorothy 6" blast furnace, there was a modern blast furnace but no caster. The reason the foregoing efforts failed is that the federal government was not about to make money available for this purpose, and the private funds that could be found were insufficient.

On the other hand, if in a desperate effort to find capital one contracts with a Wall Street investment firm, new dilemmas arise. True, the firm of Lazard Frères put together the Weirton deal, and has been engaged by the United Steelworkers of America on a continuing basis, and true, Lazard Frères has sometimes found the money. But the cost is substantial. If one lays the four above-stated principles of Polish Solidarity alongside what has been done at Weirton Steel, or projected by the Steelworkers at other sites, one finds: (1) no union pluralism, rather a tendency to cut concessionary deals with the existing union; (2) no workers' council, but the far more innocuous notion of worker "participation" on the shop floor (team leaders, rotation of work, etc., etc.); (3) no veto on the part of workers' representatives over investment decisions and the selection of management personnel; and (4) no separation between the union and management of the enterprise, but rather a tendency for the worker-director who accepts a concessionary package in the board room to be the same person who as local union president tries to sell the package at the union hall.

These conservative dynamics have a special poignancy in plant closing and reopening struggles. The closing of an enterprise literally destroys the rank and file by ejecting them from the workplace. After a first few weeks of tumultuous mass meetings, and talk of occupying things (we should more often do it!) and blowing things up, most workers in the typical situation conclude that the plant will not reopen, withdraw from collective efforts, and turn their attention to individual survival strategies.

The dispersal of the rank and file in turn has its effect on those organizing the takeover effort. The rank and file, and the local union, are no longer in being. (Alternative rank and files, such as retirees and the unemployed, are rarely explored.) The obvious available source of aid from the labor movement becomes the international union. It has lawyers. It has "contacts." Above all, it has money. In place of raucous mass meetings there come to be quiet talks with international union insiders. A place is found in movement rhetoric for the said-to-be legitimate interests of "business." A painfully constructed analysis, explaining plant shutdowns by the capitalist thirst for profit maximization, is shelved for more palatable talk about currency rates and import barriers. Whatever thrust there had been for public ownership gives way to enthusiasm for employee stock ownership, which is easier to sell in the state capital.

I suggest that these dynamics should be understood in a no-fault manner. I have myself felt their pressure. It is not a question of old friends and comrades "selling out." But we must give attention. The purpose of labor-community coalitions to save endangered plants is partly to save jobs, and partly to serve as a bridge to a new society. If the jobs can be saved only by sacrificing the values essential to the new society, we place ourselves in an insoluble quandary. We cannot get from here to there without victories in the short run, but immediate victories will not be what André Gorz called "revolutionary reforms" if, in fact, they take us in the wrong direction. What are we to do?

Toward Participatory Economic Democracy

The argument of this essay is that a *certain kind of* labor-community coalition—free-flowing, democratic, assisting rank and filers in one branch of the economy directly to encounter their counterparts in other branches of the economy—can serve as a model and stepping stone in moving toward economic democracy. Polish Solidarity remains far ahead of anything experienced in the United States in pointing the way, but examples such as the Workers' Solidarity Club of Youngstown show that what has happened in Poland is also possible here.

On the other hand, I suggest, if we build labor-community coalitions that include and make their peace with the bureaucratic, top-down undemocratic structure of existing national unions, then the economic enterprises created by such coalitions will also be bureaucratic, top-down, and undemocratic. Efforts to reopen particular closed plants under "worker ownership" or "worker-community ownership" give rise to the temptation to make this compromise, I argue. And I contend that surrender to this dynamic would be tragic, because then what we would do is to make a socialism without a human face, causing another generation of rank-and-file workers to conclude that public ownership and socialism are not what they want.

Let me try to be as specific and helpful as possible for readers who may share these concerns.

First, in the local communities where we live and work we should try to create institutions like the local branches of Polish Solidarity, or the Workers' Solidarity Club, where workers from different unions and enterprises make common cause. In some cases this will be a radicalized central labor council. In other cases it will be an ad hoc or "parallel" central labor council. Some participating local unions will be independent of existing national unions. Others will belong to national unions but *act* independently. Through these institutions, rank and filers can reinforce one another horizontally and develop a broader consciousness through supporting one another's struggles, as opposed to the typical vertical style of union operation during the last fifty years in this country, where if you belonged to a particular national union and you wanted to blow your nose you had to get clearance from the appropriate person in the national office before proceeding. Such local solidarity unions can be like "base communities" in Latin America. They can be formed independently of national movements or any particular stage of national struggle, but be ready to contribute to such movements and such struggles, and to inject into them their distinctive experience and spirit.

Second, we should talk about a form of public ownership or socialism such that *in general* the national government would fund the provision of goods and services by decentralized entities jointly managed by workers and consumers. The solidarity unions engendered during the previous phase of struggle, and continuing into the phase of ownership and management of the economy, will provide living models for such entities. When asked what we are talking about, we can respond, "You know, like the solidarity club, or the" whatever name we have given it in our locality: workers together solving common problems.

Legal Services offers an example of how national funding and monitoring can be combined with decentralized administration. Funds are allocated to the dozens of field offices in proportion to the number of persons in the geographical service areas of the various offices whose incomes are below the federal "poverty line." The field offices are required by law to be administered by boards composed in roughly equal parts of lawyers (workers) and clients (consumers). Thus, on the board of Northeast Ohio Legal Services there are three former steelworkers, each one formerly employed at a mill the shutdown of which our office struggled mightily to prevent. The board also includes three members of the Workers' Solidarity Club (two of the three steelworkers and the director of labor studies at Youngstown State University).

I have been employed in this system for the past ten years and can testify that it works. I believe that it could readily be adapted to the provision of other needed services, such as national health insurance. Thus Physicians for a National Health Program of Cambridge, Massachusetts, have proposed a program that would be "federally mandated and ultimately funded by the federal government but administered largely at the state and local level."

The labor-community coalition at the local level is the natural incubator of the various work groups that will provide nationally funded goods and services in this way. Thus, in Youngstown, the little nurses' union that organized under the name Visiting Nurses Solidarity now fully controls the management of the service its members provide, in the sense that all three agency "supervisors" are former members of the union. And the national network of labor-community coalitions is the force that can bring Congress to provide the national funding without which local ventures in participatory economic democracy can hardly be expected to succeed, at least on a significant scale.

The land trust is another attractive model. The land trust has been used to create housing where the user has most of the attributes of ownership, including the right to alienate the property by inheritance (but not by speculative resale), while the trust remains title-holder and ultimate owner. The Tri-State Conference on Steel in Pittsburgh is seeking an industrial version of the land trust, where a public development authority acquires and owns the land and buildings of an abandoned steel mill, but leases the property for operation to a more or less conventional for-profit business. Whether in housing or industry, the land trust expresses a deep critique of the capitalist idea of absolute ownership of private property. For this it substitutes the notion that the current user is, in the language of Catholic social doctrine, a "steward" of that which still belongs to God, or in Jefferson's similar vision, an embodiment of the "living generation" which, upon death, must return the property it has used to a common pool for redistribution.

Thus there is no dearth of intriguing technical arrangements that in a society that was not driven by profit maximization could happily combine centralized public funding, regulation, and ownership with localized participatory management. Cold war hang-ups about the inevitable effects of public ownership, visions of long lines of people waiting before huge, grey government office buildings, are no longer appropriate. Enough examples exist for us to be able to talk persuasively to our fellow citizens about how we, as members of labor-community coalitions, can effectively step in and do the job when profit-seeking corporations are unwilling to make steel, build low-income housing, or heal all those in need. There is overwhelming public support for national health insurance, decades of cold war conditioning notwithstanding. The times are ripe for a breakthrough into a more socialized economy.

But none of it will happen absent a certain will, an inextinguishable desire, the endurance of long-distance runners. In a sense one circles back to the stress of the Port Huron Statement on "values": on a vision of how it ought to be between people that energizes the organizer in going to one more meeting, pecking out one more leaflet. Participatory economic democracy requires participatory agitation in every stage of its creation. Upheaval from below is the best assurance of an outcome that will allow ordinary persons to participate in decisions that affect their lives.

Upstairs, Downstairs: Class Conflict in an Employee-Owned Factory

Jeremy Brecher

A hundred years ago, as large companies were supplanting self-employed artisans in U.S. industry, a burgeoning labor organization called the Knights of Labor argued that workers, instead of working for a wage, should own their companies. Conservative unionists like Samuel Gompers attacked this vision, urging workers to face reality and organize powerful craft unions within the developing business system. Left-wing unionists, conversely, attacked worker ownership as just another form of capitalism that would instill in workers an illusory identification with the bosses. Many worker cooperatives were started, but most either failed or ended up as conventional businesses.

A century later, arguments over the meaning of worker ownership have erupted again as a result of the recent spread of employee stock ownership plans (ESOPs). Dramatic headlines tell how seven unions bid $750 million to take control of the Southern Pacific railroad and how Avis employees bought their company for $1.75 billion—giving the Westray Capital Corporation, which engineered the deal, a $500 million payoff.

Originally the brainchild of business lawyer Louis Kelso, author of *The Capitalist Manifesto: How to Turn 80 Million Workers into Capitalists on Borrowed Money*, ESOPs now enroll an estimated 8 million workers. Most have been initiated by managements to take advantage of special ESOP tax breaks; often they are designed to exclude worker stockerholders from voting rights; in some cases, ESOPs originated when managers threatened to close workplaces unless the workers agree to buy them on unfavorable terms. But ESOPs have also been used by unions and community groups to buy companies in the hope of saving jobs and improving the workplace. What can be learned from their experience?

Background

One of the largest, most democratic, and longest-running of the recent worker buyouts is Seymour Specialty Wire in Seymour, Connecticut, a classic American mill town a few miles west of New Haven in the heart of Connecticut's "Brass Valley." In a region studded with abandoned brass mills, Seymour Specialty Wire employs more workers today than it did when its employees bought it nearly three years ago. But it is also marked by bitter internal conflict. The company's experience is worth examining because it reveals difficulties that will be faced not only by other democratic ESOPs, but by any effort to increase workers' power in the workplace, whatever the form of ownership.

Until the buyout, the Seymour story was in many ways a history in microcosm of American industry. Founded in 1878 as the Seymour Manufacturing Company and controlled by a prominent local family, the brass mill employed 1,400 workers by World War I.

Initially at Seymour, as throughout American industry, skilled manual workers possessed the crucial knowledge necessary for production and directed much of the production process. Frank Pochron, a retired manager who started at Seymour in 1936, recalls that "years ago they didn't have all this equipment to check out what you were doing. They relied upon the people to do it. Years ago it seemed the operators had the technicalities, were proud of their work and able to do their jobs, what the customer demanded and the shop wanted."

But all that changed as American industrialists began to redesign the work process to concentrate knowledge and authority in a management cadre whose job was to tell manual workers how to do their work. Frank Pochron described the impact at Seymour: "Now you are directed what to do. It seems the operators wait for management to tell them what to do and if it doesn't come out right, so what?"

To ensure that the deskilled workers would actually work, production standards were set for each job. Sam Kwochka, who started working at Seymour in 1935 and retired in 1979, recalls that if you met the standards "you were entitled to stay on till layoff. But if you faltered below a hundred percent, out the door you went."

Workers responded to the restructured work process with a two-fold strategy. First, they developed informal shop floor tactics for controlling the pace of work and resisting management pressure. One retired worker recalled, "They would time me; I would work normal, just like I've always been doing. But when they're not there, instead of shearing it in one or two pieces, I can shear four or five. It's my own ingenuity."

This and the many other techniques workers developed to control the pace of work were backed up by informal work groups. As Sam Kwochka recalled, "They would tell them man-to-man what to expect and what not to exceed."

Along with these informal methods, Seymour workers developed unionism. Eddie Labacz, former president of the union at Seymour, told me, "When they tried to organize a union in Seymour in the early 1940s, they had to meet in cellars or somebody's house; they were afraid that the company would let them go. . . . Once the union won the election, they told the company, 'If you fire anybody, we're all going to walk out.' So the company figured there was no use firing anybody for being active in the union."

The sharp division between a managerial cadre concentrating knowledge and authority and a unionized manual labor force paid to obey orders and not paid to think became a deeply rooted feature of the company, as of most other U.S. manufacturers. It was built into the union contract, the employees' jobs and lifestyles, and even the physical layout of the workplace and the language used to describe it. Manual workers are called "hourly" and "bargaining unit"; all others, whether typists or top managers, are "salaried." To this day at Seymour, workers refer to management as "upstairs" and to those on the shop floor as "downstairs."

The workers' strategy of combining informal resistance and union protection was so effective that management was forced to accommodate. I toured the Seymour plant in the early 1980s and was struck by the easy pace of work and the relaxed atmosphere. Tony Mazza, who started working at Seymour in 1983, noted:

"There was always that laid-back attitude on the part of the foremen. One reason was the union. The foremen never could exercise their authority. Maybe because in the past they had gone to the extreme with it. The foremen had to have a very soft-spoken, step-lightly kind of attitude. Sometimes that was not good. It opened the door for too many problems. Guys getting away with things, people not being corrected, people not doing their job right, communications not being what they should be, gripes not being settled. That went on year after year."

The tendency toward lax management was reenforced when the Seymour Manufacturing Company was bought out by a larger company, Bridgeport Brass, which in turn was purchased by the conglomerate National Distillers. Foremen and supervisors received little training; production systems remained in the precomputer era; little new investment was allowed; the facilities were permitted to run down.

Such milking was rife throughout the Brass Valley, and by the early 1980s the multinational conglomerates that owned the brass mills were closing them or selling them off to liquidators. In response, unions, churches, and community organizations in the region had formed the Naugatuck Valley Project (NVP), an experiment in using the techniques of community organization to fight deindustrialization.

When the local union in Seymour heard rumors that the company might be put up for sale, their United Auto Workers (UAW) international representative said they should think about buying the plant themselves and suggested they get in touch with the NVP. Leaders of the local were highly skeptical—but eager to explore anything that might save the jobs of the company's 250 employees, they set up a meeting with the NVP and the Industrial Cooperative Association (ICA), a Boston-based consulting organization specializing in employee-owned businesses. The local voted to go ahead and explore the buyout idea.

The Buyout

ICA began a feasibility study for a buyout. When National Distillers appeared reluctant to deal with its workforce as a serious potential buyer, the NVP mobilized a community pressure campaign, whereupon National Distillers became fully cooperative and even contributed to the costs of the feasibility study. Local white-collar officials began to participate and joined the steering committee that had been set up for the buyout effort.

After visits to less-than-democratic buyouts at Hyatt-Clark and Atlas Chain, the steering committee decided the new company should be wholly owned by an ESOP open only to company employees. It would be run by a nine-member board of directors with five members elected at an annual ESOP meeting on a one-employee-one-vote basis, plus the presidents of the company and the union and two outside directors chosen by the board.

An initial ESOP meeting was held for all employees and candidates for the board gave two-minute speeches; to the surprise of union leaders, managers were elected to four of the five seats. A search committee, after reviewing 170 responses to a blind ad in the *New York Times,* hired the current plant manager, Carl Drescher, to be the president of the new company.

Under a business plan developed with help from ICA, the workforce was to be reduced by forty jobs, all but twelve of them by attrition. All employees were to take a 10 percent wage cut. The union continued to represent the hourly workforce in the new company. Union president Mike Kearney recalls, "We went upstairs to negotiate a contract and we found we were negotiating with ourselves." While there was grumbling about the wage cut, the contract was ratified with only two negative votes.

The union and the steering committee kept workers informed of the buyout process through a series of meetings. Perhaps 40 of the

250 employees were actively involved, but most rank-and-file workers were more observers than active participants in the process.

The ESOP Experience

On April 17, 1985, Seymour Specialty Wire, an employee-owned company, took over the assets. Reporters and the governor converged for the celebration. Top company officials began setting up the accounting and other systems necessary for an independent company. But little else seemed to change. According to Tony Mazza, "On paper it was different, but in actuality it wasn't much different. What he could actually see and hear, the guy in the shop, it was no different, except he knew the company belonged to him and he had x number of shares being built up on paper. There wasn't the vehicle there yet to help him realize this really was his company."

The legacy of roles, privileges, and power bases led inevitably to a series of conflicts. Soon after the buyout, for example, several managers were given substantial raises to compensate for their added duties. Union president Mike Kearney recalls the reaction:

"I was approached by I don't know how many of the people down in the shop. What action could they take? I said, you could petition under the by-laws for a special meeting. Over 125 people petitioned. They had a full-house meeting. They demanded to know how the company could give managers a raise when everyone had taken a 10 percent cut."

Despite the protest, the board voted seven to two to confirm the raises. Kearney recalls that he told company president Carl Drescher after that incident, "You lost everybody's trust and everybody is kind of leery now. Anything that happens upstairs, 'They've only thinking about themselves.'"

Workers also continued to use their traditional weapons. In the casting department, often a stronghold of informal workgroups in brass mills, a dispute broke out between workers and a new foreman. Workers conducted a slow-down and were accused of sabotage when large amounts of unusable metal began coming out of the casting shop. The dispute continued until the foreman was withdrawn.

The evidence of sabotage in the casting shop alerted all parties to how dangerous the company's labor-management situation really was and made them ready to consider alternatives. The board brought ICA back in to organize a "goal-setting process" to draw the rank and file into a discussion of the company's future. They held a series of twenty-minute meetings with approximately twenty employees in each to list and prioritize company goals. A lot of anger was vented in the process; one lower white-collar person commented, "The first goal I would suggest is that we figure out some way to kick top management's ass."

Delegates were selected to an "ad hoc committee" which refined the various goals to five, dealing with productivity, maintenance, safety, finance, and, above all, a system to promote labor-management communication and cooperation. The ad hoc committee developed a detailed design for such a system, which they dubbed Workers Solving Problems (WSP). Under WSP, work groups would meet with their foremen for twenty minutes every two weeks to identify and solve problems; those they couldn't solve themselves would be carried by the foreman and a worker representative to meetings at a higher level.

WSP bore a resemblance to "quality circles" and also to the stages of a union grievance procedure. To its architects, however, it was intended not just to draw workers into improving production, but also to make management at every level accountable to rank-and-file employees and work groups. They had high hopes for its success. But WSP met severe resistance to both worker participation and management accountability. It was perhaps ominous when one manager asked, "Will we allow them wash up on their time or our time?"

Work groups met and chose representatives. These representatives and the foremen were trained in group process and problem-solving techniques and proceeded to run WSP meetings. Many workers were already so skeptical about the whole situation that they announced they would attend the meetings, since they were compulsory, but would refuse to say anything. Typically, after a WSP group identified a problem, the foreman and representative were told to discuss it at the next higher level and bring back an answer. If the work group did not like the answer they brought back, they had little recourse—they usually just went on to another problem, or, ultimately, withdrew from the whole procedure.

WSP turned out to be unable to hold any level of management accountable; problems were passed upstairs, but if the answers were not satisfactory there was not much workers could do about it. Workers had little interest in participating in a mechanism that gave them no real power. Blame for the failure of the program was apportioned variously to worker disinterest or abuse, foreman sabotage, and lack of leadership from top management.

Meanwhile, issues outside the purview of WSP continued to plague the company. A review of salary policy had revealed that some foremen were paid less than the workers they supervised and that some lower white-collar workers were paid below the bottom of their salary range, violating the board's salary policies. Yet proposals to give raises to these groups enraged rank-and-file workers, who felt everyone was benefiting but them.

This conflict brought in the union in its traditional role as representative of the economic interests of the hourly workforce. But the union itself was divided over the issue of an increased differential for the skilled trades workers in the maintenance department, who were receiving considerably less than similar workers in other plants in the area. Unskilled workers resented the idea that everybody but them seemed to be getting raises. The union proposed a wage reopener with something for everybody; management responded that it would cost the company too much. After nearly a year of discussion, the board agreed to a modest increase.

Meanwhile frustration about WSP, wages, and many other issues led to growing shop floor sentiment for electing hourly workers to the board. The second election chose one hourly and one salaried representative. Before the third election the bargaining unit was split over the issue of differentials for skilled tradesmen, but a union caucus endorsed two bargaining unit members who were overwhelmingly elected, giving the board for the first time a blue-collar majority.

This began to bring to a head a series of issues about the board and the role of union representatives on it that had only been hinted at when a majority of the board was drawn from management. From the beginning, company president Carl Drescher had been concerned that the hourly-waged members of the board keep apart their two hats as company directors and union leaders. In his view, the company had an obligation to its stockholders to maximize profit and equity. Pursuing other goals—whether job expansion, increasing hourly pay, or helping other buyouts—presented a potential conflict of interest with the board members' fiduciary responsibilities to the owners.

Such potential conflicts have arisen several times. When the union pushed to reopen the wage package, for example, union members on the board felt obliged to consult the company lawyer to see if they might be sued for violation of their fiduciary responsibilities. (The lawyer advised that the cost of the final proposal was too small to significantly affect the company's viability.) Hourly workers on the board voted raises for foremen over the objection of many workers because they believed it was a valid and necessary business decision. Particularly painful for union representatives on the board was a decision that they had to stop helping workers at Century Brass in Waterbury develop a buyout plan, on the ground that Seymour's interests might be hurt by the potential competition.

When only two people from the bargaining unit were on the board, Mike Kearney encouraged management board members to spend time on the shop floor talking with workers and urged workers to bring their concerns to the board members when they came through the shop. As more blue-collar people went on the board, this approach atrophied, and many workers defined the blue-collar representatives as their spokespeople on the board, through whom they channeled their communications with management. Many workers object to the idea that union representatives must act on a business basis while on the board. According to Kearney, "There was a lot of heated debate and argument up there because we're on the floor and Carl and them are up in the office. But when it came time to make decisions, I'm not going to do anything to jeopardize my job. If I'm going to make a decision that's going to shut the company down, I shouldn't be up there. People couldn't understand that. 'Hey, you should be representing hourly people!' Yeah, I know I'm representing hourly people. But remember, I don't have my union hat on when I'm up there. I've got my director's cap on."

Carl Drescher is well aware of this situation. "Union directors make decisions as directors. That's appropriate. But it's not always popular on the floor." One worker described the situation more bluntly: "Because of the way the voting has gone on the board, the people in the shop perceive the board members, especially those who are supposed to be representing them, as just oblivious to their concerns. They think they've been betrayed." There has been discussion of organizing hourly worker opposition against the present hourly worker representatives at the next election.

With the election of an hourly worker majority on the board, questions of the accountability of management to the board and the board to its electorate have been posed in a new context. The hourly workers on the board now meet weekly with Carl Drescher, creating a sort of cabinet with undefined authority. The board has created a committee on goverance and has brought ICA back in to help redefine roles. Whether a redefinition of board, management, and other responsibilities can establish the accountability that WSP failed to provide remains to be seen.

After a visit to Weirton Steel, the WSP coordinators decided to modify the program by making participation voluntary and by providing training to all participants, not just leaders. While the new plan is no longer a means to establish accountability to the shop floor, it provides a way those who want to can begin to take managerial initiative. Groups are presently working on such problems as late customer deliveries, training, and dissemination of financial data to employee owners. Says WSP facilitator Harry Francolini, "We probably had to go through the first version to get where we are today, because it was a learning process."

The first year at Seymour was a financial success. After six months, workers received a bonus and the 10 percent pay cut was restored. Then the business turned down sharply. While no layoffs occurred, and the business has now partially rebounded, there is a sense throughout the company of the compelling need for a "turnaround."

In response, management made a highly controversial decision to bring in a new consulting company, Universal Scheduling, for an intensive six-month intervention. Universal will establish a database for making production and productivity goal-setting decisions. It will conduct extensive management training designed to change the work culture and encourage foremen to set goals and define and solve problems. It will establish "ideal work centers" with optimum equipment and conditions to set productivity standards; when production falls substantially below the established standards, managers will be encouraged to take corrective action. According to Carl Drescher, "The purpose of bringing in Universal Scheduling is to install better management systems. The company needs their help in production scheduling. The managers can't run the business on a day-to-day basis and put in the time necessary to install these systems. The board voted nine to zero to hire them."

Mike Kearney explains, "There is some resistance because we've been doing the same thing for so many years. Pacing. After a while, from generation to generation it got ingrained in the different people, no matter who came in. They start like a bat out of hell, after a while they just get into a pattern. Universal is telling us, look, you guys have got a lot of idle, unproductive time in the shop you should fill. We said, we don't want to lay any people off. We came to agreement with Carl and the top managers that nobody would be laid off because of this."

The decision to bring in Universal Scheduling caused an uproar on the shop floor. Over a hundred employees petitioned for a special ESOP meeting. Management was vigorously attacked for spending money on consultants to do a job it should do itself. Some employees attacked president Carl Drescher as incompetent to run the company. The meeting itself had no authority and the board is unlikely to reverse its decision to bring in Universal Scheduling. Several people have told me they are watching to see what happens at the upcoming annual ESOP meeting when new board members are elected. There have also been rumors of a possible wildcat strike or a refusal to ratify the next union contract.

A Buyout Balance Sheet

What does the experience at Seymour so far say about the significance of worker buyouts? To answer that question it is necessary to look at what has changed because of the buyout at the company, what could change because of the buyout but has not, and what such a buyout is unlikely to change.

Some of the changes are dramatic and make a profound difference in workers' lives. Perhaps most important is the fact that workers now wield great influence over the power that unions elsewhere have had the greatest difficulty affecting—the power to make the basic economic decisions affecting the future of the company. Nobody besides those who work at Seymour can decide to close it down or make decisions that would lead to layoffs. No one can milk the company's profits and reinvest them elsewhere. As Mike Kearney put it, "You don't have to worry about National coming in and saying, we're going to have to eliminate this, Carl, cut this out, and there goes twenty jobs." Saving their jobs was the original reason workers turned to a buyout; the company is in that regard a tremendous success.

Worker ownership has also transformed what was, like most factories, an industrial autocracy into a democracy, however imperfect. Employees have voted out board members from management and replaced them with hourly workers. They have won the right to full information about every aspect of the company. Workers at Seymour, unlike those in most workplaces anywhere in the world, possess the basic human right to free expression. Roz Niezelski, who works in the accounting office, says, "People feel free to complain out loud. Normally, they don't do that in an office. The boss would fire them." Tony Mazza points out how unusual it is that "we can hold an ESOP meeting like we just did to address the grievances of the employees. Where in the world, or in any company in the United States that's not an ESOP company, could you do something like that? Management would just tell you to get out the door. You have a right to hold a meeting like that because it is your company." The political process has transformed the workforce from a fragmented mass to a contentious polity.

At Seymour, management still retains a great deal of power. But workers have far more counterpower than in a conventional company. Two top officers and at least one foreman have been demoted due to worker pressure, and the idea of "firing the boss" has been freely discussed.

Attitudes at Seymour are also very different from before the buyout. Many workers feel they still do not have an adequate share in decision-making—but they feel strongly that they are entitled to such a share. Tony Mazza indicates that the company's financial difficulties have increased that feeling: "Maybe if things were doing well financially, some of them wouldn't care. But that is just intensifying things."

If the company is financially successful and the initial loans are paid off, workers will be able to turn their share of equity into cash when they leave. While many workers consider this too remote to take seriously, some regard themselves as sitting on a potential pot of gold.

There are additional changes which worker ownership could help make possible, but which have not yet emerged. Perhaps the most important of these would be a transformation of the job structure itself, to reverse the division of labor, knowledge, and authority that developed in Seymour and other factories over the course of the twentieth century. Jobs can be redesigned to include management-type tasks as part of the responsibility of all individuals or work groups. Such a restructuring of jobs would entail a blurring of the distinctions and the differential privileges between white- and blue-collar workers. There might still be people whose primary job was managing, but there would no longer be a distinct managerial cadre which concentrated all management functions within itself. This approach would also require a democratization of knowledge, indeed, the turning of education into an everyday aspect of life in the shop, much as it was in the days when apprenticeship was society's principal means of education.

Another area that worker ownership could change but so far has not is the relation among different groups of workers. Top management remains the domain of white men; lower level office workers are almost entirely women; all but a handful of workers in the shop are male. Racial and ethnic tensions, while no worse than before the buyout, persist, with little effort to address them. Workers are still divided by skill classifications. Although they have not done so at Seymour, workers in a worker-owned company have more opportunity to challenge some of these divisions.

While the goal of saving jobs has, in fact if not in declared policy, been added to that of making money as a company objective, there has been little consideration of other, broader goals that a worker-owned company could pursue. Within the constraints of the market, such a company could seek to make the workplace and work experience as pleasant as possible, support the educational development of its workforce, emphasize socially useful products, seek to strengthen the local economy, emphasize involvement with underdeveloped countries, or pursue other objectives representing employee or social interest. Even conventional companies pursue goals in addition to making money; employee-owned companies have a greater opportunity to do so.

While the form of a private, for-profit company defines a firm as a unit of competition, there are many ways in which Seymour could reach out for more cooperative relations with others. An open house was held for workers' families and the Seymour community soon after the buyout, but since then there has been little effort at involvement with the local community. The Naugatuck Valley Project community activists who helped the company get going hoped it would be part of a network of worker- and community-owned enterprises and economic institutions. Seymour union officials are active in the project, its managers have participated in some NVP activities, and the company has contributed to the NVP's corporate fundraising campaign, but to date it has not joined the NVP despite invitations to do so, apparently due to concern that its business might be adversely affected by conflicts in which the NVP became involved.

There are other aspects of workers' powerlessness on which a buyout such as this one is likely to have little impact. The demand for the company's products and the price it must pay for its means of production are determined by a kaleidoscope of swirling global forces over which a single company can exercise no control; Seymour had to change its prices three times in one week due to gyrations in the cost of copper. Nor can the company exercise any control over the labor market; indeed, many of its most serious internal problems have resulted from the gap between the prevailing pay differentials in the marketplace and the concepts of fairness and worth held by various sectors of the company's workforce.

Worker ownership of a single company has no effect on broader social questions about what needs and whose needs get met and how. Nor can it have more than a trivial impact on the nonwork cultures and subcultures in which workers and managers live and in which most of their attitudes about work and life are formed.

The Seymour story reveals the anatomy and physiology of alienation. Workers' subordination is embedded in the institutional, cultural, and even physical structures of work and allocation. Each aspect will cause difficulties and need to be transformed or replaced—no matter what the formal structure of ownership—if work is to become an expression of free, cooperative human action.

The lessons of this experience are many, and are somewhat different for trade unionists, workers in worker-owned companies, and those looking more generally for ways to end the subordinate role of workers within the workplace and society.

Many trade unionists fear that worker ownership will achieve just what the original ESOP legislation intended: an identification of workers with their employers and with business in general. So far, the impact of the Seymour buyout on workers' class consciousness does not confirm such concerns. Indeed, workers generally seem to regard their ownership as changing little in their relationship with management. According to Tony Mazza, "The people who were pro-union before are for the union. The others not. I don't think being a buyout has affected their decisions either way. They don't think of it in terms of an employee-owned company; they just think in terms of what the union was before."

The role of the union has changed somewhat, but, except for a more positive attitude toward raising productivity, the change is more an expansion than an abandonment of its confrontive role. While retaining its grievance and collective bargaining functions, the union now also challenges management on a wide range of decisions about business policy. Management does not fully accept the legitimacy of these challenges—which is why conflict is so rampant. Indeed, one outside observer, asked what had changed at Seymour since the buyout, replied, "The class struggle is more obvious. People feel they can say things and take on issues; instead of just quietly hating someone or sabotaging, they're talking about it."

For workers faced with buyouts, however democratic or undemocratic, the Seymour experience shows that they need not abandon the weapons of union organization and informal on-the-job resistance that have helped workers survive in the past. What has yet to be found is a way to use the "withdrawal of efficiency" as a bargaining weapon while still taking advantage of the new avenues a buyout opens to increase worker's power. Perhaps some variant of productivity bargaining has a role to play here.

There are many advocates of social change who, echoing left-wing critics of the Knights of Labor, oppose worker ownership outright. Jerry Lembcke of Lawrence University, for example, writes: "For Marxists the only progressive step for moving things beyond capitalism is toward the social ownership of capital . . . a strategy to recreate a stratum of worker-owners . . . offers false hope to workers."

Workers' ownership of their own company does not in itself realize the ideal of social or common ownership of society's means of production. But the same, unfortunately, is true of the other existing models, such as government ownership or self-sufficient communes. A social or common economy requires an attack on two fronts, the control by workers of their workplaces and the coordination and control of social production as a whole by society. Direct worker ownership of a company is relevant only to the former, but does not in itself contradict the latter.

Some critics support the idea of workers taking over and running their own factories, but reject the worker-owner or ESOP models. Staughton Lynd, for example, has suggested that buyouts take the form of nonprofit corporations whose purpose is to preserve jobs, rather than of for-profit businesses whose ostensible goals are to make profits for the worker-owners. Such an approach would certainly help resolve the difficulties that arise when efforts to act in a socially responsible way come into conflict with a fiduciary responsibility to maximize profits, but the nonprofit form does not, in itself, solve some of the other major problems manifested at Seymour. Managers can be just as arrogant in the exercise of their power, and just as anti-union, in a nonprofit organization like Blue Cross or a hospital as in any for-profit business. The jobs of the lowly may remain just as lowly and oppressed. Conflict and discrimination among different groups of workers may be just as rampant. In short, nonprofit buyouts may well be superior to for-profits ones, but they will still have to grapple with many of the same problems.

The first two and a half years of worker ownership at Seymour have been a time of conflict; Mike Kearney likens the experience to "six tours in Vietnam." What does that conflict mean?

Some feel that a worker-owned company should be a harmonious whole, led by management, with everyone pulling together for the common good of the company. Others feel the persistence of labor-management conflict reveals that worker-ownership simply reproduces the evils of capitalism in a new form. To me, the existence of conflict—and the fact that conflict takes new and developing forms—shows that real issues are being addressed and that something important is happening.

The problem of popular control of managers and bureaucrats arises in governments as well as workplaces and in state-run as well as capitalist economies. This problem is real; it is unrealistic to expect it to be washed away by appeals for harmony. What is happening at Seymour produces conflict for the same reason that it produces progress: because workers are moving into fields previously dominated by others.

The Greenhouse Compact:
Why a Good Plan Failed

Daniel Weisman

In June 1984, Rhode Island voters went to the polls to decide the fate of an ambitious economic revitalization plan. Two years in the making, the plan was based on the most comprehensive study of a single state's economy ever conducted. It was overseen by a broad-based commission, including AFL-CIO leadership, and was authored by a leading authority on industrial redevelopment, Ira Magaziner, who infused it with a liberal philosophy.

Called the Greenhouse Compact, the plan was a tapestry of public policy changes and strategically targeted public investment to create jobs in selected industries, and it included concessions from both business and labor. It was presented to the electorate a half-year before the actual vote. At 800-plus public meetings and in the media, it was heralded as pro-labor, modestly liberal but balanced, appropriately priced and financed, and a can't-miss, sure thing to resuscitate the state's ailing economy. The program was actively promoted by the governor and most of the state's business, civic, political, and labor leadership. When the vote came, however, Greenhouse was defeated by a 4-to-1 margin.

The Greenhouse Compact was, on balance, advantageous for working people, the poor, and minorities. It could have been better for these constituencies, but compared to most other economic development programs, it was unusually progressive. The compact sought to create 60,000 new jobs, *at higher than prevalent wages,* and this would have represented almost full employment in this small state.

Economic growth would have been pursued without endangering the environment, weakening unions, reducing workers' standard of living, raiding other states, or eroding social services. Instead, particular Rhode Island industries with an inherent but unrealized competitive edge would have qualified for free or low-cost public investment funds. The plan proposed specific policies, governmental services, tax incentives, improved infrastructures, workforce retraining, and business management consulting to improve targeted industries' opportunities for stability, growth, and new product development.

Labor's concessions, while greater than industry's, paled in comparison with experiences in other planning efforts and in relation to the potential benefits of the package. Business agreed to closing some unproductive tax loopholes and to some accountability for how investment money would be used. Labor agreed to surrender the state's little-used but symbolic Strikers' Benefits law, which provided unemployment benefits after the eighth week of a strike. Labor also allowed a business tax freeze and, in the political process preceding the referendum, reductions in workers' compensation benefits.

One year after Greenhouse was defeated, the Strikers' Benefits law was repealed. A year later, the state was subsidizing private industry without the performance criteria or social protections contained in the compact. None of the business concessions or labor benefits has yet been enacted.

Given the complete package (jobs, higher pay, accountability, and scientific rather than random or politicized public subsidies), the plan was, overall, good for workers and meritorious of their support. The alternative was continued stagnation, low-paying jobs, dead-end careers, and the exodus of young families. Most voters abandoned their economic self interests. Why?

An analysis of the election data, collected by randomized telephone interviews within twenty-four hours of the referendum, revealed that the plan encountered fatal voter mistrust based on the planning process rather than the plan. When asked if they felt represented by the commission, 88 percent of the no-voters said "no" (compared with 39 percent of the yes-voters); about 90 percent of all voters indicated that they thought they should have been represented.

The process had begun as representative. The governor, in 1982, named a nineteen-member Strategic Development Commission (SDC), including leaders of industry, labor, and government. But SDC members built their concensus (no small accomplishment for a group representing traditionally opposed interests) by isolating themselves from their own constituencies and from the general public. The nineteen members found common objectives and made "reasonable" concessions. They released the final report as unamendable economic scripture. The public needed only to adopt it.

As a result, rank-and-file unionists, many business leaders, state legislators, and working and poor people felt alienated, and rejected the Greenhouse Compact. The planners failed to follow the rules of coalition work—involve constituents during the concession-trading process in order to ensure shared understandings and joint ownership.

Minorities, women, and poor and elderly people were not represented on the SDC. Nor, it appears, was a significant portion of the business community. When a consumer-based group formed and presented its concerns to the planners, its modest proposals for more aggressive antibias measures, day care, neighborhood revitalization, and representation were rejected. The group was rebuffed as a "special interest." Instead of supporting a plan that could only help them, consumers were disaffected and worked actively for the Greenhouse's defeat.

In sum, the plan was both feasible and fair, albeit disproportionately expensive for labor. It was also justifiably beaten. For labor, the lessons are not subtle: organize rather than exclude memberships; reach out to unrepresented workers, minorities, and others who are a prime target for anti-union sentiment; undertake internal economic education so members can critically assess economic development programs rather than relying on others; and support an open process which involves workers and citizens at every stage.

Rural-Urban Cooperation: Our Populist History and Future

Mark Ritchie

Jesse Jackson's decision to open his headquarters for the 1988 Iowa presidential primary in the tiny farm town of Greenfield came as a surprise to many supporters around the country. His decision was, however, an explicit acknowledgement of the tremendous support that farmers and small town residents had given him in both the 1984 and 1988 campaigns.

Jackson had discovered two of the best-kept secrets of the U.S. politics. The first was the fact that rural people, farmers and small town residents, make up almost 30 percent of the nation's voters nationwide. In many statewide elections rural voters often hold the balance of power between largely Democratic Party-controlled cities and Republican-controlled suburbs. America's largest pool of swing voters is in rural America.

Jackson's second discovery was that rural people respond enthusiastically to the populist economic message his campaign was built upon. His message about the "barracudas in the farm pond" touched deep-felt anger and frustration about the devastation of rural America. At the same time his message of support for basic family and community values moved many rural voters, helping to overcome generations of racial stereotypes and biases. As a result, rural America contributed a significant percentage of Jackson's staff and volunteers, supporters, and delegates to the Atlanta convention.

The political importance of rural Americans, and the populist feelings that can be tapped for progressive causes, has been recognized by the labor movement for over one hundred years. Historians Richard Boyer and Herbert Morais, in their classic *Labor's Untold Story*, reported that "trade unionism reached its greatest heights when it joined hands with farmers, small businessmen, and the Negro people in the epic populist revolts of the 1890s and later in the triumph that was the New Deal."[1] They go on to describe over one hundred years of urban and rural cooperation, including numerous examples of political and economic alliances between trade unions and farm organizations. One example was the mobilization by farmers to defend striking railroad workers in 1877, including donations of food and medical supplies. Material assistance by farmers during strikes was one of the most important parts of building a basis for cooperation in the electoral arena. In the election held in the fall of 1878, for example, there were almost 1 million votes cast for the farmer-labor candidates of the Greenback Party, enough to elect fourteen members of Congress.[2]

At the same time, the trade union movement had a profound impact on many aspects of rural organizing, including inspiration for the first national farm organizations. The first formal national association of farmers, the Patrons of Husbandry, now called the Grange, was organized in the late 1800s using many of the same basic principles as the national unions. Even some of the political language used by the Grange was borrowed from labor.

In 1892 the two largest organizations of workers and farmers, the Knights of Labor and the Farmer's Alliance, became politically united in the People's Party, also called the Populist Party. In their very first platform the Populists affirmed their belief that "the interests of rural and civil labor are the same; their enemies are identical."[3] This spirit of political cooperation held strong for over fifty years, until the McCarthy era of the 1950s pitted many segments of society against each other, including farmers and workers.

The New Deal Era

The most significant victories during this half century of close farmer-labor coalitions were those of the Non-Partisan League in North Dakota and the Farmer-Labor Party in Minnesota. These two mass movements were also central elements of the New Deal coalition that swept Franklin Roosevelt into power in 1932, ushering in an era of significant political and economic progress for both labor and farmers.

During the Roosevelt era, Congress established both minimum wages for workers and minimum parity prices for farmers. Laws were passed to protect collective bargaining for employees and supply management for farmers. Dozens of other vital social security measures were enacted. Although some argue that it was World War II that "solved" the 1930s Depression, it was the New Deal programs, primarily those which put purchasing power back into the hands of rural and urban people, that lifted out nation out of the Depression.

However, these important economic and social achievements of the 1930s provoked a vicious counterattack by industrial and agribusiness corporations. Even before the end of World War II, a campaign by these corporations to dismantle the New Deal programs was well underway. Virtually simultaneous with the surrender of Germany and Japan came a declaration of war against America's farmers and workers.

The "Red Scare" Era

Entering the White House after the death of Franklin Roosevelt, President Truman moved quickly to replace many of Roosevelt's best people with corporate leaders and "free market" academics committed to reversing the New Deal. Although their efforts were, at first, relatively unsuccessful, the unleashing of the "red scare" in the late 1940s and early 1950s gave corporations an effective way to attack a wide range of farm, labor, and social security programs. For example, by labeling the New Deal's parity farm programs "communist" or "socialist," agribusiness was able to convince Congress to repeal this legislation in the early 1950s.

Trade unions faced the same red-baiting and harassment tactics. For example, C.E. Wilson, head of General Electric and a key figure in the Truman administration, launched one of the most vicious red-baiting attacks on labor with these words: "The problems of the United States can be captiously summed up in two words: Russia abroad, Labor at home."[4] Industrial and agribusiness corporations, many of which viewed organized farmers and workers as a threat to their postwar ambitions, used the nation's fear of an "external threat," in this case the Soviet Union, as an excuse to destroy progressive farm organizations and trade unions. They would stop at nothing, including blacklisting, criminal prosecution, and physical attacks in their campaign of repression.

One of the loudest voices in the corporate-led attacks came from the U.S. Chamber of Commerce, which published an entire series of reports "documenting communist infiltration" in the labor movement, the government, and other institutions. In 1947, the Chamber of Commerce was part of a corporate-led coalition that secured the passage of the Taft-Hartley Act, the first major postwar antilabor legislation. In the very same year, the chamber joined with other agribusiness spokespeople, including the American Farm Bureau Federation, to launch a campaign to abolish the New Deal farm programs. Anticommunist hysteria was used to harass a number of leaders in the farm movement. For example, a number of the state chapter and key leaders of the National Farmers Union were driven from the organization under the accusation of "communist influence." President Truman was himself personally involved in red-baiting some farm leaders. Although farmers were able to successfully defend their farm programs until the early 1950s, agribusiness ultimately won.

Globalizing the Crisis

Simultaneous with their attack on unions and farm organizations, U.S. corporations began organizing a global campaign to impose their vision of a new international economic order onto the rest of the world. Their most important goal was to create a totally deregulated, "free trade" environment for U.S.-based export and import companies. World War II had devastated industry and agriculture in the nations of both Europe and Asia, making them heavily dependent on the United States for both food and industrial goods. The goal was to maintain this dependency. "Free trade" rules were designed to prevent other countries from rebuilding their own industrial or agricultural industries, by granting U.S. corporations the right to unrestricted access to almost all markets and sources of raw materials.

Arguing the inherent superiority of "free markets, free enterprise, and free trade," U.S. corporations enlisted the support of the Truman administration to force other nations to submit to their new rules for international trade: "free trade." By 1947, a year of intense attacks on labor and farmers, the United States was able to convince and coerce twenty-three nations to a sign a global trade treaty called the General Agreement on Tariffs and Trade (GATT). This was the first major multicountry trade agreement designed to enforce the postwar "free trade" rules demanded by the United States. This treaty, now signed by over ninety countries, continues to govern the lion's share of modern world trade.

One part of this treaty required the U.S. government to promise that it would limit its use of import tariffs or quotas to protect U.S. industries, regardless of the working conditions or wage structures in other countries. The end result was an unprecedented opening of U.S. markets to a flood of imports.

By opening up U.S. borders to greatly increased imports of agricultural and industrial products, the Truman Administration declared economic war on the standard of living and the working conditions of U.S. workers and farmers. Wages, social benefits, farm prices, safety regulations, and a whole host of other government programs were attacked as "excessive" in the name of "comparative advantage." Many basic social programs were blamed for making U.S. industrial and farm products more expensive, and therefore less "competitive" in world markets. Lobbying campaigns by U.S industrial corporations and agribusiness successfully cut wages, farm prices, and other government programs in order to make U.S. exports "more competitive."

The flood of imports allowed into the United States under these "free trade" policies continues even today to thwart efforts to solve our enormous trade deficit. Most U.S. politicians, Democrats and Republicans alike, have chosen to cling to the "free market" notion that we can balance our trade deficit simply by exporting more agricultural and industrial products. This argument has been used at times to convince workers and farmers to accept deep cuts in wages and in farm prices based on the false promise that this would make their products more "competitive," which would ultimately lead to "better days." This blind pursuit of eighteenth-century British "free trade" theory has nearly broken the back of U.S. family farm agriculture and of our steel, timber, textiles, auto, machine tools, petroleum, electronics, and other basic industries.[5] The only real solution to the trade deficit, the limiting of imports, has been repeatedly rejected as inconsistent with free trade.

In the years immediately following the McCarthy-era attacks on oganized labor, farmer-labor cooperation, along with other elements of American political life, fell to a low level. Many farmers, especially white farmers, came under intense ideological, economic, and political pressure to align themselves with conservative agribusiness interests rather than with labor. Farmers were constantly told by the government, universities, and by some farm organizations that organized labor was the cause of their economic problems. This was also a period of political retrenchment by trade unions, who ended up supporting a U.S. foreign policy based on "free trade" and military intervention, hoping to benefit from U.S. global economic dominance. However, with the inevitable decline in the U.S. position in the global economy, U.S. workers have become victims of this ideology, hard hit by the reality of foreign competition.

By the 1960s, however, a strong resurgence of political activity had begun to sweep across rural and urban America, given impetus by the civil rights and women's movements. The active support given by organized labor to the newly formed National Farmers Organization in the early 1960s was an important first step in rebuilding farmer-labor relations. Strong rural support for labor's campaign to defeat a "right-to-work" initiative in Missouri in the early 1970s was another key step in the revival of this political cooperation.

The 1970s were also important in the overall evolution of political coalitions within agriculture. The beginning of alliances between farm-workers and family farmers against agribusiness began to take shape. The clear identification of corporate agribusiness with disastrous domestic and international farm policies helped rebuild political alliances among rural farm organizations, labor, civil rights organizations, and other progressive movements.

The Farm Crisis of the 1980s

In 1979, the American Agriculture Movement (AAM) burst onto the national political scene, bringing over 40,000 tractors into Washington, D.C. Protesting corporation-dictated government policies to enforce low farm prices, AAM believed that the time had come to challenge agribusiness control over U.S. farm policy. Even during their first few months of existence, AAM gave high priority to practical and political cooperation with organized labor. One example was the emergency assistance provided by AAM farmers to striking United Mineworker (UMW) coal miners. Farmers from all over the country donated dozens of semi-truckloads of food and joined in picketlines and protests to show their solidarity with UMW strikers.

At the same time, the AFL-CIO gave strong lobbying support to the legislative demands of farmers. Two congressmen with close ties to labor, George Brown of California and Richard Nolan of Minnesota, were the chief sponsors of AAM's farm policy legislation. With help from labor and other allies, AAM mounted a national lobbying campaign to reverse the federal farm laws that were creating an economic and ecological crisis throughout rural America.

The primary objective of corporate-controlled farm policy is to provide agricultural raw materials to the industrial sector of the economy at the lowest possible price. This objective has been pursued in three major ways. The first has been to reduce labor costs in agriculture by both eliminating farmers and lowering farm family income. Chemical fertilizers and pesticides have been promoted as a way to replace labor, much like robots are promoted in factories as a way to replace labor.

Their second strategy for lowering the price of farm products is to get the taxpayers to pay for part of the cost of production. Agribusiness has manipulated Congress into supporting various types of so-called farm subsidy programs which are, in reality, subsidies to agribusiness and to their customers, many of whom are overseas. In fact, some describe current farm policies as "farmers laundering money for agribusiness."

Their third strategy for reducing farm prices is to push all environmental, health, and social costs of agriculture onto the society as a whole. The end result is that industry is able to buy farm products at extremely low prices, while current and future generations will have to pick up the tab for the damage. Agribusiness policies end up forcing taxpayers to pay for the social costs of taking care of the farm families and small-town residents who lose their farms or jobs as a direct result of corporate policies.

In opposition to these policies, a broad-based progressive farm movement has emerged. The goal is to force agribusiness to pay the full cost of production, enough to provide fair prices to farmers, fair wages to farmworkers, and to cover the full environmental and social costs of production. Second, they are demanding that agricultural research must be reoriented away from developing new chemical-intensive methods of farming to methods which are nonpolluting and sustainable. Finally, the progressive farm movement is demanding an end to so-called farm subsidies. With around 50 percent of our grain crops going to Europe, Japan, and the Soviet Union, taxpayer-paid subsidies end up largely in the pockets of the wealthiest consumers in the world, enriching the "dirty dozen" corporations who control world food trade.

The demands of the progressive farm movement were originally incorporated into legislation sponsored by Congressmen Nolan and Brown back in 1979. These have been updated and incorporated into new legislation, commonly called the Family Farm Act. In 1986 this bill was co-authored by Senator Harkin and Congressman Gephardt. It has been strongly supported by progressive forces in both the House and the Senate, including dozens of co-sponsors and the Congressional Black and Hispanic caucuses.

The Family Farm Act calls on the government to adapt the most successful of the Roosevelt-era policies to modern conditions. The central feature is the supporting of farm prices at the average cost-of-production, to protect family farmers, alongside of reestablishment of effective supply balancing to protect consumers and taxpayers. The supply balancing programs would establish a minimum national food reserve, maintained by the federal government, to prevent shortages and high food prices in times of drought or other disasters. At the same time, to prevent expensive, burdensome surpluses, total U.S. production and imports would be managed to ensure that farmers did not overproduce in times of good weather.

If surpluses did begin to build up, farmers would reduce their production, either by letting some land lie fallow or by reducing chemical and fertilizer use. If shortages became a threat, some of the land that has been kept in reserve would be brought back into production to cover the potential shortage. Under current policies, the United States bounces between shortages and surpluses, both costing taxpayers and consumers billions, while lining the pockets of the agribusinesses.

Of course the impact of this current policy does not stop at the U.S. border. Surpluses that are produced as a result of "fencerow to fencerow" policies in the United States are eventually "dumped" onto world markets, driving down world prices. These lower prices, in turn, reduce the export earnings of other nations, such as Brazil and Argentina. For those exporters who are debtor nations, this is a disaster. In addition, heavily subsidized U.S. exports make it impossible for local producers to compete in their own domestic markets against this "dumped" U.S. grain.

Labor's Stake in Solving the Farm Crisis

Labor has two direct stakes in helping farmers win their demands. The first is that farmers earning a decent living are good customers for U.S.-built pick-up trucks, appliances, and all other goods and services. Farmers "buy American" and they shop at their local merchants, which fuels the entire rural economy. Broke farmers eventually become competitors for ever scarcer good jobs in urban America.

Second, falling world commodity prices have pushed many third world countries, such as Brazil, Thailand, and Mexico, to expand their manufactured goods sector in an attempt to pay their debts. This flood of increasing manufactured goods from debtor nations, financed largely by the World Bank and multinational bankers, will continue to accelerate until U.S. farm policy allows world commodity prices to rise.

Farm-Labor Cooperation in the 1980s

Organized labor has been a major influence on the farm movement in the 1980s. In addition to providing strong financial and political support, a number of the most effective organizing strategies and themes of the labor movement have been incorporated into the farm movement. For example, one of the most basic tenets of organized labor, the belief that "an injury to one is an injury to all," has become the rallying cry for farmers who have organized "penny auctions" to stop foreclosures.

At the same time, farmers have given their active support to labor in a number of critical situations, including the Phelps Dodge mining strike in Arizona and the Hormel strike in Austin, Minnesota. Farm organizations and leaders were very active in the "Jobs With Justice" rallies organized by unions in 1987 and 1988. Support by farmers for these struggles often brought new energy and vitality. In addition, some of the farm movement's analysis of global economic issues, such as the GATT trade negotiations, has been useful to the labor movement. Much of this new farmer-labor cooperation is being consciously constructed by leaders in both movements in ways to ensure long-lasting, mutually supportive relationships. They want to make sure that these important bonds cannot be destroyed again by red-baiting or other corporate strategies.

One of the most important elements of rebuilding political cooperation has been the creation of a National Rural Caucus within the Democratic Party. With strong encouragement and support from a number of trade unions, the Rural Caucus was able to play an important role at the Democratic Party convention in Atlanta, and to make campaign contributions to a number of the progressive rural Democrats running for Congress in 1988. Educational efforts of the Rural Caucus were also effective in creating an awareness among many candidates about the key economic and environmental issues of concern to rural voters.

New and innovative farmer-labor efforts are now beginning to address growing international economic and environmental threats, such as the efforts to impose new "free trade" policies or the rapidly deteriorating condition of the ozone shield. One of the first serious joint farmer-labor campaigns on an international issue was the efforts to stop the U.S.-Canadian Trade Agreement, in 1987. Although this effort did not ultimately succeed, it laid the groundwork for greater cooperation on a wider range of global issues, including the on-going General Agreement on Tariffs and Trade (GATT) negotiations.

Perhaps it is in this global arena that the farm movement can make its most important contribution to a wide range of progressive social, ecological, and political movements. U.S. farm groups have helped to create an effective global network among farm organizations and consumers, including groups in Europe, Canada, Japan, and a number of third world countries. This "internationalization" of the farm movement has made it possible for U.S. farm organizations to alert other U.S. groups, including trade unions, environmentalists, consumer groups, and third world development activists, to the inherent dangers in the Bush administration's push for a totally "liberalized" international trade policy at GATT.

Political Cooperation into the Future

Farmer-labor cooperation in political affairs will continue to be very important in the future. Rural people will remain a significant percentage of the voters, playing a critical role as swing voters in determining the outcome of many House, Senate, and presidential races.

Many rural voters, like many urban voters, are not strongly attracted to classic liberal issues and are often sharply divided on social issues, such as abortion. What concerns them most is economics: the prices they receive for their crops, interest rates, and rising costs of production. The pressure exerted by rural voters on candidates to keep them focused on basic economic issues often benefits many others, including labor.

When progressive candidates speak out clearly on key rural economic issues, they attract the support of many independent rural voters, often a key element in getting them elected. This has been the case recently in many of the Midwest farm states, where a strong "populist" farm message from progressive candidates has generated enough rural support to defeat conservative Republican incumbents. For example, in 1986 nearly 40 percent of the voters in South Dakota cited the farm crisis as their number-one concern. Roughly two-thirds of those concerned with the farm crisis voted for the progressive Senate candidate, Tom Daschle.

Continued cooperation on electoral issues must remain central to farmer-labor relations, but as only one part of an entire range of political strategies. For example, some of the most successful examples of farmer-labor cooperation in the early to mid-1980s were the efforts to counter the upsurge in extreme-right organizing which occurred after Ronald Reagan took office. Confronting right-wing speakers, alerting the press to their activities, and counterorganizing were a few of the methods used. Perhaps most important, this activity alerted progressive farm leaders to the incredible frustration that was building up in many economically hard-pressed farmers, which needed to be channeled in a positive direction. This effort needs to be quickly expanded to meet the challenges we are likely to face in the upcoming recession. The election of New Orleans Klu Klux Klan leader David Duke appears to be only the tip of a huge, reactionary iceberg waiting for the next major economic crisis to emerge. The success of the farm-labor counterorganizing against the extreme right in the early 1980s will be a key example for responding to any new upsurges in the coming years.

Practical day-to-day cooperation on a wide range of personal and community problems must continue to be strengthened, while we are addressing the emerging global issues. It is only by combining the best visions, strengths, and leadership from the farm movement, the trade union movement, and all the other progressive economic, issue, and constituency-based movements that we can find the right solutions to the enormous, at times overwhelming, problems we must now all face.

Controlling the Land, Controlling the Future

As the multinational corporations continue to deplete our petroleum, uranium, and other mineral resources, they are being forced to increasingly rely on renewable natural resources, primarily agricultural and forestry products, to supply the raw materials needed to fuel their factories and transportation systems. Renewable natural resources, those which can be grown on the earth or harvested from the seas, are rapidly being recognized as the key future source for most of the raw materials needed by future energy, transportation, pharmaceutical, construction, textiles, health care, and manufacturing industries. As a result the struggle over "who will control the land" takes on a new urgency.

Who owns the land, and therefore who controls the raw materials of our future economy, can no longer be the sole concern of farmers. It is now of paramount importance to everyone, rural and urban alike. If the land or the seas can be directly or indirectly controlled by the multinationals, as they now control oil and many other raw materials, they will continue to hold the entire economy hostage to their demands. However, if small and medium-sized family farmers can keep the land out of the hands of these corporations, it will give us the opportunity to create a new economy for the future, one where control over the raw materials will be dispersed, decentralized, and democratic.

Notes

1. Richard Boyer and Herbert Morais, *Labor's Untold Story* (New York: United Electrical, Radio, and Machine Workers of America, 1955), p. 12.
2. Ibid., p. 63.
3. Preamble of the Platform of the People's Party, July 4, 1892, Omaha, Nebraska.
4. Boyer and Morais, *Labor's Untold Story,* p. 345.
5. For an excellent review of this dynamic, see David Morris, "Free Trade, the Great Destroyer," available from the Institute for Agriculture and Trade Policy, 3838 Blaisdell Avenue South, Minneapolis, MN 55409.

Economic Conversion As a Radical Strategy: Where Social Movements and Labor Meet

Carl Boggs

The prospects for radical social change in the advanced industrial countries will ultimately depend upon a convergence of labor struggles and popular movements around feminism, ecology, peace, and social equality—a convergence that links material and quality-of-life demands within a coherent political strategy. Probably the most fertile terrain for such an historical meeting of interests and goals is the full-scale conversion of what Seymour Melman calls the "permanent war economy" into a system of production geared to social needs rather than military waste and destruction.[1] A conversion-oriented politics would integrate the concerns of material well-being, antimilitarism, ecological balance, and general social renewal into a single project which, though diverse in its constituencies and outlooks, might crystallize the energies of *all* movements committed to a rational alternative.

Such a strategic vision contains its own dilemmas and pitfalls to be sure; but this would be true of any radical-democratic strategy built around the challenge of dismantling powerful institutions. In any case, the task is a necessary one. It rests upon several interrelated premises: (1) that any successful progressive formation in the United States, as elsewhere, will have to expand its social base across diverse classes and groups; (2) that the historic clash of interests between the left and labor, sharpened over time, will have to be transcended if real change is to occur; (3) that the U.S. labor movement, victimized by the twin forces of repression and deindustrialization, is facing its most severe crisis since the modern era of corporate integration began in the 1920s, thus opening up new prospects for a shift in priorities; (4) that the U.S. economy has become more and more militarized, generating a structure that is materially fragile, ecologically rapacious, and perpetually disruptive to peaceful international relations; and (5) that significant changes in the world economy and in the Communist world have given rise to a new international mood, to a likely eclipse of cold-war politics, which might undercut long-established ideological barriers to change.

Viewed in conventional terms, economic conversion refers to the transition from a militarized economy that is designed to mobilize

302

vast amounts of resources for purposes of "defense" or "national security" toward a system of production more attuned to social needs: education, health care, housing, public transportation, and so forth. Reform efforts, both in the United States and Western Europe, have typically conceived of this strategy as a substantial transfer of resources from one sector of the economy to other sectors, generally as part of a last-ditch attempt to save jobs where military-related firms were struggling for survival.[2] Conversion was rarely understood as an integral process within a larger scheme of social transformation. Viewed from a more radical perspective, however, conversion takes on an entirely new meaning, something more than just another Keynesian plan for reconsolidating capitalism. This approach, initially developed by the West German Greens in the early 1980s, differs from the liberal-reform model insofar as it links conversion to broad social goals (e.g., feminism, ecological renewal, grassroots democracy) and, inevitably, to an overturning of the corporate-military power structure with its inbred drive toward profits, rampant growth, and destruction.[3] Here the break with Democratic Party politics (in the United States) and social democracy (in Western Europe) could hardly be more dramatic. As the capitalist distortions of modernity accrue with each passing year, the relationship between the economy and nature, between material forces and the environment, becomes more interwoven—and more problematic. The result is that genuinely transformative initiatives will have to be carried out if perilous forms of industrialization are to be blocked. A radical-democratic strategy, therefore, suggests nothing less than a complete reversal of the logic of state-capitalist accumulation.

As Melman observes, in consuming something on the order of $10 trillion since 1950, the militarized economy of the United States severely eroded the industrial infrastructure of what was once the world's most dynamic system.[4] The results have been predictable enough: loss of jobs, decline of productivity, lopsided growth patterns, the erosion of social programs, worsening of the quality of goods, technological lag in the civilian areas compared with the military sector. Four decades of Pentagon-driven growth have contributed mightily to the contemporary crisis, which permeates every sphere of life—social, cultural, and political as well as economic. Sadly, the United States today lacks an extensive, workable railway system; even the highway system is in decline. Resources for education, housing, and health care are not close to being adequate to meet basic needs. Schooling, especially in the central cities, is abysmally inadequate and the teachers grossly underpaid. Clinics, hospitals, and emergency health care services have been closed down in many cities. Water systems are disintegrating. Poverty, homelessness, urban violence, mental illness, drug and alcohol addiction are all rampant in a country with enormous material abundance. Environmental degradation is out of control, reflected in urban blight, undrinkable water, unbreathable air, contaminated food, depleted soil, automobile congestion, and disappearing wildlife that, unfortunately, most Americans now seem to take for granted.

As these conditions worsen, public debate over what to do is virtually absent from the political arena even as the country spends well over $300 billion yearly to support a military machine that can already destroy every Soviet target sixty times over. With only a tiny handful of exceptions, both Democratic and Republican politicians routinely evade what is manifestly visible for all to see: that without economic conversion no solution to these problems is even thinkable. Indeed, continued social and economic decay is the only possible outcome, with frightening human and political implications.

At the same time, a project of economic conversion alone—even assuming that it could be realized within a capitalist framework— would still leave undisturbed the current path of development. It follows that conversion, viewed in more than strictly economic terms, needs to be incorporated into a *movement*-based strategy for long-term social transformation. As part of a struggle against multiple forms of domination (class, bureaucratic, gender, racial, ecological), conversion anticipates more than an expansion of social programs or better welfare measures on the one hand, or reversal of the arms race on the other. It also goes beyond a focus on technological innovation and industrial efficiency within the "civilian" sector, as proponents of more instrumental schemes have been inclined to favor. By contrast, conversion represents a novel path of development grounded in a drastic reordering of values and priorities along social, ecological, and local-democratic lines. From this standpoint demilitarization would be accompanied by the transition to a system of production less attuned to profits, growth, and bureaucratic efficiency (or control) and more attuned to immediate social needs, ecological balance, and human-scale interaction. In this ideal conceptualization, therefore, conversion occupies a strategic focal point where societal commitments, institutional politics, and class interests potentially converge with the rhythmic pulse of everyday life and grassroots activism.

In bringing together the immanent concerns of labor and the new social movements in this way, the conversion process can confront the logic of capital more directly as it is forced to take up a broader range of issues. The war economy assaults the natural and social environment in a myriad of ways: destruction of the natural habitat; soil, air, and water pollution; the spread of toxic wastes; massive energy consumptioin; creation of workplace hazards; the militarization of culture. As for labor, capital's incessant boom and bust cycles—on which the working class precariously lives and dies—are exacerbated to the extent that a region's economy becomes dependent on war production. A militarized economy typically excludes low- and medium-skilled workers in its demand for highly specialized forms of expertise tied to a technology-intensive system. Moreover, because war production requires a state-command structure of authority, the dictates of "national security" and secrecy tend to divide workers from each other while reproducing hierarchical norms at the workplace.

A reversal of this developmental logic—indeed of the entire state-capitalist pattern of growth and stagnation—calls for a completely new set of economic priorities. The historic progressive ideals of workers' control, democratic participation, and community renewal will mean little unless the system of production is simultaneously transformed. To the degree economic conversion is integral to this dynamic, the trajectory of change points toward post-Keynesian solutions that are far more imaginative than the statist, growth-oriented system that has failed in the United States and elsewhere.

An alternative strategy will have to counter all previous corporatist strategies (including leftist ones) engineered through a social compact among the state, corporations, and the trade unions. The growth model has proven itself incapable of stimulating economic development without severe dysfunctions. A vision of material expansion that reduces social progress to quantitative indicators while largely ignoring ecological limits can no longer be sustained.[5] What is urgently needed—and missing from traditional leftist strategies—is a clear understanding of the contradictions and limits of industrial growth itself, which revolves around not only the commodity form but the war economy, especially in the United States. New insights into the global crisis require an analysis of the growth-driven system responsible for decades of harsh resource exploitation and ecological devastation. Fresh analysis in turn suggests the need for a radical politics that presses for a fundamental shift in the forms of production and consumption, the nature of investment, the structure of work—in the very ends of economic activity.

A revision of premises along these lines brings us to what the Greens call an "ecological mode of development." The West German Greens, for example, envision a society reordered differently from both the corporate market system and the Soviet command type of statism; reliance upon nationalizations and state planning is shunned in favor of new (socialized) forms of production, expanded social priorities, ecological equilibrium, and grassroots self-management. Economic conversion is a vital lynchpin in this schema. For the Greens it is no longer sufficient to emphasize industrial output for its own sake without questioning the *content* of what is produced. Resources devoted to armaments, commodities that are environmentally harmful, and wasteful private goods are to be redirected into sectors closer to collective human needs. This could reduce absolute levels of growth while also improving living standards, enhancing the quality of life, and restoring the balance between economy and nature before it is too late. For such a dynamic to be set in motion, the old productivism and privatized consumerism would have to be replaced by an ecological thinking that puts human values and needs at the core of historical progress.

According to the ecological model, changes in the nature of production and consumption would be organically linked to the emergence of new forms of work tied to the overturning of hierarchical social relations. From this viewpoint, the prospects for creative and meaningful work for the entire adult population depend upon the full involvement of workers made possible by popular control (local committees), alternative technology, expansion of socially useful production, and more leisure time with greater cultural options. Green politics calls for a technology that emphasizes renewable (e.g., solar) energy, a democratically controlled application of technology within smaller scale units, and a system of "ecological accounting" that supplements standard financial accounting. A conceptual and strategic fulcrum of these grand objectives—and of the linkage between the struggle for peace and the vision of ecological development—is a radical conversion project that entails a progressive cutting away at the military sector and a rechanneling of those resources to meet social needs.

In this context, the fight against militarism takes on a material as well as a moral dimension; in other words, it is grounded in concrete social and political action rather than normative appeals alone. Since nuclear weaponry (like other types of weaponry) has no autonomous logic but is the product of a specific social system, the peace movement is faced with the ultimate task of overturning that system if is to achieve far-reaching goals such as disarmament. Viewed from this angle, the strategy of conversion represents yet another way in which, ideally, the struggle for peace, the new social movements, and labor converge.

The realities of American politics, however, are such as to dampen real optimism around this or any other radical agenda. Despite widespread grassroots activity over the past two decades, political culture in this country remains depoliticized, the left tiny and marginalized. Can any progressive movement hope to escape this quagmire? Can a radical-democratic strategy of the sort championed by the West German Greens achieve viability in the United States?

My thesis is that economic conversion, within an historical context of building economic and ecological crisis, offers the best opportunity for transforming heightened social contradictions into political gains for the left. Whether this strategy turns out to be a "Green" one or something else cannot be anticipated. In any case, it is not enough to posit a simple collaboration of labor and new social movements as a strategic answer to the impasse. Given the limits of American politics, there will have to be a rather dramatic reshaping of both the labor tradition and social struggles if conversion is to be more than another modest reform of the dominant structures. For labor, this requires a shift of historic proportions—a reversal of the corporatist attachment to jobs, productivity, and growth within a capitalist framework and, conversely, an embracing of the feminist, ecological, and communitarian principles associated with the new movements. Cold-war ideology has served to integrate large sectors of labor into the dominant growth–national security logic, which is associated with jobs and prosperity for those employed in the military sector; military production is regarded as both necessary and legitimate by most workers, even as its wasteful and destructive features have become more visible. This is one reason why most conversion plans to date have been instrumentally designed to restore jobs or stimulate "growth" with little reference to broader social goals.

For labor to become radicalized to the point where conversion has a genuine chance of success, there must be a break with the prevalent cold-war, anticommunist outlook. Further, there would have to be a shift from sectoral, interest-group activity to a vision of a more common, socially defined set of priorities; a willingness to reflect more intensively upon the actual content and structure of work, thereby undermining the chronic emphasis on "jobs" and "full employment"; and a view of labor that transcends the traditional focus on manufacturing sectors so that other sectors of a broadened, diversified workforce are brought into the picture. Finally, there would have to be a more active mobilization for change in place of the familiar defensive posture around material claims, plant closings, and so on. It should be added that the complex relationship between labor and social movements implicit in conversion politics—not to mention vast transformations at the workplace itself—necessarily undercuts any schema that assigns to labor a privileged role in historical change.

A change in outlook on the new-movement side of the ledger will have to be equally dramatic, and undoubtedly will be just as difficult to achieve. In the United States, the peace movement has raised consciousness about the dangers of nuclear weapons but so far has been unable to create dynamic programs that address the issue of structural change. All too often a form of moral witness has substituted for clear analysis and, above all, strategic thinking. Few leaders of the peace

movement have suggested, for example, that a reversal of the arms
race will demand a basic dismantling of the war economy—involving
conventional as well as nuclear weaponry—along with the infrastructure that supports it. Weapons systems are typically viewed as autonomous formations, detached from the larger power structure. Thus
peace-movement challenges to specific weapons systems, Pentagon
waste, or various policies, along with a preoccupation with "arms control," essentially leave intact the whole edifice of Keynesian militarism
and cold-war politics. Indeed, sizable elements of the peace movement
persist in the myth of the Soviet threat, even after Gorbachev's dramatic foreign-policy initiatives and events in the Communist world
have begun to reshape the very contours of super-power rivalry. From
this standpoint, the peace movement will have to be reconstituted
on new foundations: moving beyond either moral witness or limited
reforms, it will be forced to confront those institutions responsible
for the war economy and the arms race—the multinational corporations, the state, and the Pentagon.[6] A conversion strategy potentially
creates space for such a departure.

For new social movements in general, conversion allows for a more
effective politics that takes into account factors ignored or downplayed:
the economy, class domination, material struggles. The tension between labor and the new movements has come from both directions.
By placing the claims of peace, ecology, and women's issues, for example, over the more "mundane" concerns of labor, the new movements undercut their own viability by sidestepping the structural
component of their targeted concerns (the arms race, environmental
crisis, male domination). A conversion strategy can inject a strong
dose of historical realism into popular struggles and also offer an anti-
dote to the anti-labor bias that permeates many of the new-movement
organizations (including the Greens).

Whether a radical-democratic *theory* of economic conversion can
be translated into a cohesive, sustained political *practice* remains to
be seen. Although the numerous initiatives undertaken in the United
States (around Jobs with Peace, the McDonnell-Douglas Project, etc.)
have encountered serious obstacles—in part owing to the impasse
of strictly local efforts—they do represent a serious beginning. What
seems abundantly clear is that, without establishing linkages of some
sort between disparate oppositional forces, a rational alternative to
the present all-consuming power structure will be unthinkable. Obviously the political means for carrying out this project call for imaginative solutions and novel organizational forms, shaped by a new
(ecological) rationality. Thus, for conversion to be part of a genuine
transformative process it will have to be rooted in popular control
over all areas of production, work, consumption, and social life—in

equilibrium with nature. Under such conditions the economy as such no longer constitutes an end but rather a means to the free development of everyone according to the principles of self-activity, social equality, and ecological balance.

Notes

Thanks to Robert Koehler and Vincent Stankiewicz for their thoughtful comments on this essay.

1. Seymour Melman, *The Permanent War Economy* (New York: Simon and Schuster, 1974).
2. See the accounts of the Lucas Aerospace project in Suzanne Gordon and David McFadden, eds., *Economic Conversion* (New York: Ballinger, 1985), ch. 4.
3. For a discussion of the West German Greens' approach to conversion, see Carl Boggs, *Social Movements and Political Power* (Philadelphia: Temple University Press, 1986), pp. 186–93.
4. For the most recent elaboration of this point, see Melman, *The Demilitarized Society* (Montreal: Harvest House, 1989).
5. An excellent formulation of such an ecological mode of development can be found in Murray Bookchin, *Remaking Society* (Montreal: Black Rose Books, 1989), pp. 159–204.
6. Relevant here is Melman's insightful critique of the U.S. peace movement in *The Demilitarized Society*, ch. 2.

Jobs with Peace

Jill Nelson

Jobs with Peace is a national campaign to shift federal spending priorities away from military spending to programs which generate jobs and provide services in our communities. It is a multiracial, multiclass organization which works on the national and local levels for social and economic justice and peace. The campaign connects grassroots organizing for the empowerment of low-income and working-class people with the movement to create a new U.S. domestic and foreign policy.

Jobs with Peace responds to people's immediate concerns and also builds awareness and action around national and international issues. The goal of the campaign is to help build a movement which connects organizing at the local, state, and federal levels.

Jobs with Peace as a Common Agenda

One of the major obstacles to progressive social change in the United States has been the fragmentation of groups around separate issues. While each issue is important and deserves to be addressed separately and in depth, at the same time it is critical that we also focus on the connections between issues and begin to formulate a program which meets the needs of the majority of American people. After all, we know that no one group is strong enough to win its demands acting alone. It is only by working together, and reaching many people, that the progressive movement can build enough power to make any significant change.

The Jobs with Peace Campaign was founded with the goal of helping to provide a part of a common agenda. The campaign is based on the premise that organizing for a transfer of federal funds from the military budget to the domestic budget provides a program which addresses the self-interest and at least a portion of the issues of the labor, peace, civil rights, environmental, women's, and other social justice movements.

Jobs with Peace sees military spending not just as a moral issue but as a national problem which has severe negative effects on the everyday lives of a majority of people. The last eight years have seen a shift in the allocation of the country's resources. Between 1981 and 1988, Congress voted to spend over 52 percent of our tax dollars on the military while spending only 2 percent on low-income housing, 2 percent on education, 2 percent on the environment. This shift has involved a significant reversal of federal priorities: funds for low-income housing, to take one example, were cut by over 60 percent in constant dollars, while funds for the military were increased by over 60 percent during this period.

Under these conditions, no matter what domestic issue a group is fighting for, its demands cannot be met without reordering federal priorities. Without more federal money, innovative local programs to meet human needs in housing, health care, child care, education, transportation, infrastructure repair, and environmental preservation cannot succeed on a scale large enough to meet the need.

By the same token, unless the military budget is redirected, the goals of those people who are fighting for peace will remain illusory. The peace movement's goals of developing a noninterventionary, nonmilitarized foreign policy must be concretely reflected in a reduction of military spending.

Further, domestic and military policies are connected in deeper ways than simply the trade-offs within the federal budget. In reality, U.S. foreign and domestic policies are two sides of the same coin, though Congress, the media, and the entire "political establishment" have always tried to obscure this fact. Much of the deindustrialization of the United States has been due to multinational corporations moving operations overseas to third world countries to take advantage of low wage, regulation-free environments. Wages are low in such areas as the Philippines, South Korea, and South America not because workers are "willing" to work for less, but because military dictatorships violently suppress union and community organizing. These dictatorships are maintained through direct and indirect military and economic support from the United States. In effect, we have a situation in which U.S. taxpayers are financing the flight of jobs from their communities and the repression of fellow workers abroad.

History of the Campaign

Jobs with Peace has helped to raise public awareness of the misallocation of our tax dollars, calling attention to the little-publicized fact that *over 52 cents* of each of our income tax dollars goes to the Pentagon, while only pennies go to social programs. At the same time, through action campaigns, Jobs with Peace has helped to build the political power necessary to change this situation.

Jobs with Peace started as a local referendum campaign in San Francisco, in response to President Carter's initiation of a military build-up in 1978. The referendum, which was advisory, passed by 61 percent and asked the City Council to "call upon the U.S. Congress to make more federal funds available for local jobs and programs—in quality education, public transportation, energy-efficient housing, improved health care, and other socially productive industries—by reducing the amount of our tax dollars spent on nuclear weapons and programs of foreign military intervention, thereby creating jobs with peace."

During the Reagan years, the military build-up was further escalated. In response, local coalitions have organized successful Jobs with Peace referendum campaigns in over eighty-five cities and towns since 1980. Of those eighty-five groups, ten have made the transition from ad-hoc coalitions to established community groups, with offices, staff, budgets, and programs.

Strategy of the Campaign

The overall strategy of the Jobs with Peace Campaign is to unify in a concrete way groups working against nuclear weapons and against U.S. foreign intervention with groups working on domestic issues. Often these constituencies are at odds with each other—recall the "Peacenik versus hardhat" confrontations of the 1960s and the long-standing antagonisms between organized labor and nonunionized workers, especially minorities and women. In addition, groups working on domestic issues are often pitted against one another as they struggle for shrinking pieces of the federal budget pie.

In the beginning, many Jobs with Peace organizers were warned that "you can't organized around peace issues in working-class communities." But they have. The distinguishing feature of most local Jobs with Peace Campaigns is that they have done neighborhood organizing to build their own community bases, often centered in communities of color. They have also built coalition relationships with other groups in their area, with whom they have worked on joint action programs.

The key to this success has been the focus on a common agenda, and one which has both a national and a local component. Jobs with Peace organizers see the reprioritization of the federal budget as a key way to frame a common program which focuses on what *unites* the interests of different groups, as opposed to what *separates* them.

The National Campaign, which was started in 1982 by local Jobs with Peace campaigns, is governed by a Coordinating Committee composed primarily of the leaders of the local campaigns. Over the years, these leaders have developed a common political understanding to guide the development of national strategy, which can be summarized in capsule form as follows:

—The present economic system is unwilling and unable to adequately provide for people's needs at home and abroad.

—A 25 percent cut in the military budget and a transfer to the domestic budget (the basic Jobs with Peace demand) is not possible as long as Congress is dominated by the current configuration of Democrats and Republicans, who represent the interests of the corporate and financial elites.

—Therefore, independent political organization is needed at all levels, bringing more people into political action, empowering new leadership, and building alliances across class and race lines.

These conclusions were based on an analysis of the current allocation of political power, in which our elected officials represent the interests of their large financial backers rather than the majority of the people.

A major obstacle to changing this situation is the disenfranchisement of low-income people, especially people of color, who are systematically excluded, through voter registration procedures and many other barriers, from full participation in the political process. Another obstacle is the failure of progressive organizations to reach out to and involve those who are inactive and uncommitted. A third obstacle is the lack of a program which can inspire people to action and speaks to the connections among individual issues, as well as provide local handles on these issues.

From this assessment, the campaign came to the conclusion that it should focus its energy on *local organizing*, since it is only at the local level that we can start to bring new people into the political process and build the political power to change the current situation on the federal level. In addition, the campaign also wanted to maintain its focus on a *national agenda*, in order to make the connections between issues and groups.

Consequently, the campaign has developed a *two-track strategy* of (1) organizing *locally* for a specific local demand that could be won, while (2) simultaneously drawing the connections between the local demand and a national agenda, and building support for that national demand. Its current strategic priorities are:

—To build local community-based, multiracial, multiclass membership organizations centered in and led by those communities hardest hit by the militarization of the federal budget. To develop leadership from those hardest hit.

—To establish coalition relationships with existing groups representing human needs, labor, peace and social justice issues.

—To link together local Jobs with Peace Campaigns with other organizations in a fight for an alternative federal budget by making the federal budget a local issue.

The Development of a National Program

In 1988, the National Jobs with Peace Campaign launched the "Build Homes Not Bombs" campaign, which calls for large-scale national funding of affordable housing financed by a cut in the military budget.

The impetus for the national action focus came from the assessment by Jobs with Peace that it was necessary to develop a specific fight for a particular demand at the national level in order to make the relatively abstract concept of a budget transfer more concrete, especially at the neighborhood level.

Because of the obvious growing crisis in affordable housing, of which homelessness is only the tip of the iceberg, Jobs with Peace chose housing as the focus of a national program. During the Reagan years, the federal government abdicated its already inadequate role in providing affordable housing. Between 1980 and 1988, federal funds for housing were reduced by over 60 percent, the most severe cut of any social program. While there are many innovative local programs, there can be no adequate solution to the housing crisis without an infusion of federal funds. Further, a massive national housing construction and renovation program would create hundreds of thousands of jobs, in a host of construction and other related industries.

The Build Homes Not Bombs Campaign has several components:

—A *general demand* for an adequate affordable housing program, financed by cuts in military spending.

—A *legislative focus*—the National Comprehensive Affordable Housing Act—introduced into Congress by Representative Ronald V. Dellums in June 1988. This act is based on a three-year study, *A Progressive Housing Program for America*, developed by housing advocates from around the country and coordinated by the Institute for Policy Studies in Washington, D.C.

—A *national strategy* for pushing the general demand and the legislative focus.

—A *local strategy* which calls for developing local "winnable" housing fights, which can be linked to the overall demand for more federal money for housing.

Jobs with Peace kicked off the Build Homes Not Bombs campaign by building a symbolic house on the lawn of the Pentagon on June 3, 1988, together with leaders of the National Union of the Homeless, the National Organization for Women, the Committee in Solidarity with the People of El Salvador, the National Education Association, the United Food and Commercial Workers, and the Gray Panthers.

The following day, in thirty-five cities around the country, local coalitions gathered to build model houses on the steps of the federal buildings or in other symbolic locations. Milwaukee Jobs with Peace, for example, staged a car caravan with houses on the car roofs to visually connect the military and housing issues. The caravan started at a homeless shelter, then went from a boarded-up HUD house, to the site of a senior occupancy residency hotel which had been torn down to make way for a parking lot, to a luxury housing development built with public housing bonds, and ended up at the National Guard armory.

The strategy for Build Homes Not Bombs is to concentrate on building support at the local level for a transfer of funds from the military to low-income housing, as embodied in the National Comprehensive Affordable Housing Act. The initial targets are mayors and city councils, leading to a fight for a resolution of support from the U.S. Conference of Mayors.

Organizing for Build Homes Not Bombs has put Jobs with Peace in touch with local housing groups around the country. Similarly, it has brought local peace organizations and local housing organizations into contact with each other, usually for the first time, and helped them to connect the fight for housing to the need for peace.

Adopting Build Homes Not Bombs as a national program does *not* reflect a decision by Jobs with Peace to become a group which works solely on housing issues. Instead, Jobs with Peace's role is to continue to *make the links* between separate agendas and diverse constituencies that have not worked jointly in the past.

Changing the Terms of the National Debate

One of the goals of the Build Homes Not Bombs campaign is to help change the nature of the national debate around federal priorities and budget issues. Throughout the Reagan era, we heard constantly from our elected officials that "because of the massive deficit, we just don't have the money for human needs, be it health care, the environment, education, housing, or anything else." This refrain continues under the Bush administration. Meanwhile, the military budget has become virtually sacrosanct. There is currently no major leader on the national scene who is calling for significant cuts in military spending and no visible program which really addresses the needs of the country.

The National Comprehensive Affordable Housing Act calls for $53 billion *per year* to be spent on a broad range of affordable housing programs, whose overall effect would be to take low-income housing out of the private for-profit market and put it into various forms of not-for-profit community ownership and control.

Yet in the current climate in Washington D.C., such a demand is considered wild-eyed. As Jobs with Peace co-chair Ann Wilson says, "When I go to my congressional representative and ask him to support this bill, he tells me, 'Well, I know we have a housing crisis, and I'm concerned, but I have the health care advocates in my waiting room, and the toxic waste clean-up people are on the schedule this afternoon. Fifty billion dollars is too much for housing—what with the deficit, we just don't have the money.'" More than ever, domestic issue groups are being forced to compete against each other, while hardly anyone is pointing the finger at the military budget or other elements of a real solution.

The Build Homes Not Bombs campaign is a model of one kind of national program which can help to overcome this stalemate. Through Build Homes Not Bombs, Jobs with Peace is trying to promote the message that "we DO have the money. We KNOW where the deficit came from—from the skyrocketing military budget and from the lowered taxes on the wealthy and the corporations. Now we want that money back for our communities. Now *we* want control over how our national resources are used."

Build Homes Not Bombs addresses a concrete problem in a deliberately visionary way. It demands what is really needed, instead of what is currently possible on Capitol Hill. It identifies a source of funding— the military budget. And it proposes progressive forms of dealing with the housing crisis by avoiding the control of the for-profit sector.

It also calls for local organizing around local issues as an essential component. By building visible local power on such issues as public housing tenant councils or allocation of Community Development Block Grant funds, people get the sense that their actions do make a difference. By maintaining a focus on the need for a national solution, people also gain clarity on what kind of change is really necessary.

Jobs with Peace at the Local Level

Local Jobs with Peace Campaigns vary in their composition and agendas. Some local chapters have been initiated by organized labor, some by religious communities, some by peace groups, and others by leaders in minority communities.

While their local demands differ, all of them are united by their focus on the federal budget and by their commitment to build local power, especially in communities hardest hit by budget cuts. The diversity of the local programs of these groups, combined with a unified national demand, is an indication of the adaptability of the general Jobs with Peace agenda to different conditions. The following is a short description of how this formulation of issues has played out in four cities.

Los Angeles Jobs with Peace

The experience of Los Angeles Jobs with Peace illustrates the potential impact of the Jobs with Peace strategy. Through building their own community base and through coalition organizing, the Los Angeles Campaign has been able to make a substantial showing of political clout in the electoral arena.

Los Angeles is a city of 2.5 million people located in a county of 9 million. A center of garment, furniture, aerospace, and electronic manufacturing, it also has the distinction of having more military money than any state in the United States except California—over $18 billion in military contracts in 1987 alone. One out of six people in Los Angeles County works directly or indirectly for the military. The city's minority population—33 percent Latino, 11 percent black, and 12 percent Asian—does not benefit from military spending in terms of employment.

Twice, in 1984 and 1986, Los Angeles Jobs with Peace gathered over 140,000 signatures (a total of 300,000) to place binding ordinances on the Los Angeles city ballot—the first time in forty-five years that a citizens' group has been able to qualify an ordinance through signature gathering, and the first time ever that a group did this twice.

The first referendum passed by 61 percent and mandates that Los Angeles prepare an annual report on the impact of military spending on the city, and how the city might use the money if military spending were reduced by 25 percent and Los Angeles received its share. An indication of the breadth of the coalition support for the referendum is that the campaign was headquartered at the offices at the Southern Christian Leadership Conference and the Los Angeles County Federation of Labor.

The second referendum called for the creation of a Development Commission as part of the city government which would demonstrate how Los Angeles County could diversify its economy toward non-military job-creating industries.

Los Angeles' military-industrial complex found this second referendum so threatening that they came out in forceful opposition. Military contractors from all over the country spent over $600,000 for a massive advertising campaign to defeat the referendum. But they were not the only source of opposition. In addition, conservative sections of the leadership of the black power structure and the labor movement, as well as elements of the Democratic Party machine and some elected officials, helped to defeat the referendum campaign.

Their opposition was based on their fear of the independent, city-wide organization which Jobs with Peace was building, a structure which challenged their control because of its independence. All of these sectors of the city power structure felt threatened by Los Angeles Jobs with Peace's ability to mobilize voters, especially those who often did not vote. For example, in 1984, the campaign registered about 50,000 voters and put 700 precinct leaders into the field who turned out 29,000 additional new voters in the city that year—people who without being contacted by Jobs with Peace would not have gone to the polls.

The Los Angeles Jobs with Peace campaign has two basic components which enable it to achieve results on this scale. First, it is building neighborhood Jobs with Peace chapters which are centered in communities hardest hit by the economic downturn and budget cuts, especially the black and Latino sections of the city. These are the areas whose populations are most affected by the misallocation of federal dollars and who are most underrepresented in the political process.

Second, Los Angeles Jobs with Peace brings together a coalition of progressive organizations from around the city through "home-based precinct organizing." The precinct organizing strategy is based on the understanding that organizations can work together concretely and avoid turf battles if their activity is centered on neighborhood organizing, since in most areas, there is more than enough uncovered turf to go around (Los Angeles County has 6,000 precincts).

The precinct network's foundation is "neighbors talking to neighbors," as opposed to the traditional "invading army" approach. Each participating organization identifies and recruits people who are willing to sign "contracts" to be "precinct leaders," which means taking responsibility for the three square blocks in which they live. Precinct leaders make a commitment to have personal face-to-face contact with their neighbors, the most effective way of reaching and recruiting people.

The advantage to the precinct network is that it can create a permanent mechanism for mobilizing large numbers of people, which can be used for many purposes, including elections. It allows each participating organization to promote its individual agenda, while at the same time promoting whatever common agenda has been adopted by the coalition, such as opposition to or support for a referendum, for example.

"The development of the common agenda is the key element in maintaining the coalition's viability," says Anthony Thigpenn, director of Los Angeles Jobs with Peace. "The decisive element in building consensus is making sure that each organization feels a sense of ownership. Consensus can happen only when organizations agree to focus on the larger goals which they have in common rather than each pushing their own particular agenda. To make the consensus meaningful, the coalition must have specific requirements in terms of joint *action,* not just meetings, from each member organization. For example, each group can make their commitment real, while simultaneously building their own organization, by agreeing to recruit and train a certain number of precinct leaders."

The strength of the common agenda approach is reflected in the pattern of support and opposition from the labor movement. Despite the opposition of some union leadership, the Jobs with Peace initiatives were supported by numerous local and regional labor unions and the local Democratic Party. The strongest labor support came from service employee unions, who clearly saw the trade-off between military spending and a healthy service economy. Jobs with Peace did not receive active support from the building trade and aerospace unions, who saw their short-term self interest more tied to military spending. However, it was significant that these unions did not come out in active opposition as might have been expected, reflecting their understanding that increases in military spending could not go on forever and that their long-term self-interest lay in reinvestment in the civilian sector and retraining for military workers.

The defeat of the referendum in 1986 did not significantly weaken Los Angeles Jobs with Peace, whose precinct organization had reached a high level of development with over 800 precinct leaders. It did, however, educate people as to the nature of the power structure they were up against.

As a next step, in order to further build the precinct network and the neighborhood chapters, the campaign decided it needed to focus on a specific issue which would make the message of Jobs with Peace very concrete. Hence, the "Childcare Not Warfare" campaign was developed, which calls for a specific demand—20,000 additional daycare slots for "latch-key children," to be funded by a combination of federal, state, and local money. In addition, the precinct network was further developed into "Coalition '88," under the banner of "Humancare Not Warfare." The coalition trained 1,199 precinct leaders and continued to focus on voter registration and turnout in the 1988 elections, winning thirty-two out of the thirty-eight referendums the coalition endorsed.

The experience of Los Angeles Jobs with Peace in building its own base in economically hard-hit communities, combined with galvanizing a community coalition around a common agenda, has been reflected in Jobs with Peace campaigns in other cities. Most important, the Los Angeles experience has shown that the Jobs with Peace program can unify major elements of the progressive movement around common actions which actually build political power.

Milwaukee Jobs with Peace

Combining a focus on the federal budget with organizing in public housing has helped Milwaukee Jobs with Peace, with a membership of 2,500, become one of the most visible and influential groups in the city. Milwaukee's population is 630,000, 25 percent black and 4 percent Hispanic. With an economic base in printing, metal working, machine tools, and other heavy industry, its economy has been hard hit by the decline in manufacturing (one-third of manufacturing jobs have been lost). It has the worst black-white unemployment ratio (25 percent–5 percent) of any city in the nation.

One of the Milwaukee campaign's major projects has been to build a base centered in the city's public housing developments, which have a high concentration of people of color. Milwaukee public housing tenants in the past have been largely uninvolved in the political process and have not had effective organizations to represent their interests. Jobs with Peace concentrated resources on building strong tenants associations in several projects.

Through intensive voter registration and turnout work, Jobs with Peace raised the participation of public housing residents in several public housing developments to the citywide average. As a result, these new voters played a significant role in 1987 in electing John Norquist, Milwaukee's first new mayor in twenty-seven years.

As a result of this successful electoral activity, Ann Wilson, senior organizer of Milwaukee Jobs with Peace, a tenant in public housing, and co-chair of the National Jobs with Peace Campaign, was appointed by the new mayor to the Board of Commissioners of the Milwaukee Housing Authority, and subsequently elected the chair of the body.

Soon after his election, the new mayor announced major budget cuts in key social service programs which benefited primarily the city's minority communities. The stable base that Jobs with Peace had built in public housing developments and its strong relationships with Milwaukee's other progressive groups enabled it to organize an immediate large-scale response, called the "Save Our Services" coalition. This coalition mobilized 500 people almost overnight to attend a public hearing and organized on-going letters and calls to the mayor and

City Council. The result was that the City Council basically ignored the mayor's recommendations and kept the services largely intact.

Currently, Milwaukee Jobs with Peace is supporting public housing tenants in their fight for a citywide public housing tenants association, providing extensive leadership training and organizational support. The campaign is also concentrating on participating in elections, protesting military intervention in the third world, and leadership development. There are plans to set up a politicial action committee and lobbying arm to more directly engage in city politics.

While working for victories on the local level, Milwaukee Jobs with Peace also maintains its focus on the military budget and U.S. foreign policy. The campaign's experience in public housing has shown that "peace issues" and "immediate bread-and-butter local issues" can be complementary, not antagonistic.

As Ann Wilson says, "The managers in the housing developments basically make my case for me at meetings with the tenants. When we ask them for improvements in security or repairs, they say, 'We don't have the money—the federal government cut our funds.' It's easy then to bring up the military budget and show people that's where the money went. People then understand that *they* have a stake in seeing the military budget cut, and that it won't happen unless they get involved and get their neighbors involved."

"It would be wrong," Ann Wilson feels, "to organize tenants solely around public housing issues, because, ultimately, there are no adequate local solutions to many of our problems. Unless there is more federal money, public housing around the country will continue to deteriorate, paving the way for demolition, which is already happening in many cities. We *have* to make the connections between the local problems and the federal budget; it's a matter of survival."

Pittsburgh Jobs with Peace

As part of the nation's industrial heartland, Pittsburgh has experienced severe economic reversals due to the decline of its industrial base, especially steel. Several hundred thousand jobs have been lost, and ten thousand people leave the city annually.

Changing the alignment of local power within the city has been the main goal of Pittsburgh Jobs with Peace. In 1986, Jobs with Peace and ACORN (Association of Community Organizations for Reform Now) were the primary conveners of a coalition of over thirty local groups whose goal was to pass a referendum changing city elections to a district system. By disenfranchising the white working class as well as the African-American community (in a city whose population is 30 percent black), the at-large system had made it easier for the City Council to cater solely to the interests of the city's corporate and financial sectors.

Pittsburgh Jobs with Peace played a leading role in the district elections campaign based on the analysis that until Pittsburgh's black and working-class people had real local political power, there was no hope of having an impact on budget priorities at the federal level. Further, the campaign reasoned, even if the federal budget *were* redirected, Pittsburgh's low-income communities would not benefit from an increase in federal funds for the city unless they could direct those funds away from the powerful "downtown" interests.

The district elections referendum, which won by a large margin, was a unifying issue for many segments of the community. Jobs with Peace worked primarily in the black community, increasing voter registration and participation. Currently, the campaign's target is to change the allocation of Community Development Block Grant funds which come to the city away from the "downtown" interests and toward the black and other working-class areas.

Delaware County, Pennsylvania, Jobs with Peace

Like Milwaukee Jobs with Peace, the Delaware County (DelCo) Campaign, located near Philadelphia, has found that combining a focus on low-income housing with a program to change the federal budget had laid the framework for a broad-based coalition. In its two-year history, Delaware County Jobs with Peace has brought together a countywide organization, linking the peace movement with the homeless and low-income residents of Chester, the county's major city.

Chester has a population of 50,000 in a county of 500,000. With a population which is 70 percent black, 25 percent white, and 5 percent Hispanic, Chester is ranked by the Department of Housing and Urban Development (HUD) as the most economically depressed city of its size in the nation. Fully 25 percent of the population is below the official poverty line, with 20 percent living in public housing and 20 percent unemployed. The city's economic decline has been hastened by the erosion of its industrial and ship-building base. Penn Ship, still the city's largest employer, is currently only a small fraction of its former size.

As part of the national Build Homes Not Bombs campaign, DelCo Jobs with Peace has lobbied their conservative congressional representatives to support federal housing legislation and participated in national demonstrations in Washington, D.C., as well as locally. They also built a house on the steps of the Federal Building in Chester and occupied it for three days.

To translate Build Homes Not Bombs into a demand that can be won at the local level, DelCo Jobs with Peace organized a takeover of a HUD-owned, abandoned house in Chester, which involved civil disobedience and incurred arrests. From there, the campaign developed a proposal to renovate abandoned HUD-owned homes for a joint federal-local low-rent housing program for homeless and other low-income people.

At first, Chester's mayor refused to talk to them, telling the homeless people at a public hearing that they should just "go get yourselves a home." However, Jobs with Peace forced the mayor to reverse herself completely and become an active supporter. By organizing a series of public demonstrations, which brought together antinuclear and anti-intervention activists with homeless people, housing advocates, students, and religious people, Jobs with Peace forced the regional director of HUD and the mayor of Chester to enter negotiations with homeless people on the implementation of the program.

In addition to housing, DelCo Jobs with Peace has also had some other local victories. They organized a campaign of low-income workers in Chester to challenge Penn Ship, the county's largest company, which was hiring workers from outside the region but not locally. The campaign also challenged Fidelity Bank, which forced welfare recipients to stand in lines segregated from other customers to cash their welfare checks. By organizing the welfare recipients, the campaign raised such a stir that the Welfare Department terminated Fidelity Bank's contract.

Currently, the campaign is stengthening its alliances with public housing tenants, 20 percent of the city's population who, like many others around the country, face demolition of their housing developments. Jobs with Peace is developing a coalition to demand construction of 200 public housing units. The coalition is also demanding community control over allocation of Community Development Block Grant funds and the direction of those funds to renovation of abandoned HUD housing.

Like Jobs with Peace in Milwaukee, Los Angeles, and Pittsburgh, Delaware County Jobs with Peace has found that bringing peace activists together with low-income people around specific demands enhances the coalition's clout on many different issues. They have also found that building on the connections between local and federal issues strengthens their overall program and deepens the understanding of participants in the campaign.

It's Time to Come Together

With the global economy in a state of contraction and instability, it is difficult to envision how there can be any improvement without major shifts in power, away from elites and toward the vast majority of working people.

At the federal level, we have seen major cutbacks in domestic progams. Now we are beginning to see even more cutbacks at the state and local levels as well. Meanwhile corporations continue to attack labor's standard of living and demand givebacks and cuts in benefits.

Programs like Jobs with Peace, which magnify the power of progressive forces by building broad coalitions and by bringing new people into action, are becoming ever more crucial. Piece by piece, we need to advance toward a common analysis and vision that can unite our various movements.

To do this, we must first deepen our understanding of the real causes of some of the problems we are fighting. We need to understand where the levers of power really lie and develop strategies for changing the allocation of power. We need to examine critically the economic and social structures we live in, and develop programs which lead us to a more humane and democratically controlled society.

Current conditions in the United States and around the world make it clear that we can no longer afford to keep our organizations on separate tracks. We must link up at the national and local levels. We must find common ground which can lead us to united strategies and actions.

Concluding Essay: Labor-Community Coalitions and the Restructuring of Power

Jeremy Brecher and Tim Costello

When corporate management and its right-wing allies declared "class war" on American workers, maybe they made a mistake.

In the short run—indeed for most of the 1980s—the results were pretty much what they had in mind: plummeting union membership, falling real wages, a "new labor force" of workers needy enough to work under abusive conditions, job-hungry communities competing to offer tax concessions to corporations, and an electorate willing to tolerate pointless military waste and unlimited degradation of the environment.

The architects of the corporate-right offensive correctly perceived that those who might oppose them were divided. Where they went wrong was in assuming that workers, women, Native Americans, blacks, Latinos, Asian-Americans, other people of color, gay men, lesbians, farmers, students, the elderly, the handicapped, environmentalists, peace and development advocates, consumers, and all the others they were hurting would remain divided forever.

They failed to anticipate that troublemakers—grassroots activists—would begin to cooperate across the lines that had previously divided movements from each other. They did not expect peace groups to back strikers, unions to fight for women's rights, or thousands of previously isolated organizations to cooperate against conservative nominations to the Supreme Court. The leaders of the "corporate community" and their allies had violated one of the first rules of politics: don't unify your opposition. In so doing they sowed the seeds for the emerging alliance of labor and community.

If the oligarchs whom the labor-community alliances now challenge were unified, farsighted, and in control of global forces, they would have little to fear from such a seemingly frail foe. But in this time of global transformation, in which the rigid and unified power structures of the cold war era are breaking up and popular mass movements are reshaping entire societies almost overnight, corporations, military establishments, and political elites all around the world exercise diminishing control over events. The future significance of labor-community coalitions therefore will depend not just on the corporate-right ascendancy within the United States from which they gained their impetus, but also on the deep restructuring of power the world is now undergoing. The kinds of labor-community coalitions described in this book can help channel that restructuring in a democratic direction.

From Corporate Liberalism to Corporate-Right Offensive

For the quarter century that followed World War II, the world's power—economic, political, and military—was centered in the United States, and American corporations, government, and military establishments were closely linked. Global dominance made it possible to incorporate nonelite groups, most importantly the labor movement, as junior partners in the power structure.

This unequal partnership, dubbed "corporate liberalism" by the New Left and the "liberal establishment" by the New Right, was represented in the workplace by union-management cooperation and in the political arena by the ascendancy of the liberal wings of the Democratic and Republican parties. Given U.S. "world leadership" and a prosperous world economy, this system allowed both business and organized labor in the United States to achieve their principal goals.

During the 1970s, the corporate liberal ascendancy began to fall victim to what was—as we can understand in hindsight—a profound restructuring of social power. Its outlines are still hard to discern, but they involve simultaneous globalization and fragmentation of power. A world dominated by U.S. corporations producing in the United States was being transformed into one dominated by multinationals producing in a "global assembly line." Giant factories employing tens of thousands were being replaced by smaller, geographically dispersed units employing at most a few hundred. Cold war allies, like the United States, Germany, and Japan, were becoming economic rivals. Sovereign European nations were creating common economic and political institutions that cut across international frontiers. As a consequence, the boundaries of economic, political, military, and cultural spheres, which had largely coincided with the borders of nations or superpower spheres of influence, began to "decouple" or "disalign" from such boundaries and from each other.[1]

In the United States, the leading edge of this historic transformation was widely—if rather self-centeredly—interpreted as the premature demise of the "American Century": competition from the resurgent economies of Europe and Japan was eroding U.S. economic hegemony and the profitability of U.S. corporations; the Soviet Union was developing approximate military parity with the United States; nationalist and leftist political revolt in the third world was proving irrepressible.

For the corporate elite, corporate liberalism was no longer working. So during the 1970s, elements of the corporate leadership in the United States began shifting to an alternative designed to restore the dominance of the United States and its corporations through linked domestic and international policies.

By the latter years of the Carter administration, this alternative was clearly expressed in think tank reports and the resolutions of business organizations. These proposed to redistribute wealth and income to corporations and the rich to enable them to invest in the rebuilding of American enterprise; "free" the corporations to do whatever they want to make money, regardless of the cost to people and the environment; greatly expand the military to restore superiority over the Soviet Union, suppress revolutions, and keep allies and dependents in line. Proponents proclaimed the entire package as the restoration of "freedom" and its defense throughout the world.

Had corporate liberalism been working well, the constituency for such an approach would have been narrow, since most people would inevitably be hurt by it. But the failures of corporate liberalism during the 1970s affected ordinary people as well as the corporations. The decline in U.S. economic and military dominance was visible in everything from defeat in Vietnam to lines at the gas pumps to revolution and the taking of American hostages in Iran. The increasingly global economy had produced hyperinflation and mass unemployment in both the United States and much of the rest of the world—at the same time undermining the effectiveness of Keynesian policies designed to moderate economic instability.[2] The new corporate agenda was sold as an alternative that could succeed—where corporate liberalism had failed—in restoring global dominance and with it the "good life" for Americans.

Corporations and wealthy conservatives bolstered this new approach with a lavishly financed ideological campaign that rehabilitated ideas hardly heard in serious public discourse since the presidency of Calvin Coolidge. The "freedom to choose" bestowed by the "free markeet" was utilized to debunk every notion of human solidarity and mutual responsibility. Under this revivified doctrine of extreme laissez-faire, environment protection, laws against discrimination, health and safety regulations, consumer protection, and the right to self-organization in the workplace were all recast as unwarranted interferences with individual freedom. If people froze in the street, it must be because that was what, in our free country, they had freely chosen; certainly it was not the responsibility of anybody but themselves.

Even with such ideological bolstering, the new corporate agenda could not have been implemented had the corporate leadership not formed an alliance with a diverse group of religious fundamentalists, racists, militarists, homophobes, ultranationalists, and single-issue groups such as the anti-abortion movement.[3]

What these diverse groups had in common was primarily a desire to restore hierarchical social relations undermined during the 1960s and 1970s. They represented a reaction against feminism, against gay liberation, against autonomous youth culture, against the advances of blacks and other minorities, against labor militance, against the questioning of militarism and nationalism, and more generally against the acceptance of social diversity. Their principal goal was to resist the redistribution of power by restigmatizing and repressing those they found socially and/or psychologically threatening. Political leaders successfully obscured the obvious contradictions between this pursuit of cultural conformity and the libertarian ideology propounded by the apostles of laissez-faire.

While the corporate-right alliance celebrated its nuptials in the Republican Party with Ronald Reagan officiating, it entrenched itself in many realms besides presidential politics. Fundamentalist churches, television evangelists, the Pentagon and other government agencies, corporate industrial relations departments, think tanks, Washington lobbies, conservative members of Congress of both parties, local governments, university economics departments, organized gun owners, conservative newspapers, some veterans and women's organizations, chambers of commerce, employers associations, and diverse other institutions became resilient and seemingly impregnable bastions of the corporate-right ascendancy.

"Success" of the Corporate-Right Alliance

During the Carter and Reagan years, the corporate-right offensive was extraordinarily successful in implementing the new corporate agenda. Equality was redefined in public discourse and public policy as a hindrance to capital accumulation and economic incentives. Social services were regarded as an unacceptatble tax burden. Labor solidarity was treated as a hindrance to international competitiveness. Environmental protection became a drag on profitability.

The results were predictable. Real wages fell as corporations transferred industrial jobs to low-wage areas in the United States and abroad and as poverty-level service occupations in the United States burgeoned. "Reagan Hood" economic and social policies helped raise the incomes of the wealthiest 1 percent of the population by one-fifth—during the same period that the incomes of the least affluent 60 percent actually declined, leaving working- and middle-class Americans even more driven by economic necessity, more vulnerable to illness, poverty, and job loss than any time since the Great Depression.[4]

"Business flexibility"—the casualization of labor markets and the destruction of union protections—reduced job security for most workers to a memory. Family life—so cherished in conservative rhetoric—was disrupted as married women and even children poured into the labor force primarily in response to the economic squeeze and growing insecurity.

Whatever progress had been made by such discriminated-against groups as women, African-Americans, and other people of color began to be rolled back, while sexist, racist, and homophobic violence ran rampant. The attacks on public services predictably led to an undereducated workforce, a housing shortage, and a health-care crisis which by the end of the decade even the business community despaired of curing via the magic of the market. Economic marginalization of the poor and discriminated against led to the shame of mass homelessness and a generation of young people for whom drug dealing appeared the optimal route to opportunity.

Global warming, destruction of the ozone layer, deforestation, acid rain, soil depletion, and other unfolding ecological disasters proceeded unabaited in a political climate in which attempts to deal with them were treated as attacks on entrepreneurial freedom. Responding to right-wing zealotry, the U.S. government sabotaged efforts at global population control, helping ensure overpopulation, depletion of global resources, and uncounted deaths in poorer countries.

The worldwide proliferation of nuclear and chemical weapons accelerated as the United States set the world a sterling example of rampant military growth and glorification of the means of violence as the key to peace and security. Reverting to a "might makes right" concept of international morality, the United States intervened through overt and covert military operations in Africa, Asia, Latin America, and the Middle East; when called to account by the World Court for its illegal aggression against Nicaragua, the U.S. government showed its respect for international law by simply withdrawing its recognition of the authority of the Court. The gap between rich and poor both within the United States and internationally was aggravated by supposedly "free market" policies (actually manipulated by the International Monetary Fund, the World Bank, and other international economic institutions dominated by the wealthiest countries). These policies pitted workers of different countries against each other and encouraged the deindustrialization of the United States, a world debt crisis, and a shift in income from third world countries and American working people to U.S. and multinational corporations.

By the start of the 1990s, the dream of restoring U.S. world hegemony has faded before the actuality of a country whose economic base has been so depleted by military spending and lack of social, industrial, and infrastructure investment that it has to auction off its national assets just to pay the interest on its international debts. The dream of restoring an imagined white middle-class utopia in which women, people of color, and youth stay "in their place" and provide a pedestal of comfort for the contented "real Americans" has met a rude reality in which more and more Americans now share the problems of such denigrated groups.

While the corporate "class war" has been hugely successful, it has brought more "mourning" than "morning" in America.

Rise of the Community-Labor Alliances

The national organizations that professed to address the growing social problems—and to defend the interests of those such problems have affected—found themselves virtually powerless. Labor, civil rights, women's, environmental, and other movements saw their carefully cultivated relations with the corporate liberal leadership go for naught as the right wing captured the Republican Party and an increasingly conservative Democratic Party blamed its defeats on the power of "special interest groups." For the labor movement, a modus vivendi worked out with business over forty years was shattered; the globalization and fragmentation of power reduced the effectiveness of strikes and other conventional economic weapons as well. As such movements became less able to deliver gains to their constituents, their membership and clout fell still further.

At best, national leaders of labor and other groups hunkered down to weather the storm. At worst, they became the agents for providing the concessions that corporate management demanded. Throughout the 1980s there was little effective national-level opposition to the corporate offensive. But faced with the failure of established strategies, grassroots activists from diverse movements began reaching out to each other.

As conventional collective bargaining techniques failed to resist concessions demanded by corporations, unionists began to find support for workplace struggles from community allies. Today it would be difficult to find a major strike or organizing campaign in which support from community allies was *not* a central part of the labor strategy. While the labor movement remains severely weakened, it is far less isolated than it was for most of the 1980s. Victories at Pittston Coal,

Yale University, Colt Firearms, and other employers have been due in considerable part to community support.

When corporations began to close workplaces and move jobs, with devastating local impact, workers and communities began to form coalitions through which they could influence economic decision-making and develop alternative economic strategies. Community-labor coalitions, such as the Naugatuck Valley Project and the Tri-State Conference on Steel, filled the vacuum left by business and political leaders; they forced corporations to bargain with them over the closing or sale of plants and developed worker buyouts and industrial authorities as vehicles for preserving and developing the local economy.

Starting in the Carter years, the Democratic Party became less and less responsive to labor and other social movements, so activities from a wide range of movements began running candidates from their own ranks, often challenging conservative Democrats as well as Republicans. They created institutions, such as LEAP, Pro-Pac, and local Rainbow coalitions, to recruit and support these candidates and to keep them accountable when elected. Dozens of officials have been elected at state and local levels, caucuses of progressive legislators have been formed in several states, and the "Rainbow Coalition" campaigns of Jesse Jackson have projected an alliance of social movements into the national electoral arena.

Throughout the 1980s, any issue that did not benefit corporate management or its right-wing allies was likely to face tough sledding. That included peace, social justice, human rights, racial justice, human services, gay and lesbian rights, environmental protection, and many other concerns. Groups that had previously been able to make headway on their own found themselves going backward. So issue campaigns, too, began increasingly to take the form of coalitions. These achieved some of the few progressive victories of the Reagan era, such as plant closing legislation, Nuclear Freeze and Jobs with Peace referendums, comparable worth policies, and the defeat of Robert Bork's nomination to the Supreme Court.

The corporate-right offensive had unleashed an unanticipated process. It led grassroots activists to develop a new mode of operation or political practice, an active outreach to each other: "bridge-building."

The result is that what were once isolated movements are now beginning to redefine themselves as part of an emerging alliance. This alliance can be conceived in a number of ways, none of which is as yet definitive: a movement of movements, a coalition of coalitions, a democratic convergence, a new social bloc. Elements of this alliance call themselves community-labor alliances, Rainbow, progressive, or populist coalitions. All of these terms point to something which is emerging; none of them entirely encompasses it.

What Makes These Coalitions Different?

Cooperation among movements for social change is nothing new, and historical antecedents—from the Knights of Labor in the 1870s and 1880s to the United Farm Workers organizing drives a century later—can be found for the coalitions described in this book. But the pattern of today's grassroots alliances is strikingly different from those typical of the recent past.

In the United States over the past half-century, coalitions between organized labor and other movements have characteristically taken one of two forms. One is the Democratic Party, through which organized labor and many other groups have contested for a share of political power. The other is the "umbrella organization," such as the Civil Rights Leadership Conference, the Citizen Labor Energy Coalition, or the Progressive Alliance. Such umbrella organizations have usually been coalitions of national organizations initiated by national leaders in which the union representatives are generally the dominant partners.

The inter-movement cooperation described in this book, in contrast, results primarily from initiatives by local movement groups. In some instances, as in the case of Jobs With Justice or the campaign to defeat the nomination of Robert Bork to the Supreme Court, national organizations may provide support or a framework for action. In others, as in the case of Connecticut LEAP or the Hormel meatpackers strike in Minnesota, local affiliates may pursue bridge-building despite the active opposition of national parent organizations.

Cooperation is often initiated by one or another movement or by representatives from a number of groups; increasingly it grows out of an already established network and a legacy of past cooperation. Those directly affected by a question may have more say about how to deal with it—the workers involved in Naugatuck Valley Project buyouts, for example, or in Jobs With Justice-supported strikes, have taken much of the initiative in coalition decision-making. But it is characteristic of these coalitions that no group is regarded as having a superior right to call the shots because it has more members, more money, or some other special status. As Connecticut LEAP founder Marc Caplan put it, cooperation requires that the largest and wealthiest partners (in this case the unions) are willing to work as equal, not dominant, partners.

These coalitions differ from traditional ideological politics in that they do not demand agreement on a single "line" or even a common definition of reality. They depend on a political culture which recognizes that meanings will vary for different groups and which accepts the necessity at times to "agree to disagree."

These coalitions also differ from conventionial interest group politics: they represent not the competition among constituencies for their "piece of the pie," but rather their alignment with other movements and with broad social interests. They appeal, as one picket sign put it, to "Justice—not 'Just Us'."

What is emerging differs from several common approaches to unifying social movements, such as construction of political parties, merged organizations, or political vanguards.[5] It is different from either an electoral party or a union in that it functions in many spheres of society, not just government or workplace. It does not take the form of a single unified organization, but rather involves multiple organizations and many levels of coordination. Rather than being controlled and perpetuated by a distinct central leadership group, it is continually reconstructed by coordinating initiatives from below.

Indeed, the pattern emerging in many locations seems to be in effect a network of networks. Some portions of these networks are solidified into temporary organizations or permanent institutions; other portions remain essentially communication links that can be mobilized when needed. Some are short-lived, others long-lasting, but the "network of networks" endures.

The grassroots alliances described in this book also differ from two kinds of coalitions common in other countries. They bear little similarity to the alignments of front organizations controlled and brought together by "vanguard" parties, for one group does not reach out to control the others from within. Nor do they resemble coalitions among political parties in a multiparty parliamentary system, for their constituents are grassroots movements, not party representatives, and their primary arena of action is not within a legislative assembly.

On the other hand, the emerging labor-community alliances in the United States bear a strong affinity to movements all over the world that are attempting to link concerns of working people to what are sometimes referred to as the "new social movements."[6] Just during the months this book was being compiled, Greens and Social Democrats formed governing coalitions in several West German cities; the Italian Communist Party put ecology and feminism at the heart of its platform; an environmentalist-trade unionist alliance in Brazil resisted the destruction of the Amazon rain forest; Chinese workers and students demonstrated side by side for democracy and civil liberties; striking miners in Siberia, with wide community backing, demanded housing, anti-pollution efforts, and constitutional reform;

South African unions joined with community organizations to create a township-based strategy against apartheid; and broad coalitions of workers, human rights activists, environmentalists, and other social movements transformed the face of Eastern Europe. The efforts described in this book are part of this worldwide process.

Bases of Cooperation

The construction of community-labor alliances or coalitions has in a sense been "action research" to discover potential bases of cooperation. The results indicate that there are several, often overlapping, bases for cooperation, beyond the fact that the potential partners all were hurt by the corporate-right offensive.

Sometimes cooperation has been based on little more than a recognized common enemy—that was the principal force that brought together the vast coalition to defeat Robert Bork. Sometimes it amounts to a pragmatic "I'll-scratch-your-back-you-scratch-mine" exchange of support, as when Massachusetts building trades unions formally agreed to open jobs for minority workers in return for help on a prevailing wage referendum.

But often inter-movement cooperation has grown out of common or at least overlapping interests. Women and blacks have repeatedly cooperated to defend affirmative action programs. Employees, churches, government officials, and even merchants have often supported efforts by groups like the Naugatuck Valley Project and the Steel Valley Authority to save local plants via worker or community buyouts. Some interests, such as environmental protection, may be articulated by specific groups, but the constituency that benefits from them may be so wide as to be nearly universal.

Those who play the role of "bridge-builders" often turn out to have been personally active in several different movements, serving as crucial links in an emerging network. Overlapping membership also means that many members of one group have a direct stake in supporting the struggles of another to which they also belong: the increasing proportion of women in the labor movement, for example, has played a crucial role in bringing many unions to back women's demands for abortion rights.

Some programs have been constructed in ways which are specifically designed to help unify different groups. The New Haven Community-Labor Alliance, for example, developed and won a plan for cafeterias in local schools which united parents whose children would be fed and low-income communities for which it would provide jobs. Peace movement activists and workers in military industries jointly supported Minnesota Jobs with Peace plans for conversion from military to peacetime production—demonstrating that such a program can bring together even long-time antagonists.

Such integrating objectives are beginning to coalesce in wider programs for social change. Jesse Jackson's proposals for protection of international labor rights combined the need of American workers for protection from slave-labor competition with the concern of human rights and international development activists for the conditions of third world peoples. Plans for conversion from military production to a community sector integrate the goals of a wide range of groups.

The alliances are also fostered by a sense of common values—of human solidarity, mutual responsibility, social justice, and resistance to oppression. These are sometimes religious in origin, sometimes secular, but are most often expressed in language and symbols drawn from labor, civil rights, and other social movements. While neither their values nor their interpretation of those values are identical, the movements involved with the community-labor coalitions certainly cluster at the opposite pole from the laissez-faire individualism and antagonism to difference articulated by the corporate-right alliance.

Finally, these movements often share an identification with a wider, indeed global movement that is seen as trying to bring about a more just, peaceful, and environmentally sustainable world. As John Childs indicates, this movement is itself more of a network of ramifying connections than a single entity. As American church, labor, anti-interventionist, women's, environmental, development, and other movements have increasingly linked up with their opposite numbers abroad through sister cities and sister locals, solidarity actions, and direct contact, the bridge-building network has begun to be part of a global movement in reality as well as in vision.[7] These growing links were powerfully symbolized by the international trade union delegation that visited the coalfields during the Pittston strike and then helped pressure the United States government to intervene. As power and problems are becoming globalized, so is bridge-building.

Grassroots, National, and Rank-and-File Dimensions

While each of the movements and organizations participating in the new coalitions has its own history, there are some common patterns in their recent development. In the era of corporate liberalism, many social movements developed extremely sophisticated ways of influencing institutions and policies via national organizations. Within corporations, unions often operated as junior partners to management. Women's, civil rights, environmental, and other organizations as well as labor skillfully lobbied government agencies and played a major role in the Democratic Party.

These organizations were ill-equipped to deal with the changes that confronted them in the 1980s. The corporate-right offensive excluded them from their previous positions of influence. And the ongoing globalization and fragmentation of power rendered such influence less and less productive.

In some cases national organizations have tended to see each other as competitors for resources and influence. And as Andrew Banks, Eric Mann, and Michael Pertschuk and Wendy Schaetzel indicate, they sometimes have viewed initiative on the part of their own rank and file as an undisciplined and potentially disruptive force to be feared and repressed.

Thus the labor-community alliances have generally arisen through the initiative of grassroots activists and local leaders: their networks have provided the threads along which the alliances have grown— usually without the encouragement and sometimes against the will of national organizations. This book provides numerous examples of local efforts, from strike support to electoral coalitions, where local leaders have had to resist pressures to withdraw coming from on high.

This pattern has begun to shift, however, as national organizations have begun to see the necessity for adapting to a changing world. After considerable hesitation, a wide range of national organizations supported a united mobilization of their rank and file for the campaign against the Bork nomination. A group of national unions joined to support local coalitions through Jobs With Justice. While the strike of Austin, Minnesota, packinghouse workers against Hormel was crushed by their own national union with help from the AFL-CIO, some national unions have adopted much of the Austin strikers' approach in subsequent strikes, notably the United Mine Workers' strike against Pittston. In some cases, such efforts are essentially a way of maintaining control over a restive rank and file; in others, they are tentative first steps toward a much-needed reconstruction of movement organizations to support decentralized initiative and a wider social vision.

If the initiative for labor-community cooperation has not come from the top, neither has it come primarily from the rank and file. But rank-and-file involvement has been growing as large numbers of people have been drawn into coalition-supported efforts, such as in the

International Paper and Pittston strikes, Jobs With Justice, and the presidential campaigns of Jesse Jackson.

Cooperation Without Merger

The community-based alliances tend neither to fall back into isolated movements nor to move toward merger in a single movement or organization. Rather, they seem to be developing an increasingly rich set of social practices and organizations which reflect an attempt to synthesize cooperation and diversity.

Some of the alignments are essentially ad hoc strike support committees; some are informal networks that convene to deal with problems as they arise; some are membership organizations; some are composed of delegates from constituent organizations. Some have paid staff or officials; others are entirely voluntary. In some the active people are professional staff members or officials of other organizations; in others they are unpaid activists.

In many areas there are multiple coalitions, often with overlapping memberships.[8] Some of the organizations that participated in the Naugatuck Valley Project, for example, also belonged to a Waterbury Community-Labor Support Committee. The Naugatuck Valley Project included churches that could not engage in politics and was able to draw in wide sections of the community which would not have participated in some of the Support Committee's more militant actions. The two alliances nonetheless functioned as part of the same broad network.

The new alliances do not take the form of a single movement represented by a single party or other organization in part because many of their constituent groups value their own distinctive identities. Many important movements of the past few decades, such as the women's, black, gay, and lesbian movements, have had the assertion of identity and the construction of group culture and institutions as central goals. To submerge such identities in some allegedly broader definition, be it "worker," "progressive," or whatever, would in itself defeat a central goal of such movements. Fortunately, as John Childs has emphasized, the assertion of distinct identities is not incompatible with active outreach for cooperation and mutual understanding with others.[9]

There are also differences of interest within emerging alliances. While the United States has some of the sharpest divisions of wealth and income in the Western world, its people are not grouped into neat, homogeneous categories like "middle class," "working class," "poor," or "underclass." However these categories are defined, they have vague and shifting boundaries and most individuals and families cannot be neatly fitted into one or another group.

Nonetheless there are certainly divergences of interest within the new community-labor alliances—divergences which would be likely to split a single movement or organization. In one city, for example, a requirement that public employees be city residents recently disrupted an otherwise cooperative relationship between predominantly low-income black and Latino inner city community organizations and public employee unions, many of whose members lived in predominantly white, "middle class" suburbs.

These divergences cut across each other and operate in different ways in different contexts. Much of the corporate-right alliance's electoral success was based on appealing to whites to vote as whites, rather than on the common interests they share with blacks as workers. Women workers in a corporation may conflict as workers with women managers, but they also share common interests as women in opposing gender discrimination at all levels—an opposition that may bring them into conflict with men with whom they otherwise have class interests in common.

At times, differences on issues are virtually unbridgeable. Catholic activists and feminists may agree completely on dozens of issues, and yet find an irresolvable conflict on abortion rights. Such conflicts can be bridged creatively in many but not all instances. Coalitions allow cooperation on common goals while agreeing to disagree on others.

Other sources of division are less closely linked to movements' basic goals and values, but nonetheless restrict closer ties. Leaders may believe that their personal and/or institutional power is threatened by participation in wider groupings. AFL-CIO affiliates were ordered to withdraw from some electoral coalitions, for example, on the grounds that they would compete with the parent organization's Committee on Political Education (COPE) and its endorsement procedures.

Suspicion and hostility rooted in past conflicts and the bigotry rampant in American society also impede coalition. Overt or subtle "baiting" of bridge-builders for their association with alien forces is not uncommon; at a recent coalition meeting which included gay rights activists, for example, a labor delegate demanded to know "Why is our union making a coalition with 'life-style' groups?"

Bigotry occurs not only between dominant and oppressed, but even among groups that suffer a common racial or other oppression. This is why, as Jack Tchen points out, deliberate efforts to educate different groups about each other, to reduce fear and hostility based on ignorance by bringing individuals together, and to encourage the valuing of cultural diversity, are important dimensions of bridge-building.

In Many Spheres

Significantly, community-labor alliances are rarely located within a single social realm. They cut across the boundaries of workplace, economy, politics, and culture. Indeed, this is one of the reasons that the phenomenon of labor-community alignment as a whole has received so little recognition.

These alliances are forced to operate in a variety of spheres in part for the simple reason that the corporate-right alliance is itself entrenched in many spheres. As the miners' strike against Pittston and many other examples show, labor strength in the workplace is vulnerable if corporate-right-dominated government forces can easily be called in to defeat a strike or organizing campaign. Conversely, even after winning protective legislation, environmental groups have found that polluters can often use local administrations, courts, paid experts, and economic terrorism (the threat of job loss) to defeat the intent of the law in the absence of organized community pressure for its enforcement.

But the tendency of alliances to operate in multiple social spheres also represents a response to the globalization and fragmentation of power: the decoupling of multinational corporations from national states and the blurring of corporate boundaries through joint ventures and other alliances; the rise of television, computer networks, regional economic blocs, and other formations that cut across long-established national, economic, and cultural frontiers; the gradual, then sudden, replacement of the economic, political, social, military, and ideological confluences embodied in "East" and "West" by fluid, multiple, and overlapping networks and boundaries. This obscure but palpable restructuring of power is also experienced in daily life, an increasing proportion of which is spent moving among and trying to coordinate diverse institutions in different social spheres.

The labor-community alliances are not centered in one sphere partly because there is no single social sphere, be it economic, political, military, or ideological, whose control gives power over the rest. There are no commanding heights to storm, no Winter Palace to seize, no single center from which social power is exercised.

Even those whose goal is to maintain domination increasingly talk and operate in terms of the coordination of networks—albeit of coordination in the interest of those on top and prestructured to prevent a challenge to their power. For only through such networks can the filaments of power necessary to accomplish anything be brought together.[10] The community-labor alliances are structured in effect to apply similar techniques for coordinating the challenge to such domination.

Strategies

The community-labor alliances gather elements of power outside a given sphere and project them into struggles within that sphere. Electoral coalitions, such as LEAP and PRO-PAC, take the energy, skills, and financial resources of a variety of labor and community movements and funnel them into the political arena. Strike support operations use influence in government, media, communities, the marketplace, and other spheres to affect struggles in the workplace.

Pressure can succeed in part because the power centers being attacked are often themselves coalitions whose components are subject to pressure in other spheres. Even as seemingly unified an institution as a corporation is, in the words of Ray Rogers of Corporate Campaigns, "a coalition of individual and institutional interests that can be challenged, attacked, divided and conquered."[11] Such a "divide-and-liberate" strategy will become increasingly viable—and necessary—in a fragmenting world where no single "power structure" integrates economic political, ideological, and military power.

This strategy is currently limited by the weakness of the allies within each sphere. But much coalition effort is now directed toward building up the respective partners' power. Community organizations, for example, are increasingly serving as the base for workplace organizing, as Andrew Banks and Patricia Lee, among others, point out. And both labor and community groups are making a major commitment to joint action in the electoral arena. These efforts are pursued in part because they increase coalition power across as well as within social spheres.

Community-Labor Alliance and the Restructuring of Power

Despite its success at promoting military and economic violence at home and abroad, the corporate-right alliance has utterly failed to reestablish American hegemony—economic, political, military, or cultural. Indeed, its efforts have only accelerated the globalization and fragmentation of power.

The emerging pattern of social power is fraught with dangers. It is failing to reverse onrushing ecological catastrophe, impoverishing economic competition, or the proliferation of nuclear and chemical weapons. It is unable to rectify oppression and injustice or even mitigate their effects. The fragmentation of power may lead simply to escalating conflict among multiplying power centers, each intensifying the exploitation and abuse of those human and natural resources it controls.

The alternative cannot be the restoration of national power and/or corporate liberalism. The technological and organizational forces that have promoted globalization and fragmentation make such a reversion almost inconceivable. Besides, these forces are also opening new possibilities for human liberation.

Authoritarian hierarchical pyramids—whether communist planning bureaucracies or multilayered corporate managerial bureaucracies—are dying or restructuring themselves in the face of a desperate need for horizontal cooperation and initiative from below. Work by self-directing individuals and groups is proving more productive than work by people required to act like machines.

There is an expanding possibility—indeed necessity—for a social order in which people coordinate their activity from below, living in equality and solidarity with each other and in harmony with nature. Today's globalization and fragmentation contain some of the preconditions for an evolving social order based on self-defining social groups directing their own activity and coordinating it through a network of organs at every level from the local to the global. But those possibilities are blighted by the drive for profit and domination—protected so tenaciously by the corporate-right ascendancy in the United States.

The restructuring of power going on around us empowers irresponsible political, military, economic, and cultural elites, but it also fragments the integrated power structures of the cold war era. Labor-community coalitions are in effect putting a democratizing twist on today's globalization and fragmentation of power, striving to impose norms of justice, nonviolence, and environmental sustainability on a wide range of institutions.

Labor-community coalitions can be a vehicle for making institutions responsible both to their own rank and file and to the needs of other groups, society as a whole, and the environment. They join together both specific rank-and-file groups and the broader community. And they reflect an understanding that the goals of particular groups must be integrated with those of other groups and society at large. A paradigm of such integration: the Oil, Chemical, and Atomic Workers recently demanded joint union-company monitoring of the environment around the plants where its members work. A union official noted, "The people who live in the communities where we work, which includes us, our families, and friends, won't be protected unless we take the initiative."

The integration of rank-and-file and broader social interests requires a devolution of power both upward and downward. Economic enterprises, for example, need to be made subject to the control of their workers and the communities they affect; at the same time they need to be subject to national and global regulation to ensure that they do not destroy community and regional economies or the environment. Nation-states need to be radically decentralized with greatly increased power for local communities and regions to shape their own lives; at the same time, their predatory sovereignty needs to be restricted by far stronger international law and regulation, particularly to eliminate their military means of destruction.[12]

The coalitions described in this book can be seen as experiments in realizing the liberatory possibilities of the contemporary restructuring of power. They are models for coordinating different groups and concerns from below without imposing a central authority or a single common identity.

When Connecticut LEAP member groups join to support candidates but nonetheless retain their own endorsement procedures, or when Los Angeles activists from many organizations form a common city-wide precinct organization while retaining their distinct organizational affiliations, they gain the benefits of cooperation with minimal loss of initiative or autonomy for constituent groups; the rules and practices in effect recycle power back to the base. When a variety of groups participate in "Rainbow coalitions," they promote common interests in a way that explicitly recognizes their distinct identities.

The practice of bridge-building, and the kind of diversified, continually self-reconstructing cooperation it creates, provides a model for the kind of social organization we need.

A Labor-Community Counteroffensive?

The need for labor-community alliance will only intensify as the corporate-right ascendancy continues to exacerbate human misery, hasten ecological, military, and economic catastrophe, and stymie the possibilities for human liberation.

New technologies and organizational forms show the possibility, indeed the superiority, of decentralized, cooperative, horizontal work structures coordinated by networks of self-regulating people. But the corporate-right ascendancy strives to preserve corporations, military bureaucracies, and similar obsolescent hierarchical authoritarian organizations.

New communications technologies, worldwide ecological concern, world trade, and the flow of cultural trends across national borders create the basis for a new global consciousness based on a sense of world citizenship. But the corporate-right alliance promotes a chauvinist nationalism which cares more about the burning of a flag than the scorching of the planet.

Democratization movements in Eastern Europe open possibilities for creative experimentation with economic democracy, combining organization and freedom in an innovative "third way." But the corporate-right powers in government and business strive to impose their own brand of laissez-faire capitalism and international corporate hegemony on the region.

"People power" in every part of the globe demonstrates the capacity of mass nonviolence to overthrow repressive regimes and transform social practices. But the corporate-right alliance promotes military repression to prop up "death squad democracies" which maintain domestic elite rule by means of U.S. military support and violence against their own people under cover of the fig leaf of periodic elections.

The Soviet leadership has embraced many of the peace movement's proposals for common security and a purely defensive military. But the corporate-right alliance strives to preserve United States interventionary power projection capacity, prevent neutralization and demilitarization in Central Europe, and block opportunities for nonviolent conflict resolution in Central America, Africa, Southwest Asia, and elsewhere.

At home, widening concepts of freedom find expression in the drive for equality and self-defined identity formation for blacks, Latinos, Asian-Americans, other racial and ethnic groups, women, gay men, lesbians, and many others. But the corporate-right alliance seeks to impose a repressive uniformity that denies multicultural pluralism and seeks to punish difference.

Just as the pressures of the corporate-right offensive called the community-labor alliance into being, so they are laying the basis for a counteroffensive to assert the needs of those they have hurt. Many of the elements needed for a community-labor counteroffensive are prefigured in the grassroots coalitions described in this book. By putting them together we can begin to see what such a mobilization might look like.

Imagine, for example, the emergence in numerous cities and towns of community-labor alliances and councils designed to facilitate mutual support among labor and community groups; the creation in each of a block-by-block organization composed of activists from different movements, along the lines of the precinct organization developed by Los Angeles Jobs with Peace. Imagine the emergence of a continuing dialogue on common goals, as seen for example in the "Revisioning New Mexico" program; the establishment of institutions, such as the Los Angeles Community-Labor Strategy Center, for supporting that dialogue.

Imagine groups of activists like the Youngstown Solidarity Club ready to use direct action to back the struggles of local labor and community groups. Imagine mass mobilizations, such as those developed by Jobs With Justice and the P-9 support movement, ready to give extensive backing to a wide range of social struggles.

Imagine the development of electoral organizations, such as Connecticut LEAP and New Mexico PRO-PAC, electing social movement activists to an increasing number of city and state offices. Imagine the consolidation of a progressive power bloc within the national electoral arena growing out of the efforts of the Rainbow Coalition.

Imagine the proliferation of independent citizens organizations like the Naugatuck Valley Project and government institutions like the Steel Valley Authority supporting groups of workers and community members in taking over their economic institutions and/or creating their own. Imagine their evolution into a community economic sector, controlled by local worker and community groups, creating jobs oriented toward the real needs of the community.

Imagine a mobilization of all these elements, along the lines of the coalitions developed by Jobs with Peace, to force a shift of society's resources from military waste and environmental destruction to the reconstruction of our communities. Imagine a coordination with similar movements all over the world to bring pressure to bear from inside and outside on each nation and institution to move in the same direction.

In a world as fluid as today's, it would be foolish even to guess how successful community-labor alliances in the United States and similar formations elsewhere might be in imposing a different direction on society. But developed along the lines sketched here, they might at least give the architects of the corporate-right alliance's assault on American working people cause to wonder whether perhaps they made a mistake.

Notes

1. As Michael Mann points out in *The Sources of Social Power* (Cambridge: Cambridge University Press, 1986), such divergence has been the norm for most of human history. A distinguishing feature of the period from which we are now emerging has been the convergence of military, economic, and ideological boundaries with the political boundaries of the nation-state.

2. For a detailed examination of this economic context, see Joyce Kolko, *Restructuring the World Economy* (New York: Pantheon, 1988).

3. The formation of this alliance is brilliantly described in "The Reagan Victory: Corporate Coalitions in the 1980 Campaign" by Thomas Ferguson and Joel Rogers, in Thomas Ferguson and Joel Rogers, ed., *The Hidden Election*. (New York: Pantheon, 1981).

4. According to the U.S. Bureau of Labor Statistics, real weekly earnings in August 1989 (after years of much-touted economic expansion) were 8.9 percent lower than ten years earlier. Statistics on increasing inequality are reported in Stephen Rose and David Fasenfest, *Family Incomes in the 1980s* (Washington: Economic Policy Institute, November 1988).

5. See Richard Flacks, *Making History: The Radical Tradition in American Life* (New York: Columbia University Press, 1988), for a discussion of party and alternative forms of organization in the history of the American left.

6. This linkage is dealt with at length in Carl Boggs, *Social Movements and Political Power: Emerging Forms of Radicalism in the West* (Philadelphia: Temple University Press, 1986). Similar developments are now occurring not just in "the West," but also in many communist and third world countries.

7. The international dimension of movement networking is addressed in Jeremy Brecher and Tim Costello, "Labor Internationalism," *Zeta* I, No. 11 (November 1988).

8. Traditional theories of hierarchical organization have abhored fuzzy boundaries and overlap in organization charts. Today even prominent management theorists are calling for overlapping responsibilities in organizational design. See for example Tom Peters, *Thriving on Chaos* (New York: Alfred A. Knopf, 1987).

9. John Brown Childs, *Leadership, Conflict, and Cooperation in Afro-American Social Thought* (Philadelphia: Temple University Press, 1989).

10. Recent management literature proclaims the end of hierarchical organization even as it expounds on the transformations managerial cadre will have to go undergo in order to remain competitive. Moshe Lewin in *The Gorbachev Phenomenon* (University of California Press: Berkeley and Los Angeles, 1988) argues that it is a similar need of modern society for horizontal communication and coordination—for experts and managers in one institution to coordinate directly with those in others—which has made perstroika and glastnost prerequisites for development in the Soviet Union.

11. For a sophisticated look at states as power networks built up over time see Charles Bright and Susan Harding, eds., *Statemaking and Social Movements: Essays in History and Theory* (Ann Arbor: University of Michigan Press, 1984). Gene Sharp, *The Politics of Nonviolent Action* (Boston: Porter Sargent, 1973) shows that Gandhian and related forms of nonviolent direct action derive their effectiveness from their ability to disengage the multiple sources of social power from which political power is built up.

12. The interdependence of devolution upward and downward is explored more fully in Jeremy Brecher, "The 'National Question' Reconsidered," *New Politics*, Summer 1987.

An Organizer's Checklist
for Coalition Building

Janice Fine

Prominent national figures listed on fancy letterheads don't make a coalition. A whole bunch of national organizations coming to a conference don't make a coalition. Inspirational speeches and good intentions don't make a coalition.

If an organizer's guide to coalitions existed, it would probably list thousands of city, county, state, and national coalitions—but the number of them that are dynamic and functioning could probably be pared down to a few pages.

It's simple. In order for a coalition to work, member organizations must contribute significant resources and integrate coalition priorities into their own. And the coalition has to *do* things—it can't spend all of its time in meetings.

There are different types of coalitions:

• geographic ones—that bring together people in the same neighborhood or city or state;
• ad hoc-temporary ones that are organized to pass a certain bill or stop a development project or an eviction;
• single-issue ones that bring groups together around one very specific issue;
• multi-issue ones that bring groups together around a broad agenda of concerns;
• electoral ones which coalesce around particular candidates or are formed in order to support candidates for public office based on their positions on issues of concern to coalition members.

No one type of coalition is intrinsically better than another. In fact there are probably examples of successful coalitions of every type in the pages of this book! Most coalitions come together for a lot of the same reasons . . . and almost all of them work for a lot of the same reasons. The following is a list of eight important principles for successful coalition building.

1. *A coalition should be more than the sum of its parts—like five*

fingers on a hand that are much stronger when clenched into a fist.
Organizations form coalitions because they're after something they
realize cannot be won by working alone. That's good. But what's essential to the coalition's success is that each of the member organizations
see the coalition as one of their top priorities and invest time, money,
and people into the coalition effort. Too often this is not the case
and a coalition is formed by organizations concerned about a problem,
precisely because they cannot make that problem a priority within
their own group. That's like trying to make a fist out of a bunch
of broken fingers!

2. *Self interest is important to the success of the coalition.* Organizations must feel that they are going to derive concrete benefits from
taking part in coalitions. Particularly important are such things as
specific victories on issues; increased media attention; long-term allies;
leadership and staff development; more resources—money, staff, in-
kind services, and contributions; and an ongoing power vehicle.

3. *The coalition has to have a strategy, fun tactics, and other concrete activities.* Let's face it, large meetings are almost always a drag.
Usually they don't build in much participation, they're long and they
often lead to less participatory, longer and more boring meetings.
So, just say no! Only meet when you have to and the rest of the
time, mobilize coalition leaders to do something together—like rough
out a campaign target or testify at an open hearing. Mobilize members
not to sit in boring meetings, but to sit in at the mayor's office, or
a target's corporate office!
Remember, just as impressive organizations don't a successful coalition make, neither do fun tactics alone make a strategy. Your coalition
must see its work in terms of a campaign, with a clear beginning,
middle, and end with tactics aimed at winning a concrete victory.

4. *If the issue can't be boiled down into three essential facts, and
about as many demands, it will be harder to educate, agitate, and
organize around.* The best coalition campaigns are simple. The issues
are clear. The demands are clear. The target is clear. It's something
lots of people care deeply about. Period.

5. *Credit: From each according to their contribution. To each according to their contribution.* On this matter, I am a capitalist! Nothing
will anger organizations more than a lack of recognition, or recognition
disproportionate to their contribution to the coalition. Similarly, if
all the organizations honestly feel that they are working hard in the
coalition, there is nothing worse than all the credit going to one organi-

zation. If it's a coalition effort, when leaders are quoted in the newspaper for a coalition issue or event, they must directly credit the coalition. Not all organizations will be able to contribute the same amount of money, or staff, or people—but all of them must ante in what would be considered a major contribution considering the over-all resources they have to work with.

6. *Have a clear structure and make sure everybody knows the rules.* There are a lot of reasons why coalitions fall apart. Often it is a question of resources, but almost as often it's a question of faith—or lack of it. The coalition's leaders must always be accountable to coalition members. People have to feel like they're running the show and involved in decision-making. Especially if they are contributing major resources—which is the whole idea. Accountability and democracy begin at home: everybody antes in, everybody gets a vote . . . everybody knows the way things work.

7. *Real coalitions take real resources.* All of the above rules suggest a lot of work for somebody. Staff are usually essential to successful coalition efforts, not to *be* the coalition—staff cannot substitute for membership participation—but to maximize the coalition's effectiveness and to help coordinate participation of member groups. Organizations have to be willing to make some of their individual resources available: their money, their membership lists, their contributor lists, their media contacts, their offices, their telephones, their xerox machines, not just their brilliant ideas!

8. *Keep your eyes on the prize, hold on.* The coalition should have clear goals even if it is formed for more than a limited duration, more than one issue, on behalf of more than one candidate. These goals should not exist only in the heads of some well-meaning individuals. Thou shalt write them down. Thou shalt repeat them many times, to anyone who will listen, always at coalition meetings. Once is never enough. Neither is twice.

Being able to go back and review the original goals of a coalition will keep leaders and member organizations focused on more than just immediate objectives, and help remind them of the larger reasons they are in the fight.

Notes on Contributors

Andrew Banks, assistant director of the Center for Labor Research and Studies at Florida International University and associate editor of *Labor Research Review*, was the coordinator of the nation's first Jobs With Justice rally on July 29, 1987. He currently coordinates the Florida Jobs With Justice committee and is a strategic consultant to numerous unions throughout the United States.

Max Bartlett, formerly executive director of New Mexico PRO-PAC, is a political theorist and organizer who also teaches political philosophy at the University of New Mexico.

Carl Boggs currently teaches political science at the University of Southern California. He is the author of *Social Movements and Political Power, The Two Revolutions: Gramsci and the Dilemmas of Modern Marxism,* and *The Impasse of European Communism*. He is active in the Westside Greens in Los Angeles and the Left Green Network.

Jeremy Brecher is the author or co-author of six previous books, including *Strike!, Brass Valley, History from Below,* and *Common Sense for Hard Times* (also with Tim Costello). He is currently preparing a book and a documentary on the Naugatuck Valley Project and serving as Humanities Scholar in Residence at Connecticut Public Broadcasting.

Cindia Cameron, formerly a staff director of Atlanta 9 to 5, is currently Southeast Field Organizer for 9 to 5, National Association of working women.

John Brown Childs, associate professor of sociology at the University of California at Santa Cruz, is the author of *Leadership, Conflict, and Cooperation in Afro-American Social Thought, The Political Black Minister: A Study in Afro-American Politics and Religion,* and the broadside *Black Communities Against War*. A former community organizer in Massachusetts, he was a member of the Commonwork Pamphlets publishing collective in New Haven for five years.

Tim Costello, a truck driver and workplace activist for the past twenty years, is currently also studying and teaching at the University of Massachusetts in Boston. He is co-author (with Jeremy Brecher) of *Common Sense for Hard Times*.

Mel Duncan is director of the Minnesota Jobs with Peace campaign and director of the Minnesota Alliance for Progressive Action, both in Minneapolis.

Janice Fine was on the national staff of the Jesse Jackson for President campaign in 1988 and was campaign manager for Rosario Salerno's successful 1989 campaign for Boston City Council. A former president of the U.S. Student Association and Boston director of Massachusetts Fair Share, she is currently a member of the board of Massachusetts Citizens Action.

Jim Green directs the Labor Studies Program at the University of Massachusetts-Boston and co-chairs the Boston Labor Support Committee for the United Mine Workers Pittston strikers. He is the author of *The World of the Worker: Labor in Twentieth-Century America* and *Workers' Struggles, Past and Present: A 'Radical America' Reader*.

Temma Kaplan, feminist community activist and historian, directs the Barnard Center for Research on Women.

Patricia Lee was a field representative for Local 2 of the Hotel Employees & Restaurant Employees (HERE) in San Francisco for seven years. She currently works for SEIU Local 790 United Public Employees Union in San Francisco. A second-generation Chinese-American, she is active in the Asian-American community and in the immigrant rights movement.

Staughton Lynd, formerly a historian, is currently a legal services attorney in Youngstown, Ohio. He is the author of numerous books and articles, including *Labor Law for the Rank and Filer*, *The Fight Against Shutdowns: Youngstown's Steel Mill Closings*, and with his wife Alice Lynd, *Rank and File: Personal Histories by Working-Class Organizers*.

Eric Mann worked in auto plants from 1978 to 1986, including five years in the Van Nuys plant, where he served as the UAW's coordinator of the Campaign to keep Van Nuys Open. He is presently director of the Labor-Community Strategy Center in Van Nuys, California, and author of *Taking On General Motors: A Case Study of the UAW Campaign to Keep GM Van Nuys Open*.

Charles McCollester, associate director of the Pennsylvania Center for the Study of Labor Relations at Indiana University of Pennsylvania (IUP), was one of the founders of the Tri-State Conference on Steel. Former machinist and chief steward of UE Local 610 in Swissvale, PA, he now represents Pittsburgh on the board of the Steel Valley Authority.

Kim Moody is a staff writer for *Labor Notes* and the author of *An Injury to All: The Decline of American Unionism*. He is a member of the Newspaper Guild and the National Writers Union and has been a member of the Communications Workers of America and the American Federation of State, County and Municipal Employees.

Jill Nelson is a founding member of Jobs with Peace and has been executive director of the National Jobs with Peace Campaign for the last five years. She previously worked as a lawyer in San Francisco assisting public housing residents in organizing tenant unions and has also been active in the movement to establish progressive community-based foundations.

Michael Pertschuk, former chief counsel of the Senate Commerce Committee and chairman of the Federal Trade Commission, is currently co-director of the Advocacy Institute, a national public interest advocacy organization in Washington, D.C. The author of numerous works on the consumer movement, he most recently co-authored (with Wendy Schaetzel) *The People Rising: The Campaign Against the Bork Nomination*.

Peter Rachleff, associate professor of history at Macalester College, St. Paul, Minnesota, is the author of *Black Labor in Richmond, 1865–1890*. From 1985 to 1987 he was chairman of the Twin Cities P–9 Support Committee and is currently working on a book about the strike, entitled *P–9 Proud*.

Barbara E. Richards, director of the Community-Labor Alliance (CLA), also works for the Hotel and Restaurant Employees Union, Locals 34, 35, and 217, in New Haven on community issues and political action.

Mark Ritchie, agricultural trade policy analyst for the Minnesota Department of Agriculture, is active in raising public concern about the farm crisis. The author of numerous books and articles, he is a founding member and board chair of the League of Rural Voters, a national nonpartisan organization.

Wendy Schaetzel, a journalist and community organizer, is co-author (with Michael Pertschuk) of *The People Rising: The Campaign Against the Bork Nomination*. She currently works on media strategies for community groups for the Advocacy Institute, in Washington, D.C.

Bruce Shapiro is a freelance writer. He was co-founder and editor of the *New Haven Independent*, a weekly newspaper.

Louise Simmons, director of the University of Connecticut Urban Semester Program, is an activist in Hartford, Connecticut, where she has been instrumental in community-labor alliances and electoral initiatives.

Jane Slaughter is a staff writer of *Labor Notes*, co-author of *Choosing Sides: Unions and the Team Concept*, and author of *Concessions and How to Beat Them*. She is a member of the Newspaper Guild and formerly a member of the United Auto Workers.

Mike Stout, a printer and sales manager for the Steel Valley Printers, is project coordinator of the Tri-State Conference on Steel. Former head grievanceman for USW Local 1397 at the historic Homestead steel mill, he now represents Munhall on the board of the Steel Valley Authority. He has been active in organizing the Federation for Industrial Retention and Renewal (FIRR), a national coalition against plant closings.

John Kuo Wei Tchen is a historian and cultural activist. He co-founded the New York Chinatown History Project and the newly formed Asian/American Center at Queens College, City University of New York. He is currently working on a book about the early formation of and the development of tourism in New York Chinatown.

Daniel Weisman is assistant professor of social work and director of labor studies at Rhode Island College in Providence, Rhode Island.

Just Published

Many of our contributors have recent publications they would especially like to bring to the attention of readers of this book.

Charles McCollester and Mike Stout of the Tri-State Conference on Steel have produced a video called *Recharge South Side Steel*. This tape tells the story of the effort to restart the electric furnaces on the LTV site on the south side of Pittsburgh. The price of the tape is $20.00. For more information or to place an order, contact: Tri-State Conference on Steel, 300 Saline Street, Pittsburgh, PA 15207.

Alice and Staughton Lynd have edited *We Are the Union: The Story of Ed Mann*. Copies can be obtained by sending a check for $5.00, made out to Alice or Staughton Lynd, to the Lynds at 1694 Timbers Court, Niles, OH 44446.

Eric Mann's *Taking On General Motors*, just published by the UCLA Institute of Industrial Relations, can be ordered by sending $20.00 to: Labor Distributors, 6454 Van Nuys Blvd., Suite 150, Van Nuys, CA 91401.
"If you are serious about social change, *Taking On General Motors* by Eric Mann is a book you have to read. I have marched with the Van Nuys organizers and seen their impressive movement first hand. But *Taking On General Motors* takes you beyond where the eye can see to the complexities of how read movements are built. If you are an activist in the environmental movement, the peace movement, a labor union or community group, a high school or college teacher, or a member of the Rainbow Coalition, I strongly urge you to read this book."—Rev. Jesse Jackson

Kim Moody's *An Injury to All: The Decline of American Unionism*, just published by Verso, can be ordered from Labor Notes. Send $15.00, plus $2.00 for postage and handling to: Labor Notes, 7435 Michigan Avenue, Detroit, MI 48210.
"This is the most readable history of postwar labor I have ever seen. Moody understands that the decline of American unionism is ultimately a political phenomenon, and, thus, its revival will be unlikely without the rebirth of radical politics and social solidarity."—Helson Lichtenstein, author of *Labor's War at Home: The CIO in World War II*

John Brown Childs' *Leadership Conflict and Cooperation in Afro-American Social Thought*, just published by Temple University Press, is available from the press in cloth only at $29.95 plus $3.00 postage.

Michael Pertshuk and Wendy Schaetzel's *The People's Rising: The Campaign Against the Bork Nomination* has just been published by Thunder's Mouth Press in New York City. It is available from the press at $13.95 plus $1.50 postage and handling.

Peter J. Rachleff's *Black Labor in Richmond, 1865–1890*, just published by the University of Illinois Press, is available from the press at $10.95 plus postage and handling.

Jane Slaughter and Mike Parker's recent book, *Choosing Sides: Unions and the Team Concept*, published jointly by Labor Notes and South End Press, can be ordered from Labor Notes. Send $15.00 plus $2.00 for postage and handling to: Labor Notes, 7435 Michigan Avenue, Detroit, MI 48210.

"A timely and definitive work on management's newest scheme to change the balance of power in the workplace. This book should be in the hands of union leaders, activists, and rank and file workers."—Jerry Tucker, leader of UAW's New Directions Movement

Monthly Review Press also publishes a number of other books which readers should find relevant and interesting. Most recently:

The Power in Our Hands: A Curriculum on the History of Work and Workers in the United States, by William Bigelow and Norman Diamond, is an innovative curriculum that enables the participants to project themselves into real-life situations where they can explore concrete problems and potential solutions. $15.00 plus $1.50 for postage and handling.

Rank and File: Personal Histories by Working-Class Organizers, edited by Alice and Staughton Lynd. $10.00 plus $1.50.

Empty Promises: Quality of Working Life Programs and the Labor Movement, by Donald M. Wells, $8.00 plus $1.50.